POETS AND MYSTICS

POETS AND MYSTICS

By

E. I. WATKIN

Haec est generatio quaerentium eum, quaerentium faciem Dei Jacob

SHEED AND WARD

LONDON AND NEW YORK

FIRST PUBLISHED 1953
BY SHEED AND WARD LTD.
110/111 FLEET STREET
LONDON, E.C.4
AND
SHEED AND WARD, INC.
840 BROADWAY
NEW YORK, 3

PRINTED IN GREAT BRITAIN
BY PURNELL AND SONS, LTD.
PAULTON (SOMERSET) AND LONDON

To

MY DEAR DAUGHTER

JULIANA

PREFACE

THE STUDIES which compose this volume, *Poets and Mystics*, are partly unpublished, partly reprints. The introductory study "Poetry and Mysticism" and the four studies which conclude the book—"John Smith, the Cambridge Platonist", "The Spiritual Teaching of Sister Elizabeth of the Trinity", "Henry Vaughan", and "*Urania*: the poetry of Miss Ruth Pitter"—have been written especially for this volume. "He Wanted Art" appeared in *The Wind and the Rain*, "Drama and Religion" and "A Puritan Devotion to the Sacred Heart" in the American *Catholic World*. "Dame Julian of Norwich" and "Richard Crashaw" were published in a collection entitled *The English Way* (Sheed & Ward), "William Crashaw" (a lecture delivered at a celebration of his son's tercentenary at Cambridge) in the *Dublin Review*. "In Defence of Margery Kempe" embodies an article published under that title in the *Downside Review*. But a life of Margery has been prefixed to it. The study of Augustine Baker consists substantially of two reprinted studies, a study contributed to the collection of Catholic lives edited by Fr. Claude Williamson, O.S.C., and entitled *Great Catholics* (Messrs. Nicholson and Watson) and an article on Father Baker and Active Contemplation published in the *Downside Review*. No paper, however, has been simply reprinted as it stood. All have been revised, enlarged and corrected when necessary.

Strictly speaking neither Goodwin nor William Crashaw is entitled to a place in this collection. The religion of neither was mystical. Goodwin wrote only prose, and William Crashaw's verse rarely achieves the quality of poetry. But I did not wish to lose this opportunity of bringing to the notice of my readers Goodwin's remarkably beautiful expression of devotion to the Sacred Heart—though frankly that devotion is not my personal *attrait*—and at the same time refuting the belief generally entertained by Catholics and Anglicans that the religion of the Puritans was dour and harsh. The first step towards a better understanding among Christians is unprejudiced knowledge of one another's belief and devotion. And the study of William Crashaw, to my knowledge more detailed than anything hitherto published, throws valuable light on his son's religious progress by establishing that it started, not from a paternal Puritanism—an incipient Nonconformity—but from the zealous attachment to the Anglican worship and church government entertained by his father. The section in my study of Baker which begins on p. 203 and concludes on p. 225 marked by a spacing on each page deals with questions of mystical theology which the general reader may think too technical. If he does he is invited to skip the section.

My thanks are due to the editors of the *Catholic World*, the *Downside* and *Dublin Reviews*, for permission to reprint.

CONTENTS

CONTENTS

CHAPTER I

POETRY AND MYSTICISM

BEFORE discussing the relationship between poetry and mysticism we must first be clear as to what we mean by poetry. At first sight this might seem unnecessary. Surely we all know poetry when we see it? Verse yes, but not therefore poetry. For verse is by no means the same as poetry.

> How doth the little busy bee
> Improve each shining hour
>
> Let dogs delight to bark and bite
> For God hath made them so.[1]

Or

> Thirty days hath September
> April, June and dull November.

These are verse. For anything is verse which is written in a recurrent metre, that is with a recurrent pattern of sound, whether of accent, as in English verse, or quantity, as in Greek and Latin verse. But they are not poetry. What then is poetry?

Poetry is a branch of art. Art is the expression of aesthetic perception, intuition I would call it. This aesthetic perception is the perception of beautiful form. Beautiful form is significant form.

These definitions of course need explaining. And we must begin with form. By form I mean the nature of anything, what it is, not indeed its entire form, all it is, but its nature in some aspect of it. If it is the form of a physical object it may be its shape, its size, its colour, its scent, its taste, the sound it emits. Or the form in question may be what is common to an entire class of objects, for example the distinctive characters that belong to a species of plant or animal. Or it may be a spiritual form, a virtue, for example, or a mental quality, the attribute of a created spirit,

---

[1] Watts, however, could write genuine poetry on occasion (see below, p. 302).

our own spiritual nature in so far as it is known by introspection, what is passing in our consciousness, or an aspect of God as His creatures are related to Him and reflect the nature of their Creator, what we call an attribute of God.

All our knowledge of the nature of things is, I hold, fundamentally intuition of form. But this intuition is not always of the same kind. An important, though rough, division must be made between the intuition of clear and abstract forms and the intuition of obscure but concrete forms.

When the intuition is clear and abstract, the mind perceives a distinct clear-cut characteristic of the object to which it is directed. Thus the mathematician perceives the numerical or the geometrical aspect of things. His knowledge is clear. But it is abstract, the knowledge of characters numerical, measurable, geometrical, abstracted from the concrete objects to which they belong. Most, though not all, scientific knowledge is of abstract quantities, of what can be measured and numbered. For only this knowledge is sufficiently exact for the exact sciences.

Another type of abstract and clear intuition is logic, which in fact of recent years has been subjected to a strictly mathematical treatment. All reasoning, however, of the type called discursive, whether formally logical or not, is, in proportion to its clarity and abstraction, a process of these clear abstract intuitions.

The function of the human spirit which operates in this clear abstract reasoning was termed by the French poet Claudel the *animus* and his terminology was adopted by the historian of French Catholic spirituality Bremond in a book he wrote on our topic, the relation between Poetry and Mysticism, which he calls more widely Prayer.

But there is another type of knowledge, another kind of intuition of form, which is obscure and concrete. The intelligence perceives not a form or pattern of forms clearly discriminated and exactly determined but forms more or less indeterminate because they are not clearly abstracted from their objects. It perceives an indefinite complex of forms which compose the concrete nature of an object as it is perceived and known to be. Whereas for example scientific botany states the number and arrangement, the shape of the parts and organs of a flower, this obscure concrete intuition is aware of the flower as a whole, as a complex of forms or qualities which make it the flower whose beauty delights us but which so largely escapes the exact schedule of the professional botanist. To avoid misconception I hasten to add that the most complete and the richest knowledge of the flower possible requires a combination of both forms of intuition, the clear and abstract and the obscure and concrete. To this obscure intuition belong the knowledge of moral values, the perception that particular conduct is morally good or bad, and the kindred perception of human character. And whatever in psychology is more than a registration of nervous reactions or the study of sensory mechanism is of this obscure concrete type. Religious knowledge, from the character of its objects, transcendent as they are of the world open to exact determination and measurement, must also be obscure and concrete.

The function of the human spirit which operates in this obscure but deeper and richer knowledge Claudel, followed by Bremond, has termed the *anima* in contradistinction to the animus with its abstract and clear thought.

On no account however must we lose sight of the fact that in actual experience and knowledge, these two types of intuition are not separated. They work together, the one interwoven with the other. Moreover there are varying degrees of clarity, of abstraction, of exactness, and varying degrees of obscurity and concreteness. Even the clear reasoning of the mathematician or the scientist is often guided by obscure intuitions verifiable only later by exact discrimination. Nevertheless the two types of knowledge are roughly distinguishable and we can roughly assign to each particular branches of human knowledge.

Aesthetic perception, that is, the perception of beautiful form, belongs to the class of obscure concrete intuitions. The forms it perceives are not clear and abstract but obscure, incapable of precise definition and pregnant with an inexhaustible content, a content not fully comprehensible. The form thus aesthetically perceived I term significant form, by which I mean sensible form perceived, though obscurely, as significant of a spiritual reality beyond, which this sensible form reflects in its own lower order. These realities, these forms of the spiritual order, we may term in Platonic language—any satisfactory philosophy of beauty must be Platonist—ideas. Thus the forms which aesthetic intuition perceives are forms significant of ideas.

Art in all its branches expresses significant forms which it selects from the forms of nature and, normally at least, recombines so as to show them as significant, that is as reflecting and signifying spiritual realities, ideas beyond themselves. "There is a twofold meaning" writes Smith the Platonist "in every creature, a literal and a mystical and the one is but the ground of the other." Consciously or subconsciously the artist sees the mystical meaning in the literal and expresses it by his selection and combination of forms. But this significance which is essential beauty is obscure, nothing that can be defined and stated in precise scientific language. That is to say, aesthetic intuition and its artistic expression are operations of anima, not of animus.

It is true that, as in nature so, perhaps still more, in art, there is an important, indeed indispensable, factor of exact form, form in principle and often in fact scientifically determinable, quantitative, measurable. This is obviously true of metre in poetry, which has indeed been called numbers, whose numerical basis is obvious, and of architecture, in which proportion plays so large a part. The mathematical structure of music is equally evident. But it is also true of painting, where many masterpieces by different masters have been found to possess precise mathematical proportions between the main lines of the composition, proportions which are aesthetically satisfying.[1]

This exact mathematical factor in beauty and art is, as such, an object of scientific knowledge, the knowledge of abstract form, the knowledge and perception of animus. If and when an artist is distinctly conscious of it, animus operates consciously. If he is not distinctly conscious of it, the operation of animus is masked —a subconscious exercise. And, as I have already pointed out, in actual experience the two types of intuition and operation are inseparable and interpenetrate.

These mathematical conditions of significant form do not, however, constitute its beauty any more than the skeleton constitutes the beauty of a beautiful living body. To suppose that it does is the radical error of materialistic and purely utilitarian architecture, content to be nothing more than an embodiment of geometrical proportions. Nor, normally, are artists consciously aware of the exact mathematical structure of the beautiful patterns, be they architectural, linear, musical or verbal,

---

[1] Harold Speed, *The Science and Practice of Drawing*, Appendix, 289-91.

which they employ. Contemplating the living body, they are not normally conscious of the underlying skeleton. The artists, for example, in whose pictures a particular linear proportion has been detected, were certainly not consciously aware of it. The operation of anima which perceives the beauty, the significant form, is not therefore accompanied by a fully conscious operation of animus perceiving and intending its mathematical conditions—though this direct awareness and operation of animus may occur as, for example, when a student of art studies anatomy, a poet the laws of prosody. Moreover, a conscious collaboration of animus is required for a sustained work of art or literature, for example, the construction of a drama or an epic.

Poetry then, being an art, expresses an obscure intuition of significant form. It is distinguished from other arts by the fact that its medium is language. It employs words to express its intuition. This fact, however, gives it a peculiar, even an ambiguous position among the arts. For it employs words in two ways. It employs them for their sound and for their meaning. In so far as poetry employs words for their sound it is akin to music, is a verbal music. The sounds, like the notes in music, suggest an obscure significance incapable of conceptual formulation. But in spite of stories of poems enjoyed for their sound by hearers ignorant of their language, sound alone cannot suffice for poetry. Professor Richards proved this once for all when he rewrote a passage of Milton's Ode on the Nativity in sounds closely approximating to Milton's but without meaning.[1] This employment of verbal meaning is in fact what primarily differentiates poetry from music. But meaning in poetry is itself of two kinds, in the concrete blended inseparably, but nevertheless distinct. The meaning may be what has been called an overtone, a suggestion which cannot be exactly defined. This is the specifically poetic use of meaning to express and convey the distinctively poetic intuition, the obscure intuition of significant form, the intuition aware of forms pregnant with dim but potent reference to spiritual reality, the intuition therefore of the poet's anima. In this employment of it meaning is similar in its function to sound, with which indeed it is intimately associated, so that each reinforces the other.

[1] *Practical Criticism*, pp. 232-3.

The other type of meaning employed in poetry is the dictionary meaning of words, the grammatical, the logical meaning of their combinations. In this meaning there is no overtone, no suggestion of a dim spiritual beyond, in short no significant form in the sense in which I have used the term. For this meaning does not signify anything beyond itself, whether its reference be to a material or to an immaterial being. This employment of meaning, though contained in poetry, indeed indispensable to it, is therefore neither poetic nor aesthetic. It is the product of the poet's animus, whether or no he is fully conscious of it, and represents clear abstract intuition of the same class as the intuition represented by scientific, logical or mathematical statement.

It is most desirable, even from the point of view of his art, that the poet should be fully aware that the form he selects, combines and expresses is significant of a spiritual reality beyond. But the example of Lucretius, the express purpose of whose poem was to inculcate a materialist atomism as the ultimate truth, but who nevertheless produced a poetical masterpiece, is sufficient to prove that such conscious knowledge is not indispensable. If the poet's anima is subconsciously aware of the spiritual reality signified by the forms he expresses, he can, like Lucretius, produce poetry which is genuine and of high quality, in spite of the ignorance of his conscious mind, even the denial by his animus of what his anima knows.

The poet's distinctively poetic communication to his reader is due to his expression of the obscure intuition of anima, whether by verbal rhythms, a pattern of sounds or by the poetic employment of meaning to convey more than its superficial dictionary sense. In particular the vocal rhythm, the rhyme, the choice of words of a suitable sound, the vocal pattern, are wholly a poetic and a distinctively poetic communication to the reader of the poet's intuition of realities which elude clear formulation.

Keats originally began " Endymion " with the line:

A thing of beauty is a constant joy.

When his friend expressed dissatisfaction he reflected a little and then wrote the immortal line:

A thing of beauty is a joy for ever.

From the standpoint of precise dictionary meaning the two lines differ little.[1] Poetically they are poles asunder. For the rhythm of the second line enables it to express and convey a poetic intuition of joy and loveliness abiding eternally while the successive events of experience pass away, whereas the former merely states that a beautiful object is something relatively enduring, not ceasing after a momentary or brief experience of it.

A rose-red city—half as old as Time!

The author of this line, Dean Burgon, was not a poet nor even an outstanding writer of prose, simply a scholarly divine, one of a multitude. But this line is poetry indeed, immortal as the line of Keats' just quoted. By it Burgon achieved the possibly unique distinction of being the poet of one line. And the line is poetry, great poetry for two reasons, the assonance, the pattern of sound, and the poetic meaning of the words, their meaning over and above their simple dictionary meaning, which to the reader today is grotesque—for a city obviously cannot be half as old as time[2]—the meaning which is significant of realities of which the writer's anima was stung to awareness but which cannot be grasped and formulated by the clear intuition and expression of animus. Indeed as we have just noticed in this instance, the expression of anima's truth is often false, even absurd, from the point of view of animus.

Nursery rhymes can hardly be considered poems. Despite the authority of Bunthorne's judgment and although its preposterous juxtapositions resemble much that passes for poetry nowadays, "Hey diddle diddle" cannot "rank as an idyll". Nevertheless in a nursery rhyme there is embedded, as has been pointed out recently, a line of genuine poetry—"Over the hills and far away". Like Dean Burgon's line this is the very stuff of poetry flashing out suddenly. For the poetic intuition of an anonymous bard has seen and expressed a journey over the distant hills to the country beyond their horizon as form significant of a

[1] " Constant ", however, is not so lasting as " for ever ". And this difference of meaning undoubtedly plays its part in the difference of poetic value between the two lines.
[2] It was not, however, absurd to the animus of the writer, who presumably accepted Archbishop Ussher's biblical chronology which dated creation at 4004 B.C. According to this chronology Damascus, from its mention in Genesis, would be roughly two-thirds as old as time!

spirit's journey away and away, on and on, to a realm of spirit
incomprehensible and unbounded.

A striking example of a poetic intuition of truth, an intuition
of the poet's anima which exceeded the clear knowledge of his
animus is the passage in which Browning, in conscious belief a
Protestant Nonconformist, sees and expresses the sacramental
advent of the glorified Christ at the consecration of the Host,
and in His advent His eternity, His eternal glory shining through
the veil of a wafer and a religious rite at a particular instant
of time and in a particular place to snatch the adoring spirit away
from this temporal and local order to the presence and awareness
of this Divine Humanity.

> Earth breaks up, time drops away,
> In flows Heaven, with its new day
> Of endless life, when He who trod,
> Very man and very God,
> This earth in weakness, shame and pain . . .
>
> Shall come again, no more to be
> Of captivity the thrall,
> But the one God, All in all,
> King of Kings, Lord of Lords,
> As his servant John received the words,
> 'I died, and live for evermore'.[1]

Yet the writer's animus rejected the Real Presence in the Blessed
Sacrament. It rejected, that is to say, the truth his anima, by its
distinctively poetic intuition, saw and expressed so well.

At this point language presents a difficulty. For although, as
we have seen, verse is not conterminous with poetry, the opposite
of verse is called prose and the opposite of poetry is called prose.
I may perhaps be permitted to avoid the resultant ambiguity by
calling the opposite of verse prose, the opposite of poetry statement, understood as the clear one-dimensional statement of the
scientific type, the statement with which logical reasoning is
concerned. Because statement and language are so closely bound
up together the poet, since he employs words, is obliged to use
them not only aesthetically, artistically and poetically to express

---

[1] " Christmas Eve."

his poetic intuition of significant form but also rationalistically, at their face value as simple statement. Inasmuch, however, as he does so, his poetry is not strictly poetry but reasoned statement.

I have spoken of obligation, of compulsion. But this is gravely misleading. It is no defect in poetry, though it is a source of serious danger, that the poet must inevitably make statements not as such poetic. For a blend of the two meanings of language, the poetic and the rationalist, is of the nature of poetry, as much as a blend of spiritual and bodily function is of the nature of mortal humanity. It is only when the lower bodily function is insufficiently controlled by the spiritual, or at the other extreme when the bodily function is unduly thwarted or starved by the spiritual, that humanity is disordered and functions badly. It is the same with poetry. Poetry does not suffer because it combines clear rational statement with pure poetry, poetry in the strict sense, the suggestion of significant form. On the contrary when the blend of statement and pure poetry, the products respectively of animus and anima, is successful, then and only then is the poem a successful poem of high and sustained poetical merit. If rational statement is insufficiently inspired and permeated by pure poetry, to the extent of the failure there will be unpoetic statement in verse, such for example as Dante's elaborate explanation in the *Paradiso* of the lunar markings which, though bad science, is scientific statement pure and simple, and therefore verse, not poetry. Or if, at the other extreme, in the supposed interest of strictly poetical intuition or from some weakness of reasoning in the poet rational statement does not receive its due, though the poem may contain much beautiful suggestion, it will be more or less defective. For this reason Smart's "Hymn to David", written in madness, despite its great suggestive beauty and powerful emotional force, cannot claim equality with poems in which suggestion and statement, the obscure intuition of anima and the clear but more superficial intuition of animus, are balanced and blend harmoniously. The right proportion however between these two constituents of poetry varies indefinitely. Roughly speaking, statement is at a minimum in lyric poetry, at its maximum almost in epic poetry or drama. I say almost; for of course it must play an even greater part in didactic poetry. Here, however, it tends to become disproportionate, a tendency so difficult to overcome

that very few didactic poems have been successful. Though
Lucretius' *De Rerum Natura* in which he expounds the Epicurean
philosophy, and Virgil's *Georgics*, whose subject matter is a
farmer's manual, are outstanding examples of success, even they
are not, could not possibly have been, poetical throughout. On
the other hand a didactic purpose, and with it a corresponding
amount of statement, characterise one of the greatest poems ever
written, the *Divina Commedia*. And it is very rarely that, as
in the instance just mentioned, the statement is insufficiently
informed by the pure poetry of Dante's aesthetic and poetic
intuition.

From what has been said it should be clear that poetry is not
confined to verse. Just as there is verse which because it is pure
statement in metre is not poetry, there is poetry which lacks the
regularly recurrent metre of verse but which, because it employs
language for the suggestion and aesthetic significance of its sound
and also for the aesthetic significance of its meaning over and
above its meaning as simple statement, is truly poetry, prose
poetry it is often termed. Examples are the works of Sir Thomas
Browne and many passages of Ruskin's *Modern Painters*. Some
measure, however, of this poetry is, I am convinced, to be found
in all prose of value, not only for the notions or facts it states but
for its quality as literature. That is to say, there can be no prose
which is literature, is good prose, which does not contain some
measure of pure poetry, and no poem of any length and high
quality which does not contain some measure of the statement
which is prose as contrasted with poetry, though not, of course,
prose as contrasted with verse. We should observe, however,
that to the extent to which prose, as contrasted with verse, by
the element of poetry in it approaches poetry in the strict sense,
namely metrical poetry, it becomes itself rhythmic though its
rhythms are laxer and more irregular than those of verse. Ancient
prose indeed was intended to be declaimed. It was like a deacon
chanting the Gospel that Cicero, in the Roman courts, intoned
his speech for the prosecution or defence. Oratory therefore
assumed metrical rhythms. Cicero in fact lays it down that
"prose should be metrical, though not entirely metrical like
poetry". He recommended the use of feet little used in poetry.
Modern research has discovered the metrical structures of ancient
and mediaeval Latin prose. And the Latin collects are obviously

metrical in structure. Nor is rhythmic structure, though laxer than in Latin or Greek, absent from the periods of classical English prose. That is to say, prose is not always pure prose even in the sense in which prose is contrasted with verse. Some degree of rhythm seems to be inseparable from the poetic intuition of anima whenever it operates.

To sum up: poetry is a form of art employing words for their sound and meaning. In as much as poetry employs the sound and the suggestive meaning of words, words as they are aesthetically significant forms, it expresses an aesthetic intuition and contemplation of significant form and whether it is verse or poetic prose is pure poetry, is poetry as the product of anima. But in as much as poetry must and should use words for their meaning as simple statement, rational and in a wide sense scientific, it contains an element of reasoned statement, of prose in the sense in which it is the product of animus. This rational element, however, must be permeated and, so to speak, transfigured by the poetry. In short, what the soul in a living and healthy man is to the body, in a poem pure poetry, the poetic intuition of aesthetically significant form and of words as aesthetically significant forms, must be to the rational statement, the "prose" in that poem. As the soul the body, the anima must control and vitalise the production of animus.[1]

We should now be in a position to consider the relation between the poet and the mystic. By this I mean the relationship between the poet as poet and the mystic as mystic, between poetry and mysticism. For in the concrete a poet may be also a mystic, a mystic also a poet. There is Crashaw, for example, and Gerard Manley Hopkins. There are the great Persians Jami and Jallal u'Din Rumi. There is Luis de Leon and pre-eminently the supreme master of Christian mysticism, St. John of the Cross, who has left us poems, few it is true, which give him a place among the masters of the world's poetry. The problem, therefore, is precisely the relation between the poet's intuition and the intuition of the mystic. What the former is we have discussed already. What then is the latter?

[1] I have said nothing of poetry as expressing and conveying emotion. For emotion is but an accident and by-product of poetry, which normally invests the poet's intuition and expression of significant form. Were it otherwise, were emotion the stuff and substance of poetry, national anthems, devotional hymns and *The Red Flag* would be among the finest poems of humanity. When emotion is itself and as such is the theme of poetry, the poet intuits and expresses it objectively as a psychological form of its subject, whether himself or another.

The mystic's experience is an experience of a union with God as He transcends all forms, whether images or concepts. This union is effected by, or rather is produced in, the central self, the root of intellect and will alike, though in this case more precisely as it is the root of the will, the fundamental orientation of the will. For the spirit is a spiritual energy, a radical volition. This centre is variously named *synderesis*, the fine point of the soul, its apex, its ground. The intuition of its union with God is an intuition of contact or presence but, as it were, a touch, even it may be an embrace, in the dark. The spirit is aware of contact with Absolute Reality.[1] But because It is Absolute Reality, the spirit cannot say what It is. The essentially limited forms of its creaturely experience must all alike fail it.

Evidently these two intuitions—the artistic-aesthetic of significant form, and this mystical intuition of a union with a Reality Formless because exceeding all forms—are wholly distinct in nature. Nor can they be fused into one and the same experience. Each excludes the other. Where one is, to employ a spatial metaphor, the other cannot be.

Both, to be sure, poetic intuition and mystical, are concrete and obscure intuitions, as contrasted with the abstract and clear intuitions which are the stuff of discursive ratiocination and therefore of scientific thought.

Both are intuitions of anima. The latter, however, and this is a most important distinction, is deeper than the former. The anima which is the subject of aesthetic-artistic intuition is deeper and more obscure than the animus which is the subject of discursive and scientific thinking and of the conceptual factor in poetry. The centre or apex on the other hand which is the subject of mystical union, the union of which mystical experience is the intuition, is at a still greater psychological depth.[2] It is indeed the ultimate depth where the very being of the human spirit is grounded in God.

Accordingly the qualities common to both of obscurity and concreteness do not alter the fact that artistic intuition of significant form and mystical intuition of union with the Formless Divine Reality are distinct and cannot coincide or fuse. Normally

---

[1] In as much as this Reality is apprehended as Absolute, it is apprehended as Infinite.

[2] As contrasted, however, with the superficial animus the apex or centre may be termed, as I have termed it, the anima.

—for a reason to be stated later, we cannot say universally—both intuitions cannot so co-exist in the same subject that he is fully conscious of both at the same time. If the consciousness is engaged by the one, there can normally be no full consciousness of the other. Moreover the mystical experience of union with God since it is ultimate, and most potent, must, when the spirit is fully conscious of it, exclude the aesthetic-artistic consciousness of significant forms. If, however, experience of the presence of God, of contact with Him, is not fully conscious but is more or less subconscious, it may co-exist as subconscious awareness in the background with an artistic experience which occupies the foreground and which alone is fully conscious. This is possible precisely because the psychological locus of mystical experience is not the same as the locus of aesthetic-artistic experience, but at a deeper level beyond and behind the latter.

Aesthetic-artistic experience in fact involves, I am convinced, a background awareness, though it is extremely indistinct, indeed subconscious rather than conscious, of the Presence of Divine Reality and of the soul's union with it—either the supernatural union of Charity or at least the union it possesses in virtue of its nature as created by God, deriving existence from Him and depending upon Him for its existence. For the spiritual realities, the ideas of which the forms perceived and chosen by the artist are significant, are in the last analysis attributes of the Absolute Spiritual Reality which is God. To be aware therefore of this significance, however obscurely, is to be aware, however obscurely, of God. Aesthetic experience, that is to say, of significant form, not only may but must involve a background, and more or less subconscious, awareness of God. If the subject is not in supernatural union with God, the awareness is but the inchoate intuition of a natural mysticism, intuition of the ontological dependence of the created spirit on God and the union it involves. If the union with God is supernatural, this subconscious background awareness may be substantially identical with the intuition which when fully conscious is the intuition, the experience of the supernatural mystic.[1]

The co-existence in the poet's experience of a foreground consciousness of significant forms, and an obscure more or less subconscious background experience of the ultimate Reality has been well expressed in a sonnet by Humbert Wolfe:

[1] For the supernatural union may be too weak, too embryonic for awareness of it.

> I will tell you the poet's secret. It is this
> To trap the shadow and leave the light that cast it,
> To set a sound beside those silences
> That give the sound its glory and outlast it.
> There is a net of colour at the edge of the mind
> And the poet beats against it, as a bird
> Against a stained glass window, but, behind
> The window, distance stainless, cold, unstirred.[1]

Nevertheless the background subconscious experience of God is not the fully conscious artistic-aesthetic intuition of significant form. And normally both intuitions cannot be fully conscious simultaneously.

I have said it is normally impossible. But it cannot be said that it is never possible. For some mystics, notably St. Teresa in her *Interior Castle*, report a condition of double consciousness in which it even seems as though there were not one soul but two. Above, the soul enjoys in peace conscious union with God. Below, her attention is occupied with her human activities, is perturbed or suffering. "A soul," she says, "seems to be in some sort divided. The spirit is enjoying a delightful rest; the soul plunged in such suffering and occupied by so many employments that she cannot share the joy of the former." And St. John of the Cross corroborates her witness. "Sometimes . . . the higher and lower portions of the soul seem . . . to be so far apart; that neither seems to have anything in common with the other."[2] Nor is this double consciousness confined to the high states of prayer of which these Saints are speaking. Sensitives remote from these summits have at times had the same experience of a psychological division, of a spirit contemplating from above the equally conscious experience of the lower soul. It is therefore possible that the same person might be fully conscious at the same time of poetic intuition at a level of his personality, which though by no means superficial, is not the deepest, and of a mystical intuition of central union with the formless Godhead.

Has this possibility been in fact realised? Has any poet been simultaneously fully conscious of his poetic experience of form and of union with God? So far as I know there is no evidence

[1] Humbert WOLFE, Sonnet Sequence, *The Blind Rose*.
[2] *Interior Castle*, Seventh Mansion 1: *Dark Night of the Soul*, I, II, 23.

enabling us to return a certain answer. Most poets who have written of mystical experiences seem fairly certainly to have written after the event, when the conscious intuition of contact had passed and been replaced by poetic intuition of significant forms suggesting what they cannot express. It is a case, not of "emotion recollected in tranquillity", but analogously of mystical intuition recollected in poetic. Such, for example, were Dante's attempts in his *Paradiso*, most notably in his final Canto, to tell us something of a mystical experience which he knew to be an earthly beginning and foretaste of the heavenly vision. With the poetry of St. John of the Cross, however, it is different. Some of his poems, pre-eminently the *Noche Oscura*, seem to owe their birth directly to the mystical experience their symbolism attempts to suggest, to express a poetic intuition of the appropriate significant forms which was simultaneous with the mystical intuition at the centre. Since, however, we have no account of the actual composition of these poems, this can be no more than a probable conjecture. In any case such fully conscious co-existence of poetic and mystical intuition must be extremely rare. Normally the former alone is fully conscious, the latter more or less subconscious. And of their nature, even if experienced simultaneously, they are always distinct and mutually exclusive.

Moreover it is important to recognise that whereas artistic intuition is the substance of art, mystical intuition is not the substance of mystical prayer. The substance is the union of the soul with God, the central union of the radical will, the intuition of that union no more than an accident. Strictly therefore we should not speak of contemplation and contemplative prayer, terms which refer to the accident, but of union and unitive prayer, terms which refer to the substance. Whether and to what degree the subject of this union is aware of it, depends on circumstances of no direct religious significance, whether his psychophysical constitution is transparent or opaque, on his surroundings and occupation, on his religious beliefs, on his acquaintance with mystical literature or oral teaching. Of these factors conditioning intuition or its absence the most powerful is the psychological temperament, whether it is transparent or opaque, and the degree of its transparence. A transparent temperament is such that the central spirit and the realities with which it is in contact, normally buried below the threshold of consciousness,

become on occasion conscious as they do not—or not so easily—
when the temperament is opaque. Accordingly the union of the
central spirit, the radical will, with God, which is the substance
of mystical prayer, is the more likely to become conscious, the
object of an intuition, the more transparent the subject. This is
not to question the value of the intuition, the assistance it must
bring towards a closer union. But it does mean that the union
alone is essentially and, normally at any rate, is alone the direct
effect of Divine Action. At a certain degree of intimacy the union
with God is likely to become conscious, the subject to become
aware of it. But many factors outside his prayer may prevent this.

The relation therefore of poetic to mystical experience is a
relation between the substance of a superior, indeed a lofty
and noble, human function and fulfilment, and an accident
of the supreme. And when all is said the substance of this supreme
human fulfilment is the *unum necessarium*, the one thing necessary,
for whose sake in the last resort all other human functions and
fulfilments exist, among them therefore the artist's and the poet's.
Better darn stockings for God's glory and thereby be united with
Him than write *Hamlet* for one's own glory or profit and be
divided from Him or even retreat from Him farther, though
to write the *Commedia* for God's glory and be united more closely
with Him in doing so is even better. For, as St. John of the Cross
tells us, we shall be judged on our love.

The prayer called so misleadingly contemplative is union, an
activity of the will. Contemplation is but its by-product. Poetic
experience on the other hand is contemplation, a contemplation
of significant form. Unitive prayer lifts us above this half-
world of imperfection and disappointment. Poetic contemplation affords us a temporary escape from it. For it presents its
forms abstracted from their concrete embodiment in energies
which clash with each other and with our own, and restrict their
action and our freedom. The will, however, is not affected, much
less is its direction radically changed. It is not being transformed.
Indeed, as Schopenhauer pointed out, aesthetic contemplation,
while it occupies the spirit, lays the will to sleep. The subject ceases
for the time to will and is content to contemplate. If in fact the
will comes into action, or even an imperfect and more superficial
volition, a desire or a wish, it banishes the aesthetic contemplation.
If for example a picture of still life by a great artist arouses in a

hungry man the desire for food aesthetic appreciation of the picture is impossible. If a work of art, a picture or poem, makes too strong an appeal to the sex instinct or, on the other hand, disgusts us by the loathesomeness or horrifies us by the brutality of its theme, however fine the technical achievement, whatever its genuine aesthetic quality, it fails as art. For the positive or negative volition or desire which it provokes prevents the aesthetic intuition of its significant form. Therefore, when the will awakes from its contemplative slumber, it is precisely what it was before it went to sleep. Aesthetic contemplation does not *directly* and as such alter the moral character of the subject, increase or diminish holiness. Poetry cannot unite us more closely to God, though our employment of it may. But it withdraws us for the time from the rubs and stings of surrounding objects, be they people or things, from anxiety, ambition and superficial pleasure, to behold in their immortality, celebrated by Keats in his "Grecian Urn", the abiding forms of things which elude our grasp or slip away from it, forms resplendent with the light of their ideal significance and investing our spirits with their passionless peace. To combine in our lives this aesthetic contemplation of form and the union of unitive prayer would be the richest and most satisfactory life possible to mortal man. Many mystics have in fact been distinguished by aesthetic sensibility. For they must be sensitive, endowed with an exceptional measure of sensibility. Otherwise they would not be transparent, and a central union with God would remain unconscious. Simply by its nature as a created spirit the soul is intimately united to God. For God is immanent in all His creatures and the more fully as they approach Him closer, as they rise in the scale of being from inorganic energy through life to spirit; moreover the being of the spirit is grounded in God—its source. He sustains it in the existence He has bestowed. Indeed, He *is* its positive being. For it is His communication. And it is distinguished from Him only by its comparative lack of being, its comparative nonentity. He is therefore its being, as an object is the being of its reflection. As the late Father Stuart has explained, God's complete transcendence of His creatures, the fact that He is wholly other than they, enables Him to identify Himself with them as colour with shape but not shape with shape. A triangle may be red but it cannot be square.

A man therefore of a transparent psychophysical disposition may experience this natural union with God and God accordingly as immanent in himself, irrespective of personal holiness, without regard to the degree or even perhaps the existence of a supernatural union of the will by charity.

And since poets, like others of exceptional aesthetic sensibility, are on the whole more likely to be transparent than those not so endowed, it is not surprising that poets by no means remarkable for sanctity have been the subject of a mystic experience of a lower order, a naturally mystical experience, an experience that is to say of God's immanence in their own spirit and beyond it in the universe. Such was the experience recorded by Wordsworth in his "Lines Written Above Tintern Abbey" and in many passages of his poetical autobiography. Such Tennyson's experience of a "boundless being" into which his individuality itself seemed to dissolve and fade away—as though an image reflected in a mirror could become aware of the object of which it is but a reflection and therefore of its own comparative unreality.[1]

Even a drug, by inducing a state of transparency in a subject normally opaque, may occasion an intuition of his union with God, the presence of God in his spirit whether merely natural or even, if for example an anaesthetic is administered to a holy person, supernatural. For natural mystical experience, an intuition of the spirit's ontological union with God immanent, is an accidental concomitant of that natural union, as supernatural mystical experience, the intuition of a supernatural union with God transcendent, is, as we have seen, an accidental concomitant of that supernatural union. And as the latter union presupposes the former and is built upon the foundation it provides, the former intuition may and should be, though too often is not, the prelude to the latter.[2] Poets certainly are often natural, if rarely supernatural, mystics. But their naturally mystical intuition when it occurs is as distinct from their aesthetic intuition as is a supernaturally mystical intuition.

Almost all mystics, so far as we can judge, are sensitive to natural beauty, though many in consequence of an unfavourable environment and education have had little, if any, appreciation

---

[1] See Dom Cuthbert BUTLER, *Western Mysticism*, 2nd ed., p. 331. Cf *In Memoriam*, xcv: an experience of contact with God, " that which is".

[2] It was so in the case of Richard Jefferies. See his *Story of My Heart*.

of art. And the artist, the poet, because the forms he contemplates are significant of the ideal world and its spiritual realities, points beyond himself to the mystic who may even be himself in another aspect and on a deeper psychological level. And the poet, whether he writes in verse or prose, provides the symbols which suggest the Indescribable Reality the mystic knows.

Without prayer the spectacle of human life would be intolerable, a spectacle of folly, suffering and final frustration. Without the beauty presented to aesthetic intuition and created by art, prayer would be more difficult than it is, when the pain of the world lies heavy on the heart and there is no apparent answer. Never was this truer than today when the shadow of atomic warfare threatens mankind and we are confronted with a hideous dilemma. We must, it would seem, submit to the tyranny of a totalitarian and godless Communism, or resist it by a method of warfare plainly immoral, because it inevitably involves the wholesale massacre and mutilation of innocent non-combatants. It is the prospect of a war to be waged between those employing evil means for an evil end and those employing the same evil means for a good end. And no end however good can justify means so evil. In face of this grim outlook art offers only the respite of a temporary oblivion, though with the intimation that somehow and somewhere there must be a way of liberation and a final happiness. For it is obscurely aware of final Good, of Good at the heart of things, of Good as ultimate reality. This intimation indeed is the purification, the catharsis effected by art, by poetry, above all by tragedy.[1] Prayer can effect the liberation itself, can give us strength to refuse to take part in warfare which cannot be waged without wrong, and present union with the final and eternal Good to which art can but point from afar. It unites us to the source of the forms art displays, to the Truth which is their significance. No power outside ourselves—neither conscription nor bureaucracy nor Communism nor nationalism nor atomic warfare—only refusal or neglect to pray can sever this union, can deprive us of God.

Now therefore more than ever the society of poets and mystics should be welcome, as the former invite us to repose and refresh ourselves with the spectacle of beauty, the reflection of God's

[1] See in particular Bradley's *Shakespearian Tragedy.*

glory, the latter to climb ourselves the mount of transfiguration where humanity is glorified, deified with His glory. Even if we can but climb the lowest slope, the ascent is richly rewarding and the mystic's report of the summit assures us of the eternal life of God as present Reality. The mystic's prayer and the poet's work alike are a service of joy. For the artist's creative activity, reflecting and reproducing the glory of God, like the Divine Creation which in a true sense it completes, reproduces somewhat of the Creator's joy in His work. And the mystic's prayer is union with joy itself, the channel by which it takes possession of his spirit. The mystic therefore who is also a poet or an artist in some other medium experiences and imparts a twofold joy.

In a time when, as never since the origin of humanity, the framework of man's life is being so completely and so rapidly revolutionised that nothing of his historic heritage seems secure, it is reassuring to keep company with those concerned with the immutable, with the beauty which "is a joy for ever" and with God who throughout all human changes is the eternal present. So may be fulfilled for us the words of the Collect "O God who makest the spirits of the faithful to be of one will"— the will united with God and receptive of His will, of which mystical experience is the intuition—"grant that Thy people may love Thy commands and desire Thy promises" reflected in the poet's mirror, tasted already by the mystic's prayer, "that amid the changes of the world our hearts may be fixed where real joys are"—the joys the poet indicates, the mystic possesses.

CHAPTER II

"HE WANTED ART"

Lack of information about Shakespeare's life has left his admirers free to imagine a life and character in harmony with the creator of Hamlet. Keys to his soul have been sought, as by Wordsworth, in the Sonnets, though no one can say how much in them is personal experience, how much literary convention. Of late, however, a few but very significant facts have come to light. And they are most emphatically not what we should have expected. We find Shakespeare taking part in a flutter in knitted stockings, involved in legal wrangles, hand-in-glove with a wealthy moneylender and agreeing with an unscrupulous fellow-townsman not to oppose his encroachment on the citizens' common rights provided those attached to the poet's property are respected. In the event, though he refused a request from the townsmen of Stratford to champion their cause, the usurpation of their rights proved too flagrant for even a Jacobean court to sanction.

When he received a visitor at Stratford, Shakespeare did not discourse on the art of drama or the psychology of Hamlet. He discussed municipal politics affecting property. The ambition of the creator of Lear and Macbeth sought the higher distinction of a coat of arms such as his mother's family, but not his father's, was entitled to bear. And when he could retire from the stage to comparative affluence and the social rank of a country gentleman, he buried Prospero's magic staff and book and wrote no more. For like Prospero he thought more of being Duke of Milan, the owner of New Place, Stratford, than the master magician commanding the elements of human nature and controlling the spirits of men. If we do not allow preconceived opinion to blind us, we cannot reject the evidence of such things that Shakespeare the man was mediocre, commonplace in outlook and ambitions, a careerist, a moneylender out for the main chance, a social climber, something of a snob, the British middle-class man of property, both in getting and in enjoying it.

Father Thurston satisfactorily proved that John Shakespeare's Catholic "will" is a genuine document, and that there is equally conclusive evidence that the poet's sister, Joan, was a Catholic. Although, however, apart from the patriotic rant in *King John* about stamping on a Cardinal's hat, the plays are remarkably free from Protestantism, and a local clergyman who had no motive for deceiving us or himself about it informs us that Shakespeare died in the Catholic Church, he conformed to the Establishment during his life. He was the last man to share the suffering of the recusant confessors and martyrs. In the interest of man's artistic heritage it is not easy to regret this. But it does not suggest nobility of character. And the conformity is more likely to have been inspired by the consideration of his career than of his art. Dante in exile for his principles, Milton with his lofty, though narrow, ideals and his self-sacrificing, if chiefly wasted, labour on political polemics, Blake content with poverty and refusing to sell to Hayley his artistic soul— such men were of a higher stature.

But on the other hand there is Shakespeare. This strange, this amazing, duality is the solution of the enigma. There is Ariel Shakespeare, the poet, whose anima, moved by an aesthetic insight, poured out as sublime poetry as the world has heard, and there is Forsyte Shakespeare, of bourgeois aims, and, as we shall see, an animus that failed to appreciate and therefore to assist the achievement of anima. Only if we keep these two un-reconciled beings steadily in view can we hope to understand Shakespeare or his work. When the breath of poetry blew, awoke and moved his anima, the result was as close to artistic perfection as is possible for the workmanship of man. When it failed there was nothing but Forsyte Shakespeare, of mean will and the animus not of an artist but a successful business man. We have indeed his own testimony to the peculiarly inspirational character of his work in the well-known passage from *A Midsummer Night's Dream*:

> The poet's eye in a fine frenzy rolling
> Doth glance from heaven to earth, from earth to heaven
> And as imagination bodies forth
> The form of things unknown, the poet's pen
> Turns them to shapes and gives to airy nothing
> A local habitation and a name.

Such surely was the birth of Shakespeare's poetry, and of everything in his dramas truly dramatic. When the Spirit of the Lord
came upon Saul, "Is Saul among the prophets?" they exclaimed
as they saw the young warrior, who was not presumably remarkable for his piety, and who moreover had gone out to look
for lost asses, possessed by the spirit of prophecy. "Is Shakespeare among the poets?" we may well exclaim when we see this
careerist and moneymaker possessed, as few among the sons of
men, by the spirit of poetry, and pouring out, it would seem,
without effort, poetry as magnificent as any in the literature
of mankind and drama finer, perhaps, than any other. Yes, he
is among the poets, a poet and, one might almost say, more
than a poet, a ·veritable superman of poetry. But even so not
the perfect poet, still less the perfect dramatist, which but for
Forsyte Shakespeare he might have been.

That Shakespeare's art is inspirational rather than deliberate,
the art of anima moving animus, not of animus co-operating
with anima, was the view of it taken by Milton.

> Or sweetest Shakespeare, Fancy's child
> Warble his native woodnotes wild.

The "wild woodnotes" are the spontaneous, "native", out-
pouring of anima, "fancy" Milton calls it here, and moreover
they are contrasted with the studied and technically elaborated
art, the animus art of Ben Jonson—"Jonson's learned sock".
Milton thus testifies to the pre-eminently, we must indeed say
the exclusively, inspirational character of Shakespeare's poetry.
We have said that Shakespeare's duality affected his work. It
did, and obviously not for good. There was not, of course, a
complete divorce between animus and anima in Shakespeare.
Had there been he could not have produced the work he did.
Without a collaboration between animus and anima no work
of very high quality is possible. We must, however, distinguish
between two ways in which animus operates. When anima was
in control it seems to have taken hold of animus and made it
almost unconsciously work in its service. The great dramas
must have been the product of animus thus subdued to the
service and expression of anima's vision. But there is another,
a more conscious, operation of animus working upon the product

B

of anima when for the time anima has ceased to see and operate, or does so but feebly. And at this point Shakespeare indubitably fell short. He did not make the best use of animus he could, at whatever cost of time and labour. To a degree unique among artists of the first rank, he lacked the artistic conscience. And he lacked it because he was not only Ariel but, also, Forsyte Shakespeare, because his will (of which animus is pre-eminently the tool) cherished ambitions other than artistic perfection.

Since this is precisely what the idolaters of Shakespeare refuse to see or admit frankly, we must refuse to wear their blinkers and insist on looking obvious facts in the face. And this I invite my readers to do. Of the many unjust judgments of history, not the least unjust is the condemnation of George III as an uncultured Philistine because he said that much in Shakespeare is "sad stuff". His critics forget that in the more lucid intervals of his madness the King found solace in the woes of tormented Lear. For after all he was right. There is sad stuff in Shakespeare, and it is due to his lack of artistic conscience, a lack itself due to causes for which Forsyte Shakespeare was responsible. Sad stuff indeed. Do the speeches of ranting abuse which mar *Richard III* deserve to be called anything better? And what stuff could well be sadder than the scene in *The Winter's Tale* laid on the coast of Bohemia, in which a bear devours Antigonus on landing? Presented by a playwright to any modern producer it would mean the play's instant rejection without time spent on reading another line. But anon the spirit of poetry awakes anima and the immortal Perdita is born.

> O Proserpina
> For the flowers now that frighted thou lettest fall
> From Dis's wagon, daffodils
> That come before the swallow dares and take
> The winds of March with beauty.

Through Perdita and the scenes of which she is the central figure, *The Winter's Tale* climbs to the heaven of poetry. But the fact remains that the careless Forsyte Shakespeare's lack of artistic conscience marred the play with the preposterous rubbish about the bear. Indeed, even the lovely lines quoted seem to me to lack the finishing touch animus might have given "Dis's wagon".

Surely the hissing is unpleasant: "Dis's" like "Missis", which is probably the ugliest word in our language. I dare to think "Pluto's wagon" would have been more euphonious. A trifle, it is true, but not without significance. How unlike Shakespeare's rough and ready carelessness is the delicate artistic conscience of a Horace keeping his odes in his desk nine years for polishing, or its exaggeration even, in Virgil who because his *Aeneid* wanted the finishing touches condemned it remorselessly to the flames—from which under Providence only the Imperial command saved it for mankind. Of the saying, too commonly repeated, that genius is the capacity for taking infinite pains, Shakespeare is a striking and sufficient refutation.

What care did he take for the publication of his plays in an accurate text? None whatever. The players published them as they would from any playhouse text in hand. For the plays brought in far more money by being acted than as published for readers, and this for Forsyte Shakespeare was the important point. Certainly no artistic conscience was at work here. What sum would have bought Virgil's consent to the publication of an imperfect *Aeneid*? For this reason the reader of Shakespeare, if faced with a difficulty of language or interpretation, must ask himself whether he is reading the work of Ariel Shakespeare, the poet of anima, or Forsyte Shakespeare, of animus without anima. It might save time wasted in reading into the text what is not there.

Imagine the producer of an opera approaching Beethoven with a proposition such as this: Herr Kappellmeister, as you probably know, has begun to write an opera for the opening of next season. Having finished only the first act he has fallen very seriously ill and even if he gets over his illness will not be able to do any more work for at least a year. Would you be so kind as to help us out by finishing it? We are, of course, prepared to remunerate you handsomely. His reply, no doubt, would have been the language of a bargee and a vigorous kick for the producer. It would have been the reply, not perhaps of a gentleman, but of an artist. And Milton would have received with language equally vigorous, if possibly more refined, a proposal to complete the unfinished epic of a Puritan versifier more distinguished for piety than poetry.

This, however, was the very thing that Shakespeare did frequently and without a qualm. He began his work as a dramatist by botching up a minor playwright's *Henry VI*. He was willing, it seems, to add a page or two to a play on More by a handful of writers. His last play, *Henry VIII*, was written in collaboration with Fletcher. And the case of *Pericles, Prince of Tyre* may well have been an exact parallel to my imagined suggestion to Beethoven—but not refused. Some years ago at his Maddermarket Theatre, Mr. Nugent Monk produced *Pericles*. He omitted the first act as glaringly inferior. The remaining four despite an absurd plot made a fine play. Either the first act was the work of some theatrical hack or it was written by Shakespeare himself when his pen was not moved. In either case he was content to complete the work of a hack, were that hack another writer, perhaps the writer of an earlier play, or his own uninspired self. What dramatist of artistic conscience would consent in this way to attach his gold to brass? Forsyte Shakespeare was willing to do it, because he had no artistic conscience and Burbage no doubt paid well. Am I then saying that Shakespeare was not a great man? Yes, I am. He was a little man. He was not just a great artist, he was a supreme artist; but only when anima held him in her beneficent thrall. So long as anima controlled and fertilised animus there was a master poet and a master dramatist. When animus was free of anima there was no artist whatsoever, merely a man who used his pen among other, sometimes less reputable, tools to make money and win social rank. Shakespeare has his place among the world's greatest artists, second to none, but not among the world's great *men* or most perfect artists.

Voltaire's condemnation of Shakespeare's barbarism and his preference for the classical French dramatists, for all its injustice, was not sheer wrongheadedness. It was based on a principle of aesthetic valuation which attached most worth to what precisely Shakespeare lacked—the scrupulous, painstaking and polished elaboration of animus, aiming at perfection of formal expression. This the French dramatists, on the other hand, possessed. To that extent his criticism was justified. But he failed to see that the essence of poetry, as of art in general, is the insight of anima and its effective conveyance. These Shakespeare possessed in an incomparably higher measure than a Molière or a Racine. The latter, as Voltaire perceived, were more perfect artists than he; Shakespeare on the other hand, which he did not perceive, by far the greater artist.

Not every failure in Shakespeare, it is true, is the result of this duality of anima-inspired animus and uninspired animus. Take it all in all, *Timon* is a failure, a dreary series of misanthropic rantings. But this, I imagine, is due to the fact that the poet allowed a mood of passionate resentment to interfere with the detached contemplation which is the indispensable condition of aesthetic insight and the creation which expresses it. The majority of his failures, however, are clearly due to a failure of anima, leaving the field to an uninspired animus at the service of baser aims.

The finest plays indeed are almost wholly products of anima inspiring and moving animus. But even here there are lapses. Since producers usually and rightly omit or curtail it, the playgoer is unaware of the dull and ridiculous scene in *Macbeth* in which, during a halt in the dramatic action, the exiled Malcolm tests Macduff's honour by an impossible self-accusation. Anima has relaxed control and animus is content to copy Holinshed regardless of psychology or drama. Critics have spent much thought and ink to account in terms of human nature for Iago's diabolic and, it seems, "purposeless" malignity. It may perhaps be justified in such terms. But it is just as likely that it is the unqualified malignity of the stock villain of contemporary dramatic convention, of Marlowe's *Jew of Malta* for example, though, if this be the case, anima has certainly taken a hand and made incalculably more of him than animus originally intended. His fellow-villain Iachimo is far less successful.

The *dénouement* of *Measure for Measure*, unsatisfying, impossible, and in its staging ludicrously mechanized, is a glaring instance of Forsyte Shakespeare's lack of artistic conscience. Anima for some reason forsook the poet. The play perhaps must be ready very shortly and he could not, or would not, wait for her return. Burbage may have been pressing for it. And the public liked this sort of all-round happy ending. Well, then let the public and Burbage have it. But it is not only because its ending is so unsatisfactory that *Measure for Measure* baffles our judgment by delighting and disappointing us. Nor is the disappointment due solely to differences of opinion as to the respective value of preserving chastity and saving a brother's life, a matter of ethics, not aesthetics. The play is, in fact, a most instructive example of the dual Shakespeare. When Isabella pleads with Angelo in language finer than Portia's pleading with Shylock, and again in the prison scene between Isabella, Claudio and the ducal friar, anima is in control, and the high places of literature and drama are reached. And Lucio is a successful dramatic creation. But the remainder of the play is mainly the work of uninspired animus, and correspondingly of poor quality.

An instructive example of conflict between the utterance of Shakespeare's anima and his unanimaed animus is his attitude towards Prince Hal's behaviour in discarding Falstaff on his accession to the throne. That he had intended from the first to shake off his friend makes his conduct more consistent but no less callous.[1] The scene itself in *Henry IV* and Mistress Quickly's account of Falstaff's death in *Henry V* make it clear that Shakespeare's anima, that is to say Ariel Shakespeare the poet, saw and condemned Henry's action as heartless. But it is equally clear from the context in *Henry IV*, in particular the comments of Prince John and the Chief Justice towards the end (so that the audience may take home their view of the matter they are given the last word), that his animus, the mind of the man set on becoming a respectable bourgeois of Stratford, the judgment, that is to say of Forsyte Shakespeare, approved of the conduct whose condemnation his anima pronounced. The unresolved dualism is evident.

That Shylock at times displays nothing but pure vindictiveness, malice and greed, at others voices unforgettably the suffering of a persecuted race, that with equal sincerity he bewails the loss of his daughter and his ducats, is true to the mixture and inconsistency of human sentiments and motives. He has his place among the great creations of anima-animus in Shakespeare's work. Incidentally, an actor should not falsify the part by interpreting it exclusively in its baser or nobler aspect.[2] There is, however, an inconsistency in Shylock's conduct which is out of

---

[1] What is objectionable in the Prince's behaviour is not that when he ascended the throne he ceased to frequent such dubious company but the brutal fashion in which he publicly snubbed and abused a friend of years.

[2] Forsyte box-office Shakespeare I believe had intended the conventional villainous Jew. But Ariel Shakespeare took hold of Shylock, as he did of Iago, and made him what he is.

character and quite unnecessary. In Act I he refuses on religious grounds to dine with Bassanio. "To smell pork; to eat of the habitation your prophet the Nazarite conjured the devil into. I will buy with you, sell with you, talk with you, walk with you, and so following, but I will not eat with you, drink with you." In the following act, however, he goes to supper with Gratiano. On any reading of his character he could not have committed this particular inconsistency. Indeed Shakespeare seems uncomfortably aware of this to judge by the lame excuse for accepting the invitation he puts into Shylock's mouth. Also, as I have just said, it is unnecessary. Its purpose, to get Shylock out of his house when Jessica runs away with Lorenzo, could have been effected equally well had she informed her lover that on a particular evening her father would be dining with a Jewish friend, "Tubal" or "Chus", "his countryman". Here surely the carelessness of an inartistic animus is manifest.[1] Nor was it necessary for Portia so impossibly to hear before the merchant himself that Antonio's argosies were, after all, safe. A messenger could have brought the good news far more plausibly. In *Twelfth Night* Sebastian is solemnly betrothed to Olivia by the friar without mentioning his name, which she still believes to be Cesario—he could not even have answered to the name when she used it—a glaring absurdity if ever. "It is a standing puzzle", writes Mr. Douglas Woodruffe,[2] "how Shakespeare could ever have been contented with the absurdities, and generally easily removable absurdities, in the plots of his comic plays; but none is quite so boringly ludicrous as the *Comedy of Errors*, which involves long-separated twins and their twin slaves, brought up in Syracuse and Ephesus, being dressed exactly alike, and the wife of one not knowing him from his brother." No, not a standing puzzle but Forsyte Shakespeare. The appearance of Queen Margaret at the Yorkist court in *Richard III* is equally preposterous—and for no better purpose than to scold. But so long as the box office receipts came in well, what need to worry over such trifles as these? That is not the way an artist looks at such things, who is not, like

[1] Nor can I feel sure that it is in character for Shylock to save his life at the cost of renouncing his Jewish faith. It is certainly a question for the serious consideration of students of Shakespeare. In any case such a requirement was against the code of any Christian state of the time—absurd and unnecessary.

[2] *The Tablet*, September, 1952.

William Forsyte Shakespeare, an artist with his anima alone
and with his animus only when it is moved immediately by
anima, but an artist with his entire being. Such a man no doubt
is almost always a vastly lesser artist than Shakespeare. But he is
a purer and a more perfect artist.

This view of Shakespeare's defect is endorsed by the verdict
of a fellow dramatist who knew him well, Ben Jonson. Shakespeare, he said, "wanted art". This criticism is too often dis-
missed, most unfairly, as the spleen of conscious and envious
inferiority. In fact it hits the mark perfectly. Conscious art,
the art of animus not immediately moved by anima, the art
which seeks untiringly technical perfection and will be satisfied
with nothing short of the best, the art of the conscientious
artist—art of this kind Shakespeare did most certainly want.
If Jonson's perception of his lack of conscious artistry blinded
him as perhaps it did—and it is, after all, galling to a poet with
an artistic conscience to be so far outdistanced by a poet with
none—to the stature of his achievement as an inspired and
spontaneous artist (Voltaire's myopia), it is not on that account
invalidated. It would have been well, if students and critics of
Shakespeare had taken more notice of his illuminating remark.

The imperfection resulting from this lack of artistic conscience
is glaring in such a play as *Cymbeline* or *The Winter's Tale* and,
as we have just seen, in *Measure for Measure*, or in the absurd
introduction of an allegorical Hymen among the flesh and
blood characters of *As You Like It*. Even in *Hamlet* the clergy
refuse to accord Ophelia the full rites of Christian burial on the
ground that she had committed suicide. But not only was she
obviously insane, but her death, as the Queen informs us, was
accidental—"an envious sliver broke".

Shakespeare's endings are often the most unsatisfactory part of a
play. It is as if anima in sheer weariness after her mighty and
strenuous achievement had suddenly relaxed her hold and left
the poet bored and anxious to get the play off his hands anyhow.
The slackened grasp may be betrayed by a detail too slight to be
noticed except by readers for whom, as we have seen, the dramatist
cared little. Viola, for example, in *Twelfth Night*, is intended
to be, and is, a charming and sympathetic character. But at the
end of the play we learn that the sea-captain "upon some action is
now in durance at Malvolio's suit". How could Viola have been

so ungrateful to the man who rescued her from the waves and to whose kindness she owed her introduction to Orsino's court, as to leave him in a debtor's prison without attempting to use her influence with the Duke to secure his release? He was pledged to keep her secret. The ingratitude is even emphasised by her previous condemnation of the vice, when Antonio asked the supposed Sebastian for the return of his purse. It is not in character. Nor does Sebastian attempt to make use of his position as Olivia's husband to obtain Orsino's pardon for his benefactor. Antonio just fades out, to prison for all we know to the contrary—possibly even to death. A few words would have given him his well-deserved share in the general harmony and proved to him that Sebastian was not ungrateful. At the conclusion of *King Lear* the noble, but rather priggish Edgar, to point a moral, tells Edmund that his father owes his blinding to his half-brother's illegitimacy. Edmund agrees. What then of Lear's agony and death? Goneril and Regan were as legitimate as Cordelia. Nor does Shakespeare bother to tell us the fate of Lear's Fool. We may conjecture with Bradley that he died of exposure. But we cannot be certain.

For at the conclusion of the play the dramatist's mood was the careless and relaxed indifference which made him answer the request for a title, *Twelfth Night or What You Will*, a mood shown also in the Hymen conclusion to his previous drama and its similar title *As You Like It*. If Shakespeare's art was, as I have argued, the burning lava poured from a volcanic eruption of the spirit, an inspiration of the anima, this weariness which so frequently spoils or mars his conclusions is explicable as nervous reaction from the strain, sudden relapse from the inspired Ariel to the uninspired Forsyte. Even when in substance an ending is of the highest quality, plainly written under the full operation and stress of anima, for example, the conclusion of *King Lear*, a line or two may betray a final relapse. Consider the words with which Albany closes the immortal and heartbreaking scene that tells the story of Lear's death:

The weight of this sad time we must obey;
Speak what we feel, not what we ought to say.
The oldest hath borne most: we that are young
Shall never see so much, nor live so long.

The tension, it is true, should, as a matter of art, be relaxed at the conclusion of a tragedy and the final note be in a minor key, a note of calm and mournful relief. So it was in Greek tragedy, and so also it is in Shakespeare's most satisfactory valedictions. But such a banality as this cannot be justified. In fact there is worse than banality here, there is nonsense. Why should not the young live lives as long as their elders'? What, indeed, *is* the sense of the words? It is obviously another instance of the too common lapse from anima-controlled animus to mere animus, of the supreme artist who was nevertheless an artist but in part.

Reviewing in *The Observer*,[1] Mr. Ivor Brown calls attention to another example of a "lame and impotent conclusion". The superb poetry of the final scenes of *Richard II* is followed by the doggerel:

> Thy pains, Fitzwater, shall not be forgot;
> Right noble is thy merit, well I wot.

This, he maintains, is an obvious case of the work of two hands. We can hardly believe that so often Shakespeare left precisely the ending of his play to another writer. Moreover the doggerel is itself followed by a passing flash of the poetic fire—"With Cain go wander through the shades of night". In a sense, it is true, two hands are at work. But they are the hands not of two men, but of two Shakespeares, the hand of Ariel and the hand of Forsyte. Nor are these lapses, lengthy or brief, confined to the endings of plays.

We must not forget, however, in fairness to Shakespeare, that he inherited a bad tradition of botching collaboration and defective artistry. It was the crudity of Elizabethan drama still in the cradle, which made possible, even for Forsyte Shakespeare, his most glaring absurdities and impossibilities, in particular of plot. Marlowe's *Dr. Faustus* wellnigh baffles the modern producer by its mixture of superb poetry and rubbish. For like Shakespeare he was not consistently an artist, poet and playwright by fits, a spy in the secret service. And collaboration was a normal procedure. Nevertheless the readiness with which Shakespeare conformed to these inartistic conventions and dramatic barbarisms is the measure of his own lack of artistic scruple, a defect on

[1] July 14th, 1946.

which the little we know of his life casts an unpleasant light. After all, Ben Jonson, who became the acknowledged sovereign of English drama, hardly ever collaborated, and took pains to improve and perfect his work. That is to say, he was a more complete, though an incomparably lesser, artist than Shakespeare. A dramatist who could write or tolerate from another pen the insertion of a meaningless piece of bawdy jingle into the heart of Lear's tragedy must have lacked, when uninspired by the poetic afflatus, the artist's sensibility.[1] The groundlings were tickled by such things. The box office benefited. But art was betrayed. In this instance a trifling omission rights the wrong. But this is not everywhere possible. We cannot rewrite the final scene of *Measure for Measure*, or disengage the gold from the dross of *Cymbeline* or *The Winter's Tale*.

It is, however, commonly said, for example, as we have just seen, by Mr. Ivor Brown in his review in *The Observer*, that the doggerel and the poetry, the hackwork and the drama, were the work of two distinct persons. The poet, the genius, it has even been said was Bacon or was perhaps an unknown member of the aristocracy who dared not avow himself a dramatist and employed the hack writer and moneymaker, Shakespeare of Stratford, to sponsor his work and prepare it for the stage. Or, more plausibly, Shakespeare of Stratford was in truth the poet of genius. But he allowed his work to be staged and printed mixed in a greater or a lesser degree with rubbish by other pens. This view is untenable. The poetry and the rubbish cannot be apportioned in this way between distinct writers. No hint has come down to us of such a consistent dual or multiple authorship of the Shakespearean corpus. In the case of *Henry VIII,* the joint work of Fletcher and Shakespeare, the fact has been handed down. For this reason it must remain doubtful whether *Pericles*, for example, is the work of two authors or of two moods of the same author. And where the cleavage is less clear cut, or the alloy less extensive, or blent more intimately with the precious ore, the latter is the convincing explanation. Nor, except for comic gags, can two or three odd lines of doggerel have been inserted here and there by another hand. In any case the genius, the

---

[1] *King Lear* Act I scene 5 lines 56-7. Need I say that I am not referring to the "obscenities" in Lear's raving which are profoundly true psychologically and completely justified artistically.

author of the poetry and drama which have immortalised the name of Shakespeare, was undoubtedly Shakespeare of Stratford, the mediocre bourgeois careerist of petty ambitions and ignoble aims. For no contemporary friend or foe even hinted otherwise. Greene, for example, in his attack on "Shake-scene", has not a word to suggest that he is the mask of a hidden nobleman. But some at least must have known the truth. The entire literary and dramatic world cannot have been so completely hoodwinked. The contrast therefore between the poet and the man must in any case be admitted. Why not a corresponding contrast between the poet and the poetaster? Jonson who knew Shakespeare long and intimately says nothing of two men, a great poet and a hack. But his criticism, already quoted, that Shakespeare wanted art, proves that he was aware of the two aspects of the one dramatist, of Shakespeare the dramatic and poetic genius (even if he did not value him sufficiently) and Shakespeare the hack.

As I have already pointed out, the combination of magnificent poetry and rubbish is not confined to Shakespeare. Marlowe combines splendid poetry with the saddest of sad stuff, in his *Dr. Faustus* for example, the sublime poetry and drama of the damnation scene and the apostrophe to Helen with the vulgar clowning of the scene at the Papal Court. Yet everyone admits his unity of authorship. In more modern times, there is the contrast between the Wordsworth of "Tintern Abbey" and the Words-worth of "The Pet Lamb", between the lyrics of Tennyson's *Princess* and his "May Queen." Why is the contrast impossible only in the case of Shakespeare?

The dual authorship theory shifts but does not solve the problem. The genius who wrote the poetry, beyond reasonable doubt Shakespeare of the Globe and Stratford, was on that hypothesis willing to allow his work, sometimes to the extent of entire acts, to be completed by a hack writer or to be attached to the latter's work already in existence. He must, therefore, have combined with his genius a complete lack of artistic conscience. Only a writer without artistic conscience would permit his work to be mixed with rubbish by another hand. Such a poet, however, would be equally capable of writing the rubbish himself. And where the latter is no more than a scene or even a few verses or sentences, this would be the easier and the obvious thing to do. What such a poet could tolerate, he could produce. And for what reason did the genius allow *ex hypothesi* the hack to adulterate his work? Because the poetic afflatus which had inspired his anima and through it directed the activities of animus and had carried his work so far, had deserted him. That is to say his work depended for its poetic quality on such aesthetic inspiration, and when it failed he became artistically impotent. But this is precisely what I have said of Shakespeare—genius and hack.

That is to say, the explanation of dual or multiple authorship, if put forward as a complete account of the duality of Shakespearean achievement, is devoid of external evidence, is admittedly inapplicable to other instances of the same phenomenon in contemporary drama and leaves the problem substantially unaffected, to be solved, I submit, only by such a psychological explanation as I have put forward. But if this is accepted there is no need to assume dual or multiple authorship. Therefore, while admitting the existence in the Shakespearean corpus of work by other hands, even sometimes, as in the case of *Henry VI*, on a large scale, and the fact that Shakespeare made no objection to such admixture is further proof of his defective artistic conscience, I remain confident that Shakespeare the dramatist, poet and player, regarded by all his contemporaries as the author of the plays bearing his name, was responsible not only for the supreme poetry and drama, but directly for very much, I think most, and indirectly for the rest, of the very sad stuff which to a greater or lesser extent disfigures them.

To the same insensitivity of an uninspired animus we must as we have seen, attribute the stupid puns and coarse jestings without wit or humour which too frequently mar Shakespeare's plays. The fact that these weeds become fewer, or entirely cease, in the finest dramas or scenes where the control of anima is the most complete, plays or scenes by universal consent his finest work, supports further my view of a Shakespeare psychologically and therefore artistically, or rather artistically and inartistically, dual. For the psychology and philosophy of art and the aesthetic intuition art expresses and embodies, Shakespeare's case, the case of a divorce so glaring between the inspired poet and dramatist and the uninspired scribbler, is most

instructive. For this reason in particular I have called attention
to it here. It is to be wished that someone far better acquainted
with Shakespeare's work than I can claim to be would study
the plays in detail from this point of view. The labour would
I am convinced, be richly repaid by the understanding achieved
of a phenomenon in this degree surely unique in literature,[1]
though by no means uncommon on a smaller scale, and of the
dramas themselves as the product of an author so disconcertingly
dual.

It is further worth consideration whether this Shakespearean
duality, this disharmony in his life and work between anima
and animus in its normal operation, is not, as I believe and have
already suggested, the supreme example of a characteristic
commoner in English than in any other literature. Is not our
literature to an exceptional extent exclusively or onesidedly
inspirational, a literature therefore of imperfect and uncertain
artistry, in which the insight of anima is insufficiently worked
out, clarified and expressed by the subsequent labour of animus?
This unbalanced inspiration is surely a distinctive feature of our
literature as being found more or less, not of course in all, but
in a far greater number of English than foreign writers of
genius. As we have seen it explains Wordsworth's notorious
lapses from poetry of the highest quality into banal prosings.[2]
And in prose it is the outstanding characteristic of the typically
English Dickens. Witness the cheap and inartistic sentimentality
of Little Nell or the children visiting Smike's grave. And the
English are marked by an aversion to the clear conceptual thinking which is the province and work of animus, and are too often
careless of the technical perfection which the conscientious
employment of animus alone can bestow. English literature,
that is to say, is predominantly a literature of anima, often to
the detriment of animus, whereas French literature gives a far
greater part to animus, at some periods is even predominantly a

[1] For Marlowe, who shared even to an exaggerated degree Shakespeare's duality, was
incapable of his achievement.

[2] Wordsworth it is true did not lack industry and artistic conscientiousness. But
when anima failed him animus was incapable of doing work of high quality, and an ill-
informed artistic conscience, further blinded by conceit, could not see the failure. The
mass of unpoetic verse from the pens of Wordsworth and Tennyson was the product
of (1) a mistaken sense of the poet's mission to the public, (2) an æsthetic blindness
induced by contemporary bad taste enamoured of sermon and sentiment, and (3) personal conceit.

literature of animus, often to the detriment of anima. But this point I must leave to the reader to follow up.

I have spoken throughout as though the shortcomings of Shakespeare as a conscious artist, the poor quality of the work produced by his freely working animus, detract from the value of his work and must be accounted a regrettable defect, that it would have been finer even than it is, had he combined the animus artistry of a Racine for example, or, in our own literature, a Milton or a Pope, with the artistry of his anima controlling, moving and directing animus by its spontaneous action. In itself this is no doubt true. Had such a combination been possible it would have produced an achievement even more superb than that of Shakespeare as we have it. But it may well be that such consummate perfection was impossible. The defects which I have pointed out are indeed defects and in many cases very serious defects, and moreover bound up closely with defects of character, themselves due in part to defects of the mind's normal vision, the vision of animus. But they were perhaps the inevitable accompaniment and price of the inspiration to which we owe what for all such shortcomings, is as magnificent drama as any yet written by man, which, it may well be, could not have operated on other terms. For an attempt to carry the work further by the conscious action of animus, a serious endeavour to continue or improve by conceptual artistry and deliberate technique the achievement of anima's spontaneous operation, might possibly in the case of an artist so inspirational as Shakespeare have diminished or even dried up the spring of his inspired anima, have dimmed or even closed its sight, as the gift of a calculating prodigy is destroyed, if he is instructed in conscious, reasoning mathematics. In view of the possibility that Shakespeare could not have given us the supreme art he has, had he attempted, when inspiration failed him to perfect or complete his work by the art of animus—though we should be aware of his defect and trace its operation, for that is the way of understanding—we should not complain that he has not given us what might well have been incompatible with his actual gift. For his achievement no price of unachieved possibility, a possibility after all merely theoretical and hypothetical, could be too high.

CHAPTER III

DRAMA AND RELIGION

Hᴵˢᵀᴼᴿʸ shows an intimate connection between religion and drama. The ceremonial worship of religion has been the cradle of drama. The drama of ancient Greece sprang from the ritual pantomime of pagan nature worship, the worship of Dionysus, the spirit of vegetation and in particular of the vine; the drama of modern Europe from the Christian mystery play. And the origins of Indian and of Japanese drama—the No plays—were equally religious. For the ritual of religion has always contained a dramatic element. No doubt it was due, in the first instance, to the savage's belief in the magical power of mimicry. But when religion freed herself from magic, she did not therefore shed the dramatic element in her worship. For dramatic impersonation impresses the imagination most vividly and powerfully with the thoughts or actions of god, hero and saint. And religion, which, if it is to be complete, must make its appeal to the entire nature of man, can ill afford to neglect the unique influence over the imagination exercised by the dramatic method of presentation. This method is an invaluable instrument of teaching. Even the dullest subjects come alive, as soon as they are clothed in a dramatic form. In my own experience boys have begun to enjoy a lesson in elementary Latin grammar, immediately it was broken up into dialogue and seasoned with a little action.

Religion, therefore, whose message, though of an enthralling power over souls awake to its meaning, is obscure and often enigmatic and in any case requires a certain degree of spiritual perception in the hearer, is not likely to dispense, nor has it in fact dispensed, with the aid of the dramatic method of instruction. If the worship of the primitive savage consists pre-eminently of mimetic ceremonies, the ritual of the great religious bodies has always been largely dramatic. And among all the great world-religions none possesses a more dramatic ritual than Catholic Christianity. The central mystery of the Catholic Church—

the Mass—is a sacred drama (I use the word in its widest sense for any form of dramatic presentation), in which the celebrant enacts the part of Christ, and represents His work of redemption. Small wonder that religion has proved the cradle of drama.

But the cradle only, not the home. Everywhere, as drama grows to maturity, it is secularized, often formally, always in substance. For religious drama, the drama employed by temple or church to set forth the religion there professed, is not, in the full sense, drama. It is but the dramatic form of presentation. Dialogue and action are not sufficient to constitute drama. There can be no drama without the distinctively dramatic quality, a quality rather to be felt than defined, but the living spirit whose presence alone can render dialogue and action truly drama. And as the drama develops and this dramatic spirit produces drama, it separates itself from religion. This has not been the case with other branches of art. The finest sculpture and painting are religious, also much of the finest music; and one of the greatest epic poems, if not the greatest—Dante's *Divina Commedia*—is a poetical expression of the Catholic Faith. But for a dramatic counterpart of the *Divina Commedia*, we should look in vain. The great drama of the world is not sacred but secular.

We can watch the process of development and secularization. In ancient Greece it passes through the still deeply religious Aeschylus to Euripides, the dramatist described not unfairly by Verrall as an atheist preaching from the altar steps. For, if not strictly an atheist he was a rationalist, a sceptic. And although in Greece there was no official separation of drama from religious worship, though the yearly dramatic festivals were to the end religious festivals, though his outward form and his subject matter, and, to a large extent his *dénouement*, were still prescribed by the official religion, Euripides' treatment and spirit are rationalist. If he is an Ibsen compelled to write miracle plays, he is, nevertheless, an Ibsen.[1] A conventionally pious ending does not alter the fact that the *Ion* is a bitter attack upon the

---

[1] Not in the main the Ibsen whose plays are deeply tinged with a mystical colouring but are not so dramatic as his more positivist work, but the Ibsen of the realist dramas, dramatically his greatest achievement, the Ibsen of *Ghosts* and *Hedda Gabler*. The *Bacchae*, however, a work of Euripides' final period, is steeped in the vague but powerful " mysticism " of Ibsen's *Lady from the Sea*, *John Gabriel Borkman* and *When We Dead Awaken*.

moral character of Apollo as presented by the official mythology.
And the *Trojan Women* displays in a grim light the jealousies
and conflicts of the ruthless deities who fought them out with
human blood and tears.

It has been the same in modern Europe. There also we can
trace the development of drama from the religious mystery, which
itself began as a dramatic appendix to the choir office, to the pure
secularism of the Elizabethan stage. But Elizabethan drama was
drama, the mystery play was religious or moral teaching in a
dramatic form. The stage was divorced from the Church.
Indeed, in the Christian world there was an open conflict between
the religious authorities and the secular drama. The Puritans of
the Commonwealth closed the theatres and if Catholics did not
attempt such violence to human nature, canon law denied the
Sacraments to actors.

What was the cause of this alienation of religion from her full-
grown child? Why does the appearance and free development of
drama, the free action of the dramatic spirit, thus coincide with
its divorce from religion? Is there anything in the nature of drama,
on the one hand, and of religion, on the other, that will account
for it?

Before attempting an answer, I must dismiss as irrelevant
the Christian opposition to the stage as being more or
less sinful. For it was due to a number of accidental causes
lying outside the essence either of drama or religion. It was in
part the effect of a puritanic suspicion of amusement, which was
itself the religious reaction against the obscenity which disgraced
amusements, and especially the stage, in antiquity, and indeed
later in Christian countries. Under the Roman Empire the
drama had degenerated into obscene ballet and pantomime. And
it was also due to the official connection between the classical
stage and the pagan cultus; also, as far as the Primitive Church
was concerned, to a feeling that acting a part was a species of
lying. And the attitude of canon law was no doubt largely an
inheritance from Roman law, which treated the actor as infamous,
that is, without civic rights. All this has evidently nothing to do
with the nature either of drama or of religion.

But, although these accidental and temporary factors sufficiently
explain the official opposition shown in the past by the representatives of Christianity to the drama, they do not account for the

secularization of drama which everywhere accompanies its development inevitably, and as in virtue of a natural law. Nor do they explain the fact that the greatest drama is never sacred—that is to say sacred not only in form, as Greek tragedy was to the end, but in treatment and spirit.

These facts are, I believe, explicable only by a necessary and essential incompatibility between drama and religion, a mutual exclusion of each by the other, which is grounded in their respective natures. As I hope to show, this incompatibility is dishonourable neither to drama nor to religion, nor does it mean that, if religion is true, we ought to dispense or can dispense with drama. I may, therefore, ask my readers who are fond of the drama, as I am, to give a hearing to a thesis which may at first sight appear shocking or absurd.

A word first of comedy and religion. If comedy is seen in the light of religious truth, the spectacle of man's immortal spirit in its relation to the eternal God, only the superficial comedy of circumstance or manners remains to amuse us. The deeper comedy of characters, of perversity, inconsistency and folly, ceases to be comic. For it is seen to be the serious matter that the responsible choice of a spirit must be.[1] The only comedy, for example, in Mr. T. S. Eliot's Christian morality play *The Cocktail Party*, is on the surface. The substance of the play, the moral choice of Edward, Lavinia and Celia, is not comic. In Celia's case it involves an agonising death. If the playwright is in earnest when he calls his play a comedy, he must understand the term only in the sense of Dante's *Divine Comedy*, that its ending viewed *sub specie aeternitatis* is happy—the redemption of an unsuccessful marriage by mutual unselfishness and humility, and for Celia the martyr's crown.[2]

I suppose however that everyone, on reflection, will allow that tragedy is the supreme form of drama and the most fully dramatic, the form of drama in which the specifically dramatic quality or character is displayed most fully. There is, to be sure, plenty of it in the finest comedy, but its perfect achievement is tragedy. And the most dramatic comedies approach tragedy. The type of comedy most remote from tragedy, the farce,

[1] If the folly is sufficient to destroy responsibility, impotence of will is no subject for laughter.

[2] Her fate would in any case have been incompatible with comedy in the ordinary acceptation of the term. Without religion the play would have been tragic.

has so little of the dramatic quality that we should scarcely
admit its claim to be considered in the strict sense drama. This
point can hardly be argued. I can only ask my readers to compare
their impressions of Shakespeare's comedies, the feeling evoked
by them, with their impressions of his tragedies, and the feeling
they evoke, and then to ask themselves whether *King Lear* and
Hamlet are not more *dramatic*, do not possess a higher degree of
the dramatic quality, than *Twelfth Night* or *The Tempest*, and
further to ask themselves whether *Twelfth Night* or *The Tempest*
do not approach tragedy closer than *The Comedy of Errors* or
Love's Labour's Lost.[1] If, therefore, we would observe the
dramatic spirit in its purest expression, we must study tragedy.
And if we would examine the relation of the dramatic quality,
or spirit, to the religious, we must study tragedy in relation to
religion.

Tragedy involves the tragic conflict, and the tragic conflict in
turn involves the presuppositions of a non-religious interpretation
of life. For the tragic conflict is a conflict between values, and a
waste of values, as seen from the natural, purely human and
sub-religious standpoint.

William Archer,[2] pleading on behalf of a drama whose plot is
known already to the audience, tells us that the audience should
be as gods raised above the conflict they witness, knowing the
issues, ignorance of which alone renders the tragedy possible.
Certainly the audience should be raised above the particular
conflict of the *dramatis personae* in their particular situation. But
the audience *must not* be raised above the tragic conflict of human
life, of which that particular tragedy is but an instance. In fact,
it is precisely because curiosity as to the particular issues of the
particular conflict on the stage distracts attention from its universal
character, its exemplification of the universal conflict, in which
its purest dramatic quality lies, that I believe Archer's practical
contention to be right.

But the tragic conflict of human life depends on acceptance of the values presented in human experience, whether
positive or negative, as they are valued by the natural man, from

[1] Is there nothing tragic in Malvolio's humiliation? What if Olivia had accepted
Orsino's hand and left Viola to pine in hopeless silence like " patience on a monument "?
Antonio and Sebastian in *The Tempest* are tragic villains, Caliban expresses a human
malice incurable in its extreme of malignity, untouchable in its folly.
[2] *The Old Drama and the New*, 1923.

is purely human and earthly standpoint, and therefore implies
gnorance of their absolute, their real value. Did we *see clearly*
he real value, the value for eternity of the objects of human
lesire or aversion, of human love or human hate, we could no
onger share the joy and the sorrow, and therefore could not enter
nto the tragic conflict, of those who accept them at their apparent
value. Nor could we grieve at the waste of values which, as
Bradley[1] shows us, is one of the most essential elements in
ragedy, if we *saw* this waste as merely apparent, as a means to
he attainment of higher values fully inclusive of the values
eemingly wasted.

Religion, however, in proportion to our genuine acceptance of
ts teaching, opens up a point of view from which the values of
uman life are transformed, lifts us to a height from which we can
ook down upon the conflict of these values, therefore upon the
ragic conflict, as a battle for shadows. The truly religious man
ees the tragedies of adult humanity, as the adult sees the tragedies
of the nursery. The religious man, therefore, will, *as such*, be as
ncapable of writing or of appreciating tragedy, as the adult is
ncapable, while occupying the adult standpoint, of writing or
eeling the nursery tragedies of the broken doll and the disputed
oy. In presence of the Absolute and Eternal Worth revealed by
eligion, the values for which the tragic characters contend,
lestroy, and perish, the motives of their strife—Romeo's passion,
Othello's jealousy and Shylock's revenge, the ambitions of
Borkman, of Hedda Gabler and of Rebecca West,—wither and
lie. The only values that survive are the positive values that
elp, the negative values that hinder, the attainment of the One
Perfect Value, which religion has revealed. If Desdemona's
idelity and Iago's baseness still possess value of a positive and
legative character respectively,[2] it is no longer because the
ormer satisfied the human love of its possessor and her husband,
nd the latter wrecked that happiness, but because the former is
odlike and tends to eternal union with God, the latter is ungodly
nd tends to eternal loss of God.

I was once shown in manuscript a tragedy written by a friend.
To this tragedy two alternative endings were possible. One of

---

[1] *Shakespearean Tragedy.*
[2] Strictly speaking there is no negative value—a contradiction in terms. But it is
wkward to speak of " unvalues " or " antivalues ".

these was the suicide of the heroine, the other her final abandonment of her intention to commit suicide. I felt myself mos
strongly attracted to the suicidal ending. I was sure, and still am
sure, that dramatically that heroine ought to commit suicide. Bu
from the religious standpoint I am equally sure she ought not to
commit suicide. Why this conflict between the two standpoints
Considering the matter, I concluded the reason to be that, grante
the non-religious valuation presupposed by tragedy, suicide wa
the noblest conduct possible to the heroine. And her character ha
been so drawn that she would naturally make the noblest choic
open to her vision. That is to say, if the values of life were what
without the illumination of religion, they must appear to be, thi
heroine ought to commit suicide. If, however, the religiou
valuation is introduced, the suicide is shown to be wrong. But
and this is the important point to notice, the tragedy of he
situation is abolished at the same time. For the value whose los
has brought her to the resolution of suicide, her dead husband'
financial honour, which, so far as she knows, she can restore onl
by her death, is seen in the light of religion not to be the suprem
value possible to her, a value indispensable to the worth of he
existence. It was precisely the non-religious valuation which ha
made it appear to be the supreme value, to be redeemed even b
suicide. Thus does the "transvaluation of all values" effected b
religion destroy the tragic conflict.

    Nor do we need even a positive religious belief to destroy th
conflicting values of tragedy. A purely negative view of th
world, the religious negation of worldly values, without th
religious affirmation of positive superhuman values, is sufficient, i
apprehended with sufficient force and vividness, to destroy th
tragic conflict. An example of this is Elroy Flecker's Hassan. A
poetry Hassan is magnificent, as drama it fails. In the essenti
dramatic quality it is deficient. For we seldom feel that th
conflict before us is significant. We feel that it is comparativel
indifferent whether the immediate issue be happiness or misery
since the final issue is in any case vanity. "Vanity of vanities, an
all is vanity": this condemnation of all merely human values, i
Scripture preliminary to the proclamation of God, but her
taken as the final truth, is proclaimed so insistently throughou
Hassan, that the dramatic quality dependent on our sense of th
significance and value of the issues at stake is unduly weakened

If it is not altogether destroyed, it is because the love between the doomed lovers which makes them prefer a death of torture to separation is not, and in spite of himself the poet shews us that it is not, empty and vain like the false culture of Haroun or Yasmin's selfish lust, but intrinsically valuable, even in the hour of torment and death. Nevertheless the portrayal of their fading ghosts, by which his pessimism attempted to undo his own work, pronouncing even upon this heroic love the sentence of universal vanity, is patently undramatic because it refuses abiding value and significance to what we are sure is abidingly valuable and significant. And where, as in Shakespeare's *Timon of Athens*, the pessimism is complete and unrelieved, drama has perished in the universal shipwreck. *Timon* is a bad play. If even the negative aspect of religion, its preliminary denial, is so potent to destroy tragedy, the action of a positive religion must be far more fatal.

But even if the exterior conflict be destroyed by religion, will not religion leave intact, indeed even enhance, the interior conflict, the conflict of those moral and spiritual values which condition man's attainment of God? Why can there not be a religious drama whose conflict is purely interior, fought in the realm of the spirit? Maeterlinck's religion was no doubt extremely vague, an atmosphere, not a creed. But such as it is, it made him reject the drama of exterior values and conflict. In an important passage quoted by Mr. Allardyce Nicoll[1] he says:

"Is it beyond the mark to say that the true tragic element, normal, deep-rooted, and universal . . . only begins at the moment when so-called adventures, sorrows, and dangers have disappeared? Must we indeed roar, like the Atrides, before the eternal God will reveal Himself in our life? . . . When I go to a theatre . . . I am shown a deceived husband killing his wife, a woman poisoning her lover, a son avenging his father, children putting their father to death, murdered kings . . . in a word, all the sublimity of tradition, but alas *how superficial and material.*"

Maeterlinck, however, though his mystical religion has rendered him unable to accept the values which condition the

[1] *British Drama*, 4th ed., 1947.

exterior conflict of tragedy, thought it possible to construct tragedies whose conflict is purely interior. And indeed the most dramatic scene in Flecker's *Hassan* represents the interior conflict in the souls of the condemned lovers—as they hesitate between the alternative of separation and life, or love and a death of torment. And Mr. Eliot has given us dramas of interior conflict —*Murder in the Cathedral* and *The Cocktail Party*. But insofar as Maeterlinck's tragedies are tragedies of purely interior conflict, they are deficient in dramatic quality. Because a drama by Maeterlinck, for example, or *Hassan*, is of high literary quality, is good poetry, it does not follow that it is therefore good drama. For a conflict purely interior is insufficient for drama. It lacks the action which appears to be indispensable for drama in the full sense of the term. Maeterlinck's tragedies are not in fact devoid of external conflict. There is no lack of external conflict in *Hassan*. Mr. Eliot's *Murder in the Cathedral* and his *Cocktail Party* culminate in murder, the martyrdoms respectively of St. Thomas and Celia the nursing sister. The distinction indeed between dramas of exterior and dramas of interior conflict is merely relative, a matter of emphasis. For the traditional tragedy of external conflict and disaster is also concerned with interior conflict, particularly in the soul of the protagonist. In *Hamlet* the latter at least balances the former, in *Macbeth* it predominates. But even if I am mistaken and a drama of purely interior conflict should after all be created as dramatic as the older drama of exterior conflict, religion, if sufficiently clear and powerful, would render even this drama of interior conflict impossible. Mr. Eliot's plays of interior conflict, for example, are of high literary quality and exterior conflict, though subordinate, is not wanting. But they are imperfectly dramatic, certainly not tragic. For the playwright presents the interior conflict in the light of his Christian faith and by so doing converts a tragedy into a mystery or a morality play. And if there is a considerable element of drama in the plays of Maeterlinck,[1] his religious vision, unlike Mr. Eliot's is dim and uncertain.

When religion reveals the presence of a supreme and eternal value, it reveals the supreme reality. But if the Divine Object of religion is the supreme reality, Its triumph over any forces

---

[1] Not, however, in the too-popular *Bluebird*, an unconvincing morality no more dramatic than *Peter Pan*, and no less sentimental.

which oppose and with apparent success Its purpose in the
world is inevitable, a foregone conclusion. Religion is necessarily
optimist. "To them that love God, all things work together
unto good." In one of the great religious classics—the
Revelations of Dame Julian of Norwich—Our Lord declares,
"I may make all thing well, and I can make all thing well, and
I will make all thing well." This is the religious answer to the
apparent tragedy of mankind, the religious solution of the tragic
conflict.

Convince yourself of this faith, steep yourself in it with every
fibre of mind and heart, and penetrated by religious optimism,
possessed by religious faith, watch or read one of the world's great
tragedies, *Œdipus Tyrannus, King Lear, Rosmersholm*. Either the
faith will kill the tragedy, or the tragedy will banish the faith.[1]
Both cannot subsist together. Nor even is there place for a
tragedy such as *Dr. Faustus*, the tragedy of the man who finally
loses the Supreme Good. For once we admit the fundamental
equation of religion, the equation of value and reality, if we
once *see* that the highest value is the fullest, the most real Reality,
we see that a man can miss it only by his own freely willed fault,
and miss it in the precise measure of his free rejection. And,
however terrible, this is not tragic. Goodness affirms itself, and
evil is shown to be, what it always and necessarily is, failure and
impotence.

This mutual exclusion of religion and tragedy will, I believe,
be understood more clearly, if we consider what has often been
falsely regarded as the world's supreme tragedy—the earthly life
of Our Lord as it ended in His Passion and Death.

Many years ago, an advanced New Testament critic, Dr.
Albrecht Schweitzer, a leader of the so-called apocalyptic school
of Gospel criticism, published his view of the life of Christ in the
brilliant book known in English as *The Quest of the Historical
Jesus*. Like many other critical reconstructions of the life of Jesus,
Schweitzer's is based on an arbitrary selection and utilization of
selected data from the Synoptists. But the result is a consistent
and living picture of a quite possible human enthusiast, though a
figure remote from the Christ of Christian faith. For Dr. Schweitzer is endowed with the imagination which makes the
creative artist. For him Jesus was from the outset of His ministry

---

[1] I mean, of course, as consciously *felt*.

the victim of an illusion, the belief in His own supernatural vocation to be the Messiah. He expected that God would suddenly intervene in the course of His Galilean ministry and introduce the new Messianic Kingdom in which He would reign. Since this failed to happen, He came to believe that His voluntary sacrifice was required to atone for the national sin which held back the Divine hand. If He died, the hindrance would be removed, and the immediate advent of the Messianic Kingdom would be forced. In this faith He went up to Jerusalem and provoked the religious authorities to procure His death. Only when He hung dying on the Cross did He discover that His belief was a terrible mistake, that no heavenly intervention would manifest His Divine mission. He died with a cry of despair on His lips: "My God, My God, why hast Thou forsaken Me?" The Gospels, on the other hand, depict Jesus as in truth the Divine Messiah, whose Death was the divinely ordained means whereby He redeemed mankind and opened the Kingdom of God to humanity, not His failure but His supreme triumph, followed, as He foreknew, by His Resurrection.

Of these two pictures of the life of Jesus, the former, I submit, is dramatic, but is not religious;[1] the latter of supreme religious value, but not dramatic. The dramatic and religious values of both stand in inverse ratio one to another. Dr. Schweitzer's account, especially as told by himself with a dramatic emphasis of the turning points of his story, is a great tragedy. It is the tragedy of a hero whose splendid faith and noble purpose are overthrown by the remorseless logic of the reality against which he dashes himself to pieces. And by his concentration of the entire public life of Christ within a few months, Dr. Schweitzer has gained the dramatic unity and tension of tragedy. But where is the religious value in all this? The non-religious reality proves itself more powerful and therefore more real than the religious value of Jesus' ideal and faith.[2]

On the other hand, the orthodox account of Our Lord's life,

---

[1] Dr. Schweitzer is, nevertheless, a deeply religious man. His heart and life are a protest against his intellectual negations. Shortly after the publication of his book, he gave up his work and position as a scholar of European reputation, to hide himself in the depths of Africa that there, by his medical work among the natives, he might devote himself to the service of the Master whom he understood so ill. *Vicisti Galilæe.*

[2] Dr. Schweitzer believes that somehow Christ triumphed in spite of His final and utter disillusionment. This, however, is a religious belief which does not arise from the portrait which he has drawn of the tragic Jesus, nor indeed is compatible with it.

just because it is religious, because it presents an inevitable and foreknown triumph of the Divine Reality apprehended by religion over the hostile forces which sought to destroy its revelation, is not drama. And the Passion plays which present this Christian life of Christ are not drama. From the outset the readers or spectators, like the Divine Sufferer Himself, know that the Passion is not the loss and defeat, but the gain and victory, of Jesus and mankind—the way to the Resurrection. And this knowledge destroys the dramatic conflict and the tragic failure. Further, in the Passion play, the scene most entirely devoid of dramatic worth is precisely the Resurrection. Why? Because we do not believe that it happened? That is certainly untrue, of, at least, a large proportion of the audience. The true reason for this dramatic failure of the Resurrection is that the Resurrection reveals even to the sensible imagination the religious value as triumphant, and thereby *totally* eliminates the tragic conflict and defeat. We see before our eyes the conflict solved, the defeat shown to be the very reverse of the failure it had appeared to be. "All great tragedies" remarks Mr. Nicoll,[1] "present a problem but never give a solution." And religion is the solution of the universal human tragedy of which all particular tragedies are instances.

My thesis is, I believe, confirmed by another feature essential to tragedy, which Mr. Nicoll also points out. The tragic hero must not be faultless. Mr. Nicoll gives no reason. I would suggest that the reason is that a faultless character would reveal the Divine Goodness so clearly, and therefore also the power of that Goodness, that the religious value thus displayed would abolish the tragic conflict; for it would abolish even the possibility that the hostile forces could finally triumph. In Dr. Schweitzer's view of Jesus—the *non-religious* and tragic view—He is not faultless, but the victim of a defect of character, the proud credulity that claims a false Messiahship, just as Hamlet is the victim of his native irresolution, Lear of his autocratic temper.[2]

Does it follow that the religious man can dispense with drama? That he will employ it only for his recreation, or as a method of educational presentation? Yes and no. In so far as he is religious,

---

[1] *British Drama.*
[2] I do not mean that Dr. Schweitzer sees his portrait in this light. He obviously does not. But it is nevertheless what he has portrayed.

and in so far as he is actually partaking the religious vision of the universe, he can neither compose nor enjoy tragedy. Dante could not have written *Hamlet*, nor St. Teresa have appreciated it. And the literature of a period dominated by religion will not be dramatic. The supreme literary expression of the Ages of Faith was not drama but epic—not Shakespearean tragedy but the *Divine Comedy*. Indeed, the very title of the latter, explained by Dante as denoting the happy ending of his poem, indicates the impossibility of religious tragedy. The drama of ancient Greece, Elizabethan England, and modern Scandinavia are products of ages whose religious sight is dim, men's vision bounded by the *flammantia moenia mundi*.

But the vast majority of mankind neither has been, nor is, able to live uninterruptedly in the light of God, and upon the religious level. For the Divine Object of religion is so transcendent of human vision that it must be at best obscure—the apprehension of faith, not clearly seen. Its existence is known only by metaphysical insight or religious intuition. Even the Christian revelation is of necessity obscure, a glimpse of incomprehensible mysteries veiled by symbols, by human manifestations as such necessarily inadequate. If, indeed, it were otherwise, if God were clearly seen by any soul in this life, or even apprehended with the intense and vivid faith, the powerful intuition, of the saint, or even of the ordinary religious man at his most religious moments, tragedy would certainly be impossible. As it is, tragedy is both possible and valuable. To claim a perception of religious truths clearer, more constant, or more powerful than we in fact possess, to pretend even to ourselves that we always possess the religious vision of life, would be hypocrisy. This pretence is indeed an element of that insincere religiosity which has disgusted so many with religion. And when we do not actually possess the religious vision, do not see life from the religious point of view, why should we not contemplate it from the standpoint next in order of value and truth—the dramatic, the tragic? Obviously, our religious belief ought to remain and will remain in the background and will prevent our acceptance of the tragic standpoint as final. But we shall be able to adopt it sufficiently to appreciate the tragedy. The composition of a tragedy would be impossible to a deeply religious soul. When Calderon devoted himself to religion, his plays became sacred mystery

plays, magnificent literature but not tragic drama. Since, however, neither all men nor all geniuses are thus impregnated with
religion, mankind will not lack tragedians. Had Shakespeare
possessed Dante's religious conviction, we might, instead of a
Hamlet, a *Lear*, a *Macbeth*, or an *Othello*, have had another great
poem of the nature of the *Divine Comedy*, perhaps a finer *Paradise
Lost*. The literary wealth of mankind might not have been
diminished. To be sure, drama would be the poorer. But all
men of literary genius could not be religious, unless mankind as a
whole were equally religious. And if that were the case, there
would be no need of tragic drama or room for it. Meanwhile, since things are as they are, since the very height of the
religious truth renders its access so difficult, its vision so
obscure—alike for the race and for the individual—even those
who have sufficient religious faith to find a deeper vision and a
truer representation of reality in Dante than in Shakespeare, may
be grateful that we possess Shakespeare as well as Dante.

Nor is this all. In his *Shakespearean Tragedy* Bradley points out
that, although Shakespeare never directly affirms the truth of
religion, he gives us broken hints of it, for example in Horatio's
farewell to his dead friend. Why are these hints of religion so
appropriate? Why do they seem so natural, so perfectly in place?
And, above all, why does a great tragedy leave us not depressed
but exalted, almost rejoicing? For answer I appeal to the experience of the sensitive spectator. From the very spectacle of tragic
disaster, the spectacle of values wasted, good defeated by evil, the
apparent supremacy of chance or an amoral or unintelligent fate,
in short of a universal meaninglessness, there arises, as it were in
despite of reason, a conviction that somehow this is not after all
the final truth, that behind the negation there is an affirmation,
beyond the evil good, beyond the failure triumph. Whence then
this impression, powerful, even for many compelling, though
vague, unargued and often unformulated? Because this is in fact
the case; because this final Good is the ultimate, the Absolute
Reality and the spirit is more or less subconsciously aware of it.
And, in particular, because the nobility of character displayed in
tragedy, the worth of the human soul, its inner triumph in
outer defeat, bring us to the threshold of religion. For the values
thus manifest are dim hints of a Divine Value, more real and
therefore more powerful than the forces which have apparently

destroyed their human embodiment. Because for all his faulti-
ness the tragic hero presents a spiritual value that transcends his
earthly life and conflict, we are vaguely but powerfully aware that
his death cannot, after all, be his final failure, that somehow he is
the conqueror, not the victim, of the forces that have destroyed him.
We cannot believe that a worth so excellent has been eliminated
from the universe, and therefore do not feel the pain of its waste,
as we should for example feel, proportionately to the lower value
in question, the waste of a work of art, destroyed without even a
copy to suggest what it was. And when, as in *King Lear*, we have
witnessed the hero purified and exalted by his sufferings, this
impression is strengthened. In the wreck of human values, in the
darkness covering the human scene we are dimly but powerfully
aware of an Absolute Reality and Value beyond, whose veiled presence produces a peace, even a vague joy. It is an affirmation in the
heart of negation. It is "the repose of the abyss" of which Elizabeth
of the Trinity speaks—the catharsis Aristotle attributed to tragedy.

As the Russian philosopher Soloviev shows, every order of
values, as we rise in the scale from the inanimate to the supernatural, anticipates at its highest the order of values immediately
above it. The anthropoid ape, for example anticipates and foreshadows man. But in the hierarchy of values the religious values
alone are higher than those with which tragedy is concerned. It
is, therefore, no matter for surprise that tragedy foreshadows
religion, points beyond itself to the Divine Worth it cannot
reach, and therefore tends at its highest to pass over into literary
forms appropriate to the expression of religion, as *King Lear*,
according to Bradley, tends to pass from tragedy into epic.

The development of Ibsen's drama illustrates the process of
which I am speaking. Because Ibsen possessed the vision of the
tragedian of genius, he was not content to remain to the end
within the limits of tragedy. The plays of his final period from
Little Eyolf through *John Gabriel Borkman* to *When We Dead
Awaken* are no longer realist dramas but are steeped in a quasi-
religious symbolism. By this symbolic treatment the dramatist
passes beyond the sphere of the tragic conflict and the values which
condition it, breaks through the barriers which confine the sub-
religious vision of man, and opens vast, if cloudhung, vistas of a
strange country—"the land that is very far off"—the boundless
world of Divine Reality. Already in the drama which introduces

and anticipates the symbolic plays, *The Lady From the Sea*, this
window upon the infinite has been opened. The power exercised
upon the heroine by the Stranger, or rather by the mysterious
and boundless sea which he embodies and symbolises, presents
the twofold character of terror and fascination which, as Otto
has pointed out, are the two fundamental characters of the Divine
Mystery. "I feel that I must plunge into it [life with the Stranger]
because it seems terrible . . . the terrible is that which repels and
attracts . . . the terror is the attraction in my own mind . . .
the life that terrifies and attracts." It is a "craving for the boundless, the infinite, the unattainable". That is to say the sea and the
Stranger who comes from it, in the last analysis the unbounded
and uncharted life which they represent for Ellida, are experienced
by her as an awful yet fascinating mystery, the *mysterium tremen-
dum* and *fascinans*. This invasion of a human sex conflict by an
apprehension of Deity which belongs to an order transcendent of
these purely human values and conflicts and is forced violently
into this framework by investing a man with the mystery and
infinity of God, ruins the dramatic quality of the play and renders
the *dénouement* flat and unconvincing. The play in fact suffers
from the conflict between drama and religion. It is the same
mystery in its terror and charm which lures the Master Builder
to his fatal ascent of the tower. Here, however, the Builder's
ignorance of the power which draws him on and the doom which
he incurs for seeking it amiss—he embodies the attempt of man
to achieve infinity by his own strength and in his own right—is
profoundly dramatic, precisely because this lack of religious
vision has hidden from the hero his goal and the way to reach
it. Nevertheless the symbolism of the play is religious rather
than strictly dramatic. Borkman's escape from the room where
he has paced to and fro for years like a caged beast, to die in sight
of a wide panorama of mountains and sky, also expresses this
transition from drama to religion. It is not a purely dramatic
effect, but it is epic, it is a religious symbol. It is the same with
the climb and death of the Sculptor and Irene which close *When
We Dead Awaken*, and with it the work of Ibsen. Indeed in this
last play drama is wholly sacrificed to symbolism.

Because tragedy at its greatest thus stands at the door of religion
but cannot enter (or it would no longer be tragic) it is the achievement of cultures in which religious faith has been weakened but

not widely destroyed. There is still sufficient religion for the dramatist to be aware dimly but powerfully of religious values— an infinite mystery beyond, man's aspiration towards it and the reality and value of the human spirit supreme among the creature of our experience as being capable of this Divine Mystery and touched by it. But religious insight has grown too dim for him to know that this mystery is the God who made man and for whom man is made, that the human spirit can attain God and in that attainment escape the bondage of change and mortality. Thus Greek drama flourished when the nature worship of the Hellenic cults had ceased to satisfy and convince thoughtful men but was still the atmosphere in which they lived and worked. Elizabethan drama was the birth of an age in which the undisputed certainty of Catholic faith had been lost, and conflicting versions of Christianity tempted to scepticism, but the mental atmosphere was still impregnated with the beliefs and values of the Catholic religion and culture.[1] And the drama of Ibsen was the drama of a country which, lying hitherto on the outskirts of European culture, was now for the first time invaded by the rationalism of modern Europe. In the penumbra between religion and secu- larism, theism and humanism, tragedy, the quintessence and perfection of drama, in which humanism reaches out to a religious faith beyond itself, has flourished and borne its finest flowers.

Evidently, then, if religion destroys drama, it destroys it, only as the Gospel destroyed the Mosaic Law, by fulfilling it. And as the law was a schoolmaster to bring men to Christ, the drama may well be a schoolmaster to bring to religion many whose faith is weak or wanting, the theatre thus an antechapel to the church. And even when the church is entered, only the saint— and saints are few—can pass his entire life before the altar. The majority will be glad from time to time to revisit the theatre. While we are watching or reading the tragedy—*Agamemnon*, *Œdipus*, *The Trojan Women*, *Hamlet*, *Ghosts*, or *Nan*—our religious faith must not thrust itself into the foreground of con- sciousness, or the dramatic world in which alone the tragedy is possible will be destroyed. The saint, therefore, would doubtless find the theatre dull. But its presence, firmly held, if unrealized,

---

[1] And apart from the consequences of this religious upheaval and conflict the secularist movement which has gathered momentum ever since had already begun with the humanism of the Renaissance.

in the mental background, will quicken our perception of that dim subreligion, never expressed and never expressible, which is the atmosphere, conclusion and fruit of tragedy.

And when the tragedy has reached its close, our religion will enable us to interpret its hints of a God beyond itself. For it will provide that solution of the tragic conflict towards which tragedy points but which it can never reach. For if it could reach it it would destroy itself. And, in turn, our vision of the tragic conflict, as it is displayed by the tragic artist, will help us to a deeper understanding, a fuller appreciation, of the solution of the tragic problem—that is of the problem of human life—which religion and religion alone can provide. Though the saint may stand in no need of this assistance, we who are not saints would be ill-advised to reject it. Thus, if the mutual incompatibility between religion and drama renders a religious drama in the full sense of the latter term an impossibility, even a contradiction in terms, it not only permits, it encourages, a fruitful interaction of both in a human life which, though made for God and tending to God is still on the road and still far from the goal.

C

CHAPTER IV

A PURITAN DEVOTION TO THE SACRED HEART

NEVER was the hostility between Catholics and Protestants more bitter than in the seventeenth century. But the first half of that century was everywhere a period of religious revival, a revival which extended and strengthened the reaction already begun from the naturalism which, though not the sole, had been the predominant movement of the preceding century, to the supernatural sphere and object of religion.

This religious revival made itself felt without distinction of ecclesiastical frontiers. In Catholic France it took the form of a widespread movement towards a more interior spirituality, that "Invasion of the Mystics," to use the description of Abbé Bremond, whose triumph he depicts in successive volumes of his *Histoire Littéraire du Sentiment Religieux en France*. Externally the revival embodied itself in a reform of the established religious Orders, for example the Benedictine convents, and the Cistercian reform of La Trappe; in the introduction of new Orders, such as the Discalced Carmelites, who brought with them the mystical tradition of St. Teresa and St. John of the Cross; in the Sulpician training of the secular clergy; and in the religious and charitable activities of laymen such as M. De Berniers and M. De Renty and his fellow members of the Company of the Blessed Sacrament, which attempted to mould even political life in the interest of the new devotion.

In the Protestant countries the religious reaction gave birth to a series of movements whose common aim was a more intense and a more spiritual religion, a religious regulation of life: the pietist movements in the Calvinist and Lutheran Churches,[1] the Puritan movement in England. Lacking the fullness of Christian truth contained in the teaching of the Catholic Church, and dispossessed of a public religious authority divinely instituted, these movements were unable to restrain excesses of individual

---

[1] The term " pietism " is used in a wide sense. The Lutheran movement strictly so called initiated by Spener was a later development.

evotion, vagaries of individual interpretation. But, despite
ese misinterpretations and excesses the student of seventeenth-
entury religion who considers, not the theological statement or
ultus in which religious experience is embodied—matters which
annot be determined by personal experience but must be decided
y the social authority of the Church—but that religious experi-
nce itself, sees it as substantially one throughout all diversities of
xpression.

And even the theological statement of religious experience, for
ll its divergence, displays in the spiritual movement of the seven-
enth century a remarkable assimilation, an assimilation due to a
ndency among the Protestants to return to the Catholic type of
pirituality rejected by the Reformers, a return evident even
mong many who, in other aspects of their theology, are most
ercely anti-Catholic.

From every quarter of the Protestant world this movement of
eturn to Catholic spirituality presses on. Among the Dutch
Calvinists are religious leaders like Hermann Witsius, who draws
or his spiritual teaching on St. Bernard and other Catholic
ystics, and Jodocus von Lodensteyn who laments the decay of
evotion since the Reform and desires for its renewal a restoration
f Catholic practices—Matins and Vespers, fasting, some kind of
rivate confession and direction—even looks back with regret
n Transubstantiation. In the following century one of the most
nfluential German pietists, the Calvinist Gerhard Tersteegen,
ublishes three volumes of religious biography, in which all the
ves are those of Catholics, and Catholics of the Counter Reform.
nd among the Lutherans, early in the seventeenth century,
ohann Arndt bases a standard book of Lutheran devotion, *Das
Vahre Christentum*, on Catholic asceticism, and on a doctrine of
anctification and good works which is substantially Catholic.
Henceforward—such is the paradoxical revenge of truth—the
urrent of Lutheran spirituality is, however unconsciously, of a
Catholic rather than a Lutheran type.[1]

In the English Puritan movement, the same reaction crosses
nd largely overcomes, in the centre of the religious life, the
nti-Catholic current on its surface. The Puritans may spill ink

[1] For all this I am indebted to the study of this devotional movement among German
nd Dutch Protestants by the Lutheran theologian Albrecht Ritschl—*Die Geschichte
es Pietismus*. Ritschl is himself uncompromisingly hostile to Pietism precisely *because*
was a return to Catholic spirituality.

and energy in abuse of the "Roman Antichrist", smash stained
glass windows, fast on Christmas Day—their devotional leader
are all the while preaching a spirituality substantially Catholi
and, to a considerable extent, even consciously drawn from
Catholic sources. John Everard, imprisoned by James I for h
violent opposition to the marriage of Prince Charles with
Catholic bride, is also the translator of mystical writings by th
Areopagite, Tauler, and Cardinal Nicholas of Cusa. Gile
Randall translates the third part of La Règle de Perfection, a mysti
cal treatise published a few years earlier by the Capuchin conver
Benet Canfield.[1] Here is an immediate derivation of contem
porary Catholic spirituality into the stream of Protestant piety
Francis Rous, an influential Puritan leader, the author of sever
books of devotional teaching, is a student and disciple of th
Fathers of the Church, Dionysius, Bernard, Tauler, à Kempi
Peter Sterry, one of the Independent leaders, driven from h
pulpit by the Restoration, acknowledges his debt to the exampl
of holiness set by the Catholic de Renty, an "example fixed wit
much dearness and esteem upon my heart". And in a sermo
preached to the Commons in celebration of the victory of Dun
bar, while attacking Roman legalism which he compares wit
Presbyterian, he admits that the Catholics "take and give
large scope to the understanding and affections in generou
contemplation, in mystical divinity". Indeed he prefaces h
Discourse on the Freedom of the Will by a magnificent prose hym
in praise of a universal charity and inviting to its practice, a charit
in particular which is to embrace theological opponents howeve
erroneous their tenets.[2]

Among the Protestant spirituals, however, with their bar
worship, sacramental poverty, and a weak and inadequate belie
in a Church body incorporating the invisible soul of the Church
there might seem little place for devotion to the Sacred Humanit
of Christ. And yet, a tender, a deeply Catholic, devotion to Jesu
is characteristic of much Puritan religion. Once, at least, th
devotion to the humanity of Jesus takes the same form as it wa

---

[1]During the Quietist controversy, an Italian translation of this work was placed on th
Index, for fear, doubtless, of Quietist misinterpretation. But Bremond has show
that, understood according to the author's evident meaning, the treatise is free fro
Quietism.

[2] See Vivian de SOLA PINTO, Peter Sterry, a study of his life and beliefs, with extrac
from his works, among them the preface in full which I have mentioned in the text.

ortly to take among the French Catholics, a devotion to
e Sacred Heart of Jesus, and a devotion whose spirit, as
remond remarks, is akin to the spirit of Paray-le-Monial.[1] And
is Puritan devotion to the Sacred Heart, the first book specifically
eating of devotion to the Sacred Heart,[2] is the devotion of one
f the leading Puritan divines, of a favourite preacher before the
ong Parliament, duly exhorted by him to the eradication of
very vestige of popery, the devotion of a chaplain to Oliver
Cromwell, Thomas Goodwin. "The Spirit bloweth where It
steth."[3]

"The Puritans thought people couldn't be happy as well as
ood and they thought God was terrible and frightening and was
lways watching to see if He could catch them out".[4] There
ere of course many Puritans of whom this is true, as indeed
here have been only too many Catholics. Wust, for example,
e Catholic philosopher, has told us that he grew up with this
rim picture of God: "My teachers from boyhood—parents and
riests—drove me into an almost insane terror of God."[5] But as
egards the Independents at least, it is the reverse of the truth.
Holiness and happiness are both one thing in God and the soul.
ach is an elevation above all inferior corrupting or corruptible
ings and an habitation in the supreme good." "All the goings
orth of Wisdom in thy spirit are peaceful and pleasant. If Wisdom
nlighten thy way, all the outgoings of thy soul into things and
ll the appearances of things to thy soul will be like a sweet tune
r pleasant dance. All the goings forth of God in His Wisdom
re paths of peace and pleasantness." "If thou hadst any taste
r glimpse of the glory of God in thy soul, thou wouldst feel
sweet peace within thee, with thy God, with thyself and with
ll things. The soul that dwells in this love thinks no evil of
God, of itself, of anything but is at peace with all, hath sweet
houghts of all. For God is its eye by which it sees and its heart
y which it thinks." "Comprehend all, thyself and all in the
comprehensible mystery of God. There see, hear, taste, enjoy

[1] *Histoire Littéraire du Sentiment Religieux en France*, Vol. III, p. 691 note.
[2] Ibid.
[3] Ibid .Bremond speaks of Goodwin's book as " one which deserves to be read in its
tirety "—he has quoted several passages—and as " fort beau." And he quotes the
dgment of Principal Alexander Whyte: " It is a gem of the purest water."
[4] Joan WINDHAM, *New Six O'Clock Saints*, p. 10.
[5] Letter to Fr. Pfleger, published by the recipient, Karl PFLEGER, *Dialog mit Peter Wust*,
204.

Him as beauty itself, sweetness itself, music itself, joy itself
all. See, hear, taste, enjoy all as that beauty, that music, th
sweetness, that joy in Him." "The Wisdom of God is the mus
of love." "The love presence of God is a light of glory shinir
round about thee." "Mercy is the circle of Divine love as
cometh forth from heaven and eternity goeth down to the lowe
depths of time and the creation, then ascendeth again, till lil
the sun it return thither where it first arose. Poor broken spiri
who lie mourning as outcasts, hope evermore in the etern
love, wait for it. The love of God will find you out. It will me
with you and take you in its way. For Divine Love is etern
It encompasseth heaven and earth, time and eternity." " A
motions in the heart of God and in the creature, of grace ar
nature are founded upon the unmoveableness, the unchangeabl
ness of eternal love. O blessed love, O blessed God who is th
love!" "The heart of God the divine Nature is all love. All th
wonders of God are wonders of love. What joy is this to unde
stand that all that we cannot understand in the nature of thing
which is as a thick darkness round about us, is a glorious myste
of Divine Love! That all that everywhere, of every creature,
every providence of the Creator Himself in which our spiri
are swallowed up and lost is an abyss of love, a great and shinir
deep of Divine Love!" "Divine Love is the most universal ar
importunate beggar. It cometh to the door of every spirit.
knocketh. It presseth in." "Abide in the Father's love t
spiritual joy. Joy is love flaming. One saith, that laughter is th
dance of the spirits, their freest motion in harmony and that th
light of the heavens is the laughter of Angels. Spiritual jo
is the laughter of Divine Love, of the eternal Spirit, which
love, in our spirits."[1] These are the words of a Puritan of th
Puritans, Sterry, Cromwell's favourite divine, to whose influen
I am disposed to attribute the increasing toleration by the Pr
tectorate even of Catholics, and who assisted the Protector o
his deathbed. And the precise scope of Goodwin's tractate is
assure sinners of Jesus' love. I recommend both to Miss Wine
ham's consideration. And unfortunately she expresses the view
Puritan religion almost universal among those who have had
contact with the Puritan tradition. What was wrong with th

[1] Peter STERRY, *The Rise, Race and Royalty of the Kingdom of God in the Soul of M*
1683, pp. 134, 165, 88, 282, 334, 319, 324, 325, 327, 305, 390.

religion of these left-wing Puritans was not that it was harsh, legalistic, terrorist—it was spiritual, tender and loving, often mystical in tendency—but that it was excessively and onesidely individualistic, thereby cutting the ground from beneath its feet.[1]

"The Heart of Christ in Heaven towards Sinners on Earth, or a Treatise demonstrating the Gracious disposition and tender Affection of Christ in His Human Nature, now in Glory, unto his Members, under all sorts of Infirmities, either of Sin or Misery, by Thomas Goodwin, London, 1642." So runs the title of the first treatise devoted to the Sacred Heart of Jesus, and the title states already the meaning and attraction of the devotion. Nine years earlier the French Jesuit, St.-Jure, had published his book on *The Knowledge and Love of Jesus Christ*. Not yet precisely devotion to the Sacred Heart, but the principle of it and the way to it.

The purpose of the *Discourse*, Goodwin tells us, is to lay open "the *Heart* of Christ, as now He is in heaven—how it is affected and graciously disposed towards sinners on earth that do come to Him, how willing to receive them, how ready to entertain them, how tender to pity them in all their infirmities, both sins and miseries . . . The drift of this discourse is therefore to ascertain poor souls that His Heart, in respect of pity and compassion, remains the same it was on earth, that He is as meek, as gentle, as easy to be entreated, so that they may deal with Him as fairly about the great matter of their salvation, and as hopefully and upon as easy terms obtain it of Him, as they might, if they had been on earth with Him and be as familiar with Him in all their requests, as bold with Him in all their needs."[2]

Goodwin divides his treatise into three parts. The first of these is devoted to "Extrinsical demonstrations of the gracious dispositions of Christ's heart towards us". He turns first to the

[1] Sterry tried in vain to win back a son who went to the bad at Eton by pressing upon him the devotional prayer which meant so much to himself. Individual devotion is not enough.

[2] For this loving familiarity with God compare utterances by other Puritan divines. " Christ taught us to call God our Father; children cry Dad and Mam," (Hollingworth). " If thou call on God with fear and canst not cry abba, abba, that is as much as daddie, daddie, as our babes use to say, thou art spoiled and undone. Desire God to teach you this lesson." " A child can command his father and say, I must have a new coat, I must have a new book or I must have a ball to play with. So a Saint can say Father, there is a covenant, thou art my Father and I am thy child, it cannot stand with Thy truth, Thou wert not just, if Thou shouldest deny me anything that is good: O this is a holy boldness " (W. Craddock). These quotations are taken from Dr. Geoffrey Nuttal's study, *The Holy Spirit in Puritan Faith and Experience*, pp. 58, 63–4.

last discourse of Our Lord with His disciples, as told by St. John:

> Jesus having loved His own which were in the World, He loved them unto the end, knowing that the Father had given all things into His hands, and that He was come from God and went to God, He washed His Disciples' feet. Now this preface was prefixed by the Evangelist, on purpose *to set open a window into Christ's heart,* to show what it was then at His departure and so withal to give a light into all that follows, the scope whereof is to show what His affections would be to them in heaven.

"A window into Christ's heart"—this phrase, of a rare felicity, describes not only the preface to this farewell sermon, but its entire character, and may remind us that in her devotion to the Sacred Heart the Church does but take to herself her Master's parting consolation.

"What," continues Goodwin, "was Christ's heart most upon in the midst of all these elevated meditations" of His return to God? "Not upon His own glory so much, but upon these thoughts. His Heart ran out in love towards His own, that is, His own children, His own members, His own wife, His own flesh . . . Surely the scope of this speech is to show how Christ's heart and love would be towards them even for ever", "to the end", "when He should be gone unto His Father, as well as it was to show how it had been here on earth. They being His own and He having loved them, He alters not, He changes not, and therefore will love them for ever. And in the midst of these thoughts of His approaching glory He washed His disciples' feet. And what was Christ's meaning in this, but that, whereas when He should be in heaven, He could not make such outward visible demonstrations of His heart, by doing such mean services for them; therefore, by doing this in the midst of such thoughts of His glory, He would show what He would be content to do for them, when He should be in full possession of it . . . It is to show His heart to them. So that you see what His heart was before He entered heaven, and you see what it is after He has been in heaven and greatened with all His glory, even content to wash poor sinners' feet and to serve them that come to Him".

Turning to the revelation of Our Lord's Heart in the mission of the Holy Ghost, Goodwin writes:

> What His heart would be towards them He expresseth by the order He takes for their comfort in His absence. I will not leave you as orphans, I will not leave you like fatherless and friendless children at sixes and sevens. My father and I have but one only Friend, Who lies in the bosom of us both, and proceedeth from us both, the Holy Ghost, and I will send Him to you . . . and all the comfort He shall speak to you will be from the expression of My heart towards you. Him I shall send to be in my room and to execute My place to you My Bride, and He shall tell you, if you will listen to Him and not grieve Him, nothing but stories of My love . . . (For He dwelleth in Christ's heart and also in ours, and lifts up from one hand to the other what Christ's thought are to us, what our prayers and faith are to Christ.) So that you shall have My heart as surely and as speedily as if I were with you, and He will be continually breaking your hearts either with My love to you or yours to Me.

Goodwin then speaks of the promise to answer prayer as a further manifestation of Our Lord's Heart towards us and concludes with the love expressed in the prayer for the disciples. He then considers the love displayed by Jesus, after His Resurrection, towards the disciples who had forsaken Him in His Passion.

> When Christ came first out of the other world, clothed with that heart and body which He was to wear in heaven, what message sends He first to them? We would all think His first words shall be to rate them for their faithlessness: but here is no such matter: His first word concerning them is, go tell My brethren . . . He carries it as Joseph did in the height of his advancement, when he first brake his mind to his brethren; I am Joseph your brother. So Christ says here, tell them you have seen Jesus their brother: I own them as brethren still. . . . He minds them not of what they had done against Him . . . Poor sinners who are full of the thoughts of their own sins, know not how they shall be able at the latter day to look Christ in the face when they shall first meet with Him. But

they may relieve their spirits against their care and fear, by Christ's carriage now towards His disciples who had so sinned against Him; Be not afraid, your sins will be remembered no more. And to show that His heart was longing to be at work for them in heaven, He tells them, I ascend, and He expresseth His joy to be, not only that He goes to His Father, but also that He goes to their Father to be an advocate with Him for them. And is, indeed, Jesus our brother alive? And doth He call us brethren? And doth He talk thus lovingly of us? Whose heart would not this overcome?

Goodwin next considers the revelation of the Heart of Christ in the work of His Spirit among Christians.

This Spirit is still in our preaching and in your hearts in hearing, in praying, and persuades you of Christ's love, and is in all these the pledge of Christ's love still in heaven unto sinners. He takes Christ's prayers when He prays in us, He takes the words as it were of Christ's mouth, or heart rather, and directs our hearts to offer them up to God. He also follows us to the Sacrament, and *in that glass* shows us Christ's face smiling on us, and through His face *His heart*, and thus helping of us to a sight of Him, we go away rejoicing that we saw our Saviour that day.

These words are poignant reading, so beautifully do they describe the Real Presence of Jesus in the Blessed Sacrament, which yet their writer never believed. Indeed they anticipate modern Catholic devotion to the Eucharistic Heart of Jesus. The tragedy of divided Christendom is in these words, yet a comfort also and a hope: a comfort, that even when error had removed Jesus' sacramental presence, the Christian heart of a lover of Jesus yearned after it, and his desire rose to an act of spiritual communion which partook of the unknown Eucharist even when physically bread was eaten and wine drunk; a hope, that this spiritual communion of devout Protestants with our Eucharistic Lord shall finally become a sacramental Communion in the Church of His foundation.

The conversion of St. Paul by the ascended Jesus, and His final promise to come quickly, conclude Goodwin's extrinsical demonstrations of Christ's heart towards us.

"The Intrinsical Demonstration shewing the reasons" why Christ's heart must be thus disposed, is a sermon on the text, "We have not an High Priest which cannot be touched with the feeling of our infirmities, but was in all points tempted like as we are, yet without sin."

I have chosen this text [says Goodwin] as that which above any other speaks His heart most, and sets out the frame and workings of it towards sinners, and that so sensibly that it doth (as it were) take our hands and lay them upon Christ's breast, and let us feel how His heart beats, and His bowels yearn towards us, even now He is in glory.

Goodwin argues that Christ, being by nature the Son of His heavenly Father, must possess His Father's mercy.

If we as the elect of God, who are but the adopted sons, are exhorted to put on bowels of mercy and kindness, then much more must these dispositions needs be found in Christ the natural son, and these as natural to Him as His sonship is: God is Love: and *Christ is love covered with flesh, yea, our flesh.* And it is certain that as God hath fashioned the hearts of all men, and some of the sons of men unto more mercy and pity (naturally) than others, and then the Holy Spirit, coming on them to sanctify their natural dispositions, useth to work according to their tempers, even so He tempered the heart of Christ and made it of a softer mould and temper than the tenderness of all men's hearts put together into one.

The Holy Spirit, continues Goodwin, dwells for ever in the Sacred Humanity. In the Gospels the Spirit, as the Spirit of Jesus, is shewn to be the Spirit of mercy and love. And the manner of His ministry revealed this meek love of His Spirit.

John had the voice of a crier; he was a man of severe spirit, but Christ came piping and dancing; all melodious sweetness was in His ministry and spirit; and in the course of His ministry He went so tenderly to work, He was so heedful to broken souls, and had such regard to their discouragements, that it is said, He would not break a bruised reed.

And the Spirit which is now possessed by the members of Christ must be in its fullness the abiding possession of the Head.

The same Spirit dwelling in Christ's heart in heaven that doth in yours here, and always working in His heart first for you, and then in yours by commission from Him, rest assured that that spirit stirs up in Him bowels of mercy infinitely larger towards you, than you can have unto yourselves. So He hath now an heart adequate to God's own heart.

Goodwin then argues from the love men bear to their kindred. No accession of glory or power destroys a man's love to wife, parents, child, brother. But Christ

is the founder of all relations, and affections that accompany them. Shall not He Who put all these affections into parents and others suitable to their relations, have them much more in Himself? He is the subject of all relations which no creature is. If a man be a husband, yet not a father or a brother, but Christ is all; no one relation being sufficient to express His love wherewith He loveth us. All those relations and the affections of them and the effects of those affections, which you see . . . to have been in men, are all, and were ordained to be, shadows of what is in Christ. Though Christ be now in glory, He hath the heart of a husband towards you, being betrothed unto you for ever, and the idea of that beauty which from everlasting was ordained you is so imprinted on His heart, that He will never cease to sanctify and to cleanse you, till He hath restored you to that beauty which once He took such a liking of.

Besides the essential glory and bliss of Christ's human nature in its personal union with the Godhead,

God hath bestowed upon Him another capacity of glory and a revenue of pleasure to come in another way, and answerably another fullness, namely from His Church and Spouse which is His body. So that, although He of Himself personally be so full, the fullness of the Godhead dwelling in Him, that He overflows to the filling all things, yet He is pleased to account, and it is so in reality, His Church and the salvation of it, to be

another fullness unto Him, superadded to the former. As Son
of God He is complete, and that of Himself; but as an head,
He hath another additional fullness of joy from the good and
happiness of his members. The superadded glory and happiness
of Christ is enlarged and increased still, as His members
come to have the purchase of His death more and more
laid forth upon them. So when their sins are pardoned,
their hearts more sanctified, He is much more pleased and
rejoiced in this, than themselves can be. And this must needs
keep up in His heart His care and love unto his children here
below, to refresh them every moment.

For, to sum up the argument, Christ is the Husband of the
Church and "He that loveth his wife, loveth himself".

The organic and interior view of the scheme of salvation thus
beautifully explained and employed to express the love of the
Sacred Heart, is far removed from the forensic scheme of a
justice externally imputed, which was the original dogma of the
Reformation.

Goodwin's final demonstration argues from the assumption
by Our Lord of human nature "to the end He might be merciful".

But was not the son of God as merciful without the taking
of our nature? I answer, yes, He is as merciful; but yet this
human nature assumed adds a new way of being merciful;
it assimilates all these mercies of God and makes them the
mercies of a man. It makes them human mercies, and so
gives a naturalness and kindliness unto them to our capacities.
So that God doth now in as kindly and as natural a way
pity us, who are flesh of His flesh and bone of His bone, as a
man pities a man; thereby to encourage us to come to Him,
and to be familiar with God, and treat with Him for grace
and mercy, as a man would do with a man . . . knowing that
God's mercies work in and through His heart in a human way.

The third part of Goodwin's treatise discusses the manner in
which the glorified Humanity is able to feel with our sorrow
and for our sin. It is marked both by learning and by subtlety
of thought. But I prefer to conclude Goodwin's exposition
with the words just quoted. For they express so well the meaning

of devotion to the Sacred Heart, and show it to be no novel devotion, but the natural consequence of the Incarnation; indeed devotion to the Incarnation itself.

Certainly neither Goodwin nor any other Protestant approached a practical cultus of the Sacred Heart, a form of worship directed to the Heart of Jesus. In this understanding of the term a Protestant devotion to the Sacred Heart is impossible. But a devotion in this sense is, after all, subordinate, a method by which we propagate and practice the devotion to Our Lord's Humanity as the incarnate manifestation of the Divine Love, which is the essential devotion to the Sacred Heart.[1] The serious defect of Goodwin's presentation lies elsewhere. It is the lack of belief in the Sacramental Presence of that Heart in our midst. At the outset of his treatise Goodwin thus defines his object in writing:

> The scope will be to hearten believers to come unto such a Saviour, when they shall know how sweetly and tenderly His heart is inclined towards them, and so to remove that great stone of stumbling in the thoughts of men, that Christ being now absent, and withall exalted to so high and infinite a distance of glory, they cannot tell how to come to treat with Him about their salvation so freely as those poor sinners did who were here on earth with him. His disciples, they think, beheld Him a man like unto themselves and He was full of meekness and gentleness. But now He is gone into a far country and hath put on glory and immortality and how His heart may be altered thereby we know not.

"He is gone into a far country." To cross the distance is the object of Goodwin's treatise. The Sacred Heart is therefore depicted as the same Heart of human love It was on earth. And this purpose appears most evidently in the passage quoted earlier, where the Spirit is shown as the medium of communication, the bond of union between Christ's Heart in heaven and our hearts on earth. But this is to make devotion to the Sacred Heart a substitute for the doctrine of the Sacramental Presence. The

---

[1] And in practice the value of the devotion has been seriously impaired by gross sentimentality and artistic insensibility in its expression. The average statue or picture is an unintentional blasphemy.

gulf Goodwin seeks to bridge does not exist. Jesus has not gone into a far country; for He is present in our churches. Here on earth we can approach Him and treat with Him as directly as of old His disciples in Palestine. For Catholics, devotion to the Sacred Heart is not a medium of union with an absent Christ, but an illumination of Christ sacramentally present. We have seen Goodwin approach this standpoint for a moment, when he speaks of the Spirit showing us the heart of Jesus in the glass of the sacrament. But it is only a passing movement of his devotion. For him the Sacrament is at best but a mirror in which the Sacred Heart is reflected, not, as for Catholics, that Heart itself.

This painful sentiment of Christ's absence adds a pathos of unfulfilled desire to the beauty of this first treatise on devotion to the human Heart of Jesus. The devotion is explained with a charm and a tenderness that do not descend to sentimentality, because they are sustained by an earnest strength of character, and founded on a theology wide and deep, though incomplete. Catholics remember only too well the evil aspect of Puritanism, its unlovely fanaticism, its iconoclasm, its persecution of their religion. These memories widen an inevitable separation of creed into a gulf of misunderstanding and hostility. It is time to turn our gaze to the good aspect of that Puritan movement, its strong and earnest and tender devotion, its personal love of Jesus. This love of our common Lord is a unity behind our differences. From the very heart of Puritanism comes this beautiful utterance of that love. Devotion to the Sacred Heart, first preached by the Puritan Goodwin, first practised by contemporary Catholics, is a power that can unite all Christian believers in the Church which the Sacred Heart loves so deeply.

CHAPTER V

DAME JULIAN OF NORWICH

*H*abent sua fata libelli. Most writers address only their contemporaries. A few obtain a further audience of future generations. But there are also those whose message is apparently lost, and who must wait for their audience till a more or less remote posterity. Of these were Henry Vaughan and Gerard Manley Hopkins among the poets and among mystical writers Dame Julian of Norwich. Within a restricted circle, indeed, she possessed her contemporary disciples. But it can never have been large and it must soon have passed away. Of her *Revelations of Divine Love* in which she records her visions of God's truth and love and her ruminations of their meaning, but four manuscripts survive, of which only two are anterior to 1600, only one possibly was written in her lifetime. It was not until the seventeenth century that the record of her religious experience was first printed by Dom Serenus Cressy, in 1670. And it was only in the closing years of the last century that her book became at all widely known. Now interest is awake; her readers are many. Evidently her message is specially adapted for *our* reception, is a spiritual food which *our* constitution is peculiarly fitted to relish and assimilate.

Of Julian's biography we know little that is certain. Two or three days of a life covering at least seventy-one, presumably eighty-two or eighty-three years, stand out in vivid light. The rest is darkness. Of her origin we know nothing. An allusion to "the seaground" with "its hills and dales green seeming as it were most begrowing with wrake [seaweed] and gravel"[1] suggests perhaps that her home had been on or near the coast.[2]

The warmth and tenderness with which Julian speaks, in her *Revelations*, of a mother's love—when she speaks of fatherhood

[1] *Revelations of Divine Love*, Ch. 10.
[2] If I am right in concluding that her home was the scene of her illness and revelations (see below) it was probably in the neighbourhood of some house of male religious to which her visitor belonged.

her language is far cooler in tone—suggest that she lost her father in early childhood, or that he was one of those harsh and autocratic fathers too common in mediaeval England, a father such as one meets in the Paston letters. In any case her mother was still living when her daughter was thirty.

"The place in a high manner dignified by her abode", as her first editor Cressy writes, "was the City of Norwich". She was an anchoress living in a cell against the south wall of St. Julian's Church. The majority of anchorages were placed on the north wall. It is pleasant to know that Julian, whose writing is so remarkable for its spiritual sunshine of confident joy, was not debarred from the cheer of physical sunlight. The cell was demolished in the eighteenth century by those who did not share Cressy's view of the dignity conferred by her inhabitation. Its foundations, however, have been laid bare.[1] It is usually supposed that this cell was the scene of her revelations. Evelyn Underhill however in her valuable study "Julian of Norwich"[2] points out that the presence in her room of many persons makes it more probable that this experience occurred before she entered the anchorage, and suggests that she was then a nun in the Benedictine Abbey at Carrow. For St. Julian's cell was in the gift of the Abbey. It is, indeed, extremely unlikely that even at a deathbed the cell of an enclosed anchoress would have been open to a large number of bystanders—including Julian's mother and "a religious person" other than her confessor. When Richard Rolle visited his friend the recluse, Margery, in her illness, he did not enter her cell. On the other hand there is no mention of an Abbess as present, or of any nuns. Her mother closed Julian's eyes when she was believed to be dead. Surely the Abbess would have performed this office for one of her nuns? And it was not a convent chaplain, but the parson, "my curate" (parish priest), who was summoned to her death-bed. Carrow therefore is most unlikely. If the sickness and visions took place neither at Carrow Abbey nor at St. Julian's anchorage we may conclude —a conclusion borne out by the mother's presence and prominence—that they occurred while she was at home.

[1] St. Julian's was gutted, even the tower destroyed, in an air raid in 1942. It is to be restored as a centre of Anglican devotion.
[2] In her *Essentials of Mysticism*.

It is usually taken for granted that because Julian was an anchoress at St. Julian's Church, Norwich, she was a Norfolk or possibly a Suffolk woman. The manuscript evidence, however, seems incompatible with the supposition. For the only manuscript written in her lifetime is not in the Midland dialect used in East Anglia but in the Northern dialect not spoken south of the Humber. Moreover it is the manuscript which contains a shorter version of her revelations which, we can hardly doubt, is, as its editor concludes, the original version, much closer to the actual "shewings" than the longer version. Whether Julian wrote or, as is practically certain, dictated her book, the use of this northern dialect by an East Anglian author or an East Anglian scribe is surely incredible. Her home must have been north, not south, of the Humber. Since this "northern" manuscript is certainly not the manuscript written or dictated by Julian—was not indeed written before 1413 at the earliest, many years no doubt after the composition of the original manuscript,[1]—it may be objected to my conclusion that it is not written in the dialect she employed, but is a later translation. To my mind the supposition is hardly plausible. There seems no evidence for the deliberate translation of entire texts from one English dialect into another. A northern reader annotated in his own dialect the sole surviving manuscript of Margery Kempe's Book. But he obviously found no difficulty in reading her Midland and East Anglian dialect.[2] Manuscripts of the *Cloud of Unknowing*, written in the northern area by scribes using the Northern dialect, do no more than introduce a number of northern forms. The book is left substantially in its original East Midland dialect. No manuscript of the *Cloud of Unknowing* has the least claim to be regarded as the autograph or even approaches it closely in date. Nevertheless study of the manuscripts from the point of view of their dialect has enabled Miss Phyllis Hodgson, editing the *Cloud* for the Early English Text Society, to conclude that it was written in the East Midland dialect, which therefore was the dialect spoken by its anonymous

---

[1] Later contents are held to show that the MS. was not written till many years after 1413. In face of the note that Julian is " yet on life ", I am not convinced. If, however, this is the case, a scribe who copied a note now so obviously irrelevant must have copied most faithfully his exemplar of 1413.

[2] *The Book of Margery Kempe*, edited by Prof. Sanford Brown Meech in collaboration with Miss Hope Emily Allen (E.E.T.S.), Introduction, p. xiii.

uthor.[1] We are surely entitled to conclude in the same way
hat Julian dictated her book in the Northern dialect to a northern
cribe.

Moreover Julian refers to St. John of Beverley as a "kind
eighbour and *of our knowing*".[2] This, it is true, need mean no
nore than that he was a fellow countryman. "Our Lord shewed
im . . . for countrey sake".[3] But when taken in conjunction
rith the dialect of our oldest manuscript it not only corroborates
er northern origin but suggests that she came from York-
hire. And the suggestion is further strengthened by a reference
o "the plenteous miracles doing about" St. John's body con-
nuously.[4] An East Anglian would be unlikely to possess this
nowledge of events at a shrine whose celebrity was local
ather than national. Thus convergent evidence points to the
ast Riding of Yorkshire as Julian's home, probably the district
etween Beverley and the sea, on or near the coast. That her
cribe also wrote in the Northern dialect is a further indication
hat the scene of her shewings was not the Norwich cell but
er north-country home. How was it then that she became
n anchoress at Norwich? What could have taken her to Nor-
olk? It cannot have been the sanctity of a shrine. For she did
ot settle at Walsingham or Bromholme. I can think of
o reason except a marriage. There is no evidence for her
ccupation of the Norwich cell earlier than 1404, thirty-one
ears later than her "shewings" in 1373. Meanwhile she could
ave married and been left a widow. In the Middle Ages mar-
ages were apt to be dissolved quickly by death. In view
owever of her claim to have given to God "the service of her
outh" it is more likely that her mother remarried a Norfolk
an or perhaps a brother or sister married a Norfolk bride or
ridegroom and Julian went to live with the newly wedded
ouple.

The service of her youth however need not mean an eremitical
* technically "religious" life. It is quite possible that Pepwell
as well informed, and that the mystic of Lynn, Margery
empe, ended her life as an anchoress. But even so her dedication
* God's service began many years earlier and most of it, at
ny rate, was passed in the world. What to me is inconceivable

---

[1] *The Cloud of Unknowing*, E.E.T.S., Introduction, p. 1. (50).   [3] ibid.
[2] *Revelations*, Ch. 38.   [4] ibid.

is that the revelations of a Norfolk woman should have bee
dictated and written in the Northern dialect. That the long
version is in the Midland dialect, though one manuscript sign
ficantly contains Northern forms, shews that this version w;
dictated and written later when Julian had spent many years i
Norfolk and moreover employed a scribe whose dialect w;
Midland.[1] It is also another proof that the longer versio
is the later. For we know that Julian did not leave Norwich f
the north.

Our evidence that Julian occupied her anchorage in 1404 is
will discovered in Archbishop's Arundel's register by my so
Dom Aelred Watkin. Its date is May 19th 1404. Thom;
Emund, chaplain of Aylsham, bequeathes "to Julian an anchore
at St. Julian's Church Norwich 12d pence and 8d to Sara livin
with her", either a servant or a fellow anchoress. A note attache
to the manuscript of the shorter version of the *Revelations* stat
that she was still living when it or its exemplar was written i
1413. In a will found in Archbishop Chichele's register for 141
John Plumpton of Conesford at Norwich bequeaths "40d to tl
anker in the church of St. Julian at Conesford at Norwich'
12d to her maidservant and 12d to a former maid Alice. U
fortunately the "anker" is not named. But a will of La
Suffolk in the same register for the following year leaves ;
shillings to Julian "recluz" at Norwich. We can hardly dou
that the beneficiary of both wills is the same and is Dame Julia
On the other hand it is not easy to know what to make of a w;
of 1423 in which Walter Daniel bequeaths a legacy to an "inclus
at St. Julian's—on the face of it a male recluse. As the cell w
inhabited by a succession of anchoresses, *incluso* is presumably
scribal error for *inclusæ* and since Dame Julian Lampet did n
take possession of the cell until 1426 the beneficiary is probab
our Dame Julian.[2]

It was in the seclusion of this anchorage—not a comple
solitude for it was shared by a servant—that Julian ponder
the significance of her shewings and by her meditations upon
prepared the longer version which embodies them. It was
the cell at St. Julian's that she learned her theology.

---

[1] For this information about the dialect of the MSS. I am indebted to Sister Ar
Maria (Reynolds), C.P.
[2] A similar mistake was undoubtedly made in Thomas Emund's will in which t
church " Sct*i* Julian*i* " is called " Sct*e* Julian*e*."

Nor was she dependent solely on her own prayerful thought.
ae was no doubt an influential member of a circle of Norwich
ntemplatives, a Norwich school of mysticism centuries before
e Norwich school of painting. Prominent among them was
ichard Caister, vicar of St. Stephen's, after his death venerated
cally as a saint, and the Carmelite William Southfield, favoured
ith visions of Our Lady.[1] She was therefore visited by a friend
d protégée of Caister's, Margery Kempe of Lynn. Margery
d separated from her husband and devoted herself to a religious
e in the world. Her unusual vocation however—outbursts of
ud crying in Church, exclusively religious conversation, and
buke of her neighbours' faults—had made her unpopular
nong people with no understanding of the spiritual life or
mpathy with it, and often disposed to scent Lollardy in any
ceptional or unusual devotion. She told Julian of the favours
anted her in prayer, hoping to be assured that they were
nuine. For Julian "was expert in such things and good counsel
uld give". She gave Margery the assurance she sought.
ae told her "to fulfil with all her might whatever God put
her soul if it were not against the worship of God and profit
her even Christians. For if it were, it were never the moving
a good spirit. The Holy Ghost moveth never a thing against
arity, for if He did He were contrarious to His ownself, for
e is all charity." She urged Margery to stand steadfast what-
er her critics might say. For "when God visiteth a creature
ith tears of contrition, devotion or compassion he may and
ght to believe that the Holy Ghost is in his soul. Such tears
e devils hate and fear. I pray God grant you perseverance.
t your trust in God and fear not the language of the world.
r the more despite, shame and reproof that ye have in this
orld the more your merit in the sight of God".[2] This report is
invention of Margery's but the authentic voice of Julian with
hoes of her *Revelations*. The sobs, we should notice, which
andalise Miss Allen as they scandalised Evelyn Underhill,
ified Dame Julian. Margery and Julian spent "many days
gether". Julian calls herself "a simple creature unlettered".
the manuscripts report correctly her Latin exclamation:
3enedicite Domine" (or "Dominus"), this description of herself

[1] See *The Book of Margery Kempe*, ed. Meech and Allen, pp. 276, 278, 320.
[2] *Book of Margery Kempe*, pp. 42–3.

was not simple humility.[1] In her conversation with Marger
however she quotes the Epistle of St. James and appeals to th
authority of St. Jerome, though indirectly it would seem,
quoted, authentically or otherwise, in a devotional treatise
Besides Scripture the *Revelations* also show acquaintance wi
St. Gregory's Life of St. Benedict, from which she quote
Richard of St. Victor's *Benjamin Minor*, translated by Julian
contemporary the author of *The Cloud of Unknowing*, ar
presumably the mystical writings of the Pseudo-Areopagite. C
English mystical writings she certainly knew the *Ancren Rewl*
Parallels have been found with fourteenth-century mystics c
the German and Flemish school, with Ruysbroeck, Tauler ar
Suso. And it has been claimed—not to my mind convincingly—
that she was influenced by Eckhardt.[3] Her knowledge howev
may not have been obtained by reading. A priest at Lynn rea
perhaps also translated, mystical books to Margery Kempe
Caister or some other member of the group of Norwich spiritua
may well have rendered Julian the same service.

If she did not die until 1426, Julian must have been eighty
three years old at her death. In place of epitaph on her unknow
tomb we may inscribe the judgment of an eighteenth-centu
French Protestant, Pierre Poiret, in his catalogue of mystic
writers—*Theodidacta, profunda, ecstatica*—Taught of God, Pr
found, Ecstatic.

Julian tells us that in her youth she desired "three gifts k
the grace of God". The first was "mind of the passion". By th
she meant not only an intense realization of the Passion but eve
an actual vision, "a bodilie sight". The second was an illne
grave to the point of dying without actual death. This illne
she desired for the age of thirty. "And this meant I, for I wou
be purged by the mercy of God, and after live more to th
worship of God because of that sickness." The third was t
receive three spiritual wounds, a number suggested by th

---

[1]The exclamation however was derived from the words at the end of Prime—
Benedicite R. Dominus—the Sarum equivalent of the Roman v. Benedicite R. Deus.

[2] Miss Hope Allen's quotation from the *Speculum Christiani* (*Book of Margery Kem*,
p. 279) differs considerably from Julian's reported words. If it is the source her memo
embroidered upon it.

[3] For all this I am indebted to a brochure by Sister Anna Maria (Reynolds), C.
" Some Literary Influences in the Revelations of Julian of Norwich," in *Leeds Stua*
in English and Kindred Languages, nos. 7 and 8, 1952. For Eckhardt see below, pp. 87–

[4] *The Book of Margery Kempe*, pp. 322–3.

three bodily wounds of St. Cecilia's martyrdom. These were true contrition, "kind compassion", that is a feeling of Our Lord's suffering, and "wilful longing to God".[1] This wilful longing is for Julian the substance of religion and of prayer. It is "the affectuous stirring of love to God for Himself", the "sharp dart of longing love" on which the anonymous mystic who wrote *The Cloud of Unknowing*, insists and of which he says "this is only by itself that work that destroyeth the ground and the root of sin" and that "all virtues shall be subtly and perfectly conceived, felt and comprehended in it, without any mingling of thine intent".[2]

In the May of 1373, when Julian was thirty-and-a-half years of age, the illness she desired was granted.

Six days and nights she lay ill, during half that time in a critical condition. On the seventh night death seemed certain. On the following morning, Saturday, May 8th,[3] her body was paralyzed from the waist downward. She was propped upright in bed and the priest set a crucifix in front of her eyes. As she gazed on the crucifix, the room grew dark about her "save in the image of the crosse wherein held [continued] a common light [ordinary daylight], and I wist not how". If this was a pathological symptom, it was a symbol also of a world whose meaning is dark, except for the light yielded by the Cross. The paralysis crept upward. She was now scarcely conscious, when suddenly all feeling of pain passed away (she had suffered from difficulty in breathing) and from the waist upward "I was as whole as ever I was before". The second spiritual wound came into her mind, her desire for compassion with her crucified Saviour. But she no longer desired any "bodilie sight".[4] All this while her gaze was focused on the crucifix before her. "And in this, sodeinlie I saw the red blood running down from under the garland, hot and freshly, plentuouslie and livelie, right as it was in the time that the garland of thorns was pressed on His blessed Head." "And in the same shewing, sodeinlie the Trinitie fulfilled my heart most of joy; and so I understood it shall be in heaven without end to all that shall come there."[5]

[1] Ch. 2.
[2] The *Cloud of Unknowing*, Ch. 12. Cf. *The Epistle of Privy Counsel*, Ch. 7.
[3] May 13th rests on a mistaken reading of the Paris MS., xiii for viii.
[4] Ch. 3.
[5] Ch. 4.

This was the double beginning of a series of revelations which lasted from four in the morning "till it was noon of the day or past".[1]

When they ceased and Julian was left to physical pain and the listless aridity of an exhausted nervous system, she began to doubt their reality and told a religious who visited her that she had raved. It would seem that the chief matter of her doubt was the series of sensible visions of the Passion. But she is careful to add, "I believed truly for the time that I saw."[2] That night another "shewing", an intellectual apprehension of Jesus' presence in the soul, together with a comforting utterance, reassured her belief for the remainder of her life.

"All this blessed teaching of our Lord God", Julian tells us, "was shewed by three parts; that is to say, by bodily sight; and by word formed in my understanding, and by ghostly sight. For the bodily sight, I have said as truly as I can: and for the words I have said them right as Our Lord shewed them me; and for the ghostly sight I have said some deal, but I may never fully tell it." There are three kinds, three modes of "shewing"— apparently external, whether seen or heard; images or words recognised as formed by or at any rate in the imagination of the subject; purely mental perceptions. In the technical language of mystical theology the vision of objects apparently external to the subject is termed "corporeal"—misleadingly, for it is in fact the hallucination of a corporeal vision. The vision recognised to be imaginative is termed "imaginary". And the vision which consists of ideas without images is termed "intellectual". Of the first, the so-called corporeal vision, the vision of the bleeding crucifix is an instance; of the third, the intellectual, the joyful intuition of the Trinity. Julian's "bodily sights" are partly "corporeal", partly "imaginary" though the distinction is merely apparent. Some of her shewings lack any "corporeal" or "imaginary" vision and consist entirely of spiritual intuition. And the great parabolic vision of the Lord and the Servant is partly imaginary, partly intellectual. "The sight", Julian informs us, "was shewed double." "One part was shewed *ghostly in bodily likeness*"—was an imaginary vision. "The other part was

---

[1] Or perhaps " it was nine of the day overpast," as Miss Warrack's edition reads from another manuscript.
[2] Ch. 66.

shewed more ghostly without bodily likeness"—was an intellectual vision. And in her account of the vision she distinguishes precisely between the imaginary and the intellectual shewings.[1]

As Evelyn Underhill points out, these physical "shewings" reflect contemporary art and devotional literature. Moreover, modern studies of subliminal activity have shewn that the images out of which visions and locutions are woven, and even the concepts that explain them, already existed in the subconscious of the visionary, and are derived from environment, education, or reading. But this fact does not disprove an objective contact with God as the ultimate stimulus giving birth to these visions, words and ideas and even to some extent determining their arrangement. Whether or no this Divine stimulus or arrangement is present, and if so, to what degree, can be judged only from the religious value of the teaching thus conveyed, or from the spiritual effect on the mystic or his disciples. Since we are embodied beings, intuitions of the Divine are likely to clothe themselves in the sense-derived images and the concepts laid up for their vesture in our subliminal wardrobe. The extent to which mystical experience thus translates itself will no doubt vary with psycho-physical constitution. But if we are theists, we shall see no reason to deny that it may also depend on the intervention of God.

The supreme revelation of God's love in face of the evil in the world is the crucifix. Therefore Dame Julian's "shewings" begin with a vision of the Crucified and continue with a series of visions of the Passion. Of these there were five.

"Our courteous Lord", Julian writes, "shewed His passion to me in five manners. Of which the first is the bleeding of the Head; the second, discolouring of His blessed Face; the third is the plenteous bleeding of the Body, in seeming of scourging; the fourth is the deep drying" of our Lord's Body on the Cross by an inner parching of thirst and a drying wind. (This feature was probably suggested by the withered and meagre figure of the mediaeval crucifix.) "And the fifth is that was shewed for the joy and the bliss of the Passion."[2] This fifth vision was the

---

[1] Ch. 51. From her account of them the words heard by Julian, her locutions, were "imaginary"—an imagined utterance, "word formed". When therefore she says "in my understanding", "understanding" is used in a wide and loose sense to include the imagination.

[2] Ch. 23.

sight of a sudden change in the dying Christ to "a blessedful cheer". With this change she heard the words " 'Art thou well apaid [satisfied] that I suffered for thee?' I said 'Yea, good Lord, gramercy; yea good Lord blessed mote thou be.' Then said Jesu our good Lord 'If thou are apaid, I am apaid: It is a joy, a bliss, and an endless liking to me that ever I suffered passion for thee: and if I might have suffered more, I would have suffered more.' "[1] And here we must remember that as Julian tells us elsewhere, the "thee" for whom Our Lord would if possible have suffered even more than He did is not distinctively the individual Julian but each and all of the saved. "All that I say of me, I mean in person of all mine even Christian."[2]

The Passion series closes with a vision already half an intellectual apprehension, in which was shewn to "the understanding" the wounded side of Jesus opened to provide a "fair and delectable place large enough for all mankind that shall be saved" and within the wound "His blessed Heart cloven in two".[3] We are already on the road to Paray and St. Margaret Mary.

The second mode of revelation experienced by Julian is purely intellectual, spiritual. Supreme in this mode is the immediate experience of the Absolute Godhead—mystical experience in the strict sense. For this is the intuition of union with God which is the essence of mystical prayer. Inextricably blended with this intuition is a series of distinct conceptions, "understandings" of the Divine Attributes and of the Divine Action in man and in creation as a whole. These intellectual visions blend in their turn with the visual or audible "shewings" already considered. Julian's revelations are a gospel to her "even-Christians" rather than an account of her personal union with God, or of the way by which she attained it. She therefore says little of the formless concept-transcending prayer-union which exceeds even these intellectual apprehensions of the Divine attributes and operations. For, of its very nature, it lacks a content communicable to others. But she speaks of "an unperceivable prayer" which is evidently this indescribable union, and hints at it as presupposed by her inability after years of reflection to express her "ghostly sight".

We cannot suppose that all the significance she found in her intuitions of Divine truth was distinctly present to her mind

[1] Ch. 22.   [2] Ch. 8.   [3] Ch. 24.

in those first hours of their apocalypse. Their interpretation is
largely due to later reflection upon an intuition originally too full
and too indistinct for understanding. In the shorter version
of the *Revelations* contained in the fifteenth-century MS and
published by the Rev. Dundas Harford, the theological develop-
ments of her "shewings" are for the most part absent. There
is nothing corresponding to Chs. 44–63 of the longer version, the
section most exclusively a theological treatise. The editor's
contention may therefore be accepted that this version is the
earlier form of the revelations before later reflection had worked
over their material. Moreover, this shorter version contains several
homely details absent from the longer, for example that the
priest brought his serving boy, that Julian was propped up "with
clothes", that her mother was present and "lifted up her hand to
lock her eyes" believing her dead, that the bystanders bathed her
temples. There are also a few bold sayings and ambiguous phrases
absent from the longer version. On the other hand, many of the
absent passages are spoken of in the longer version as direct
revelations. It is likely that in the years of prayerful contemplation
during which her revelations were pondered by Julian many of
their interpretations came to her, not as conscious reflections of
her own mind, but as intuitions or illustrations apparently the
direct gift and illumination of God. In any case we are bound to
ascribe a considerable portion of her theological explanations
to her own reason, whether operating consciously or subconsciously. But we should not conclude that this "use of kindly
[natural] reason" led to an arbitrary remodelling or misinterpretation of the intuitional material. For, as she says, the intuition,
the immediate experience, "the inward gracious working of the
Holy Ghost" and the "use of man's kindly reason" are both
"of one God".[1] And as regards the human medium, a psychology
which forgets the unity of the soul and draws too sharp lines of
demarcation between the intuition in the central depth, raised
into consciousness, of its contact with God, and the normally
more conscious intuition of discursive reasoning, must be
artificial and sterile—a dissection, not a picture, of the living
organism. Without these distinctions and dissections we cannot
understand the organism. But they cannot reveal its living reality.
Its unitary and individual life eludes their analysis.

[1] Ch. 79. As also is " the common teaching of Holy Church " (ibid.).

Julian's attempt to translate her obscure but vivid intuition into terms comprehensible by the understanding sometimes takes the form of a parable. These parables range from simple illustrations that occurred to her mind, "came into her head" as we say, to visions or locutions that appeared to be the direct work of God. They deserve our special attention since they are not only one of the most attractive features of the book, but present in an imaginative and therefore impressive form its sometimes difficult and always profound theology.

As the bodie is clad in the cloath and the flesh in the skin and the bones in the flesh and the heart in the bulke, so are we soul and bodie clad and enclosed in the goodness of God.[1]

He shewed a little thing, the quantitie of a hazel nut, lying in the palm of my hand . . . and it was round as a ball. I thought, "What may this be?" and it was answered thus "It is all that is made."[2]

He shewed this open example: "It is the most worship that a solemn king or a great lord may do to a poor servant, if he will be homely with him: and namely, if he shew it himself of a full true meaning, and with a glad cheer both in private and openly.[3]

In this time I saw a body lying on the earth: which body shewed heavy and fearful, and without shape or form, as it were a swilge [foul] stinking myre. And suddenly out of this body sprung a full fair creature, a little child full shapen and formed, swift and lively and whiter than the lily, which sharply glided up into heaven. The swilge of the body betokeneth great wretchedness of our deadly [mortal] flesh: and the littleness of the child betokeneth the cleanness and the pureness of our soul. And I thought with this body bliveth [remains] no fairness of this child, ne with this child dwelleth no foulness of this body.[4]

A picture curiously reminiscent of Blake.

And there is the parable of motherhood, which occupies the sixtieth and sixty-first chapters. The services of a mother to her baby are applied to the service of Jesus to us in the birth and

[1] Ch. 6.   [2] Ch. 5.   [3] Ch. 7.   [4] Ch. 64.

infancy of our supernatural life. But the most developed and the most important parable—a parable which condenses Julian's central teaching—is the parable of the lord and the servant. To this we must return later. The majority of these parables are wanting in the shorter version. Perhaps some of them suggested themselves later, perhaps Julian feared these secondary pictures might distract her readers from the primary visions and teaching.

Such then are the media of her revelations—intuition, speculation, subconscious art. It remains to consider the religious doctrine they convey.

To the double character of the revelations, in part visions and words, in part intellectual contemplations, correspond roughly the two poles around which their doctrine revolves. One pole is the incomprehensible and infinite Godhead, eternal and immutable; the other the redeeming Humanity of Christ with Its extension the Church. This bi-polarity is indeed the distinctive feature of Christian mysticism. For Christianity is the religion of the Incarnation of Godhead in humanity, of the Absolute in the relative, of Eternity in time.

The Eternal Godhead, Its incarnation in humanity in Christ and His Church-body, are thus the two poles alike of the universal Christian revelation and these private revelations of Dame Julian. The bi-polarity is present already in the first shewing where the joyful apprehension of the Trinity represents the pole of eternity, the vision of Christ's bleeding Head the pole of time. This double vision of eternity and time—not of eternity as annulling time or depriving it of significance, nor of time as possessing a significance independent of its manifestation and incarnation of Eternal Being—runs through the revelations. Julian's doctrine of the soul, of prayer, of redemption, her treatment of the problem of evil, is unintelligible, unless this twofold point of view is always before the mind. The same problem or fact wears a different aspect, as it is regarded from the lower standpoint of time—its phenomenal aspect, though real enough in its own order—or from the higher standpoint of God's eternity—its ultimate and therefore truest reality. And both aspects are seen to be harmonious and complementary, though Julian, not possessing the unveiled vision of God, cannot always explain how the harmony is effected.

To eternity belong "the substance of the soul" and God's "higher doom [judgment]" upon it; to time "the sensuality" of the soul and the lower doom passed upon it by the Church on earth.[1] Unless this double standpoint is grasped Julian may seem to teach doctrines which she would in fact have abhorred. Keeping it always in mind we will consider her doctrine of God, of the human soul, of evil and its redemption and finally of prayer.

Julian sees God immanent in all things. "I saw God in a point; that is to say in my understanding [she saw Him thus] by which sight I saw that He is in all thing."[2] The point here would seem to be the centre of Dionysius' circle which contains and unites all the radii—and thus represents God as the central unity which contains and unites all the created communications of His Being.[3]

But though present everywhere, God is not present in equal measure. The soul being most Godlike—capable even of the beatific vision of His Infinite Being—is His special seat. In the sixteenth revelation Julian sees Christ both in His Godhead and in His Manhood specially present in the human soul.[4]

As God is immanent in all things, so is He their value, their positive being.[5] It is indeed their inherent limits as contingent and relative beings which constitute them creatures essentially distinct from God. As God is thus the goodness, the ultimate and truest reality of all things, He is also the agent of their activities. "I beheld that He doth all that is done. Wherefore all things that are done, are well done; for Our Lord God doth all: for in this time the working of creatures was not shewed; but of Our Lord God in creatures . . . and *all* He doth. There is no Doer but He."[6] "Man beholdeth some deeds well done, and some deeds evil: and Our Lord beholdeth them not so, for as all that hath being . . . is of God's making, so is all thing that is done, in property [really, in the ultimate truth of it] of God's doing . . ." "See I am God See I am in all things. See I do all things . . . How should anything be amiss?"[7]

[1] Ch. 45.
[2] Ch. 11.
[3] I owe this interpretation to Sister Anna Maria (Reynolds), C.P., " Some Literary Influences in the Revelations of Julian of Norwich," p. 24.
[4] Ch. 68.
[5] Ch. 26.
[6] Ch. 11.
[7] ibid.

Consider the limited existence of creatures; it is unintelligible save as contingent upon Absolute Being and grounded in it. Consider causation and activity, they also are unintelligible as independent and self-explanatory. They are essentially contingent upon the One Absolute Cause and Agent and relative to it.

And the positive existence and activity of creatures are good. For as positive value and energy they are communications of the being and activity of God.

If Julian sees God in all things and especially in the human soul, she also sees all things and especially the soul in God who transcends their being which He gives and preserves. "As the body" to recall the little parable already quoted "is clad in the cloth and the flesh in the skin—so are soul and body clad and enclosed in the goodness of God."[1] "God is more nearer to us than our own soul—for He is the ground in whom our soul standeth[2] . . . Our kind is in God whole [our specific and our individual nature are contained in His universal being]; in which He maketh diversities flowing out of Him to work His will."[3] "Verily I saw that all our substance is in God." The complement of the vision of God in a point is the vision of the universe as a ball, the size of a hazel nut, lying in the palm of her hand. "I marvelled how it might last: for methought it might suddenlie have fallen to pieces for littleness. And I was answered in my understanding, 'It lasteth and ever shall: for God loveth it.' And so hath all thing being by the love of God. In this little thing I saw three properties. The first is that God made it. The second is that God loveth it. The third is that God keepeth it."[4] Our immanence in a transcendent God is for Julian a truth even more valuable than the immanence of God in us.[5] So deeply in fact is the soul grounded in God that she can even say that we can know our own soul only by first knowing God—"It is more easy to come to the knowing of God than to know our own soul. For our soul is so deep grounded in God . . . that we may not come to the knowing thereof, till we have first knowing of God . . . We should be in deep longing . . . into the time that we be led so deep into God that we verily and truly know our own soul."[6]

[1] Ch. 6.   [3] Ch. 57.   [5] Ch. 54.
[2] Ch. 56.   [4] Ch. 5.   [6] Ch. 56.

Julian distinguishes between "the substance" of the soul
grounded and dwelling in God and "the sensuality" of the soul
in which God dwells. The sensuality is the soul as informing
the body, its life principle and the subject of our psycho-physical
experience. It begins to exist "what time our soul is inspired in
our body".

Her concept of the higher part of the soul, the substance, is
more difficult. After comparing different passages I have reached
the conclusion that by the substance of the soul she means the
soul as a spirit existing independently of its function as the soul,
the formative principle and life of the body. And in particular
she has in view its inmost depth or centre from which the will
and understanding take their rise. The ground of the soul, the
apex of the soul, the *synderesis*, are other terms current among
mediaeval mystics. This centre, normally subliminal, is, mystical
writers agree, the peculiar seat of the mystic's contact with God.
For it is most free from the limitations of the more or less
superficial psychical functions and their sense-conditioned
experience.

For Julian the substance is united with God so immediately
that in those who will be saved it is never separated from Him
however grievously the soul sin in her sensuality. In the shorter
version she says "Prayer ones the soul to God. For though the
soul is ever like God . . . in substance, it is often unlike in condition through sin on man's part. Then makes prayer the soul
like unto God when the soul wills as God will. And then is it
like to God in condition as it is in substance."[1] She even says
(in the longer version) "I saw no difference between God and
our substance but as it were all God." She hastens however to
add that "my understanding took that our substance is in
God, that is to say, that God is God and our substance is a creature
in God".[2] To the substance belongs a "godly will that never
finally assenteth to sin ne never shall, that may never will evil
endlessly but ever good". This is opposed to a "beastly will in
the lower part that may never will no good".[3] For the lower
will, even when the particular object of its choice is good, is
self-asserting and selfish and as such contrary to God's will and
the self-sacrificing and unitive love by which the higher will can
and should and, so Julian thinks, in the elect always does, deny

[1] Cf. longer version, Ch. 43.   [2] Ch. 54.   [3] Ch. 37.

tself and receive the will of God. Hence arise the two dooms mentioned above, God's higher doom of approbation on the good will of the substance, the Church's lower doom of censure on the sinful will of the sensuality. This doctrine of an indefectible union between the elect and God in the fundamental orientation of the will is, as far as I know, peculiar among Catholic mystics to Julian and Coventry Patmore.[1] It may even seem identical with the Protestant teaching of the indefectibility of grace. But Julian also teaches that a soul that shall be finally saved may fall into mortal sin: "I saw how sin is deadly for a short time to the blessed creatures of endless life."[2] This seemingly inconsistent doctrine of a substantial will-union persisting despite even mortal sin is, I believe, Julian's vision of the ground of the soul as outside the time series in the eternal Now of God. However a soul sins in time; if it is finally saved for eternity, in eternity and therefore in the present vision *and reality* of God —more real than the time series and its phenomena—it is now what it will finally become. *Sub specie aeternitatis*, and therefore in God, the will is fundamentally, indeed essentially, its final choice. Moreover the central self is present to the entire succession of choices, from childhood until death, therefore to the final decisive choice. Consequently, if that choice is the right one, the central self *is* throughout present to it as being its final choice, even though one or many of its previous choices may be grievously sinful. Further, as we shall see, Julian does not separate any elect soul from the solidarity of Christ and His saints. God sees all souls saved in Christ as an indissoluble unity, one "man" with Him and in Him and therefore as good and united to Himself in the one will of the Total Christ. "In Him [the Second Person of the Trinity] we have this godly will whole and safe without end."[3] Sister Anna Maria Reynolds believes that Julian was indebted for this doctrine of the indefectible will to Eckhardt

---

[1] " Remembered Grace ":

> Whom God does once with heart to heart befriend,
> He does so till the end: . . .
>
> Of his sad errors none
> Though gross to blame,
> Shall cast him lower than the cleansing flame,
> Nor make him quite depart
> From the small flock named " after God's own heart".

[2] Ch. 71.
[3] Ch. 59.

D

from whom she quotes a passage she considers parallel.[1] Her doctrine however is not Eckhardt's. For Eckhardt is speaking of a natural orientation of the will to good, a permanent tendency to good, even in hell inclined to good. This is nothing but an Eckhardtian, that is to say a paradoxical, expression of the truth that the only possible object of any will must be good. Evil can be willed only *sub specie boni*. Julian on the other hand is speaking of the elect alone, in as much as God sees their final union with Himself already present in His present eternity.

Flemish and German mystics had spoken of the Divine Idea of each soul as its uncreated ground or substance. When a soul has fulfilled God's purpose in its creation, it corresponds to its type-idea in the Divine Mind and is wholly united to it. Since the soul is the expression of an idea of the Divine Wisdom, which contains the exemplars of all creatures from which they derive their natures, the created substance thus the reflection of the uncreated, and since that Wisdom for Christian theology is the Second Person of the Trinity incarnate in Jesus Christ, that Divine-Human Person is for Julian "our Mother in kind [nature], in our substantial making, in whom we be grounded and rooted".[2] Jesus thus in His Godhead our mother by nature, has become by His Incarnation our mother by grace. "Our very Mother Jesu."[3] For as natural humanity is contained in its exemplary cause, the Godhead of Jesus, thus the womb from which it has emerged, redeemed humanity, is contained in the Sacred Humanity, as the body of which Jesus is the Head, contained therefore in the Total Christ—"Christ having knit in Him every man that shall be saved, is perfect man."[4] Moreover in the mysteries of His Incarnation Jesus has performed the part of a mother towards us. "He dight Him all ready in our poor flesh Himself to do the service and office of Motherhood in all thing. He sustained us within him, in love and travail, into the full time that He would suffer the sharpest throes and grievousest pains that ever were, or ever shall be, and died at the last." "The mother may give her child to suck her milk; but

---

[1] " Some Literary Influences in the Revelations of Julian of Norwich," p. 27.

[2] Ch. 58.

[3] Ch. 63.

[4] Ch. 57. In the same passage, however, Julian also speaks of Our Lady's universal motherhood: " Our Lady is our Mother in whom we be all beclosed and of her born in Christ."

ur precious Mother Jesu He may feed us with Himself and
oth full courteously and full tenderly with the blessed Sacra-
ent." "This fair lovely word Mother," she concludes, "it
so sweet and kind in itself that it may not verily be said of
one, ne to none but of Him, and to Him, that is very Mother
f life and of all."[1]

Julian has perhaps confused to some extent the uncreated sub-
ance of the soul with the created. Hence she speaks of the
ork of redemption as a re-union between the sensuality and the
bstance. There are however two distinct unions—the union
etween the created and uncreated substance both natural and
ter a higher fashion, by supernatural charity—and the perfect
bordination of the sensible functions of the soul to its central
round itself united to God. She also speaks as though super-
atural gifts, especially faith, derive from the substance of the soul.
his can be true only of God as the ground and *ideal* substance
f the soul. Of the created substance it is true only in the sense
at faith—with hope and charity—is directly given to the root of
e soul's central functions and thence attains the more superficial
henomenal functions. Further Julian once says the substance
as "made fro without beginning" a statement true only of the
ncreated substance—its Divine Idea. Yet we have noticed her
xplicit statement, that the substance of the soul is a creature
istinct from the eternal Godhead. This portion of the book
aves the impression that she has been unable to achieve a suf-
ciently clear understanding and expression of her intuition. Per-
aps she has misunderstood hard sayings of mystical writers
ad or heard during her years of reflective elaboration. We
ust remember that the fourteenth-century German-Flemish
chool with whose teachings Julian must have been directly or
idirectly acquainted, derives from Eckhardt who *did* speak of
e ground of the soul as somehow uncreated and Divine. And
is pantheistic language,[2] though abandoned by his disciples,[3]
ft traces in ambiguous phraseology.

But there remains clear enough for Julian's readers the teaching
at our true nature and life, even our personality consist in the
nion with God and life in Him for which we are created. We

---

[1] Ch. 60.
[2] In Fr. Copleston's judgment it was a pantheism of expression only, not meaning.
Mediaeval Philosophy, p. 156.
[3] Tauler is careful to distinguish between the created and the uncreated ground.

came forth from God to express in our unique individuality :
unique aspect of His Wisdom. However we fail, unless w
deliberately and whole-heartedly reject Him, we are in th
centre of our being united with Him; if the root of our wil
cleaves to God, our feelings about Him matter little. The proces
of redemption is thus a return to our origin, a return by grac
to our true nature, that aspect of Divine Reality eternally presen
in the Wisdom of God which from eternity we are predestine
to express.[1]

But this return can be no simple ascent of unchecked progress
Redemption implies the restoration of something lost, the cur
of an evil. Julian's intuitions of redemption presuppose, there
fore, a doctrine of evil. When she saw God in all things "Si
was not shewed and I saw verily that sin is no deed."[2] Elsewher
"I saw not sin; for I believe it had no manner of substance, n
no part of being, ne it might not be known but by the pai
that is caused thereof." In the shorter version she says: "Sin i
neither deed nor liking."[3] These words, omitted later, no doub
owing to the danger of misunderstanding, mean, I believe, tha
sin is no positive act or desire. For a sinful act is, *as a positiv
activity*, good. Its sinfulness consists in its exclusion of anothe
and a worthier choice that should have been made. And a sinfu
desire is always for something possessed of a certain value withou
which it could be in no way desirable. Its sinfulness consists i
the undue imperfection of that value. Thus the object of si
differs from the object of a good will by a defect of being, an
the sinner is, as such, one who chooses nothingness. Toward
the end of the shorter version is an eloquent declamation agains
the "naught" of sin. But Julian does not therefore regard si
lightly, as in the concrete unreal or unimportant. "If it were lai
before us all the pain that is in hell and in purgatory and in earth
to suffer it rather than sin, we should rather choose all that pair
than sin; for sin is so vile and so mickle for to hate, that it ma
be likened to no pain; which pain is not sin."[4] Baron Vo
Hügel found these utterances inconsistent, ascribing the forme
to Neo-Platonic theory, the latter to Christian experience.

[1] Chs. 58, 62.
[2] Ch. 11.
[3] Ch. 27.
[4] Ch. 40.
[5] *The Mystical Element of Religion*, 1st Ed., Vol. II, p. 294.

There is no inconsistency. That which has no substantial existence may be in another sense very real. A famine is a terrible
reality. Yet it is not positive, no thing—simply the undue absence
of food. And if evil *had* a positive reality, there must either be
an ultimate principle of evil—a bad God—or God must be
partly evil.

Cold comfort, you may think, before the hideous countenance
of the world's sin and our own, this abstract consolation of its
metaphysical nonentity! But it has its practical importance.
For it means that despite appearances the universe is ultimately,
fundamentally, essentially good. Wrongdoing therefore cannot
be truly profitable, or finally triumphant. But Julian has further
comfort. She sees sin as God's scourge for our discipline. It
humbles us and increases our knowledge of His love.[1] For
redeemed humanity sin is an occasion of greater good. "Sin is
behovely",[2] that is, has its part in the Divine economy of good.
"Adam's sin", she insists, "was the most harmful that ever
was done" but the satisfaction made for it by Christ "is more
pleasing to the blessed Godhead and more worshipful for man's
salvation without comparison, than ever was the sin of Adam's
harmful".[3] God will bestow on redeemed mankind a better
gift than we should have enjoyed had man never fallen. And
this is true also of the individual sinner.[4] "God shewed that sin
shall be no shame but worship to man; for right as to every sin
is answering a pain by truth, right so for every sin to the same
soul is given a bliss by love. Right as divers sins be punished
with divers pains after that they be grievous; right so shall they
be rewarded with divers joys in heaven after that they have
been painful and sorrowful to the soul in earth."[5] We are
reminded of the bold words placed by Dante in the mouth of
Folco in Paradise: "Here we do not repent, but rejoice, not in
the sin which is forgotten, but in the Goodness that ordained
and provided."[6]

[1] Ch. 39.
[2] Ch. 27.
[3] Ch. 29.
[4] The *Exultet* in the York and Sarum Missals which Julian will have heard reads " O
certe necessarium Adae peccatum *et nostrum* " ("Necessary indeed Adam's sin and our
own".)
[5] Ch. 38.
[6] *Paradiso*, ix, 103–5. In this connection I would call attention to a problem which, so far
as I know, has escaped notice hitherto. God " brought to my mind, first Magdalen, Peter

Like St. Catherine of Genoa, who saw no wrath "in tende
love", Julian is insistent that there is no anger in God. Possibl
she is thinking primarily of the saved, and means that God'
continuous love towards them without anger for their sin i
His prescience of their good end in His eternity. But the scop
of her words is universal. "I saw verily that Our Lord wa
never wrath, ne never shall: for He is God, He is good, He i
truth, He is love, He is peace . . . I saw truly that it is agains
the property of His might to be wrath [anger is due to impotenc
temporary or final before an obstacle to the will]; and agains
the property of His wisdom, and against the property of Hi
goodness. God is that goodness that may not be wrath, fo
God is not but goodness."[1] "I saw no manner of wrath in God."
"I saw no wrath but on man's part."[3]

Of the origin of sin she says little. To debate the questio
she considers a waste of time and thought; for "it is a hig
marvellous privity (secret) hid in God: which privity shall b
known to us in heaven. In which knowing we shall verily se
the cause why He suffered sin to come."[4] And "all that is beside

and Paul, Thomas and Jude, St. John of Beverley and others; how they are known in th
Church on earth with their sins; and it is to them no shame, but all is turned them to wo
ship. . . . And St. John of Beverley Our Lord shewed him full highly in comfort of us f
homeliness and country sake and brought to my mind how he is a kind neighbour and
our knowing: and God called him plainly St. John of Beverley . . . shewing that he is a fu
high saint in his sight . . . and that in his youth and in his tender age he was a dear worth
servant to God . . . Nevertheless God suffered him to fall . . . And afterward God raise
him to manifold more grace; and by the contrition and meekness he had in his livin
God hath given him in heaven manifold joys overpassing that he should have had, if I
had not sinned or fallen" (Ch. 38). Jude—the reference no doubt is to the unbelief c
Our Lord's brethren. But St. John of Beverley? History and legend, so far as I can di
cover, know nothing of any fall into sin. On the contrary St. John is represented as
man of consistent holiness. Is the reference perhaps to his opposition to St. Wilfre
his accepting episcopal consecration by Archbishop Theodore in violation of his metro
politan's rights? And is his subsequent repentance, his reconciliation with Wilfred ar
resignation of his see? There is, however, no evidence that St. John or unbiased conten
poraries regarded his action as wilful, much less as grievous, sin. In any case it is difficu
to believe that Julian was acquainted with Eddius' partisan life of St. Wilfred or indee
with the details of ecclesiastical history in the seventh century. Though the quarrel wit
St. Wilfred seems the only possible explanation, it hardly seems to account sufficient!
for Julian's picture of St. John of Beverley as notoriously a converted sinner. It is wort
notice that his feast was May 7th, the day before Julian's shewings began. There is anoth
feast on October 25th, three days before SS. Simon and Jude. St. John is not mentione
in the shorter version. Possibly the introduction of his festival into the Sarum calend
under Henry V revived devotion to a patron of her youth.

[1] Ch. 46.
[2] Ch. 49.
[3] Ch. 48.
[4] Ch. 27.

our salvation . . . is our Lord's privy counsel, and it longeth to the
royal lordship of God to have His privy counsel in peace.   And
it longeth to His servants for obedience and reverence not to
will to know His counsels."[1] Her theology is practical, concerned with the achievement of our salvation. Of merely
theoretical questions she is impatient.

Julian's doctrine of man's fall and redemption is condensed in
her parable of the lord and the servant.[2] Though stated to have
been a direct "shewing" and of cardinal importance, it is strangely
absent from the shorter version. The reason is, perhaps, that,
as she herself hints, she found it very difficult to understand,
and that, until she had satisfied herself of its interpretation, she
judged it better to omit it. It consists of a vision with an intellectual illumination which in part explains it; in its present
state doubtless the product of subsequent contemplation. Julian
saw a lord seated on the earth, clad in a blue cloak. His eyes were
"black most fair and seemly, shewing full of lovely pity". On
his left hand stood a servant wearing a labourer's kirtle, "white,
single, old and all defaulted, dyed with the sweat of his body".
The lord looked with love on his servant who "for love having
no regard to himself nor to nothing that might befall him,
hastily did start and run at the sending of his lord, to do that
thing which was his will and his worship". "There was a treasure
in the earth which the lord loved . . . a meat which is lovesome
and pleasing unto the lord." As "the servant runneth in great
haste for love to do his lord's will, anon he falleth in a slade
[ravine] and taketh full great sorrow and then he groneth and
moneth and walloweth and wrieth; but he may not rise nor help
himself by no manner of way. And of all this the most mischief
was failing of comfort; for he could not turn his face to look on
his loving lord, which was to him full near, in whom is full
comfort; but as a man that was full feeble and unwise for the
time he entended to his feeling and enduring in woe". "And I
beheld . . . if I could perceive in him any default: or if the
lord should assign him any manner of blame. And verily there
was none seen, for only his good will and his great desire was the
cause of his falling. And he was as unloathful and as good inwardly, as he was when he stood before his lord, ready to do
his will." " Then said this courteous lord in his meaning, 'Lo,

[1] Ch. 30.   [2] Chs. 51 et sqq.

my beloved servant, what harm and disease he hath had and taken in my service for my love, yea, and for his good will Is it not reason that I reward him, his frey and his dred, his hurt and his maim and all his woe? And not only this, but falleth it not to me to give him a gift, that be better to him and more worshipful than his own heal should have been; or else me-thinketh I did him no grace." [1]

The lord is God, and His constant love for the servant is His eternal love that no temporary state of sin can change. He sit on the earth, Julian tells us, because His dwelling is in human souls. The complex figure of the parable is the servant. He is at once Adam in his fall, Jesus Christ in His Incarnation and Passion, and all souls that are finally saved. For they with their natural head Adam are the mystical body whose Head is Jesus Christ. Redemptive solidarity in the body of Christ, the cardinal doctrine of Christianity, is thus the key to this central parable of the Revelations, if not indeed to the entire book.[2] "The servant", Julian here explains, "I understood was shewed for Adam; that is to say, one man was shewed and his falling to make thereby to be understood how God beholdeth all man and his falling, for in the sight of God all man is one man, and one man is all man."[3] But later, "When I say the servant, it meaneth Christ's manhood which is rightful Adam . . . When Adam fell, God's Son fell, for the right oneing that was made in heaven God's Son might not be separate from Adam; for by Adam I understand all man."[4] Again the double point of view. In present eternity as opposed to time Christ's Incarnation and Re-demption are already effected in Adam's fall in virtue of the solidarity between them in the Divine decree. And in its solidarity with Christ redeemed mankind is loved with God's love for His Son. This then is the treasure, the meat sought by the servant, His own body natural and mystical in one, the worship rendered by it to God—His human glory. Finally in the risen and ascended Christ Julian sees the servant, mankind, crowned and robed in the heaven of transcendent Godhead. This is the

[1] Ch. 51.
[2] Cf. Ch. 9. "If I look singularly to myself, I am right nought; but in [the] general [body] I am, I hope, in onehead of charity with all mine even Christians. For in this onehead standeth the life of all mankind that shall be saved."
[3] Ch. 51.
[4] Ch. 51.

return by grace to God of that which came forth from Him by nature (for her the entire creation is recapitulated in humanity)[1]: a return already effected in Christ the head—in process of accomplishment in His members. Beneath the picture of the lord and servant might be written the text, true of the total as of the individual Christ: "I came forth from the Father and came into the world; again I leave the world and go to the Father."

But after all, this servant whose fall never lost him the love of his Lord, this servant destined to share the Divine Life, this servant one with the Son of God, is not for Julian the entire human race. He is saved humanity, the elect. What then of the finally lost—the reprobate? How does their loss consist with a God who is Love? Here Julian stands out from her environment in a light peculiarly sympathetic to modern feeling. The doctrine of eternal damnation presented no difficulty to the mediaeval mind. On the contrary, mediaeval Catholics invested it with an imaginative garb of physical tortures and seemed almost to delight in their contemplation. For their feelings were those of schoolboys, during those years of a cruelty due to an undeveloped imagination, vigorous indeed, but shallow. On the left of the chancel arch were depicted the nude files of the damned dragged by demons to flames and boiling cauldrons, or devoured by the yawning mouth of a hideous monster, the symbol of hell. The number of the lost was universally believed to exceed enormously the number of the saved. Dante's hell is comparatively as crowded as a football match; his heaven as empty as a church at a weekday service. Almost alone, Julian is afflicted by this triumph of evil. Despite a nightmare of the grinning fiend,[2] her contemplations turn away from hell and its inhabitants. She would have us put them out of our mind as far as possible. "As long as we be in this life, what time that we *by our folly* turn us to the beholding of the reproved [the damned] tenderly Our Lord toucheth us and blissedfully calleth us, saying in our soul, 'Let me alone my dearworthy child; intend to me, I am enough to thee, and enjoy in thy Saviour and in thy salvation.' "[3] And when she affirms vigorously a

---

[1] A view not yet disproved by astronomy.
[2] Chs. 67, 69.
[3] Ch. 36.

final damnation—partly perhaps in view of the misunderstanding that she disbelieved it—it is the negative aspect on which she insists, the exclusion of the devils and lost souls from the society of God and His saints. "I saw the devil is reproved of God and endlessly damned. In which sight I understood that all the creatures that be of the devil's condition in this life, and therein ending, there is no more mention made of them before God and all His holy ones, than of the devil; notwithstanding that they be of mankind; whether they have been christened or not."[1] She finds it hard to conceive human wills of this obdurate malice against her "dearworthy" Lord. In the shorter version she appears momentarily at least to indulge the hope that no man will in fact make this final choice of evil. "If such there be" she says. But this bold doubt, which can scarcely have represented her more deliberate attitude, is significantly absent from the longer version.

Nevertheless, the simple dismissal of the damned from the life and mind of God in which she loves and lives is not her last word. She has a further intuition of inexplicable hope. "Our good Lord answered to all the questions and doubts that I might make saying full comfortably, 'I may make all thing well; and I can make all thing well; and I shall make all thing well; and I will make all thing well; and thou shalt see thyself that all manner of thing shall be well[2] . . . There is a deed, the which the blessedful Trinity shall do in the last day, as to my sight: and what that deed shall be, and how it shall be done, it is unknown of all creatures which are beneath Christ and shall be till when it shall be done."[3] She cannot reconcile the promise with eternal punishment, which weighed the heavier on her mind because she understood it to involve the innocent heathen. "Standing all this, methought it was unpossible that all manner of thing should be well, as Our Lord shewed in this time, and as to this, I had no other answer in shewing of Our Lord but this: 'That, that is unpossible to thee, is not unpossible to me; I shall save my word in all thing and I shall make all thing well'."[4] Assuredly no answer this to reason—for Julian the final triumph of love is God's ultimate mystery— but an intuition of infinite hope. Eternity is on a different plane

[1] Ch. 33.
[2] Ch. 31.
[3] Ch. 32.
[4] The entire chapter should be read.

from time, and the truth of a lower plane may be somehow included yet transcended in the fuller reality of a higher. It is unreasonable to deny facts, be they physical or spiritual, because we cannot also see their harmony. The problem of evil is the riddle of the universe, whose solution is attainable only in the universal vision of Divine Wisdom.

Besides these theoretic intuitions of God and His redeeming work, Julian has much immediately practical instruction. She warns us, for example, against the thought of other people's sins, which makes as it were a thick mist before the eye of the soul, points out that the penance God sends is more salutary than any we can take on ourselves,[1] that it is the service of youth, when the world is still attractive, that has special value in God's sight,[2] that "there is no dread [fear] that fully pleaseth God in us, but reverent dread" which "is soft", and "the more it is had, the less it is felt for sweetness of love".[3]

But I can discuss here only her doctrine of the practical means of union with God—her doctrine of prayer. Like all mystics, she reduces prayer to something at once very simple and very profound—the adherence of the soul through the will to God, whether we are conscious of His Presence or apparent absence, whether we find delight or dryness in our devotion. Julian does not reject "means", that is, special devotions. But she would have us regard them not as isolated and independent ways of prayer, but as manifestations, partial aspects of one Love-Will accepted by the soul, that Love being the Nature of God, Absolute Goodness, indwelling its secret depths, and at the same time enveloping it as our clothes our body. And, as this is understood by the soul, a multiplicity of special devotions tends to be replaced by a simpler prayer of adherence to the Divine goodness, which is the substance of them all. "We use, for unknowing of love, to make many means. Then saw I verily that it is more worship to God that we faithfully pray to Himself of His goodness and cleave thereto by His grace with true understanding and steadfast belief than if we made all the means that heart may think. For if we make all those means, it is too little and not full worship to God: but in His goodness is all the whole; and there faileth right

---

[1] Ch. 76. A truth on which Fr. Baker strongly insists. See *The Confessions of Father Baker*, 134 et sqq.
[2] Ch. 14.
[3] Ch. 73.

nought." We pray by the mysteries of the Incarnation and Passion and they derive from the Divine Goodness as do the intercession of Our Lady and the saints which we invoke. But "to the goodness of God is the highest prayer and it cometh down to us to the lowest part of our need . . . it is nearest in kind [nature] and readiest in grace."[1] Confidence in the Divine love, as the ultimate reality of the Universe and the key to its history, is the foundation of Julian's prayer.[2] Later she returns to the subject of prayer with a Divine locution "brought suddenly" to her mind. "I am the ground of thy beseeking. First it is my will that thou have it: and sithen I make thee to will it, and sithen I make thee to beseek it, and thou seekest it, how should it then be: that thou shouldest not have thy seeking?"[3] In her explanation Julian again employs the double point of view—the Eternal Will of God, the successive series of human dispositions. She points out that, though our prayer cannot alter the Eternal Will, this is no reason to abstain from praying, but the reverse. For that Will is to grant our prayer through the means of our prayer.[4] Moreover to be efficacious prayer must be confident. The reason, no doubt, why so much prayer is, so far as we can see, ineffective, is our lack of confident trust when we offer it. Far too often prayer, even the prayer in itself the most powerful, the official prayer of the Church, is made without genuine conviction that it will be answered, will make any difference. We are like those passengers in a storm who, when the Captain advised them to pray for safety, replied: "Oh Captain, are things really as bad as that?" Fainthearted prayer is not likely to be effective. Genuine prayer is assured of its answer. "Then meaneth He thus: that we see that He doth it and we pray therefore; for that one is not enough. For if we pray and see not that He doth it, it maketh us heavy and doubtful and that is not His worship. And if we see that He doth it and we pray not: we do not our duty . . . But to see that He doth it and to pray forthwithall: so is He worshipped and we speed. All thing that Our Lord hath ordained to do it is His will that we pray therefore, either in special or in general. And the joy and the bliss that is to Him and the thank and the worship we shall have therefore, it passeth the understanding of all creatures in this life . . .[5] Prayer oneth the soul to God."[6] Like other contemplatives Julian insists upon the

[1] Ch. 6.   [2] Chs. 6, 41.   [3] Ch. 41.   [4] Ch. 41.   [5] Ch. 42.   [6] Ch. 43.

unitive nature of genuine prayer. "Prayer is a witness that the soul will as God will and comforteth the conscience and ableth man to grace. And thus He teacheth us to pray and mightily to trust that we shall have it."[1] But this prayer whose answer is the Will of God is not any petition we may choose to make. It is what "Our Lord hath ordained to do"[2] and that is whatever is profitable for ourselves or others and assists our salvation.[3] For we may ask for the wrong thing or in the wrong way or at the wrong time. "Either we abide a better time, or more grace, or a better gift."[4]

And in the last resort this better gift is nothing less than God Himself. Infinite Love can be satisfied with no gift short of Itself. Nor can man's need be satisfied by anything less. "God of thy goodness give me thyself, for thou art enough to me; and if I ask anything that is less, ever me wanteth, but only in thee I have all."[5] "I it am, the high sovereign goodness of all manner thing: I it am, that maketh thee to long: I it am, the endless fulfilling of all true desires."[6] And this gift of God Himself is given to the entire body of saved humanity through that work of redemption and sanctification in whose consummation all our prayers will find their fulfilment. This work is already in process of accomplishment—but God wills to forward it through our prayer.

Thus prayer is a participation by the human will in God's will to manifest Himself in redeemed humanity. And it is increasingly a direct grasp by the centre of the soul of that Centre where all the lines of our partial desires and petitions converge: the Centre of the world process which is Its revelation.

As a fundamental will union this prayer is continual. But from time to time it becomes a conscious union with God, directly experienced. Though Julian gives no systematic account of the character and degrees of her prayer she speaks of these conscious contacts. One form of mystical experience is the apprehension of some truth about God and His Work—the revelation of a

[1] Ch. 43.
[2] Ch. 42.
[3] What is in fact profitable to us is indicated by the liturgical prayer of the Church. What the Church prays for, illumination for example, freedom, peace, health and security, and for the community even prosperity, must be good for us.
[4] Ch. 42.
[5] Ch. 5.
[6] Ch. 59. Cf. *The Cloud of Unknowing*. " To them that be perfectly meeked [humble] no thing shall be wanting, neither ghostly thing nor bodily. For they have God, in whom is all plenty and whoso hath Him he needeth nought else in this life " (Ch. 23).

particular aspect of God. This purely intellectual apprehension of Divine truth, the ghostly sight, is fuller, deeper, more valuable, she insists, than the apparently sensible manifestations. But it is therefore impossible to translate it adequately into the terms of conceptual thought, "the ghostly sight I cannot shew as openly ne as fully as I would".

And above these ghostly sights is the direct but necessarily unintelligible touch of God Himself. For God is the end and perfection of prayer. Prayer, in its highest form the prayer of experienced union, is thus a veiled foretaste of the perfect and unveiled possession of God in heaven. "Prayer is a rightwise understanding of that fullhead of joy that is for to come . . . savouring and seeing our bliss, that we be ordained to."[1] The contemplation of God's "deed" of universal love leads Julian to experience of the Doer. "When our courteous Lord of His special grace sheweth Himself to our soul, we have that we desire; and then we see not for the time what we should more pray; but all our intent with all our mights is set whole into the beholding of Him. And this is a high unperceivable prayer [our experience of the incomprehensible Godhead necessarily lacks a clear and intelligible content, whether of sensible images or ideas] for all the cause wherefore we pray is to be oned into the sight and beholding of Him." And "in this contemplation [the veiled and dim, often almost imperceptible, dawn of heaven's noonday vision] we pray marvellously, enjoying with reverent dread and so great sweetness and delight in Him, that we can pray right nought but as He stirreth us for the time".[2] "And truly to enjoy Our Lord is a full lovely thanking in His sight."[3]

But in this world the Divine light cannot shine steadily. It must fade again into that other light, by comparison darkness, of common day, as the vision faded from the Mount of Transfiguration, or that passing flash of God which crowns the *Divina Commedia*. As experience the prayer even of the mystic must vary between intuition and ignorance, delight and dryness. For Dante's "lofty sight power failed". "But my desire and will were being driven on, as a wheel is evenly turned, by the love that moves the sun and the other stars."[4] What Dante relates, Julian commands. "He saith thus, 'Pray entirely, inwardly,

---

[1] Ch. 42.   [3] Ch. 41.
[2] Ch. 43.   [4] *Paradiso*, xxxiii, 142-5.

though thee think it savour thee nought, yet it is profitable enough . . . pray entirely, inwardly though thou feel nought, though thou see nought: yea, though thou think thou might not; for in dryness and barrenness, in sickness and in feebleness, then is thy prayer full pleasant to me, though thou think it savour thee not but little: and so is all thy living prayer in my sight.' "[1] For whether perceived or imperceptible, felt or unfelt, love is that Divine Will which is the law of the universe and with which our union is prayer. This is the repeated and the final text of Julian's gospel, the key to her Revelations. "Fro the time that it was shewed, I desired oftentimes to wit in what was Our Lord's meaning; and fifteen year after and more, I was answered in ghostly understanding . . . saying thus: 'What? Wouldest thou wit thy Lord's meaning in this thing? Wit it well, love was His meaning. Who sheweth it thee? Love. Wherefore sheweth He it thee? For love. Hold thee therein, thou shalt wit more in the same. But thou shalt never wit therein other without end.' Thus was I learned that love is Our Lord's meaning. And I saw full surely in this and in all, that ere God made us, He loved us; which love was never slacked, ne never shall be. And in this love He hath done all His works: and in this love He hath made all thing profitable to us: and in this love our life is everlasting: in our making we had beginning: but the love wherein He made us was in Him fro without beginning. In which love we have our beginning. And all this shall we see in God without end."[2] As Crashaw will proclaim, "Love, thou art absolute, sole Lord of Life and Death."[3]

In face of all we know of the pain, cruelty and folly of mankind, Julian's message of love may sound a mockery of human woe. She may appear the victim of a pitiful illusion for whose sake she has flung away even those few poor pleasures this wretched and fleeting life might have given her. Then indeed is the world without God, its meaning not love, but the despair of an un-heeding and unconscious silence, of a void in which re-echoes the cry of man's torment. But she comes to us with the credentials of a personal experience whose authenticity we cannot doubt. She comes to relate, though with a unique beauty of manner, an

[1] Ch. 41.
[2] Ch. 86, the concluding words of the *Revelations*.
[3] " Hymn to St. Teresa."

experience common in its fullness to a multitude scattered through diverse lands and epochs, and implicit, even indirectly and obscurely manifest, in the religion of millions. Can illusion produce, not only a deep and lasting happiness, but a wisdom lofty indeed, but broad and sane, doctrine of so rich and so full a content, given in an experience of widespread even worldwide occurrence and substantial identity? M. Henri Barbusse, himself lacking all religious belief, says of its most evident obstacle: *La souffrance, c'est la profondeur même.* And *if* Julian's revelations are the truth; if, for all its ugliness and seeming power, evil is without positive and therefore without final reality; if human history, despite its piteous record of sin and suffering, is the course of a servant who has come from God and is returning to Him again; if the soul can pass beyond the changes, frustrations and disappointments of time to an eternal Goodness that dwells in its depths, wraps it about on all sides and comes down to the lowest part of its need, *if* love *is* His meaning—

BIBLIOGRAPHICAL NOTE

Four MSS of the *Revelations* exist.

A. Shorter version.

(1) Brit. Mus. Addit. MS.37.790. This is the earliest extant MS, seen by Blomefield and subsequently lost. It was recovered, however, in 1909. Its editor, the Rev. Dundas Harford, ascribes it to the middle of the fifteenth century. As, however, the copyist tells us that Julian "yet is in life anno domini MCCCCXIII", the natural inference is that it was written in that year. It is in the Northern dialect.

Printed edition. *The Shewings of Lady Julian* (originally *Comfortable Words for Christ's Lovers*), Rev. Dundas Harford, H. R. Allenson, 1911, 1912, 1925.

B. Longer version.

(2) Brit. Mus. Sloane 2499 (late seventeenth century). Printed editions:

(a) Rev. P. H. Collins, *Mediaeval Library of Mystical and Ascetical Works*, Richardson, 1877.

(b) Miss Grace Warrack, Methuen & Co. 1st ed. 1901.

(c) Dom Roger Hudleston, O.S.B., Burns Oates and Washbourne (Orchard Books), reprinted 1952.

(3) Brit. Mus. Sloane 3705 (mid-eighteenth century). (The language has been modernised.) Not published. Is it a transcript of one one of the other two?

(4) Paris, Bibliothèque Nationale, Fonds anglais, 40. Sixteenth century.

Printed edition. Dom Serenus Cressy, O.S.B., 1670. Re-edited from Cressy's printed text by (1) G. H. Parker, 1843. (2) With an introduction by Father George Tyrrell, Kegan Paul, 1902. This is the text I have employed.

The critical edition of the *Revelations* for which we have been waiting so long is at last being prepared by Sister Anna Maria Reynolds, C. P., and will be published under the auspices of Leeds University whose generous support has made it possible. She will, I understand, print both versions, the longer and the shorter. It is appropriate that the work of a mystic whose special devotion was the Passion should be edited by a Passionist.

CHAPTER VI

IN DEFENCE OF MARGERY KEMPE

Mr. ALDOUS HUXLEY has justly charged those responsible for arranging university examinations in English Literature with obliging students of eighteenth-century literature to study the brilliant superficialities of Addison and Steele while not requiring any acquaintance with the magnificent prose in which William Law clothed his presentation of Boehme's mysticism studied in the light of his own prayer. The same must be said of the attitude of our literary pundits towards mediaeval English literature. If there is a book which deserves the close study of all concerned with English history or literature in the fifteenth century it is the *Book of Margery Kempe*. Yet there is little sign that its value has been appreciated. For, like the writings of Law, it is concerned with the communion of prayer between the soul and God. And that in the eyes of the modern secularist is enough to damn a book, whatever its literary merit or historical importance.

Margery's book is the first autobiography in our language. It throws a vivid light on the England of Henry IV, Henry V and Henry VI. Bishops and burghers, friars and pilgrims, local officials and jailers, the man in the street and his womenfolk, men and women of many classes—all these appear in these pages as they thought, spoke and behaved. Her honest record of facts has given us a picture of mediaeval England as illuminating as the imaginary portraits of the *Canterbury Tales* and *Piers Plowman*. As such it ranks with the Paston letters. But the latter lack depth. The inner life, spiritual and psychological, is beyond the ken of their earthbound writers.

The *Book of Margery Kempe* has come to us risen "like Alcestis from the grave" not twenty years ago. Before 1934 it was known only as the source, since lost, of twenty-eight short extracts, all concerned with Margery's spiritual experience, printed by Wynkyn de Worde about 1501 and reprinted in 1521 by Henry Pepwell as part of a collection of mystical writings reprinted in

)10 by Edmund Gardner under the title of *The Cell of Self-
nowledge*. Pepwell calls Margery "A devout ancress of Lynn."

In the appendix to her classic *Mysticism* Evelyn Underhill calls
Margery "The first English mystic we can name with certainty,
probably writing c. 1290), the anchoress of Lynn."

Then, like a bolt from the blue, her book came to light, dis-
overed in the library of Colonel Butler Bowdon, whose family
as possessed the sole surviving manuscript from time imme-
norial, probably since the dissolution of the monastery for which
was written, the Carthusian priory of Mountgrace.

An edition was first published in modern English with the
assages recording Margery's mystical experiences relegated to an
ppendix. In 1940 the Early English Text Society published the
ook in its original language and spelling, edited by the American
cholar Professor Sanford Brown Meech, assisted by Miss Hope
Allen, who contributed a prefatory note and many additional
otes to the text. It is written in the third person about "the
reature" as Margery calls herself.

Whether she ended her days in an anchorage we cannot
ell. For nothing is known of her after the second part of her
ook, an appendix relating her journey to Prussia, was written in
438.

In any case her life as made known by her book was anything
ut eremitical. Converted to God and wearing the signs of her
ledication, she lived in the world and moreover travelled widely.
That is why her book is a picture of the contemporary world.

Unfortunately Margery tells her story with little regard for the
order of events, though facts are related which have made it
ossible to draw up the chronological framework which Professor
Meech gives us in the Introduction. Moreover, it is but inciden-
ally, even accidentally (from her report of a reply to a question),
hat we learn that she was the mother of fourteen children, of
whom only one, a son, plays any part in her Book. Many, we
nay surmise, did not survive childhood. But in a locution
orobably to be dated fairly late in her life we hear of "thin owyn
hilderyn". Otherwise the freedom of action she enjoyed would
e hard to explain. For she was a woman married for almost
orty years, though after the first twenty she separated from her
ausband, both taking vows of chastity, and she returned to him
only to nurse him in his decrepitude.

Margery was the daughter of John Brunham (Burnham), fiv
times mayor of what is now Kings, then Bishops Lynn, which h
also represented in Parliament. Lynn was a flourishing po
trading with the countries on the North Sea and the Baltic. An
Brunham was a rich man. In 1393 or 1394 she married Joh
Kempe, the son of a wealthy merchant, for his father was presum
ably the merchant whose goods, confiscated with those of othe
merchants by the Prussians, were valued by the English govern
ment in the official claim for redress at the large sum c
£300.

She was twenty or a little more when she married. Prou
of her wealth and social position she spent freely on person:
adornment; "gold pipes" in her hair and fashionable and costl
dresses. To her husband's expostulations she replied that sh
intended to live in a style suitable to her family and that i
marrying him she had married beneath her. To support he
extravagant way of living she tried to increase her income b
trade, first by brewing, then by a horsemill. Both undertaking
failed. The ale was spoiled and the horses refused to draw
Five centuries before the Married Woman's Property Act
Margery had full control of her money—how I do not know. I
consequence of these failures she was impoverished and consider
ably indebted. Only her father's death restored her to solvenc
and some degree of wealth. Her father-in-law had presumabl
lost heavily from the Prussian confiscations. The birth of her firs
child, painful and dangerous, her suffering aggravated by a refusa
to confess a grave sin on her conscience, led to an attack of mad
ness when she believed herself the sport of fiends. It must no
prejudice us against her, as though she were a permanent victim
of religious mania. The madness did not recur. It was cured by :
vision of Christ seated on her bed and saying "Dowtyr why has
thou forsakyn me and I forsoke never the." This must have bee
the beginning of her conversion. But it was not completed fo
many years. Unfortunately the chronology of these years canno
be made out. We know only that one night, presumably afte
her losses had done much to disappoint her with the world, sh
heard, as she lay in bed, music so sweet that she thought it th
music of heaven which she was in danger of forfeiting by he
sins. Her conversion was now definitive. She fasted, prayed
wept, wore a hairshirt and tried, though for long in vain, t

persuade her husband to renounce his marriage right. Two years of peace were followed by three years of temptation when she believed herself abandoned by God, surely the Dark Night of Sense. It was at this time that a friend, to test her virtue, asked her to be his mistress. Throughout Vespers she turned his offer over in her mind. Then in despair she consented, only to be told that he had never meant the suggestion seriously. The episode is told with a rare psychological detail and subtlety—yet with complete discretion.

The darkness was ended by a vision of Our Lord who gave her detailed instructions for her spiritual life, among them to receive Communion every Sunday, a practice extremely rare at this period. About the same time she finally broke off marital relations. Her parish church was St. Margaret's and she foretold that attempts to grant its chapel of ease St. Nicholas parochial status would prove unsuccessful, an issue which pleased her affection for the church where she worshipped. When she was hearing Mass a large stone fell from the roof and struck her, but, by a miracle she believed, she took no hurt. The same summer (it was 1413), she went with her husband to visit a number of shrines and holy persons. On Midsummer Eve, as they were returning from York, where she had made friends with an anchoress, on the road between York and Bridlington, Margery carrying a bottle of beer, her husband a cake, she persuaded him to renounce formally any claim to matrimonial relations. In return she undertook to pay his debts.

Her father, as we know from the archives of Lynn, died a few months later. It was only then that she redeemed her promise to her husband. When she made it she no doubt knew that he was a dying man and promised to pay the debts from her inheritance.

At one monastery, unnamed, which they visited, Margery won over a hostile monk, told him of secret sins he had committed and, on the authority of Our Lord's word to her, promised him salvation if he amended his life, which he did. At Christchurch, Canterbury, on the other hand, she had much to suffer from monks and people. The populace wanted her burned for a Lollard. Her suffering was followed by words of love and consolation from Our Lord, of the type offensive to those who lose sight of the value attached by God to souls that love Him.

She visited Lincoln with her husband and they took vows c
chastity before the Bishop, Philip Repingdon. He invited thei
to dinner. But he refused Margery's request to invest her wit
a mantle and ring, saying that, as he was not her diocesan, he coul
not do so without the approval of the Archbishop of Canterbury
to whom he referred her. They went on to Lambeth, wher
Archbishop Arundel received her kindly, approved her way c
devotion, gave her a sealed letter empowering her to choose he
confessor and go to Communion every Sunday and talked wit
her, her husband patient in the background, till the stars cam
out.[1] But he does not seem to have done anything about th
mantle and ring, though we hear later of her wearing the latter
Those who picture the mediaeval Catholic in servile dread of th
clergy should notice that Margery told the Archbishop it was hi
duty to prevent his retainers swearing as she had heard them d
and rebuked them for doing, and had already told Bisho
Repingdon that he placed human respect before the love c
God. Her book in fact confirms the impression made by th
more or less contemporary lives of St. Bridget, St. Collette, S
Catherine of Siena and St. Joan; that in the mediaeval Church th
balance between the prophetic and the priestly office was bette
observed than, for obvious reasons, it has been since th
Reformation.

The narrative now turns back to the time when Margery'
last child had just been born and by Divine command sh
went to the saintly Vicar of St. Stephen's, Norwich, Richar
Caister, and told him of her life and prayer, of God's com
munication to her soul. The Vicar believed her an
became her staunch friend, as also the Carmelite Willian
Southfield. And it was at this time that she visited Dam
Julian, the visit of which I have spoken in my study of her.
That is to say, she was accepted by the Norwich group o
contemplatives. But here, as elsewhere in England, the peopl
were hostile. Her campaign against profane swearing, he
particular *bête noire*,[3] was confused with the Lollards' objectior

[1] Though I have followed the order of Margery's narrative there can be no doubt tha
the visit to Bishop Repingdon at Lincoln immediately followed the journey from Yor
to Bridlington and that the visit to Canterbury followed the visit to Archbishop Arundel
[2] See above, p. 75.
[3] Mediaeval oaths were in fact shockingly profane, by God's body, wounds, blood o
death.

to oaths of any kind. Her preaching, the more so that it was interlarded with quotations from Scripture, suggested the lay-preachers of Lollardy with their Wycliffite Bible. Nor should we forget that her former parish priest, Sawtree, was the first man to be burned as a Lollard. No theologian, however, still less any bishop, pronounced her guilty of heresy, certainly not after examination. It was from the ignorant laity that she had so much to suffer. At Lynn, though one confessor distrusted her, another, the anchorite at Black Friars, supported her and foretold future events in her life, which presumably he saw in her subconscious present. Once at the Elevation she saw the Host flutter like a dove. Our Lord informed her that it foretold an earthquake and on the same occasion that every word in St. Bridget's revelations was true. Here her subconscious adulterated whatever Divine communication may have been made to her soul. For no earth-quake occurred. Nor does she say that the prophecy was fulfilled later. And it is impossible to accept St. Bridget's reve-lations as literal truth. Margery indeed would have profited greatly by the instructions and warning of St. John of the Cross, that the recipient of locutions and visions should not attach himself to their letter but pass through them to the spiritual substance beneath. But she cannot be blamed for what she did not and could not know. And if, like so many down to the present day, she took for infallible a guidance only infallibly profitable,[1] with her knowledge and in her environment she could scarcely have done otherwise.

We are told of private revelations made to her, revelations of future deaths or recoveries, of the state of particular souls after death. The former can be explained naturally by the abiding present of the central spirit, the latter of their nature cannot be verified. Twice she warned a friendly priest against men who sought to abuse his charity.

In the late autumn of 1413 Margery set out on a pilgrimage to the Holy Land. According to Professor Meech's calculations she cannot have left Lynn later than November 1st, 1413. Her father had just died, before October 16th. Before her departure she had it given out from the pulpit that she was prepared to settle any debts owed by her husband or herself. Evidently her father's death had given her the money required to pay her debts,

[1] See below, pp. 229-30.

defray the cost of her pilgrimage and fulfil the promise made to her husband the previous midsummer. She sailed from Yarmouth to Zierickzee in Holland and from there set out for Venice.

Her loud sobs at her Sunday Communion, her abstinence from meat and above all the fact that she would talk of nothing but religion, even at meals, annoyed her fellow pilgrims who like Chaucer's were holydaymakers and tourists as well as pilgrims. They refused to allow her to remain with them and, when by humble entreaty she persuaded them to let her travel with them as far as Constance, they heaped insults on her, forcing her to wear ridiculous clothing and sit in disgrace at the foot of the table. At Constance she went to an English friar who, she says, was a Papal legate, but who has not been identified. Perhaps there is a slip of memory. He took her part with the pilgrims. His intervention, however, only exasperated them further and they left without her, taking with them her maid and sixteen pounds of her money—the sum no doubt she had paid for her share of the expenses. A Devonshire man, William Weaver, came to her rescue and escorted her as far as Bologna where she caught up her company. No woman could travel without a male escort. They consented to receive her back if she would agree not to talk of the Gospel "That ye schal not speke of the Gospel wher we come but ye schal syttyn stylle and maken mery as we don bothin at mete and at soper".[1] She consented and went with them to Venice where they waited for the galleys to sail next spring. During her stay in Venice she broke her agreement by repeating a text of the Gospel at table and said she could no longer refrain from speaking of her Lord Jesus Christ. They finally left her and she sailed in another galley. A priest stole one of her sheets and swore it was his. She spent three weeks in Jerusalem and its neighbourhood, visiting the Holy Places and seeing in imaginary vision the events enacted there. As she approached Jerusalem she almost fell off her donkey, overcome with a vision of the heavenly Jerusalem. It was on Mount Calvary that the sight of Jesus on the Cross wrung from her the first of the loud cries which became increasingly frequent and which, though she struggled against them, she could not prevent. As always the English pilgrims were hostile, the friars in charge of the Holy Places and even the Moslems friendly. A Saracen for a

[1] *The Book of Margery Kempe*, Cap. 27.

small tip helped her up the Mount of Temptation when her fellow pilgrims refused. But she did not, like Brydenbach seventy years later, see the field of red clay at Hebron from which God fashioned Adam's body—a refutation of Darwin—or the remains on Mount Thabor of the three tabernacles St. Peter wished to erect. Nor did she, like him, go on to Mount Sinai to glimpse the distant sight of a unicorn and picnic on the summit.

On her return her fellow-pilgrims abandoned her. She found an Irishman named Richard, a man with an injured back but evidently a strong man who, as the Lynn anchorite had foretold, agreed to guide her to Rome. With her went two Franciscans and a woman who had brought from the Holy Land an image of Our Lord which she offered to the veneration of women on their way. Lammas Day 1414 found her at Assisi for the Portiuncula indulgence of August 2nd. There she met a wealthy lady, Margaret Florentine. She was an Italian unable to speak English. We must surely understand—Margaret, a lady of Florence, a Florentine. Margery's stay at Rome was marked by persecution from her fellow countrymen. An English priest caused her to be turned out of the hostel of St. Thomas of Canterbury. There were spiritual consolations among her trials, a mystical marriage to the Heavenly Father,[1] who solemnly wedded her with a formula based on the Sarum ritual and using some of its words. Obviously all this imagery derived from Margery's subconscious, though it clothed an interior union between God and her spirit. It is in this connection that we hear of a burning fire of love felt as physical heat and continuing sixteen years, and of sounds heard over a space of twenty-five years—a sound like bellows blown which became the sound of a dove's coo and finally the note of a robin, "the voys of a lityl bryd whech is callyd a reedbrest that song ful merily often-tymes in her ryght ere".[2] She was told that it was the utterance of the Holy Ghost.

She found friends and helpers, among them Margaret the Florentine who supported her with food, wine and money. Finally her edifying behaviour convinced the Master of St. Thomas' Hostel of her holiness and she was received back. In Rome she met a former servant of St. Bridget's and through an interpreter heard reminiscences of the saint. She was favoured by an appearance of St. Jerome in the chapel where his relics lie.

[1] See below, pp. 127–8.   [2] Cap. 36.

She left Rome after Easter 1415 and reached Norwich the week before Trinity Sunday, which fell that year on May 26th.

From her account of her experiences it is clear that the Italians, indeed even the Moslems of Palestine, had more understanding of her emotional type of religion and sympathy with it, than her own countrymen. "God yaf hir grace to have gret lufe in Rome bothyn of men and of women and gret favowr among the pepyl."[1] The Church in England was free from the gross scandals which, as we know from Salimbene's *Chronicle* and St. Catherine's *Dialogue*, disfigured the Italian Church, such as the rape of a penitent at Confession or the use by a priest of the Sacred Host as an ingredient of a love charm. English Catholicism was comparatively respectable. But Margery's book and the Paston letters depict hard heads and cold hearts. The warm Italian devotion and human kindness, though Margery was struck by the poverty in Rome, were rare. The sin of the *ecclesia Anglicana* was the sin of the Church of Laodicea and in the following century it would incur the same doom.

She was greeted by Caister with a friendly welcome. But the hermit at Chapelfield refused to believe her denial of slanderous gossip. A Norwich friend provided her with the white clothes she believed it was Our Lord's will that she should wear. At Lynn she was brought to death's door by an illness and anointed, and had more to suffer from the people for her cries in church, now far louder. In the spring of 1417 she set out on a pilgrimage to Compostella. Her former journey however had left her so poor that only the alms received from friends enabled her to pay her debts and undertake this new pilgrimage. At Bristol she waited six weeks for a ship. Here also the "plentyuows terys and boystows sobbyngys wyth lowde cryingys and schille [shrill] schrykyngys"[2] at her Sunday communions aroused great indignation. A man named Thomas Marshal of Newcastle[3], struck by her devotion, paid her fare to Santiago and prepared to accompany her. But a wealthy burgess tried to prevent her sailing, and she was brought before the Bishop of Worcester for examination. The Bishop, a native of Suffolk who had known her father, was satisfied of her orthodoxy and treated her kindly. He entertained her at his table and gave her an alms. She made

---

[1] Cap. 39.   [2] Cap. 44.
[3] Newcastle-under-Lyme, Prof. Meech thinks.

the pilgrimage, returned to Bristol, visited the Precious Blood of Hailes and from Hailes proceeded to Leicester. Of her experiences on the voyage and in Spain she tells us nothing.

Here further and serious trouble awaited her. While Marshal was writing a letter for her to her husband to come and fetch her home to Lynn, she was arrested by order of the Mayor and brought before him. He ordered her to prison as a Lollard. But he allowed the jailer to keep her in his own house, since there was no accommodation for her among women prisoners. The jailer treated her kindly, gave her meals at his own table and allowed her to go to church. Then the Earl's Steward sent for Margery to examine her. He took her apart and with obscene language and gestures tried to seduce, almost to rape her. Finally, however, when she told him that her words and conduct were inspired by the Holy Ghost, he let her go back to the jailer's house. The episode shews the gulf which for good and evil divides us from pre-Reformation England. That any government official or officer of justice should behave to an accused person as the Steward behaved to Margery is inconceivable. Unfortunately it is equally inconceivable that his conduct should be influenced by belief in the presence and action of the Holy Ghost. She was publicly examined in All Saints' Church by the Abbot and the Dean of Leicester and other clerics about her sacramental belief and other points of faith. Her orthodoxy established, she was released on the undertaking that she would procure from the Bishop of Lincoln a letter to the Mayor guaranteeing her Catholic faith. She did not return, as she had intended, to Lynn, but went to York, the object of her journey being to visit the shrine of Saint William. She arrived at York in the autumn of 1417. Here also there were friends and foes, the latter produced by her white robe and cries at Communion. A doctor of divinity examined her as to her faith in the chapter house and remanded her to the Archbishop, Bowet. She was brought before him at his palace at Cawood. She told the Archbishop to his face that he was reputed a wicked man, and that if report were true, unless he amended his life he would be lost. She refused to swear to leave the diocese or refrain from admonishing the people with whom she might come into contact.

Finally the Archbishop appointed a man to conduct Margery out of his diocese. She went with him to Bridlington to see her

confessor, who had formerly been the confessor of St. John of
Bridlington, canonised by Pope Boniface IX sixteen years before.
Had he been her regular confessor at Lynn it would point to
close relations obtaining between this eastern district of Yorkshire and Norfolk, and thus make in favour of my conclusion
that Dame Julian was born and brought up in this neighbourhood.[1] But more probably she had confessed to him only when
she was at Bridlington four years earlier. As she was about to
cross the Humber from Hull she was arrested by two yeomen in
the service of the Duke of Bedford on the usual charge of being
a Lollard and taken to Beverley where she was imprisoned in an
upper room. Nothing daunted, she leaned out of the window
and addressed the passers-by. At this juncture the Archbishop
turned up and once more she stood before him, accused now even
of being a daughter and emissary of the archheretic Oldcastle.
The Archbishop, however, who, whatever his faults, was evidently a just man, set her free and sent her across the Humber.
She had scarcely crossed when she was again arrested on the
same charge but was released when a man who had been present
at her examination by the Archbishop testified to her orthodoxy.
There was evidently a Lollard scare at this time. She sent for her
husband to meet her at West Lynn and asked him to go with
her to London to ask the Archbishop (now Chicheley) for a
sealed letter attesting her faith, which, she said, she had promised
the Archbishop of York she would obtain. She was given her
letter and stayed some time in London. On the way home they
were once more arrested near Ely but released when the Archbishop's letter was produced.

    There followed a period of illnesses and in particular an inter-
mittent pain in her right side which continued for some eight
years. For years also there were loud shrieks at Communion and
on Good Friday. She was helped by a priest who came to live
in Lynn. He read to her the Bible with commentaries and many
mystical books, among them St. Bridget's revelations, Hilton's
Scale of Perfection, Bonaventure and Rolle's *Stimulus* and *Incendium
Amoris*. The readings continued seven or eight years, so that she
must have become learned in spiritual literature. For twelve days
she was tormented by obscene thoughts, no doubt a reaction of
the nerves, though she believed it to be Our Lord's punishment,

---

[1] See above, pp. 72–3.

through the agency of devils, because in the spirit of Dame Julian she had refused to credit what appeared to be revelations that particular persons would be lost. She visited Norwich and wept aloud, in St. Stephen's Church, at the tomb of her former friend Master Caister. An important Franciscan preacher identified by an annotator as William Melton refused to allow her to be present at his sermons because she interrupted them with her crying. And he preached against her publicly, which cost her many friends. Later the loud cries ceased though tears and sobs continued. She heard Our Lord bid her once more to eat meat and Our Lady discharged her of a weekly fast in her honour. In the January of 1423 a great fire broke out in Lynn. St. Margaret's was in danger. Margery prayed earnestly. When she agreed with the suggestion her parish priest and confessor took the Blessed Sacrament and bore it to meet the advancing conflagration. Still the sparks flew in. At the last moment a fall of snow saved the church.[1] If a leading Franciscan opposed her, a Dominican doctor defended her weeping at a chapter of the Friars held at Lynn. Indeed, of all the preachers whose sermons she disturbed with her sobs, only Friar Melton attacked her. Even the Bishop raised no objection. She cured a woman who had gone out of her mind at child-birth.

Her husband, who had lived apart for years, slipped on the stairs, hurt his head badly and was found lying in his blood. Margery, encouraged by words of Our Lord, took him to her home and tended him till his death. His last years were a second childhood.

Like so many contemplatives of her imaginative and pictorial type, she saw in turn the scenes of the Passion and Resurrection and other Gospel episodes as they were represented by mediaeval literature and art. There was a vision of the Ascension during the procession before Mass on the festival. As we know neither the date of the locution, nor the date of Margery's death, we cannot tell whether the words were fulfilled which she took to be Our Lord's telling her that fifteen years must pass before death would unite her to Him in heaven. They may perhaps have been suggested by the fifteen years added to the life of King Hezekiah—the story is told in the Lesson for the first Thursday in Lent—but

[1] The nave was ultimately destroyed in the eighteenth century, by the fall of a spire, to be replaced by an amazingly good example of Gothic in the late Perpendicular style.

more probably by the fifteen years which, as the locution continues, Our Lady lived after her Son's Ascension. We can hardly take them more seriously than the statement attributed to Our Lord on the same occasion that He loved Margery *as dearly* as He loved St. Mary Magdalen, doubtless Margery's imaginative clothing of a communication of the Divine Love to her soul.

The priest who rewrote and revised the extremely unsatisfactory manuscript first written added a short second part, "Secundus Liber", in which the story is told of her journey to Prussia.

Margery, we are now informed, had a son, the only one of her fourteen children of whom we hear anything. He settled in Prussia, marrying a Prussian wife. He came with his wife to England to visit his parents, only to die a month after his arrival and a month before his father's death. The widow remained in Lynn with her mother-in-law till letters from her friends or distaste for life abroad decided her to return home. What had happened to their little daughter we are not told. Probably she had died in infancy.

Margery had her confessor's leave to accompany her daughter-in-law to her ship at Ipswich. As she was hearing Mass on the way a Divine command thrust itself into her mind to return with her to Prussia. She visited the shrine at Walsingham and so proceeded to Norwich where a Franciscan Doctor of Divinity told her to obey the interior command as being from the Holy Ghost. How she defrayed the cost of the journey so suddenly decided, we are not informed. Probably Norwich friends and admirers provided the necessary funds. Storms drove the vessel onto the coast of Norway where it stayed from Good Friday until Easter Monday. At midday on Easter Sunday she saw the Cross containing the Host taken from the Easter sepulchre, later than in the English use. The master of the ship proved her friend, supplying her with food and additional clothing—a partial solution of the financial problem. A fair wind brought them to Danzig, her daughter-in-law's home, where she spent five or six weeks. Her daughter-in-law wanted to be rid of her and made herself disagreeable. And the inner voice of Our Lord told her it was time to leave. A man offered to take her on pilgrimage to the miraculous Hosts of Willsnack at his own expense and from there escort her to England at her expense. She went by sea to Stralsund, then overland to Willsnack where she saw what was believed to be the Precious Blood sprinkled miraculously on the Hosts. From Willsnack she set out for Aachen—Aix-la-Chapelle. But her sobbing had irritated her guide so much that he left her. Some unworthy priests frightened her with their indecent language and suggestions. The landlady put two of her servant girls to sleep with her. Next day she fell in with a band of poor pilgrims with whom she travelled to Aachen, though distressed when her companions stripped themselves naked to pick the vermin from their bodies. At Aachen she was able to witness a special exposition of famous relics, among them Our Lady's smock. A wealthy London widow promised to take her back with her but went off without her. She managed however to find escorts, some English pilgrims returning from Rome, until she finally caught up with the widow, who bluntly refused her company. A friar escorted her on foot to Calais. At Calais she met with kindly people, a woman who gave her a new smock, others who invited her to meals. On board ship her prayer to be kept from seasickness was granted, so that she was able to help her fellow-passengers, among them the widow who had treated her so badly. Since elderly people are less liable to seasickness than younger persons, there is no reason to see anything miraculous or even surprising in Margery's immunity. In spite of her services the passengers left her behind at Dover. She knocked up a poor man early in the morning who consented to escort her to Canterbury. From Canterbury she found her way to London.

In London she had to endure slanderous abuse from some Lynn folk who recognised her. And her constant rebuke of swearing and lying made her many enemies, not least among the clergy, who disapproved of this informal preaching in their churches. On her return to Lynn the confessor who had given her leave only to go to Ipswich scolded her for what he accounted disobedience. But he was reconciled to her and she found many friends. This journey, which probably took place in 1433, to be concluded in 1434, is the last episode of her life known to us. She was undoubtedly alive in 1438 when her book was completed and may well have been the Margery Kempe admitted that year as a member of the Guild of the Holy Trinity at Lynn.

In one respect at least Margery's desire to share the life and sufferings of her Lord has been amply fulfilled. Like Him she has been a sign that shall be spoken against, *signum cui contradicetur*. During her life she was denounced as a hypocrite, threatened with death as a Lollard, insulted, imprisoned, excluded from churches, abandoned by fellow-pilgrims and fellow-travellers, and, also like Our Lord, was particularly persecuted by her fellow-countrymen and fellow-townsmen. The promise which she claims was often made to her in prayer, that she should be exalted correspondingly by the praise of those who would recognise God's work in her soul was, it seemed, belied by the complete oblivion which for well-nigh half a millennium buried her memory. And when at last her "book", her spiritual auto-biography, came to light in a solitary manuscript, the detraction and hostility were renewed. If not a wilful hypocrite, this woman who disturbed her fellow worshippers by loud sobs and louder cries, who censured their dress and oaths, and was so full of herself that the record of her prayer is chiefly a record of God's pledges of peculiar favour, was at any rate an hysterical and fanatical person, a typical example of self-centred and morbid religiosity.

Such is the view taken of her by Miss Allen, whose notes lose no opportunity of exhibiting her as the rival and copyist of other woman visionaries, and who on several occasions calls her plainly a fanatic.

What are we to think of her? Shall we endorse this verdict of condemnation or hold with those who in her life time supported and honoured her? My intention is frankly to undertake her defence, not simply in the hope of obtaining the heavenly reward promised, she tells us, to her champions(!) but because after careful study of her life I am convinced that she loved God and her neighbour with a genuine, deep and wholehearted love. And this after all is the sum and substance of sanctity.

"But she distracted the prayers of others by her sobs and cries." True. But she could not help this. She prayed that her public crying might cease—finally the loud cries were taken from her—and would gladly have refrained had she been able. The loud cry or roar first wrung from her on Mount Calvary as she saw in spirit the Crucifixion—and which for years recurred with increasing frequency—she resisted to the utmost of her power. "When sche knew that sche xulde cryen, sche kept it in as long as sche mygth and did al that sche coude to withstand it . . .

til sche wex as blo as any lede." And, as she points out, every day you might see "men and women . . . cryen and roryn and wryngyn ther handes as yf thei had no witte" when parting with a friend or for the loss of possessions.[1] Since for one edified by her cries, there were numbers who insulted her, she had no motive to feign them even subconsciously. "Exhibitionism," you say. That was what two priests suspected until they took her to a lonely chapel and found that she cried and sobbed as she did in the crowded church. The woman that was a sinner sadly disturbed Simon's banquet by her unbecoming behaviour when she rushed in uninvited and washed Our Lord's feet with her tears. But "her sins were forgiven because she loved much". And this in effect is what He said to Margery also.

"But she censured others." She believed God laid this upon her. And she could hardly have spoken more severely than the Prophets. On one occasion she was ordered to tell a widow to change her confessor. The widow indignantly refused. She was then told in prayer that "thow this creatur [herself] came nevyr in hir [the widow's] howse, it plesyd God ryt wel".[2] When first I read this I thought it a hard saying. For I took it to mean that she would no longer call on one who refused to credit her revelations. This however would have been unlike her usual charity. And I am now convinced that it was the widow who had forbidden Margery her house or at least had threatened to do so, unless she ceased meddling with her spiritual affairs. The answer was that God had rather she did not visit the widow than pander to her obstinacy.

We should not forget the rich lady who slipped away from Aachen after promising to let Margery travel home with her to England and snubbed her when she caught up with her. When she suffered from a bad attack of sea-sickness on the boat between Calais and Dover Margery repaid her by special attention.

Père Joseph du Tremblay, Aldous Huxley's Grey Eminence, lamenting the sufferings of Jesus, by pursuing a bellicose policy renewed them in His members without a qualm of conscience. Margery, reminded of His Passion by the spectacle, wept when she saw a child or animal beaten. For her compassion saw and felt His pain and theirs in a universal solidarity of suffering. This penetrating and wide pity is surely remarkable, precious at any

[1] Cap. 28. [2] Cap. 19.

E

time and rare in an environment so insensitive to cruelty as Margery's. She obtained her confessor's leave to kiss lepers. "Now gan sche to lovyn that sche had most haytd beforetyme, for ther was nothyng mor lothful ne mor abhomynable to hir while sche was in the yerys of werldly prosperite than to seen a lazer whom now throw Our Lordys mercy sche desyred to halsyn [embrace] and kyssyn for the lofe of Jhesu."[1] When lepers are kissed by St. Hugh of Lincoln or St. Francis we are invited to revere this triumph of Christian charity over natural aversion. Is it less admirable in Margery?

Moreover, she found supporters and champions among those particularly conversant with the spiritual life, contemplatives and other men and women of prayer, and among those learned in theology. Among the numerous clergy she had to deal with only one, a Franciscan, who was probably a well-known preacher called Melton, publicly preached against her. A preacher denounced Madame Acarie, now a *beata*. The hermit at the Lynn Black Friars was her director. Master Richard Caister, Vicar of St. Stephen's, Norwich, whose holiness led to the beginnings of a posthumous cult, and above all Julian of Norwich believed in her and encouraged her. And their verdict was based on personal knowledge. It should weigh with us. In particular, as I have already had occasion to point out, Julian attached great value to those tears found so disedifying today. And her judgment of Margery was the judgment of an acknowledged mistress of contemplative spirituality.

In a note Miss Allen writes: "It may be said that Margery profoundly violates the principles of contemplation laid down by Hilton in his *Scale of Perfection*". In fact he also justifies her weepings: "In this spiritual sight [of the Passion] thou mournest and weepest and *cryest with all thy might of body and soul* . . . know well . . . that it is . . . by the grace of the Holy Ghost."[2] In this passage he describes Margery's prayer exactly and by anticipation defends it. Miss Allen's note is seriously misleading.

But Margery's revelations are, almost to monotony, concerned with herself. This surely was largely due to the fact that what she believed to be God's messages to her were so widely discredited and attacked. For the same reason Jeremiah's prophecy is far more personal than Isaiah's. And the Church has canonised

---

[1] Cap. 74.   [2] *Scale of Perfection*, 2, 2, 1.

any visionaries whose revelations were every bit as much
cupied with themselves as were Margery's. Since prayer is
ove all personal and God communicates Himself in and through
e personality of His servant, that personality tends to come to
e fore, particularly when the fact of the Divine communication
widely challenged. A tension is thus produced between the
f-assertion of a man or woman convinced that he or she is
d's instrument and the recipient of His commands, and the
mility of a creature convinced of sinfulness and created
thingness. It was no doubt this deep conviction of her nothing-
ss as created, owing all she had or was to God, that made
argery write of herself as "the creature".

This tension found expression in the well-known passage of St.
ul's self-vindication in which he is led to relate the favours
anted to him by God which he ascribes to a man in Christ, to
eak of his sufferings for Christ and apologise for the folly of a
asting he cannot avoid. It is discernible in Margery's colloquies
th Our Lord in which a keen sense of her own sinfulness and a
nuine desire to be despised for His love and in satisfaction for
r sin, alternate with His declarations of special love to her and
dges of glory in heaven and honour on earth. Surely in this
e was not so unlike "The *little* flower of the *little* way" who
vertheless saw her name written among the stars.

Moreover, the promises made to Margery in prayer to protect
r from danger, help a son or friend, or extricate her from the
any tight corners in which she found herself, were in fact
filled.[1] Her foreknowledge can, it is true, be naturally explained
the presence of her abiding self to these superficially future
ents. But the providential guidance is another matter. Here
e must surely see the hand of God.

"But if God were indeed guiding Margery and speaking with
r in prayer why were the disturbing tears and cries permitted?"
o doubt they were not, as she not unnaturally believed, the
sitive work of God. They were the effect of a morbid
ggestibility, which we may, if we like, call with Father Thurston
quoted in Miss Allen's introduction—hysteria. He points out
wever that it is now recognised that this abnormal suggesti-
ity may co-exist with high intellectual, moral or spiritual

[1] This, however, is not always certain. Cf. the locution foretelling fifteen more years
life. See above, p. 115.

endowments. If in this understanding of the term Margery was
hysterical, her hysteria was shared by Dame Julian, St. Teresa
of Avila, St. Philip Neri and even, though to a lesser degree, by
the Doctor of Mystical Theology, St. John of the Cross. For they
were all subject to psychophysical experiences produced, instru-
mentally at least, by the operation of suggestion upon the subconscious. I cannot believe that God directly and positively will:
anything unhealthy, whether psychological or physical. But He
certainly permits disease and overrules it for a greater good. O
this the lives of saints, from St. Paul and his goad of the flesl
onwards, are ample proof. Margery's tears were, I contend, permitted because they were an expression and as such, as Willian
James has shewn, a stimulus, of her love for her suffering Lord
Such love, even the least increase of it, is so precious in the eyes o
Christ that it must more than outweigh any disturbance to th
comparatively cold and perfunctory devotions of the averag
worshipper. In any case a mediaeval church was not a quiet hom
of prayer. Groups recited aloud the Office of Our Lady, othei
less devout chattered, children scampered around laughing and, a
the Paston letters shew, a client met his lawyer in church, as to
day in his office. Under such circumstances the scandal given b
Margery's exuberance of holy grief strikes me as a little pharisai
But the chief reason why Our Lord permitted her cries wa
surely that actually given to her—to purify her soul by th
suffering it caused her, the same function that was performed b
the bodily illnesses which were also permitted, though not sen
to afflict her.

Understood in Father Thurston's sense as morbid suggestibilit
I have accepted the term hysteria as applied to Marger
Hysteria normally produces gross, if unintentional, untruthfulnes
Miss Allen, however, as a result of most careful scrutiny and whe
possible checking of Margery's statements, is convinced that sl
was scrupulously truthful.

Ardent love of God and her neighbour in and for Hir
humility, truthfulness—these are not such common virtues th
we should refuse to see in them an operation of Divine grace.

Margery did not assume without further question that t
communications made to her in prayer, gratifying as they
often were in their assurance of special favour, were genuir
On the contrary, with the humble prudence of a Teresa s

bmitted them again and again to the judgment of those expert
theology and the spiritual life.[1] Moreover the joy she records
henever a Divine promise or prophecy was fulfilled proves
at, until it was fulfilled, she gave it only provisional credence.
er attitude was more cautious and sober than that of the Oxford
roups who seem to accept at once and without hesitation any
d every guidance in their "quiet hour".

When she was told that certain people would be damned, she
fused to believe that it was Our Lord who had told her, until
r disbelief had been punished by abandonment for twelve days
obscene visions sent by the devil. For like her greater contem-
rary Dame Julian, Margery's universal charity revolted against
e doctrine of everlasting punishment, though she accepted it as
vealed truth. "I have gret marveyl in myn hert Lord, that I
hech have ben so synful a woman and the most unworthy
eature that evyr thu schewedist Thi mercy onto in all this
erlde, that I have so gret charite to myn evyn-cristen sowlys
at me thynkyth, thou thei had ordenyd for me the most
hamful deth that evyr myth any man suffyr in erde, yet wolde
foryevyn it hem for Thi lofe, Lord, and han her sowlys savyd
o evry-lestyng dampnacyon."[2] How then, is the obvious
iplication, canst Thou who art love itself condemn any soul to
ell? "Lorde, I wolde I had a welle of teerys to constreyn The
yth that Thu schuldist not takyn uttyr veniawns of mannys
wle for to partyn hym fro The wyth-owtyn ende, for
is an hard thyng to thynkyn that any erdly man schulde be
parted fro Thi gloryows face wyth-owtyn ende."[3] Had
ese words been found, as are others to the same effect, in
lian's Revelations, everyone would have admired their
ide and tender charity. When they are uttered by egotistical
d hysterical Margery, it is an altogether different matter—
num cui contradicetur.

As "egotistic" as her zeal for the salvation of souls was
r zeal for the glory of God. She would fain have founded
any abbeys filled with monks and nuns praising God, and

[1] It may perhaps be thought that if St. Teresa and Margery had been content with
e approval of the first competent director or adviser it would have served better the
ace of spirit so desirable in the life of prayer. But if excess there were, it was the excess
a humble and prudent distrust of personal judgment.
[2] Cap. 57.
[3] Cap. 57.

provided many priests in her town of Lynn, to "syngen and redyn night and day for to servyn Me, worschepyn Me and preysyn and thankyn Me".[1]

"But like many other visionaries, many of them beatified or canonised, Margery believed herself God's favourite and, moreover, because He told her so." This, for modern critics, is the gravamen of the charge against her. We can see from the tone of Miss Allen's notes how it annoys her. A false equalitarianism transferred from the political field (and even here it is true only in the sense of equal opportunity) denies that a just God can have favourites. But throughout nature inequality, not equality, is the rule of Divine government. It is not otherwise in the order of grace. Our Lady alone is favoured with an Immaculate Conception. The Baptist is greatest of the sons of women, the Apostles are to sit on judgment thrones as their Master's assessors and John is the beloved disciple, privileged to recline on Jesus' breast. St. John of the Cross can even say that as damage to a masterpiece is worse than the destruction of many daubs, the frustration of a contemplative vocation is worse than the loss of many ordinary souls.[2] To quarrel with Margery for believing that she was specially favoured by God is to quarrel with God's dispensation as made known by reason in the natural, by revelation in the supernatural order.[3]

We cannot indeed share Margery's belief that the words spoken in her soul and the visions seen were directly and immediately spoken and shown by Our Lord, Our Lady or the saint in question. Saints Catherine and Margaret, for whose existence modern hagiology can find no proof, spoke with her. Her visions of the Infancy and Passion were, as such visions always are, closely bound up with contemporary religious art and devotional literature.

Huysmans, who loved the Flemish primitives, remarking the resemblance between St. Lydwine's visions of heaven and the pictures of it, concluded triumphantly that heaven is as they depicted it. We cannot follow him in this. The words and images of these colloquies and visions have been formed by a subconscious mind steeped in contemporary art and religious beliefs. But does not follow that the Divine action has not set this su-

---

[1] Cap. 84.
[2] *Living Flame of Love*, Stanza 3, viii. Edicion Critica, Padre Gerardo, Vol. 2, p. 9.
[3] This does not mean, however, that we need credit the assurance that Our Lord loved Margery as dearly as He loved Mary Magdalen.

conscious artistry in motion. If God is to address a soul through
the imagination, a method adapted to many temperaments, how
else could He do so? Divine truth, as reason and the mystics
assure us, is beyond the imaginative sphere. If an adult speaks to
a child he must speak in language familiar and intelligible to it.[1]
Why should God speak to His human children otherwise? If He
receives the answer He seeks, the answer of obedient love, the
communication is successful and He is content.

Since Margery lacked the intellectual endowment of the greater
mystics, their penetrating intelligence, she cannot speak as they
do of the profound spiritual truths. She cannot, like St. Catherine
of Genoa, throw any light on the nature of purgatory or, like
Dame Julian, on the economy of human salvation. Beyond the
sphere of imagination she has no language and must keep silence.
In consequence there is an undeniable monotony and a disappointing limitation of scope in her account of her spiritual experience.
But intellectual capacity is no measure of holiness, nor holiness
of intellectual capacity. Holiness is measured only by the degree
of charity, and that God alone can measure. He alone knows
whether Margery or Julian was the holier. But we can be certain
that Margery loved much and was therefore holy and dear to God.

Beneath and through the images and words formed in Margery's mind—for her visions and locutions were not hallucina-
tions of the senses but recognized as what mystical theology
terms imaginary—what was the essential Divine communication
to her soul? Since her psychological machinery, so to speak,
could not work except in and through words and visual images,
she can tell us little of what lay beyond, of the work God was
doing in the depth of her spirit, the "fine point" of the French
mystics. Nevertheless a few indications escape. She felt a compulsion upon her not to pass all her time of prayer in the vocal
prayer to which by nature she was drawn, but to cultivate a
purely mental prayer, and moreover a prayer of passive receptivity. "Dowtyr I wyl thow leve thi byddyyng of many bedys
[saying vocal prayers, not necessarily the Rosary, to which in
fact no allusion is made in the book] and thynk swych thowtys
as I wyl putt in thi mend. I schal yeven [give] the leve to bydden
tyl sex of the cloke to sey what thou wyld. Then schalt thow

---

[1] Cf. John Smith's observations on the veiling and condescensions of Divine Truth,
below, p. 256.

ly stylle and speke to me be thowt and I schal yeve to the hey medytacyon and very contemplacyon."[1]

The direction given her, as she reasonably believed, by God, was in fact interior, spiritual and in conformity with the traditional wisdom of Catholic spirituality. "Whan thu suffyrst Me wilfully to spekyn in the, dowter . . . this lyfe plesyth Me mor than weryng of the haburion [habergeon worn for penance] or of the hayr [hairshirt] or fastyng of bred and watyr, for, yf thu seydest every day a thowsand Pater Noster, thu schuldist not plesyn Me so wel, as thu dost whan thu art in silens and sufferyst Me to speke in thy sowle . . . To byddyn many bedys it is good to hem that can no bettyr do and yet it is not parfyte . . . I have often-tymes, dowtyr, teld the that thynkyng, wepyng and hy contemplacyon is the best lyfe in erthe."[2] Though in spite of the Mass for the Gift of Tears, weeping, we may think, were better understood of the disposition expressed by it, these words are the expression of a spiritual wisdom simple, sane and balanced, for Margery is not told to give up vocal prayer altogether.[3] Had they been written by Hilton, Rolle or Julian they would have been recognized as such. But unfortunately they are from the Book of Margery of whom we must remember only that she interrupted the sermon by her howls.

Per Christum hominem ad Christum Deum. That this was Margery's path she tells us herself. "Aftyrwardys . . . owr Lord of hys hy mercy drow hir affecyon in-to Hys Godhed, and that was mor fervent in lofe and desyr and more sotyl in undirstondyng than was the Manhod. And nevyrthelesse the fyr of love encresyd in hir and hir undirstandyng was mor illumynyd and hir devocyon mor fervent than it was befor whyl sche had hir meditacyon and hir contemplacyon only in Hys Manhod."[4] This passage is easily overlooked. For in fact we hear no more of the Godhead, much of the Manhood. The

[1] Cap. 5.
[2] ibid., 35, 36.
[3] For vocal prayer can be contemplative. In a period, however, when the nature and function of liturgical prayer were little understood, even great contemplatives failed to perceive this. Of vocal and even of liturgical prayer *as they were then commonly understood and practised* the locution is undoubtedly true. Even so the author of the *Cloud of Unknowing* says that " true workers in this work worship no prayer so much as those of holy Church; and therefore they do them in the form and in the statute that they be ordained by holy fathers before us " (Ch. 37).
[4] Cap. 85.

human Jesus, as an infant in the cradle or as enduring His Passion, fills the foreground of Margery's prayer, so that we see nothing beyond. We cannot however discount her explicit statement. We must conclude that the "mor subtyl undirstandyng" of Margery's contemplation of the Godhead escaped the capacity of her most unsubtle mind to express, and further, as indeed the word "only" implies, that she did not contemplate our Lord's Godhead without a simultaneous contemplation of His Humanity, that, even when passing beyond it and within the Divinity, she needed a bambino, crucifix or Man of Sorrows in her imagination to support her prayer.   To cavil at this is to cavil not only at the Church's employment of images but at the principle of both, the Incarnation of the Word.

In his sixty-second Sermon on the Canticles St. Bernard says that the Church presents Christ Crucified to the contemplation of those feeble and sluggish souls who cannot rise to a purely spiritual contemplation.[1]   It is difficult to believe that this passage represents the considered view of a saint so remarkable for his devotion to the mysteries of the Word Incarnate.   Though for St. Bernard, as for all the mystics, the Humanity of Christ is but the road to the Eternal Word who is the Bridegroom of the mystical marriage, he can hardly have maintained that no soul that has once attained to contemplative union with the Word should contemplate the Sacred Humanity.   It is a matter surely not so much of progress in the spiritual life, as of the psycho-physical temper of the individual and his corresponding *attrait*. A soul of Margery's emotional and imaginative stamp will not and cannot dispense with much devotion to the Human Jesus, however high and close its union with the Godhead.[2]

The most interesting and at the same time most unexpected episode in Margery's spiritual experience is her mystical marriage on the feast of the dedication of the Lateran, November 9th, in the Apostles' church at Rome—not, as we should have expected, to the Second, but to the First Person of the Trinity. This is counter

[1] *In Cantica*, Sermo LXII, 6.
[2] Here the contrast is striking indeed between Margery and Dame Gertrude More, whose " propensity . . . to seek after the simplicity of the pure Divinity " made her " unable to use the image of the humanity of our Saviour at all ". When her director Fr. Baker tells us " she treats of created things, however noble, as the humanity of Our Lord apart from His Divinity . . . you will at once feel how she is straitened and cold in comparison with her language when speaking of the pure Divinity" (*Inner Life of Dame Gertrude More*, Ch. xx. See below, p. 200–1).

to the teaching of mystical and indeed of dogmatic theology, that the Bridegroom alike of the Church and of individual souls is the Divine Word.[1] Why of all mystics should Margery, whose devotion was so centred upon Christ, experience this union with the Father?

It is true she tells us that she had already informed the mystical Vicar Richard Caister, that "Sumtyme alle thre Personys in Trinitye and o [one] substawns in Godhede dalyid to [conversed with] hir sowle" and that "Sumtyme the Feder of Hevyn dalyd to hir sowle as pleynly and as veryly as o frend spekyth to another".[2]

Margery's memory for dates however must have played her false[3] and she must have told the Vicar this when she saw him again on her return from Rome. For when the Father tells her that He will have her wedded to His Godhead she is amazed and frankly disconcerted. She "kept sylens in hir sowle and answeryd not therto, for sche was ful sor aferd of the Godhede, *and sche cowde no skylle of the dalyawns of the Godhede,* [had no experience of converse with the Godhead] for all hir lofe and al hir affecyon was set in the manhode of Christ and thereof cowde sche good skylle and sche wolde for no thyng a partyd therefro". When our Lord presses her to answer His Father she remains silent. "Sche wold not answeryn the Secunde Persone but wept wondir sor, desiryng to have stille Hymselfe and in no wyse to be departyd fro Hym."[4] Christ then answered for her and His Father espoused Margery in the words of the Sarum marriage service.

This strange episode is the picturing by a powerful but untutored and simple imagination of a Divine operation in her spirit, the drawing of it beyond the Humanity of Christ into the Godhead. Her very reluctance, so naïvely expressed, proves the objective reality of this Divine Action. She shrank from exchanging, as she obviously thought she must, her human devotion to the Human Jesus for a plunge into the desert of a purely spiritual Godhead. In fact, as we have seen, she retained the former side by side with the latter, thus exemplifying in her prayer the abiding condescension of the Word everlastingly Incarnate.

[1] Since however all exterior operations of the Godhead are common to all three Persons, union with the Son involves union with the Father and the Holy Spirit.
[2] Cap. 17.
[3] She tells us herself that she does not relate events in the order of their occurrence.
[4] Cap. 35.

Parallel with this experience of Margery's and her reaction to it is an episode in Dame Julian's revelations. "I had a proffer in my reason, as it had been friendly said to me: 'Look up to heaven to His Father!' . . . I answered inwardly with all the might of my soul and said: 'Nay, I may not, for thou [Christ crucified] art my heaven.'" Julian however adds: "I saw well with the faith that I felt that there was nothing between the cross and heaven that might have diseased me",[1] that is to say she realised what Margery did not understand so clearly, that whether the soul is consciously united with the Human Jesus or more directly with the Godhead, it is united with the *one* God. And Margery in fact tells us that she attained a permanent awareness not of the Sacred Humanity, but of God everywhere present; an abiding prayer of the central self united to God and conscious of His Presence. "Be processe of tyme hir minde and hir thowt was so joynyd to God that she never forgate Hym in alle creaturys."[2]

Dame Julian received her more spiritual and interior intuitions of Divine truth in concomitance with a series of imaginative picturings of the Suffering Jesus and His Mother of the same type as Margery's, though depicted by an imagination of incomparably finer artistic quality. But, unlike Margery, she was able to speak of this higher teaching also. When we read of such experiences as Margery's, we should consider not the imaginative envelope but the interior significance, the operation God is effecting by their means. In short we should treat such recorded experiences as St. John of the Cross bids the contemplative treat personal experiences of this kind, that is, we should pass through and beyond them to the inner spirit which God intends to convey. And if the means are homely, instead of taking scandal, we should rather with Julian rejoice that God is so "homely" with His creatures, else we should be crushed beneath the weight of His Majesty—and that His goodness thus "cometh down to the lowest part of our need".[3]

Miss Allen has no liking for the odours smelt by Margery

---

[1] *Revelations of Divine Love*, ch. 19.
[2] Like many Catholics uninstructed in theology, Margery was possibly an un-intentional tritheist.
[3] Or as John Smith puts it speaking of Scripture: "Truth is content . . . to learn our language, to conform itself to our dress and fashions . . . it speaks with the most idiotical [simple unlearned] sort of men in the most idiotical sort of way." See below, pp. 256.

during her prayer, the sweet music she heard, the heat as of a physical fire in her breast. To these psychophysical phenomena so natural in a "sensitive" like Margery we should apply what has been just said of her visions and locutions, not forgetting that since the soul is the formative principle of the body, any powerful affection of the former is likely to affect the latter. Even the supreme experiences of the transforming union, St. John of the Cross tells us, may overflow in physical delight.[1] Yet, because he has much to say of heat and melody, the singularly attractive mysticism of Rolle is dubbed "fanatical" in one of Miss Allen's notes. Anyone less like a fanatic than the gentle and poetic Rolle is difficult to conceive. We are invited, it would seem, to subscribe to the intolerant and indiscriminate denunciation of emotional and psychophysical experiences by the *Cloud of Unknowing*, whose outstanding value as an account of substantial contemplation, unitive prayer, does not justify its author when he forgets that God draws souls by many paths and that Wisdom is justified of all her children. So far as my personal preference is concerned I had rather lose the entire writings of Margery, Rolle, Hilton, St. Catherine of Siena and at a pinch would even part with Dame Julian's *Revelations* rather than lose the *Cloud*. But I cannot therefore subscribe to its exclusiveness. Baron Von Hügel tells us that Father Faber, preaching at Farm Street on the feast of St. Ignatius, ended his sermon by saying, "This, then, was St. Ignatius's way to heaven. Thank God it is not the only way." Adapting his words I would say: "This then was Margery Kempe's way to Divine union. Thank God it is not the only way." Yes, but thank God also it *was* her way and the way of countless other souls of similar temper and *attrait* and that it brought them to the goal, which after all is the only thing that really matters about any road.

What then of that white dress she was told to wear, which on a matron caused so much scandal and misunderstanding and even exposed her to be mistaken, as Miss Allen shows, for a flagellant? It was, I suggest, ordered or perhaps, since the words of Christ took shape in her subconscious, permitted for the reason that Our Lord suffered Himself to be clothed in a white robe by Herod's soldiery, to be worn as a fool's garment of scorn, permitted that is to say for the same purpose as the public tears and cries.

[1] *Living Flame of Love*, Stanza 2. Edicion Critica, Padre Gerardo, p. 420.

But there is her decidedly encratite attitude towards the use of marriage, which led to complete separation from her husband and in which Our Lord seems to have supported her. In this delicate matter personal vocation must be the deciding factor and of that only God, Margery and her spiritual adviser could judge. So intense in fact was Margery's longing to possess Our Lord and be possessed by Him that the mutual possession of sexual love had become intolerable to her. That her vocation found expression, as it did, in terms of an attitude towards sex which, though never the official teaching of the Church, indeed implicitly condemned by her, was unfortunately widespread in mediaeval Catholicism, indeed is far from extinct even today, —the Sarum calendar could celebrate St. Perpetua and St. Felicitas as virgins—should not surprise us who know that God speaks to souls in the language of their religious environment, as it influences the activity of the subconscious mind.

Professor Meech's Introduction speaks of Margery as illiterate. She certainly could not write and was obliged to have her *Book* written for her, first by a man better acquainted with German than English and later transcribed into decent English and completed by a priest. But what of reading? For her biblical knowledge she was, as she informs us, dependent on sermons and what was later read to her. And she had other spiritual books read to her by the same priest. He read her St. Bridget's *Revelations*, the *Stimulus Amoris*, then attributed to St. Bonaventure, both of course in English translations, Rolle's *Incendium Amoris*, and Hilton's *Scale of Perfection*. The Revelations of her friend Dame Julian are not mentioned nor the *Cloud*. Evidently she could not read these books for herself. On the other hand she had a book, a prayer book, in her hand when struck by the stone falling from the roof of St. Margaret's church. And she once refers to reading in church—"thu redist"—and speaks of saying her Mattins, no doubt Mattins of Our Lady. And in defence of her weeping she quotes from the "Sawter": *Qui seminant in lacrimis et cetera euntes ibant et flebant et cetera*. The Psalm from which this is taken, Psalm 125, is read in the Little Office at Sext. There no doubt Margery became acquainted with it. She could then read a book of hours, presumably the book she was reading, when the stone fell. I suggest that, though able to read a text read every day and written in large and clear letters, she could not read the small and much more difficult letters in which Bibles and spiritual books were written. I can read a fifteenth-century book of hours as easily as a book printed yesterday, but I have been baffled by a contemporary manuscript of sermons and treatises.

It is often said that before the Reformation sermons were few and far between. To this belief Margery's book gives no support. Sermons seem to have been both frequent and appreciated by the people. Margery loved them no less than any Puritan. She suffered acutely when the Franciscan preacher refused to allow her to attend his sermons. She begged Our Lord to prevent her weeping during the sermon. "That I be not putt fro heryng of thin holy prechyng and of thin holy wordys, for grettar peyn may I not suffyr in this worlde than be put fro thi holy worde heryng. And yif I wer in preson, my most peyn schulde be the forberyng of thin holy wordys and of thin howly sermonys."[1] She even appears to value the sermon more than the Mass, of which also imprisonment would have deprived her. And in fact her Italian contemporary St. Bernardine said that, if a man must choose on a Sunday between hearing Mass or a sermon, he should choose the latter. These sermons however would seem to have been either devotional or moral and to have dealt with theology no further than to inculcate the articles of the creed or a few other elementary doctrines. The detailed instruction now given was regarded as quite unnecessary for laymen. Hence the theological ignorance which left Catholics so easy a prey to the Reformers' propaganda.

In Margery's religious world we can recognise, roughly speaking, three classes. There were the devout, those definitely leading a life of prayer, men and women who read spiritual books and cherished a devotional and often a mystical type of religion. These were the people whose society and encouragement Margery sought. There were the great mass of Catholics who practised their religion obediently, desired the help of Christ, His Mother and His saints and valued Masses and prayers after their death but were worldly, hard, unspiritual, engrossed with pleasure or with money-making, with maintaining or improving their social position. Such were those who, when Margery said "It is ful merry in Hevyn", replied: "Why speke ye so of the

[1] Cap. 77.

myrth that is in Hevyn; ye know it not and ye have not be
ther no mor than we". And it was they who on pilgrimage to the
Holy Land consented to readmit Margery to their company only
when she promised to speak no more of "the Gospel" in their
presence but "syttyn stylle and makyn mery, as we don, bothin
at mete and at soper", a promise she found impossible to keep.
And there were the pioneers of future Protestantism, the Lollards,
among whom was Margery's parish priest William Sawtree.
They seem in the main to have been confined to the eastern
half of Britain. For it was only there that Margery was suspected of Lollardy. But they were more numerous, more
influential and above all more persistent than is often thought.
This I think accounts for the fact that whereas western England
and Wales clung to the Faith for many a year after the Reformation, East Anglia was already predominantly Protestant when
Kett rose in 1549.[1] The ground had been prepared. It was not,
I must repeat, the bishops, abbots and theologians who condemned Margery as a Lollard, though some of them, like the
Archbishop of York, regarded her as a nuisance and were glad
to see the last of her. They knew too much for that. It was the
laity whose religion was of the ignorant and conventional type
of which I have just spoken, who scented heresy in anything
unusual and confounded Margery's objection to profane swearing
with the Lollard objection to oaths of any kind. Like the Mayor
of Leicester they were eager to burn her. The bishops on the
other hand always gave her defence a fair hearing and even
allowed her to speak most frankly about their personal shortcomings. She told the Bishop of Lincoln he feared man rather
than God, a view of his character which there are other grounds
for believing. And when the Archbishop of York told her "I
her seyn thu art a ryth wikked woman", she replied, "Ser, I her
seyn that ye arn a wikkyd man. And yif ye ben as wikkyd as
men seyn, ye schal nevyr come in Hevyn les than ye amende
yow whil ye ben her."[2] That she returned home safely says
much for the justice of the mediaeval bishops and their fear of
taking drastic action against one who might after all be God's
servant and messenger.

Archbishop Arundel of Canterbury not only talked with her
in his Lambeth garden till night fell, though she had warned

[1] G. CONSTANT, *The Reformation in England*, Vol. II, p. 116   [2] Cap. 52.

him to restrain the bad language of his retainers, but gave her a privilege at the time extremely rare, though no privilege should have been necessary, permission to receive Communion weekly.

I have, I hope, shown Margery as she was, a woman whose intelligence was mediocre but whose strong will was surrendered in loving devotion to her Divine Lord, a woman whose charity was as wide as suffering humanity, who forgave her enemies from her heart, who sought by her words and example to spread the Kingdom of Christ. Though it cost her dear she was ready to curtail the prayer that meant everything to her to nurse her husband when he had become a hopeless invalid and required attentions of an extremely unpleasant nature. Though she often identifies by name or office those who supported or helped her, she never mentions the name of an enemy or his office save when, as in the case of the Mayor of Leicester, it is unavoidable. It is only through the marginal notes of a later scribe that we conjecture the name of the Grey Friar who denounced her from his pulpit. Like St. Thérèse of Lisieux she believed that God would finally make known her sanctity. She may even, as Miss Allen thinks, have anticipated a shrine in her parish church. But she took no credit to herself. She recognised that she was an unworthy sinner to whom God had shown unmerited love. She wrote her book only when she believed God bade her do so, and forbade its publication in her lifetime. And in it she made known that she had offered herself to a man who snubbed her. A confession so humiliating to natural pride is surely unique in autobiography. Profound love of God, all-embracing love of men and women in Him, and a humility that took no credit for Divine favours and promises which she felt obliged to believe and put on record: these things surely are proof of a genuine holiness and merited to advance her far on the road of mystical union, farther indeed than her ability to speak of her experience. Therefore I have joined the ranks of her champions against her critics and invoke her prayer. Margery Kempe, pray for us.

BIBLIOGRAPHY

Printed extracts (19) from the *Book of Margery Kempe*, Wynkyn de Worde, 1501. Reissued (A) Henry Pepwell 1521; (B) (Text modernised) Edmund G. Gardner in *The Cell of Self-Knowledge*, 1910. Wynkyn de Worde's text is reprinted in the Meech-Allen edition of the *Book* as Appendix II.

The Book of Margery Kempe, A Modern Version, W. Butler-Bowdon, 1936. The mystical passages are printed in an appendix.

The Book of Margery Kempe. The text from the unique MS. owned by Col. W. Butler-Bowdon. Edited with introduction and glossary by Prof. Sanford Brown Meech with prefatory note by Sanford Brown Meech and Emily Hope Allen, E.E.T.S., 1940.

That I disagree with Miss Allen's estimate of Margery does not of course detract from the admiration and gratitude due to her for the extensive and detailed scholarship which she has contributed to this edition of her *Book*, a gratitude equally due to its editor Professor Meech.

CHAPTER VII

RICHARD CRASHAW

THE LIFE of the poet Crashaw may perhaps be thought to embody something of the paradox so dear to the *Seicento* culture of which his poetry is, as we shall see, so perfect an expression. For the singer of Catholic devotion, in its most exotic and Latin form, was the son of a minister of North Country birth, remarkable for his virulent hatred of popery—a hatred which, not satisfied with pouring out a flood of controversial abuse, found final utterance in William Crashaw's will, in which he writes: "I account poperie (as nowe it is) the heap and chaos of all heresies. I believe the Pope's seat and power to be the power of the great Antichrist and the doctrine of the Pope to be the doctrine of Antichrist." But we must not think of Richard Crashaw's religion as simply a reaction to his father's. The author of a *Manual of Devotion* and the translator of Catholic hymns did not confine his religion to the hatred of Rome. His heart was filled by a strong and, one would gather, a tender love for God and Christ. Nor was William Crashaw a Puritan if by a Puritan we mean one who regarded the Anglican liturgy and Church government as insufficiently Reformed. On the contrary, as I shall show in the following study, he was a convinced, even a zealous adherent of the Anglican Church and her practice and teaching, as they were in his lifetime. Richard Crashaw inherited from his father his devotional temper, his bent towards religious poetry and his aptitude for learning.

William Crashaw was twice married, but both wives died shortly after marriage. Richard, born 1612 or 1613, son of the first marriage and the only child, was therefore brought up almost entirely without a mother. To this Dr. Praz ascribes the craving for a mother's love, which for its satisfaction attracted the poet to his "mother" Mary Collet, to Madre Santa Teresa, to Our Lady and finally to Mother Church.[1] That the poet felt this strong longing for a mother's care and love is shown, I think, by the peculiar

[1] *Secentismo e Marinismo in Inghilterra*, pp. 152, 188.

ondness which he displays for such images as "nest," "breast,"
id "bosom". Professor Martin even finds in the use of "nest"
 sign-manual of Crashaw's authorship, and points out how he
mploys it as a rhyme-word no less than five times in his hymn
) the Name of Jesus.[1] But with his tender half-feminine nature
e would probably have felt and expressed the same longing
ad his mother lived till her son's maturity.[2] The boy was given
place as foundation scholar at Charterhouse, then in its infancy,
'here, however Spartan the life, his headmaster, Dr. Brook,
'ould appear to have reserved his rod for young Roundheads,
is favour for young Royalists. Crashaw, so far back as we can
'ace his writing, probably to scholastic exercises in Latin and
nglish verse, was a fervent Royalist and he addressed a Latin
oem of obviously sincere gratitude to his former master. For
is father had been a Royalist and this Royalist school was the
1oice of the guardians appointed by his will. In 1631, at the
ge of eighteen, he went up to Pembroke College, Cambridge,
) be elected four years later to a fellowship at Peterhouse. He
'as probably ordained to serve Little St. Mary's, a church
tached to the college. At that time Peterhouse was a centre
f Laudian high churchmanship—not the Anglo-Catholicism of
)day, Catholic in everything but membership of the Catholic
hurch—but a deliberate *via media* between Catholicism and
eneva. Cultured, devout, liturgical, in intention and in some
spects actually primitive and patristic, Laudianism possessed
1 undeniable charm for Crashaw's studious and poetic piety.
s fundamental lack of logic troubled very little a temper more
'tistic than speculative; but its cautious moderation, whose
:presentative in poetry was George Herbert, must, we should
1agine, have conflicted with the ardour and abandon of his
evotion. But until 1644 we have no glimpse of his interior
fe, and even then it is only an obscure and passing glimpse.
Vhatever he thought of its position as against Rome, in its
pposition to Geneva, its insistence on a dignified worship, and
s appeal to the fathers, Laudianism had his hearty support.
.e took an active part in the adornment of the new Peter-
ouse chapel—a centre of Laudian worship. To aid the appeal

---

[1] *Poetical Works*, p. 463.
[2] Moreover, Dame Julian, who enjoyed a mother's love until at least the age of thirty,
eaks even more warmly of motherhood than Crashaw. See pp. 70-1, 88-9.

for funds he composed two Latin poems, not published unt
1648. During these Cambridge years of study, poetry an
prayer—"the little contentful kingdom" of his Peterhou
fellowship—he was in close contact with a unique and certain
the most gracious manifestation of Anglican religion, the con
munity—a blend of family and religious life—directed b
Nicholas Ferrar, at Little Gidding in Huntingdonshire. Thoug
the type of devotion there practised was of the more tempera
type represented by Ferrar's friend Herbert, rather tha
the ecstatic fervour which inspired his poetry, and Ferrar
theology fell short of the more advanced Laudian school, th
Little Gidding community exercised a great attraction ove
Crashaw, may even have held him back from the Catholi
Church. It consisted of Nicholas Ferrar, a London merchar
who had retired from the world to devote himself to the servic
of God, his aged mother, his brother John with his wife an
family, and his sister with her husband, Mr. Collet, and thei
family. Assisted no doubt by the masterful personality whic
he shared with his mother, Ferrar had fashioned the life of h
relatives on the model of a strict religious house. Yet it was n
servile copy, but an individual creation with a beauty all i
own. There was service thrice daily in the little church outsid
the manor house, an hourly office throughout the day divide
among the members of the community and every night a watc
from nine till one, during which two men or women recite
the entire Psalter on their knees. These watches were relieve
from time to time by singing or soft music on the organ. Ferra
himself watched two nights a week, and, when he did not watcl
rose at one to spend the remaining hours of the night in praye
and meditation. To prayer was added a full round of study an
work. Three schoolmasters were kept to teach the childrer
There was an almshouse for poor widows, surgical dressing b
the ladies, exquisite bookbinding, the compilation of biblic
concordances illustrated by the best engravings of the period
and from 1631 a little academy based on an Italian model (fo
Ferrar had studied in Italy), to which the various members of th
household, each taking a particular name—for example, th
Guardian, the Visitor, the Humble, the Affectionate, the Submi
—contributed a hymn or edifying story, told in the vigorous an
flavoured idiom of contemporary English. A charming picture o

ᴴe Gidding life, though inaccurate even in important details, is
ᴼ be found in Shorthouse's once-celebrated novel *John Inglesant*.
  Crashaw was one of a little band of friends who from time
ᴼ time rode over from Cambridge to spend a few days at
ⁱidding. There, we are told, he took part in the night watches
-congenial to one who, as the notice prefixed to his poems
ₐforms us, "like a primitive saint, offered more prayers in the
ⁱght than others usually offer in the day". But we may be
ⁱclined to agree with Dr. Praz when he says, "Perhaps the
ᵉature [of the Gidding life] which attracted him most was the
ʳesence felt everywhere at Little Gidding of womanhood in
ₛ most noble and comforting aspect". Mary Collet, brought
ᵖ from infancy with her Ferrar grandmother, had determined,
ᵏe her younger sister Anna, to live a life of perpetual virginity.
ⁿdeed, the sisters would have taken a vow of virginity had not
ⁱishop Williams, their diocesan, dissuaded them from so "popish"
  step.[1] On her grandmother's death she became officially the
Mother" of the community, as such presiding over the meetings
f the Academy. In a letter of which we shall have to speak
ₐter—the only piece of prose by Crashaw which has survived—
ᵉ calls Mary Collet his "Mother", his "good and gracious
ᴹother". "He, too had accepted the rule of the congregation,
ₐd found the tender mother which his earliest years lacked,
ₐ this devout young woman, who, when she first met the poet,
ʰen aged nineteen, was thirty-two years old. The difference of
ᵍe and the type of office with which she had been charged con-
ⁱbuted no doubt to make Crashaw's relationship with her a
ᵒmage and service of spirit in which the affection and respect
ᵘe to a mother were blent with the tenderness inspired by a
ⁱster and the knight's devotion to his lady."[2]
  The mutual complement of the two sexes transcends the
ⁱological sphere, and neither poet nor saint has been moulded
ᵛithout the aid of a woman's hand. The day indeed must come
ᵛhen Crashaw's path will diverge far from Mary Collet's.
ᴮut she is not to let him go until he will leave her for an even
ⁿore spiritual mother.
  What poetry Crashaw wrote during these years we can only

[1] *Nicholas Ferrar, his Household and his Friends*, pp. 143–6. I agree with the anonymous
ₐuthoress in accepting Hacket's account of the matter.
[2] PRAZ, op. cit., p. 188.

in part determine. Elegies, all skilful and more or less inspire
by genuine feeling, on Cambridge dignitaries or friends—
paraphrases of two psalms—a host of Latin epigrams publishe
in 1634, English translations of many of these—other Lat
poems, including a Sapphic hymn to Venus never published—
and the charming *jeu d'esprit* on a bubble to which Dr. Pr
has called attention—also no doubt the famous "Wishes to h
Supposed Mistress", may with certainty be attributed to th
period. There are also the verses prefixed to Nicholas Ferra
translation of Lessius' book on temperance—the jibe at th
"oraculous doctor's mystic bills" has lost little of its poi
in the intervening three centuries—and the verses prefixed t
Shelford's *Five Discourses*, published in 1635. The conclusio
of the latter is a caustic fling at the great negative dogma o
Protestantism that the Pope is Antichrist. It could not hav
pleased his friend Ferrar who believed it. It reveals in fact
significant divergence already existing between Crashaw an
many at least of his Anglican friends. To these years also w
must ascribe his "Ode Prefixed to a Little Prayer-Book Give
to a Young Gentlewoman" and its companion "To the Sam
Party concerning her Choice". Here we are in the full flood o
Crashaw's mature style, and that note of ecstatic mystical devotio
is struck which will re-echo throughout his later religious poetry

But the storm fell in the shape of Dowsing and his iconoclas
who visited Cambridge during the winter of 1643 and brok
down, as Dowsing's diary gleefully records, a host of "supe
stitious" cherubim, crucifixes and popes in Crashaw's homes o
prayer, Peterhouse Chapel and Little St. Mary's. It drov
Crashaw from his "contentful kingdom" into lonely wandering
which we cannot even trace. A letter written on February 20t
1644 to one of his Gidding friends—probably John Ferrar o
Mr. Collet, Mary's father—a solitary lightning flash in th
midst of darkness, discovers him at Leyden. He had accompanie
his beloved "Mother" on a visit to some Dutch relatives. Fo
some reason not specified—presumably his Catholic sympathi
—they had closed their house to the poet and left him solitar
and poor in the uncongenial atmosphere of a Calvinist cit

---

[1]The anonymous authoress of the Life of *Nicholas Ferrar*, published in 1892, argues ve
plausibly from an allusion to bookbinding, suppressed in the first edition, that the M.
to whom these two poems are addressed was one of the Gidding family, and sugge
Margaret Collet or *Mary* Mapletoft.

In the principal church, he remarks bitterly, there was no figure of a saint—but "the plaine Pagan Pallas Cap-a-pee with speare and helmet and Owl and all—so that I am neither not scholler enough or not Pagan enough for this place". This rambling letter, an awkward composition and deliberately obscure, is an attempt to salvage part of his Peterhouse fellowship by resigning it to his old pupil, Ferrar Collet, who could in turn pass on a portion of the emoluments to his tutor. Shortly afterwards, however, Crashaw was formally deprived of the fellowship for non-attendance to subscribe the Covenant. It is probable, but not certain, that he returned to England, joined the Royalists at Oxford, and was admitted to membership of the university. The reasons advanced by Mr. Martin seem convincing.[1] If so, he would there have met Queen Henrietta Maria and the patroness to whom he later addressed his moving appeal to join the Catholic Church, Susan Countess of Denbigh. When he himself became a Catholic we do not know. Obscure hints in the letter of 1644 indicate that he was contemplating the step— but shrinking back on the brink. A reference in the Queen's letter recommending him to the Pope shows that his conversion cannot have been later than 1645. Not to speak of the ill-natured sneers of contemporaries at the toadying client of pious Catholic ladies, a more reputable criticism has regarded the step as due to despair at the collapse of Laudian Anglicanism. Shorthouse, in his hauntingly beautiful but subtly misleading romance, represents Crashaw as remarking to the hero "that he feared the English Church had not sufficient authority to resist the spread of Presbyterianism, in which case he saw no safety except in returning to the communion of Rome". "He lacked the courage and patience to wait for better days" writes the authoress of *Nicholas Ferrar*. Had it not been for the débâcle Crashaw's conversion might well have been delayed; but had he lived long enough, there could surely have been but one goal to a predetermined development. The devotion which inspires his poems is not the moderate and restrained piety of Anglicanism. It is the flaming passion, the mystic fervour, of counter-reformation Catholicism. "His faith", writes Dr. Praz, "is utterly different to that of the Protestants. Entirely made up of contemplation and exultant awe in the presence of divine marvels, it does not delay over

[1] *The Poems of Richard Crashaw*, 1927, Introduction.

sermons and pedestrian discourse. It is faith of a southern and Latin type, the faith of an *anima naturaliter catholica*."[1]   Apart from the misuse of the term "faith" to signify what would be more correctly designated devotion or spirituality, we may agree with Dr. Praz.

It would be interesting if we could determine exactly what poems were written before and after conversion. For this, however, the data are insufficient. The hymn on the Assumption, which *a priori* we should certainly ascribe to the Catholic period, was, as is certain from MSS evidence, written before his conversion. But we must not forget that the Laudian Stafford, in his book in honour of Our Lady, *The Female Glory*, taught the doctrine. Car, in his posthumous edition of Crashaw's sacred poetry, adds to the title of the "Apology for the Hymn on St. Teresa", "as having been writt when the author was yet among the Protestants". But the poem thus labelled has no reference to the writer's Protestantism. In the editions of 1646 and 1648 published in England, the title was respectively "An Apologie for the Precedent Hymne" and "An Apologie for the Precedent Hymnes on Teresa".[2]   What is surprising is the open publication in England during the Puritan regime in 1646 and again in 1648 of poems so undisguisedly Catholic—many of them paraphrases of Catholic hymns.[3]   One cannot conceive the publication of Protestant poetry in Spain. It is another proof among many that English devotional life, even when Catholicism was most hated, was being fed from Catholic sources.

Whatever his movements, whatever the date of his conversion, our next certain information finds Crashaw in the autumn of 1646 among the English exiles in Paris—in touch with his old friend Cowley and under the patronage, for what it was worth, of the Countess of Denbigh and the impoverished Queen. His patronesses would seem to have made a collection to defray the cost of his journey to Rome furnished with a letter of recommendation from the Queen to the Pope. Unfortunately for the poet, the papacy had no interest in pleasing the wife of a

[1] PRAZ, op. cit., p. 273. "Protestant", however, is too sweeping. See pp. 153-6.

[2] Having given us the three titles correctly in his edition of the poems it is surprising that in his biography of Crashaw Mr. Martin should assume that the 1652 title had been printed already in the edition of 1646, which not only contradicts his own text and note, but would have been impossible in the edition of a Protestant publisher.

[3] Not like the pieces translated by his father in conformity with Catholic and Protestant theology.

fallen monarch, and nothing or nothing of any consequence
was done to assist him. Though in such ecstasy of spirit that in
the words of his friend Car he "had wholly call'd his thoughtes
from earth, to live above in th'aire a very bird of Paradise", he
could not dispense with a minimum of subsistence—though it
were only "what might suffice to fitt his soul to heavenly exercise". A story was told years later to Sir Robert Southwell, that on
receiving from Pope Innocent the paltry sum of twenty pistoles,
Crashaw remarked to a friend "that if the Roman Church be
not founded upon a rock, it is at least founded upon something
which is as hard as a rock". Gossip, no doubt, but possibly
enshrining a genuine reminiscence. After a long period of
poverty and illness he was taken into the service of Cardinal
Palotta, who finally in 1649 gave him a subordinate canonry
in his gift at the Cathedral of Loretto. According to Dr. John
Bargrave, the Cardinal was compelled to send Crashaw away
from Rome to protect him from the hostility of fellow-members
of his suite whose misconduct he had denounced. Of the truth
of this report we have no means of judging. From the Cardinal's
Letter of Appointment "Crusio sacerdoti Anglo", it seems clear
that Crashaw was now in priest's orders—but the date and place
of his ordination are unknown. Already in ill-health, a frame
never very robust worn by years of privation, the journey
through the heat of an Italian summer proved too much for his
strength. Shortly after his arrival at Loretto he died. The archives
record his burial "in tumulo sacerdotum", further evidence
of his priesthood. He was thus interred beside the Holy House,
the symbol of a Divine Infancy and fit resting-place for a soul
pure and simple as the idealised child of tradition.[1]

How well (blest Swan) did Fate contrive thy death;
And made thee render up thy tuneful breath
In thy great Mistress' arms, thou most divine
And richest offering of Loretto's shrine!
Angels (they say) brought the famed Chapel there,
And bore the sacred Load in triumph, through the air.
'Tis surer much they brought *thee* there, and they
And thou, their charge, went singing all the way.[2]

[1] Since the official entry of Crashaw's death mentions only his last confession and anointing he must have been unable to receive viaticum.
[2] COWLEY, " Ode on the Death of Mr. Crashaw."

Dr. Praz introduces what is, to my knowledge, the best study of Crashaw yet written, by an illustrated description of Bernini's celebrated sculpture in Santa Maria della Vittoria, representing the transverberation of St. Teresa's heart. "In Rome", he writes "there is a work of art which may be regarded as the epitome of the religious spirit of the *Seicento*. The angel, whose visage glows with the radiance of a triumphant smile, launches his gilded dart at the heart of the saint, stretched in languorous abandonment on a pillow of cloud. The alluring violence of the seraph's gracious and cruel gesture, the voluptuous bliss in which the saint's entire body is dissolved from a countenance inebriated with heavenly delight to the heel of the naked foot, soft and flaccid like a flower whose strength has been sapped by the sun, suggest a blend of the human and the divine, possibly best defined in a Shakespearian phrase dear to Swinburne, 'spirit of sense . . .'" "There is", he continues, "a refined and Alexandrine quality in this Christian Love which displays, not the savage violence of a conflagration, but the lambent caress of flame, so tender and so feminine is his nature. The angel's gesture is graceful, gallant, his violence adorable as the wrath of a youthful cherub. He seems to be engaged in a delightful and cruel game with the saint and twists his dart as though he were playing a madrigal. And his victim surrenders herself with a consuming pleasure to the inebriating martyrdom; transformed by her ecstasy into a weary Maenad, not visited by a fury, but caressed by the grace of God."[1] The literary counterpart of this typical Baroque masterpiece he rightly finds in Crashaw, the supreme poetic expression of the Baroque culture, the Baroque poet *par excellence*, who celebrated St. Teresa and her ecstasy in verse, as Bernini in marble.

Having visited the original I cannot agree with Dr. Praz that the saint is depicted in "voluptuous bliss" and "consuming pleasure". I saw rather the suffering of a mystical death, the ecstatic pain of soul and body crucified with Christ. Crashaw's poetical counterpart, his "Hymne to St. Teresa" balances, as Bernini's does not, the pain and the pleasure of St. Teresa's ecstasy such as she describes it herself.[2] Nevertheless all that is said of the sublimated passion,

---

[1] PRAZ, op. cit., pp. 145–6.
[2] There is bliss in the ecstatic St. Scholastica, modelled in stucco by Feichtmayer (1709–72). But it is too profoundly peaceful to be passionate. It is the ecstasy of the Bride in St. John's *Noche Oscura*, the ecstasy of total self-oblivion. See Sacheverell SITWELL and Anthony AYSCOUGH, *German Baroque Sculpture*, Plate 21.

the "spirit of sense", is equally true of sculpture and poem. And Dr. Praz's interpretation of Bernini's masterpiece expresses most felicitously the quality of Crashaw's devotional poetry and in general of Baroque religious art and literature.[1]

It is unfashionable to defend the sensuous and passionate religion which inspired Baroque culture, and, since a religion is the form of every genuine culture, constituted its form, the form therefore which its art must apprehend and express. First the Victorians, "those virgins queer with garments grimed and lamps all gone to snuff; who", continues Patmore, "tear their clothes and bawl out blasphemy" if their God is called Bridegroom, then from the opposite camp the Freudians who, for all their talk of sublimation, value what is sublimated solely in terms of its material, have made us ashamed and frightened of sense and sex in religion. A Belgian Jesuit can even denounce Bernini's statue as indecent! And the late Canon Beeching "can imagine" not unsympathetically, "a police magistrate characterising" the poems of ecstatic devotion addressed by Crashaw to the young gentlewoman at Gidding "as poems that no gentleman should have written".[2] If we have no sympathy or understanding for such devotion we shall never understand Crashaw. *Deliciae sapientiae de amore*, "wisdom's delight of love" is indeed the burden of his song, as of no other English sacred poetry, till Patmore recaptured once more this religion of mystical passion. The *directly* sexual does not, indeed, play so important a part in Crashaw's poetry as in Patmore's; and compared with St. John of the Cross he makes very little use of the *Song of Songs*. Yet Patmore's employment of the language of nuptial love is more external and theoretical—a faith defended with passionate conviction rather than lived with passionate experience. The passion of the much-married poet was perhaps too preoccupied with an earthlier love. The lesser flame can scarcely burn side by side with the greater; the sun quenches the starlight. But the unwedded Crashaw, whose sole Love was the God to whom he so readily surrendered all, put into his devotion and into the poetry which enshrines it, the entire ardour of a flaming heart. His prayer is passion, and his passion prayer. Prayer, passion,

---

[1] As such I have used it elsewhere in my account of the Baroque religion-culture (*Catholic Art and Culture*).

[2] Introduction to M. R. Tutin's edition of Crashaw (*The Muses Library*), p. xxxiv.

poetry—their unison is the formula of Crashaw's religious art. His entire writing is steeped in a spiritualised sensuousness, that "spirit of sense" of which Dr. Praz speaks, and in a diffused passion, ardent, tender and delicate, an indefinable all-pervading atmosphere, warm and fragrant. If spirit is the negation of sense, we must of course condemn Baroque art, condemn Bernini, condemn Crashaw. But this is a false philosophy, doubly confuted, by the Creation and its fulfilment, the Incarnation. All events and patterns of the biological plane are reflections of events and patterns of the spiritual plane. Whereas the Freudian sees religion as disguised sex, mystical wisdom, to which the views of Jung here approximate, sees sex as reflected religion, sexual union as the shadow of which the union of the spirit with God is the substance, the fulfilment and the significance.[1] And if God is closer to the soul than one human being can be to another, and united with her in the supreme mystic union more intimately than soul with body, religion must be essentially nuptial—the physical nuptials of earth its least inadequate reflection and image.

> That sacred store
> Of hidden sweets and holy joyes.
> Words which are not heard with eares
> Effectual wispers, whose still voice
> The soul itselfe more feeles than heares;
> Amorous languishments; luminous trances;
> Sights which are not seen with eyes;
> Delicious deaths; soft exalations
> Of soul; dear and divine annihilations;
> A hundred thousand goods, glories and graces,
> And many a mystick thing
> Which the divine embraces
> Of the dear spouse of spirits with them will bring,
> O happy and thrice-happy she
> Who ere she be,
> Whose early love
> With winged vowes
> Makes hast to meet her morning spouse
> And close with his immortal kisses.

[1] See Victor WHITE, O.P., *God and the Unconscious*, in particular pp. 55 sqq., 217.

She shall have power
To rifle and deflour
The rich and roseal spring of those rare sweets
Which with a swelling bosom there she meets
Boundless and infinite
Bottomless treasures
Of pure inebriating pleasures.
Happy proof! She shall discover
What joy, what blisse,
How many heav'ns at once it is
To have her God become her Lover.[1]

This "nuptial song"[2] of the soul was reserved by the austere
Milton for heaven, but for the mystic the expression of a present
experience, utters the heart both of Crashaw's religion and in
general the Baroque religion of which he is the poetic interpreter.

Nor shall we understand the Baroque culture if we oppose
it to the mediaeval, or its art to Gothic art. In all its manifestations
Catholic culture has always been of necessity an incarnation
of spirit in sense and has made use of the old pre-Christian
culture. Christian art hitherto has been classical art transformed
by Christian faith.[3] The literature of Christian antiquity before
the barbarian conquests of the West, for example, the prose and
verse of a Sidonius Apollinaris—was curiously Baroque in quality.
Later, though these conquests considerably reduced the classical
ingredients of Western culture, they never ceased to be present
and active. The Renaissance brought a further supply of classical
material which for a short time in Italy threatened to stifle the
Christian form and produce a neo-paganism. But that was a
passing and superficial phase, and with Baroque the Christian
form re-established an unquestioned supremacy. There is
simply a larger proportion of classical elements in the edifice
than in the Middle Ages. Not even the sensuousness is new.
The Cistercian sermons on the Canticles, begun by St. Bernard,
are as erotic as anything in St. John of the Cross, primitive

---

[1] An Ode which was prefixed to a little " Prayer-book given to a young Gentle
Woman ". In the edition of 1646, " Mrs. M.R." " Mrs." (Mistress), it may be added,
did not in the seventeenth century necessarily signify a married woman. Crashaw's M.R.
was certainly a virgin.
[2] *Lycidas.*
[3] Even Gothic architecture includes classical features and traces of classical descent.

Franciscan devotion as passionate, tender and personal as Crashaw's. To reject, minimise or apologise for Baroque devotion is logically to reject, minimise or apologise for the entire devotion and culture of Catholicism. But "the feelings, the senses are dangerous—religion should be of the mind and will alone". Away then with sacred art, with symbolism, ritual, images, sacraments. Be thorough-paced Puritans—nay, more Puritan than they—for the Puritan sermon and devotion were far from dispensing with the emotions or even—witness Rous, Sterry and Goodwin—with the sexual. But the senses, the emotions, the affections will revolt against such a religion. The entire man must live with that intense life and concentrated experience we call ecstatic. If religion is too "pure" to afford this ecstasy, man will turn elsewhere. But since religion is the highest value, final truth and most abundant life, it has always produced this ecstatic experience.

Such "a sweet inebriated ecstasy" was pre-eminently Crashaw's religion. He does not preach; he does not torment himself over his sins; he does not worry about his prospects of salvation; he adores—adoration is the soul of religion—contemplates, exults, dances, sings, fiddles, disports himself. He can carry off the most preposterous conceits—even the notorious "walking baths" and "voluntary mint" of "The Weeper"—for they are not frigid exhibitions of ingenuity, but the toys with which he plays before the shrine. "They came to him naturally," writes Mr. Shepherd, "these teeming multitudes of figures and fancies. They crowded upon him and would not be denied. So he gathered them up in armfuls and shed them upon his pages as a child does rose leaves on anything it loves. He brought them with him like little crowding brownies, to surround the manger where Jesus lies. They surged with him in sorrowing fearful confusion up the hill of Calvary."[1] And he could toy with these conceits the more lightly because they refer to a body of know-ledge—literary, theological, historical, legendary, or pseudo-scientific—common to all educated readers. To-day one reader will have specialised in one department of science or literature, another in another. In the *Seicento* knowledge could still be universal. A poet's allusions, therefore, would be dark only to ignorance, his most far-fetched similes within the compass of his

[1] Introduction to *Crashaw's Religious Poems*, Manresa Press.

eader's knowledge. Indeed, of all Crashaw's more important
poems only one can fairly be called frigid—"The Epiphany
Hymn"—not for its conceits, but because adoration is, quite
exceptionally, replaced by a long-drawn comparison between
the false cult of the sun and the true religion of the Sun of Justice
now dawning on the world. Not even such lines as—

> O prize of the rich spirit, with what fierce chase
> Of his strong soul, shall he
> Leap at thy lofty Face . . .

can reconcile us to the legend of the Areopagite told by the kings
before the crib. But the rest are on fire!

If Bernini is Crashaw's counterpart in sculpture, assuredly St.
Philip Neri was his prototype among the canonised saints. St.
Philip passes long hours in his private oratory sipping the con-
secrated chalice, the Blood-Wine of Love—with such fervour
and sweetness that his teeth have left their impress on the metal
lip. So Crashaw:

> O! let me suck the wine
> So long of this chast vine
> *Till drunk of the dear wounds,* I be
> A lost Thing to the world, as it to me.[1]

Even in the sorrowful things of religion—Our Lord's wounds
and death, the tears of Magdalen's penitence and Mary's desolation—his contemplation finds nothing but joy. For he sees
in them only the love they express. It is the same with death.
The shadow of death lies over the literature, the art, and the
devotion of the seventeenth century. The death bell tolls from
time to time in the measure of its verse, as in Bishop King's
"Exequy" on his deceased wife. The elegy is a conventional
form of poetry. Everywhere death's-heads, skeletons, a dwelling
upon the accidents of death and the tomb, even such macabre
foretaste of corruption as the famous statue of Donne for which
he dressed in his grave-clothes. Austin must needs compose his
own funeral sermon,[2] and in the *Epicedium* attached to it—a

[1] " Sancta Maria Dolorum."
[2] AUSTIN *Meditations*, 1635: " The Author's Own Funeral made upon Himself."
Poem appended to the *Epicedium*.

poem not wanting in sombre and quaint beauty—he finds the grave everywhere.

> The Wombe was (first) my Grave: Whence since I rose
> My Body (Grave-like) doth my soule enclose:
> That Body like a Corps with Sheets ore-spread
> Dying each Night lyes Buried in my Bed.
> My close low-builded Chamber to mine Eye
> Showes like a little Chapel where I lye:
> While at my Window pretty Birds doe ring
> My knell and with their Notes, my Obiits sing.

Vaughan's thought is constantly returning to the tomb and death is a recurrent theme in the conversations of the Gidding Academy. Not so Crashaw. At Cambridge indeed he compose elegies. It is expected of him as a budding poet. But even ir these he dwells rather on the gifts, real or imagined, of the deceased, than on death itself. For to his ardent devotion deatl is already swallowed up in the victorious love-life of eternity.[1] The death which he celebrates is the mystic death "of love" ever renewed as a renewed life, the death—

> in which who dyes
> Loves his death, and dyes again . . .
> And lives, and dyes; and knowes not why
> To live, But that he thus may never leave to dy.[2]

It is "the wine of youth, life and the sweet deaths of Love" Wine
> That can exalt weak earth; and so refine
> Our dust, that at one draught, mortality
> May drink it self up, and forget to dy.[3]

Spinoza, reacting against his century's preoccupation with death, would banish it from the thought of the sage. Of thi

[1] One poem, it is true, " Death's Lecture at the Funeral of a Young Gentleman," contemplates death from the conventional seventeenth-century standpoint. But it is quite exceptional and belongs to Crashaw's early period, before he had completely found himself. It contains, however, splendid lines worthy of their author.
[2] " A Hymne to Saint Teresa."
[3] " An Apologie for the Fore-going Hymne."

reaction and the universal *memento mori* Crashaw's attitude is the higher synthesis. He will think of death, but only in terms of life. And Our Lord's death he will envisage only as the source of this new deathless life:

So from His living and life-giving death,
My dying life may draw a new and never fleeting breath.[1]

And the deaths of martyrs, "thy old friends of fire"—as Dr. Praz points out, their cultus was a favourite topic of *Seicento* devotion, though in truth it is wellnigh as old as Christianity itself—are but fresh victories of life and love.

What did their weapons but with wider pores
Inlarge thy flaming-breasted Lovers
          More freely to transpire,
          That impatient Fire

The Heart that hides Thee hardly covers
What did their weapons but sett wide the Doores
For Thee: Fair, purple Doores, of love's devising;
The Ruby windows which inricht the East
Of Thy so oft-repeated Rising.[2]

Sorrow, suffering, death are but expressions, occasions and victories of love. Even a cursory glance at Crashaw's favourite phrases is revealing. Wounds, blood, weapons are recurrent themes. Here too he is Baroque. *Seicento* imagination loved to dwell on blood and wounds and darts, but the blood and wounds that attest love and the weapons wielded or vanquished by love. The preoccupation may be profane, a dwelling on the archery of Cupid or a woman's eyes or on the wounds of fleshly passion, even at times perverted and decadent, but it may also be sublimated into a contemplation of Divine Love wounded and bleeding and its human return in bodily or spiritual martyrdom. Blood, wounds, weapons—all are love's. The most obvious symbol of passionate love, because, being a genuine symbol, it is its corporeal reflection and counterpart—fire or flame—recurs abundantly in Crashaw's vocabulary. And, as we already

---

[1] " The Recommendation."   [2] " To the Name of Jesus."

F

know, wine. The apology for the hymn on St. Teresa is chiefly a panegyric of this inebriating wine—"The king has brought me into his wine cellar." Crashaw's muse is seldom sober. " 'Let my soul swell' ", quotes Dr. Praz,[1] " 'with the strong wine of love.' " "The images of blood, wine and fire" he continues, "recur in our poet with a frequency which seems extraordinary even in a Catholic accustomed to meditate on the mystery of the Eucharist, a frequency which he has in common with the poet whose inspiration seems so akin in temper to his, Swinburne. They are devices or emblems of the inflamed imagination of these poets, in the one associated with profane objects, in the other with sacred. Blood of love's martyrdom, wine which is the intoxication of sense, fire of dionysiac frenzy in the singer of Anactoria, blood of religious martyrdom, wine of heavenly vintage, fire of ecstatic ardour in the singer of Saint Teresa." As common, however, as fire and flames are images of the opposite element water, floods, showers, rivers, seas. It is as though the heat of Crashaw's passionate imagination sought by a subconscious psychological necessity the cooling of water. This surely is the psycho-physical background of such a verse as this.

> Can these fair Flouds be
> Freinds with the bosom fires that fill thee!
> Can so great flames agree
> Eternal Teares should thus distill thee!
> O flouds; O fires! O suns! O showres!
> Mixte and made freinds by love's sweet powres.

Thus in the Weeping Magdalen the complementary contrasts meet,[2] and in

> that breast
> Of thine [the Mater Dolorosa] the noblest nest
> Both of love's fires and flouds.[3]

And of all forms of water his favourite is the tear. Thirty-one melodious stanzas of "The Weeper" compose a chaplet, whose beads are a series of images and conceits—quaint, charming, often lovely—told in honour of the Magdalen's tears.

[1] PRAZ, op. cit., p. 273.   [2] " The Weeper."   [3] " Sancta Maria Dolorum."

Heavens thy fair eyes be;
Heavens of ever-falling starres.
Tis seed time still with thee
And starres thou sow'st.

.   .   .   .   .

Does the day-star rise?
Still thy starres doe fall and fall.
Does day close his eyes?
Still the fountain weepes for all.

Does thy song lull the air?
Thy falling teares keep faithfull time
Does thy sweet-breath'd praire
Up in clouds of incense climb?

Still at each sigh, that is, each stop,
A bead, that is, a tear, does drop.[1]

The rhythm of these verses is the telling of a rosary, the rhythm
of beads slipping in turn from the fingers. Vaughan, it is
true, a poet of very different inspiration, recurs as frequently
to the thought of tears. But they are the bitter tears of personal
penitence or sorrow for the overthrow of the Anglican Church.
For Crashaw, as we have seen, tears—even the tears shed at the
foot of the Cross—are sweet, even happy, but another expression
of all-triumphant love. The Magdalen is "a flaming fountain,
a weeping fire"—her tears jewels of love's adornment, wine for
the Beloved.

An instructive parallel to Crashaw's spiritual passion, to his
nuptial symbolism, his wine and his fire is to be found in the
mystical devotion of a prominent Puritan, Francis Rous. Its
author's reputation as a virulent foe of Anglicanism may possibly
have prevented Crashaw from reading a little book published
in 1635, Rous's *Mystical Marriage or Experimental Discourses of
the Heavenly Marriage between a Soul and her Saviour*. Yet its
passionate mysticism was far closer to his poetry than any production of an Anglican pen. The verse of a Herbert, even of a

[1] "The Weeper."

Vaughan, is pale by comparison with these prose fervours. The parallel between Rous and Crashaw proves that mystical devotion of this erotic and Baroque colour was in the spiritual atmosphere of the time, and from this point of view repays notice by students of the poet.

"By often visitations", writes Rous, "put Thy own image and beauty more and more on my soul and then love Thy own beauty in my soul and my soul for Thy own beauty which Thou hast put on her and let my soul love Thee infinitely for being infinitely more beautiful than that beauty which Thou hast put on my soul and therefore infinitely more lovely than that which Thou lovest in my soul." "Thy being is loveliness itself and Thy being is love itself, for God is love. Come therefore into me O Thou who art love and love Thyself in me." I am reminded of St. John of the Cross in his *Spiritual Canticle* "Let me be so transformed in Thy beauty that being alike in beauty we may see ourselves both in Thy beauty: I now having Thy very beauty, so that, one beholding the other, each may see his own beauty in the other, the beauty of both being Thine only and I being absorbed in Thy beauty, and I shall see myself in Thee in Thy beauty, and Thou Thyself in me in Thy beauty and so shall I seem to be Thyself in Thy beauty and Thou myself in Thy beauty; my beauty shall be Thine Thine shall be mine; and thus I shall be Thou in Thy Beauty and Thou myself in Thine own beauty; for Thy very beauty will be my beauty and so we shall see each other, in Thy beauty." Though Rous insists on the transcendence of God's beauty over His communication of it to the soul the likeness is striking. And although we cannot be certain that Crashaw read St. John of the Cross, his devotion to the other great Spanish mystic makes it probable.[1]

As we have just seen, Crashaw is addicted to spiritual intoxication. "Inebriating pleasures," "A sweet inebriated ecstasy."

> By all thy brimfilled bowls of fierce desire:
> By thy last morning's draught of liquid fire.[2]

> Let my soul swell with the strong wine of love

---

[1] *Spiritual Canticle*, 36.
[2] "The Flaming Heart." Lines added in the edition of 1652.

155

Some drink from men to beasts. O Then
Drink we till we prove more, not less than men:
And turn not beasts but Angels. Let the King
Me ever into these His cellars bring:
Where flowes such wine as we can have of none
But Him who trod the winepress all alone,
Wine of youth, life and the sweet deaths of love,
Wine of immortal mixture which can prove
Its tincture from the rosy nectar, wine
That can exalt weak earth and so refine
Our dust that at one draught mortality
May drink itself up and forget to dy.[1]

"Let the soul", Rous wrote, "drink plentifully that she may
be mounted up in a divine ecstasy above her carnal and earthly
station." "Let the measure sometimes be not only full but
running over to a spiritual drunkenness but not unto drowning:
for these ecstasies and excesses of love shall somewhat increase
my ability of loving Thee. For when my understanding, will
and affections are all overflown, overcome and amazed, then
shall my wonder gaze on Thee and my very faintings shall be
inflamed towards Thee and melt me into Thee."
In the same vein is Rous's beautiful saying: "When
the wine of natural joy is spent and there is nothing left
but the water of affliction, then doth Christ turn this water into
wine."
Like Crashaw's, Rous's religion is on fire.
"The spirit of union is fire, and fire turns that into itself to
which it is united." "He and she are met in the heats of a
spiritual conjugation and the excesses of a fruitive union."
Thus Rous's prose and Crashaw's verse are alike examples of a
mystical and ecstatic religion, felt and expressed with that
Baroque passion and sensuousness, that "spirit of sense" noted
by Praz in Bernini's sculpture of St. Teresa's ecstasy and in
Crashaw's poetry. Crashaw was an unworldly scholar who
sacrificed all for the Catholic faith and died prematurely, the
victim in all probability of long continued privation. Rous
was a Puritan zealot, a successful politician, Provost of Eton,
Speaker of the Barebones Parliament and a Cromwellian peer,

[1] " An Apologie for the Fore-going Hymne."

fortunate even in his death on the eve of the Restoration. No contrast could well be greater.

Yet their kinship in the interior life and its expression is evident In what Rous called *Interiora regni Dei* they meet and are reconciled.

Another quality of Crashaw's perception is his sense of space As his fire demanded water, his ardour, like the fire in St. Philip' breast which to find scope for itself forced out a rib above his heart, demands room. Weapons *"inlarge* God's flaming breasted lovers *more freely* to transpire their *impatient* fire." He dwell on St. Teresa's *"large* draughts of intellectual day" and *"large* draughts of love." "Glory flames in her own *free* sphere." The song of praise is *"spacious," "unbounded,"* and "all *embracing,"* and the martyrs' *"spacious* bosoms spread a throne for love *a large* to fill." We should also notice Crashaw's predilection for the east and the dawn. Vaughan indeed also loved it and paid his tribute in an exquisite poem. But whereas he loves the dawn for its fresh purity and clear light, Crashaw dwells on the rich colouring, the pomp of sunrise. His dawn, I fancy, is later than Vaughan's. He contemplates "the rosy windows" "the ruby portals of the east" "the purple East" "the purple pride" that "laces the crimson curtains" of morning's bed. Always, as Dr Praz has also remarked, comparing in this respect his poetry with Rubens' painting, an opulence of brilliant colour—purple, red ruby, rose, crimson—rose of dawn, purple of blood. Vaughan' favourite colour on the other hand is not red but white, and for him day and the sun mean light rather than heat. In his *Henry Vaughan* Dr. F. E. Hutchinson observes that "we are safe in relating Vaughan's fondness for the word 'white' as an epithet for all that he values most to the rich connotations of the Welsh word *gwyn*, which signifies not only white but fair, happy holy, blessed. There is no more frequent epithet in Welsh poetry",[1] and Welsh, he tells us, was Vaughan's native language Even so the word must have expressed a personal preference for a colour temperamentally dear. And Dr. Hutchinson proceeds to remark that "Next after white Vaughan's special fondness is for green." Cool colours both, in contrast with the warmth of Crashaw's palette. White light—or if gold at all the sober gold of "calm golden evenings," the green of cool shades and

[1] *Henry Vaughan*, p. 162.

moist meadows—red fire, ruby and purple—in this contrast we
have in epitome the difference between Vaughan's devotion
and Crashaw's. Vaughan is pure because he loves purity and
has achieved it, apparently, by a struggle. Crashaw is consumed
by a fire so intense that the conflagration has extinguished earthlier
flames. Mr. Aldous Huxley has analysed sexual love into
tendresse and passion.[1] Its spiritual prototype also comprises these
two ingredients. And if Crashaw's love is spiritual passion,
expressed by the wine and the fire, the blood, the purple and the
red—it is also *tendresse*. If he thinks of God as the lover or bridegroom of other souls—of the martyrs, St. Teresa or the anonymous
gentlewoman—to himself Divine Love is primarily perhaps
maternal. Nor is this surprising. The love of a man for a woman,
when richest and most complete, contains this element of filial
love, and she is a mother to her lover. Mother-love colours
Crashaw's devotion; there is little, if any, of it in Thompson or
Patmore. Whatever the cause, whether Dr. Praz is right or
mistaken in ascribing it to lack of a mother's love, it runs a
powerful current through his verse. It finds verbal expression
in his fondness for breast or bosom—not only as the source of
food but as a warm place in which to nestle and find shelter.
And we have already noticed another favourite image, akin in
feeling to the breast with which it is frequently rhymed, the
nest. A place of shelter and warmth beneath the wing of maternal
affection. This, no doubt, is the underlying motive of his choice.
The tenderness thus expressed is not, however, in any bad sense
effeminacy—for it goes hand in hand with the strength of a
mighty passion of spirit. The reader of St. Teresa's works—

> Feels his warm heart hatch'd into a nest
> Of little eagles and young loves, whose high
> Flights scorn the lazy dust and things that dy:

the "low mortality", the "dull mortality" of which he speaks
elsewhere.

This is not, perhaps, Crashaw's finest poetry; it is the quintessence of his religion. And this blend of tenderness and the
strength of passionate aspiration is also shared with the Puritan
leader. "Let the soul," wrote Rous, "often go out of the body,

[1] *Point Counter Point.*

yea, out of the world by heavenly contemplation, and treading
on the earth with the bottom of her feet, stretch herself up to
look over the world into that upper world where her treasure,
her joy, her beloved dwelleth."[1]

Crashaw's predilection for nest and breast suggests Keats and
the two poets are, in fact, akin. Both are richly sensuous.

In his lectures on Keats,[2] Professor Garrod points out that he
is a poet who used all the five senses. This is equally true of
Crashaw. His employment of imagery "practically never fails
to justify itself by a genuinely sensuous quality favourable to
strong contrasts of light and shade and colour and appealing
almost as much to the faculties of smell and touch as to the
faculty of vision."[3] Sight plays indeed a minor part. As we
have seen, Crashaw prefers heat and colour to light, and
his sense of form is so inferior to his sense of colour that his
poems possess little structure. As though conscious of this
defect he likes to find his design ready made and to get under
way by the paraphrase or, as in the opening of his "Hymn to
St. Teresa," at least by the suggestion, of some existing poem or
hymn.[4] But there is the sight of colour. And all the other

---

[1] Op. cit.

[2] Heathcote William GARROD, *Keats*, 1926, 2nd Ed., 1939.

[3] MARTIN, op. cit., Introduction, p. lxvii.

[4] The opening stanzas of the " Hymn to St. Teresa " are based on the office hymn for
the Vespers of her feast.

> *Terris Teresa barbaris*
> *Christum datura aut sanguinem . . .*

> So shall she leave amongst them sown
> Her Lord's blood or at lest her own.

> *Sed te manet suavior*
> *Mors, poena poscit dulcior*
> *Divini amoris cuspide*
> *In vulnus icta concides.*
> *O caritatis victima.*

Hence with a slight transposition Crashaw's

> Sweet, not so fast! lo thy fair Spouse
> Whom thou seekst with so swift vowes,
> Calls thee back, & bidds thee come
> *T'embrace a milder martyrdom . . .*
> *Thou art love's victime: & must dy*
> *A death* more mysticall & high.
> Into love's armes thou shalt let fall
> A still-surviving funerall
> *His is the dart* must make the Death
> Whose stroke shall taste thy hallow'd breath . . .

senses. Sound: his poems are full of music. Witness "Music's Duel"—the fantasy, taken from a Latin poem by the Jesuit Strada, of a nightingale attempting to outsing a lute-player's music and dying of the attempt. It is a veritable *tour de force* in the verbal translation of musical effects. "All things that are or what's the *same* are musicall."[1] Smell: perfume and incense are favourite symbols. Touch: in the Christmas hymn you feel the texture of the Seraphs' fiery down—the softness of the snow-flakes. Taste: sweets, nests of sweets for taste and scent com-bined—and for taste alone—the wine so often at his lips. And we taste the cream, the breakfast of Magdalen's tears. This sensuousness is Keatsian and in places the very rhythm anticipates Keats.[2]

> The sweet-lip't sisters musically frighted,
> Singing their feares are fearefully delighted.
> Trembling as when Appollo's golden haires
> Are fan'd and frizled in the wanton ayres
> Of his own breath. . . .

> Those parts of sweetnesse which with Nectar drop,
> Softer than that which pants in Hebe's cup . . .[3]

> *Enthusiasticke* flames, such as can give
> Marrow to my plumpe Genius, make it live
> Drest in the glorious madnesse of a Muse,
> Whose feet can walke the milky way, and chuse
> Her starry Throne; whose *holy heats can warme*
> *The grave*, and hold up an exalted arme
> To lift me from my lazy Urne, to climbe
> Upon the stooped shoulders of old Time,
> And trace Eternity.[4]

With the exception of the few words in italics these lines might well have come from Keats' pen. Extravagances and all, they are his vein. If the resemblance is most striking in Crashaw's secular verse, it is because the pagan Keats could never clearly distinguish the delights and experiences of sense from the

[1] " To the Name of Jesus."
[2] On the other hand a touch of Shelley has been remarked in the " winged moments", gathering Magdalen's tears.
[3] " Musick's Duell." The entire poem is prophetic of Keats.
[4] " To the Morning. Satisfaction for Sleepe."

spiritual experiences and joys which surpass them. Sensation and the intuition of the spirit are not adequately distinguished. Rightly dissatisfied with the former, Keats can find no alternative except thought or moral endeavour. But these are alien to his genius. Hence mistakes and disappointments, frustrations and gropings. Crashaw, inferior in poetic genius, escaped this error. As sensuous as Keats, as little a thinker or preacher, he is free of that higher realm of mystical intuition which fulfils the promise of sense, a joy "whose hand is" not "on his lips bidding adieu," a beauty as immortal as the loveliness of art celebrated in the *Ode to a Grecian Urn* but living and personal:

> More happy love! more happy, happy love!
> For ever warm and still to be enjoyed,
> All breathing human passion far above.

But the picture of love is not love. Hence the melancholy, almost disillusioned tone of the last stanza on which Professor Garrod remarks. The love which Crashaw sings, "young loves" which "scorn the things that die", is above all merely human passion. It possesses the eternity of Keats' Urn, is as timeless and deathless as the frozen immortality of art. But warm and living in fact not fancy, it breathes the breath of the Spirit, burns with the fire of God. Crashaw thus fulfils Keats, achieving the goal he sought in vain. I am not claiming for Crashaw a place in the first rank of poets. For that his fire lacked the necessary light, his colour the indispensable mastery of architectonic form. Only the clear conceptual background furnished by Catholic theology and philosophy—often assisted by the borrowed form of the hymns and poems on which he embroidered—saved him, as indeed it saved the Baroque devotion and culture of which he is the typical poetic exponent, from the deliquescence which is the malady of feeling, as aridity is the malady of thought.[1] Still less was Crashaw among those artists of sovereign genius who mount upon the common form of their culture and climb above it to achieve a more universal yet more individual art. Such was Milton among his

[1] Intuition, the more concrete and obscure it is, is the more liable to the danger which attends the emotion that invests it; the more abstract and clear, the more liable to the danger attendant upon conceptual thought.

contemporaries and Shakespeare in the age before him. But in virtue of a perfect adaptation of temperament and genius to contemporary Baroque culture he was enabled to voice it as no other. In a detailed comparison between Crashaw's paraphrase of Marino's *Sospetto d'Herode* and the Italian original, Dr. Praz shows how the English poet filled in Marino's too rigidly classical framework with a Baroque luxuriance of fantastic imagery which the Italians, bound in this field too tightly by the classical tradition, never attained in poetry, as they did in painting and architecture. England was cut off by her Protestant iconoclasm from the full flowering of Baroque art. Though we must not underrate Wren, Vanbrugh or Gibbs, not even Wren's work is so perfect an expression of Baroque as the work of Bernini, Borromini or the great Germans—the two Fischers, Zimmermann or the brothers Asam. But in Crashaw's work she produced the finest Baroque poetry.

This achievement however compelled Crashaw to pass beyond the provincial and fragmentary religion of his country to the complete religion which fashioned and ensouled the Baroque culture of Western Christendom. His bodily departure to Italy was but a symbol of this inner pilgrimage. Whether with better health and kinder treatment he would have produced lovelier and more perfect poetry than in those years before his arrival in Italy is a question more painful than profitable. He seems to have produced nothing or almost nothing during the last two or three years. Perhaps he was too ill; perhaps he wrote; but if he did his poems have perished. Certainly what would seem to be his final surviving utterances, the magnificent conclusion added to his lines on St. Teresa and another splendid passage inserted into his appeal to the Countess of Denbigh—the latter saved only by the chance of a single copy—show a simplicity, directness and concentration of force beyond his earlier scope. Life was now perhaps too stern even for the holy play of his earlier poetry. But love is as ever the theme of his singing. The austerity which has dispensed with love's trappings has but emphasised love.

> O thou undaunted daughter of desires!
> By all thy dowr of lights and fires;
> By all the eagle in thee, all the dove;
> By all thy lives & deaths of love;

By thy large draughts of intellectual day,
And by thy thirsts of love more large than they . . . [1]

When love of Us called Him to see
If wee'd vouchsafe His company,
He left His Father's Court, and came
Lightly as a Lambent Flame,
Leaping upon the Hills, to be
The Humble King of You and Me."[2]

When Dame Julian pondered the rich obscurity of her revelations, it was to learn that love was God's meaning in all. Crashaw's message is no other. In the teeth of a world full of hate and folly, of cruelty and death, the *Seicento* poet and the mediaeval anchoress proclaim the same simple but inexhaustible message —the omnipotence of Love.

Love was His meaning.

Love thou art Absolute sole lord
Of Life and Death.

This, the heart of religion, is the burden of Crashaw's religious poetry. What is religion? Ask Crashaw. What is mysticism? Ask Crashaw. What is love—the love which is religion and mysticism religion's crown? Ask Crashaw. His answer will not be a theological disquisition, but the music of a soul drunken with the ecstasy of God.

BIBLIOGRAPHICAL NOTE

The Poems English Latin and Greek of Richard Crashaw. Ed. L. C. Martin. Oxford: The Clarendon Press, 1927. The only adequate critical edition—also containing the most complete biography available. But Mr. Martin need not search the collections of Mone and Daniel for a hymn contained in the Little Office of Our Lady.

The Poems of Richard Crashaw. Ed. J. R. Tutin. Introduction by Canon (later Dean) Beeching (The Muses Library). A fairly sufficient edition for slenderer purses and more portable use. Beeching's introduction is on the whole sympathetic and understanding—though

[1] Lines added to " The Flaming Heart".
[2] " A letter from Mr. Crashaw to the Countess Denbigh."

Crashaw's Catholic and Baroque devotion proves at times too strong meat for this Anglican and Victorian Dean.

The Religious Poems of Richard Crashaw. With an Introductory Study by R. A. Eric Shepherd. Manresa Press, 1914. Mr. Shepherd's introduction is certainly the best critical appreciation of Crashaw in English, besides being a fine piece of English prose—in fact a little masterpiece. But we must agree with Dr. Praz's criticism that Crashaw's enthusiasm was not simply, as Mr. Shepherd suggests, the enthusiasm of the convert,—indeed, it demonstrably preceded his conversion—but the natural quality of his temperament and devotion.

Secentismo e Marinismo in Inghilterra. John Donne: Richard Crashaw. Dr. Mario Praz. Florence, 1925. If Mr. Shepherd's introduction is the best *English* study of Crashaw, the far longer study which forms the second half of Dr. Praz's book is to my knowledge absolutely the best. I have been indebted to it at every turn. Dr. Praz places Crashaw in his cultural and religious environment. I would call attention in particular to a charming sketch of the community of Little Gidding. See also for the Anglican period of Crashaw's Life:

Nicholas Ferrar, His Household and Friends. Anonymous. Ed. Rev. T. T. Carter, 1892.

Also for background only:

The Story Books of Little Gidding. 1631, 1632. Ed. E. Cruwys Sharland, 1899.

Contemporary Editions

Epigrammatum Sacrorum Liber. Cambridge University Press, 1634.

Steps to the Temple with Delights of the Muses. London, Humphrey Moseley, 1646. Anonymous preface probably by one of the poet's Gidding friends.

Slightly enlarged, but less accurate re-edition. Same publisher, 1648.

Carmen Deo Nostro. Paris, Peter Targa, 1652. Ed. by Crashaw's friend, T. Car. Crashaw's religious poems omitting, however, the translation of Marino. New pieces added and many enlarged or remodelled. The text is illustrated by engravings (reproduced in Mr. Martin's edition) which, if not as Car claims, wholly of Crashaw's designing, are in part his work. (See Martin, p. xlviii–ix.)

Expanded version of the *Address to the Countess of Denbigh.* Ascribed in MS. to 1653. London, N.D. Only one copy known, B.M.

Steps to the Temple with Delights of the Muses. The 2nd Edition (sic). London, Henry Herringman, 1670. *Poemata et Epigrammata Edicio Seconda.* Cambridge University Press, 1670. Reprinted 1674.

CHAPTER VIII

WILLIAM CRASHAW'S INFLUENCE ON HIS SON

THE WILL of Crashaw's father, William, a minister, as Anglican clergymen were then commonly called, of Yorkshire birth who held a Yorkshire living—Agburton— and at the time of his death was rector of St. Mary Matfellon, Whitechapel, contains his final profession of anti-Catholic faith. "I account [popery] as now it is, the heap and chaos of all heresies and the channel whereinto the foulest impieties and heresies that have been in the Christian world have run and closely emptied themselves." "I believe the Pope's seat and power to be the power of the great Antichrist and the doctrine of the Pope, as now it is, to be the doctrine of Antichrist, yea, that doctrine of devils prophecied of by the Apostle, and that the true and absolute Papist so living and dying debars himself of salvation for aught that we know."

The latest notice we have of his son, the poet, is the record of his death at Loretto as a Canon of the Holy House "strengthened by Holy Unction" and the burial of his body "in the priests' sepulchre". A long road was traversed between the religion of his father, with which he began, to his end as a priest of the Church so hated by his father. It is not surprising that students of Crashaw have seen his entire course as a reaction against his father's religion—not only his final Catholicism, but his Anglicanism of the Laudian School—and have regarded his father as representing the opposite doctrinal pole to Catholicism, that is to say, as a Puritan such as those who—Presbyterian or Independent—later overthrew the Anglican Church in favour of their more radical forms of Protestantism. This view is a misconception. The poet departed from his father only as he began to turn away from Anglicanism, and his earlier Anglican religion, far from being a reaction against his father's Puritanism, was substantially in agreement with his belief. That is to say his father's religion was in fact not just a starting point from which his son immediately began to depart, but the determining influence of his earlier faith and worship, and the father bequeathed to the son not merely the negative anti-Catholicism he would soon repudiate—as he did between the Latin verses on the Gunpowder Plot composed at school and the poem he prefixed to Shelford's *Discourses* in 1635—but a positive Anglican Christianity which, when he became a Catholic, he would not deny but complete. Indeed the sensitive boy could not fail to have been influenced profoundly by a father who—except for the year-and-a-half of his second marriage—was, probably from his infancy, in sole charge of him, an only child moreover. And there is every reason to believe that the elder Crashaw was a most conscientious and devoted father, deeply concerned for his son's welfare.

Certainly there is no question that William Crashaw was obsessed by "no popery". In almost all the many writings he has left us this phobia appears. It was a passion with him far more powerful than it was with such Puritans as Sterry or the Cambridge Platonist John Smith—the latter avoids the topic entirely, even when discoursing on superstition, and the former, so far as I am acquainted with his writings, treats it only once, and then to argue that, if not so false as Catholicism, Presbyterianism is uglier and more inhuman. William Crashaw, on the other hand, cannot keep this King Charles's head out of his Memorial.

In a sermon preached before the Honourable Lord de la Warr, Lord Governor of Virginia, important in several respects —we must return to it later—he wishes "that the name of Pope and Popery might be buried as they long ago deserved". He exhorts the Virginia Company: "Suffer no Papists to nestle there, nay, let the name of the Pope nor Popery be never heard of", to which the retort is obvious that had he gone out to the colony as chaplain, it would have been heard in well nigh every sermon. On another occasion he speaks in the Maria Monk vein of the unwanted infants murdered by monks and nuns, and he swallows—for his personal honesty is transparent—a cock-and-bull story told him by a certain Strickland of Bridlington of a dispensation he had been granted in Mary's reign to stay away from Mass.[1] He also tells us that a dispensation had been granted to keep two wives and by Martin V for a brother to marry his sister.[2] The Catholic Church, he declares, "professes

[1] *A Mittimus to the Jubilee at Rome or the Rates of the Pope's Custom House.*   [2] ibid.

to be a loving mother but proves a cruel stepdame". She promises the pure manna of God's word but feeds her children "with legends, lies, tales and traditions". In 1617 he published *The Parable of Poison in five Sermons of Spiritual Poison*, the first of which was preached before the Prince of Wales, the future Charles I. "Popery," he declares, "profaneness and the lusts of the flesh are all of them spiritual poisons and may not be touched, not as it were with the tip of the finger without danger to the heart and the whole body." But the Catholic clergy, certainly the Jesuits, are adepts in the use of other poisons of a less spiritual nature, delayed-action poisons whose victim cannot suspect his murderer. "The Italians have poisons, especially, since the Jesuits were hatched, that will kill after a day, a week, a month, a year, and so far from killing presently, that generally at first they are pleasant but at last they are deadly." Referring to the murder of Amnon he observes, "Oh foolish Absalom, say the Jesuits, what a stir and tumult he made by such a silly kind of invention, for could not he, having him at a banquet, have given him a dram in his drink to have wrought a week after that the feast might have had no interruption, the state no trouble and Amnon never have known, no, nor once suspected who had hurt him?" "A thousand Jews," he continues, "tried in vain to kill St. Paul. Our Italianated Papists would laugh at the folly and pity the simplicity of these men, that so many should trouble themselves in such a fashion, whereas he might have been by one poor fig despatched without noise or tumult." The Jesuits are "the devil's darlings, his youngest beloved sons". "The sin among Protestants is the fault of our men not of our religion. But in Popery I blame not so much the men as the religion . . . their practices, their doctrine . . . their people practise sin and their doctrine maintains them in it. The Romish Church and religion is a poisonful church and religion."

All this "no popery" however does not prove William Crashaw a Puritan in the sense of an embyro Dissenter, whether Presbyterian or Independent. His hatred of Rome was shared by most Anglicans. His son, it is true, had discarded as early as 1635, years before his conversion, the doctrine that the Pope is Antichrist, as the verses prove which he prefixed to *Five Pious and Learned Discourses* by Robert Shelford, priest, published in that year.

Nor shall our zealous ones still have a fling
At that most horrible and horned thing,
Forsooth the Pope: by which black name they call
The Turk, the Devil, Furies, Hell and all
And something more. Oh, He is Antichrist.
Doubt this and doubt (say they) that Christ is Christ.
Why 'tis a point of faith. Whate're it be,
I'm sure it is no point of charitie.
In summe no longer shall our people hope,
To be a true Protestants but to hate the Pope.[1]

But in this he had departed not only from his father but from his friend, the founder of that unique combination of domestic and religious life, the family community of Little Gidding, in whose devotions he delighted to share. For only the previous year Nicholas Ferrar had told an inquisitive visitor to Gidding that he "believed the Pope to be Antichrist as firmly as any article in his creed". It is indeed impossible to understand Crashaw's religious development, if we suppose that seventeenth-century Anglicanism, even Laudian, was Anglo-Catholic, as we know Anglo-Catholicism today. Laud himself on the scaffold gloried in the name Protestant. Even the Laudians rejected prayer to Our Lady and the saints. George Herbert in pathetic lines says that he would gladly have prayed to the Mother of his God had not God forbidden it. Their Eucharistic theology is less easy to determine. It was certainly remote from transubstantiation. A canon passed by Convocation in 1640 under Laud's influence, when inculcating, to the ire of the Puritans, a bow of reverence towards the altar, states that it does so "not upon any opinion of a corporal presence of Jesus Christ on the Holy Table or in mystical elements".[2] Yet Laud's theology was higher than that of the Ferrars, and their diocesan and warm friend Bishop Williams of Lincoln repudiated even the Eucharistic theology of Laud, in particular prohibiting the Laudian practice of placing the Communion table altarwise against the east wall. At Little Gidding, Communion was celebrated only once a month, as against the weekly celebration which is now normal even in Evangelical churches and which indeed Calvin would have

---

[1] These lines were not reprinted when the poem was re-published in *Steps to the Temple*.
[2] Bishop Goodman, on the threshold of the church, refused to subscribe these canons.

instituted in Geneva had not the secular authorities forbidden it
George Herbert does not ask even for monthly Communions
Ferrar even said that, if somehow Mass had been said in hi
house, he would pull down the room in which it had been said
a sentiment, surely, in harmony with William Crashaw':
"Monster of Transubstantiation".[1]

We must not then conclude from the elder Crashaw's violent
hatred of the Catholic Church, that he was hostile to the definitely
Anglican school of thought or disliked the established liturgy
and Church government. We should also notice an undercurrent
of conflict between his hatred of Popery and a genuine Christian
charity which shrank from the consequence he affirmed in the
more truculent mood of his will, that no Papist could be saved.[2]
For there are admissions, scarcely consistent, that Catholics, at
any rate simple lay folk, may after all be saved. And in a book
of devotional translations from Catholic sources, his *Manual
for True Catholics*, he explicitly states more than once that this
is the case. "Here followeth the means and manner how our
forefathers in the time of Popery prepared themselves to die:
by which it may appear that, though they were misled by the
crafty Romish clergy in divers errors and superstitions, yet in
the great point of the means of salvation they were of our
religion and were saved by it. Behold here our religion practised
in the most misty times of Popery: behold here the true Catholic
and ancient way to heaven." In the sermon preached before
the Virginia Company he grudgingly but honestly admits the
zeal shown by Catholics for the conversion of the heathen, greater,
it could not be denied, than that displayed by the Reformed
Churches. "If" he says, the Papists " . . . seek the Pope's and
their own glory why should not we seek God's? If they seek
God's glory," a supposition not denied, "we have cause to seek
it more than they: in such works we would go with them to
convert the heathen. . . . We must confess that in the last

[1] *Sermon preached at the Cross*, 13 *February* 1607.

[2] It must, however, be frankly admitted that at least the overwhelming majority of
Catholics, including the professional theologians, were convinced that no one who
died outside the visible Church could be saved; and moreover that their opinion was a
revealed truth taught by the Church. De Lugo's contrary opinion, to which von Hügel
recurred so often, was altogether exceptional. When the Benedictine martyr, Bl.
John Roberts, was awaiting execution at Tyburn, he turned to some felons about to be
hung with himself and told them: "We are all come hither to die, and, if you die in
the religion now professed in England, you shall *undoubtedly* perish everlastingly"
(CHALLONER, *Memoirs of Missionary Priests*, Ed. 1924, p. 318).

undred years the Papists, such is their government and such
heir devotion to their superiors, wherein we may worthily
earn of them, have sent many men to the West and East Indies
o preach Christ, which if they had done without other abomin-
ble idolatry and superstition their fact had been most honour-
ble."[1] The conflict of feeling which finds expression in these
wkward sentences is evident. "Some of you English Papists
re graced with great devotion in your kind."[2] Elsewhere
e calls Claudius Espencaeus, Doctor of the Sorbonne, "this
opish yet honest Bishop".[3] He even claims Cajetan, despite
is Cardinal's hat, as substantially a Lutheran, in his intention
f course a compliment.[4] To show the power of prayer he
ppeals to Henry V's words before the battle of Agincourt that
ictory was assured because "at this hour they are praying
or us in every church in England".[5] We should hardly have
xpected him to believe that the idolatrous devotions of Papists
ould have been so powerful with God.

Unfortunately the authorship is doubtful of a brochure which
he writer of the elder Crashaw's life in the *Dictionary of National
Biography* seems to accept as his. For, if it is from William
Crashaw's pen, it presents him in an attitude of Christian charity
nd impartial judgment, even where Catholics are concerned,
vhich it is not easy to reconcile with the usual tenor of his
tterances. It is a pamphlet published in 1623 based upon
nother by a writer named Goad: *The Fatal Vesper or a True
nd Punctual Relation of that lamentable and fearful Accident happening
n Sunday in the afternoon being 26 of October last by the Fall of a
Room in Blackfriars in which were assembled many people at a Sermon
hich was to be preached by Fr. Drury a Jesuit*. It bears only the
nitials W.C. Its text is Our Lord's words, "Except ye repent
e shall all likewise perish." Far from being the paean of triumph
ve might have expected, if it is by Crashaw, the writer warns
is readers against the judgment that the victims were peculiarly
inful. "Gentle reader," he writes, "whether Protestant or
apist, Reformed or Romish, thou seest an object presented unto
hy view full of pity and compassion. 'Judge not that ye be not

---

[1] *Sermon preached before the Virginia Company.*
[2] *Romish Forgeries and Falsifications.*
[3] *A Mittimus to the Jubilee at Rome or the Rates of the Pope's Custom House.*
[4] *Romish Forgeries and Falsifications.*
[5] *Sermon preached before the Virginia Company.*

judged.' Neither think you that are readers of this mournf
object that the men who perished thus together were great
sinners than yourselves, for unless ye repent ye shall likewi
perish." "The truth of this discourse is set forth according t
the best intelligence the author could procure" (in fact h
account is substantially taken from Goad's) "without leanin
partially either to the Protestant or Papist." The writer defen
himself against the charge of indifferentism in religion, a supe
fluous defence, surely, if he is William Crashaw. "Neith
inveigh against him because he doth not speak invectively again
the sufferers, for it is a case that deserves elegies, mournful ditti
rather than satires and invective speeches." And of the preache
a priest and a Jesuit to boot, he says, Father Drury, "was held b
the generality of our nation both Protestants and Papists wh
knew him and could make a true estimate of his virtues an
vices to be a man of good moral life and of a plausible and lau
able conversation"—a man in fact most unlike a delayed-actio
poisoner.

Frankly I am perplexed. It is difficult to think that such sent
ments came from a pen elsewhere so vitriolic against Papis
and Jesuits. On the other hand we have noticed, in work cer
tainly authentic, recognitions, however qualified, of Catholi
virtues and devout Catholics and Catholic hymns and devotio
are translated for the benefit of Protestant readers. We ma
therefore reasonably opine, though we cannot be certain, th
in view of the tragedy the genuinely and profoundly Christia
Crashaw overcame the No-Popery Crashaw. The writer in fa
shows a vein of tenderness which reminds us of the poet, probabl
at least, his son. If William Crashaw wrote this pamphlet th
fierce bigotry expressed in the previous year by his will ha
yielded under the influence of pity to a more charitable moo
Possibly the use of initials, for the first and last time, indicat
that the author was somewhat ashamed of his better self or a
least lacked the courage of his convictions. I might add that th
detailed account of the disaster, taken from Goad, is a vivid piec
of journalism, well worth reading for its own sake.

Not only is there no evidence that William Crashaw was
Puritan in the sense of a man so radically Protestant that he dis
liked the Anglican Prayer Book and the episcopal governmen
of the Anglican Church; there is positive evidence to the contrary

n his Virginia sermon he exhorts the Council: "Suffer no Brownists nor factious separatists. Let them keep their conventicles elsewhere", in which he was more zealous for Anglicanism than the treasurer of the Council, Sir Edwin Sandys, who would have permitted the Mayflower Puritans to settle in the Colony. In one of the poison sermons he says, "Despise not the Church of God nor the congregations of the Saints, run not with the schismatics into corners and conventicles." In a sermon preached at the Cross (Paul's Cross) on February 13th 1607, he joins Brownists with Papists in his condemnation. He defends the Church of England against the Brownists "as lawful and holy", "because it brings salvation". It is approved, he urges, by the Calvinist Churches of the Continent. "Tell us not of France, Scotland, Geneva, Zurich, Basle—for they be all ours and not yours: they do all approve us as a glorious Church and condemn you as factious and schismatical. What remains for you to go unto but unto your own corners and conventicles where you are your own carvers, your own judges, your own approvers, but have not one Church in Christendom to approve you." The Brownists so vigorously condemned would later under the title Independents (today Congregationalists) dominate English religion for a few years under Cromwell. Crashaw, it is true, does not condemn the other influential, and at this time by far the stronger, form of Puritanism, Presbyterianism. On the contrary, as we have just seen, he speaks of the Presbyterian Churches abroad in terms of the warmest eulogy. But there is nothing to make us believe that he therefore wished to substitute in England the Presbyterian for the Episcopalian form of Church government. The philosopher and apologist of Anglicanism and the defender of her polity against the Presbyterians, the judicious Hooker, did not unchurch the foreign Presbyterians. Nor in his view is episcopal ordination indispensable by Divine ordinance for a true Church and valid ministry. Nor did King James unchurch the continental Protestant Calvinist bodies for their Presbyterian government. For he sent an official delegation to the Dutch synod of Dort which, rushing in where the Pope refrained from pronouncement, defined and imposed under penalties an uncompromising form of predestinarianism. But no one can question the attachment to Episcopacy of the author of the saying "No Bishop, no King." When, about 1643, Ferrar's niece, Mary Collet, paid a lengthy visit to a merchant in Leyden, there is no reason to suppose that she refused to worship in the Dutch Calvinist churches. Laud, it is true, did unchurch the non-episcopal churches. But this was an unusual and still an extreme position to adopt. William Crashaw was as faithful and devoted an Anglican as any Laudian could be. If therefore by a Puritan we mean one for whom the Anglican hierarchy and liturgy were too Popish, he was most emphatically not a Puritan. In his study of Crashaw, Dr. Mario Praz concludes that, because he had contributed appreciative verses to William Crashaw's *Manual for True Catholics*, Benjamin Lany, Master of Pembroke College, Cambridge, Richard's college, must have been converted from an original Puritanism to his later Laudianism.[1] On the contrary, Lany's friendship with the elder Crashaw, and his appreciation of his most Catholic work, is a further indication that the latter, though not a Laudian, was no Puritan, but a devoted and zealous Anglican. Nor is it without significance in this connexion that Richard went up to the college over which his father's High Anglican friend presided or indeed that the guardians appointed by his father's will sent him to a school, Charterhouse, markedly Royalist and Anglican.

Moreover, William Crashaw rejects private judgment in religion in favour of ecclesiastical authority. The principle at any rate of the Church's doctrinal authority, from which the younger Crashaw would later draw the logical conclusion, was first learned from his father. "Woe to him," William preached, "that despiseth his godly Pastor and learned teacher, for he despiseth the means and minister of his salvation, and the very dust that cleaves to the minister's feet shall be a witness . . . to testify the due deserved damnation of such caitiffs."[2]

And in his *Manual for True Catholics* he translates with full approval for his readers' use questions taken from mediaeval forms for use at a deathbed—one of which he attributes to St. Anselm, the other to Gerson. "Dost thou believe all the principal articles of faith and all that is contained in the whole body of scripture according to the exposition of the Catholic and orthodoxial Doctors of the Holy Church? And dost thou detest all heresies and errors and superstitions condemned or reproved by the Church and art thou glad that thou diest in the

---

[1] *Secentismo e Marinismo in Inghilterra*, p. 165. [2] *The Parable of Poison*.

faith of Christ and unity and obedience of thy mother the Church? It is a sign that the dying man will be saved if he believe the articles of Christian faith as many as are determined by the Church." Here the translator seems to have in mind not so much the common faith of the Reformed Churches, though he would not of course exclude it, as the faith of the primitive Church such as he conceived it to have been before it was clouded over by the "mists", to use his own term, of Popery, and such as it continued, a saving and indefectible doctrine and faith beneath these obscuring and distorting vapours. And because this essential faith has been continuously preserved he remarks, "How truly Christ performed His promise, namely that the gates of hell should not prevail against the true faith, for, so we see, that in the vilest times this faith hath been preserved." Evidently a regard for ecclesiastical authority and ancient tradition must have been early impressed on his son's mind to be developed later on lines so alien to his father's.

Moreover, as King James's dictum pithily expressed it, the Puritan was on the side of Parliament as against the monarchy. William Crashaw speaks, like his son later, the language of a fervent Royalism. "God", he says, has shewn his favour to the Virginia Company ". . . by inclining the hearts of our mighty King and noble Prince [Henry] to make themselves fathers and founders of this plantation and thereby shewing themselves new Constantines or Charles the Greats. The ages to come will style them by the glorious names of James the Great and Great Henry." And he dedicates his Paul's Cross sermon to Prince Henry. "Go forward, princely Solomon, and walk still in the ways of David your kingly father." We are reminded of his son's poetic tributes to Henrietta Maria and her offspring, her "nest of phoenixes".

William Crashaw has left a statement of his positive beliefs, a catechism he compiled: *Milk for Babes or a Country Catechism made plain and easy to the Capacity of the Simplest.* It ran into several editions. Its most interesting feature is perhaps the treatment of justification and sanctification. While enunciating the fundamental Protestant doctrine of justification by faith, the author proceeds to correct it in such fashion as to reach in substance, though not in theological statement, the Catholic position. We must be saved, he writes, "by a special saving and justifying faith by which a man believes his own reconciliation with God and salvation by Christ". But he adds shortly:

> This does not suffice for salvation. We cannot be saved unless we be sanctified as well as justified. Q. What is the work of sanctification? A. A work of the Holy Ghost by which such as are redeemed are made new creatures and enabled to do good and holy works. Q. How does the Holy Ghost sanctify? A. By His own work and blessing, the Word of God and Sacraments. Q. What are the parts of sanctification? A. Two, mortification and vivification. Q. What is mortification? A. The killing of our corruption and weakening of sin in us. Q. What is vivification? A. The quickening of grace and holiness in our souls. Q. How are these wrought in us? A. By the virtue of Christ, His death and Resurrection applied unto us in the Word and Sacraments.

Evidently there is no question here of being saved by a faith in Christ's merits imputed externally. Those alone are saved who are sanctified by an interior holiness made evident by good works. The ultra-Puritan Rous, it may be added, expresses in other terms what amounts to the same doctrine. For he identifies justification with sanctification. Whatever their theological formulas, Protestants did not in fact believe that an adult, whatever his conduct might be, could be saved by a merely external imputation of Our Lord's holiness, by simply believing that Christ is his Saviour.

The Puritans disliked kneeling to receive Communion. When they could they received it seated, a posture against which the Anglican poet Vaughan protests indignantly. "Some sit to Thee and eat Thy Body as their kitchen meat." On this point also William Crashaw was opposed to them. "What gesture," he asks in this catechism, "is fittest to receive in? A. That which is most humble because then we shew the Lord's death."

The Puritans, like later Protestants, whether Anglican or Nonconformist, disliked auricular Confession. Crashaw, faithful to the teaching of the Prayer Book, was in favour of it, provided it were not obligatory. In one of his many anti-Catholic writings he says: "Touching confession to man, howsoever God's Church knows no reason" (notice once more the ecclesiastical appeal) "to enjoin it to be practised by all Christians, as is the Pope's auricular confession, because it is simply necessary to confess to God, but to man not so, yet our Church and doctrine not only allow but advise and *exhort all men* to use it even to man for their consolation or direction when they find cause. And we deny not but it may be of great use and hath ever been practised in God's true Church by such as tendered the quiet state of their own souls. And we doubt not but many do grievously burden their consciences and carry sore troubled and full heavy hearts about them, because they do not open their minds and discover the spiritual state of their souls unto their godly Pastors whose duty by our doctrine is not only readily, lovingly and patiently to hear them but with all his [sic] power and best skill to direct, advise and comfort them and faithfully to keep secret whatever is thus in confession made known to them as ministers of God." Unfortunately, however, thoughts of Father Garnet and the Gunpowder Conspirators made him add that the magistrate may be informed if some mischief is intended.[1] It is a little surprising in view of the writer's devotion to Anglican doctrine that in spite of the plain language of the Prayer Book conferring on priests power to remit or retain sin and providing in the Visitation of the Sick a Catholic form of absolution, he treats Confession here as wholly a matter of direction and says nothing of absolution. I can hardly think, however, that he would have refused to employ the Prayer Book formula. And in any case the value he attaches to private Confession aligns him with the Anglicans as against the Puritans.

His attitude towards Our Lady seems to me very much the same as that which inspired those verses of Herbert's in which he says how gladly he would have prayed to her, had it been lawful to do so. He allows that "she is the most blessed of all Saints". "This blessedness far be it from us to impeach, and who would not yield her all blessedness and honour that a creature may have of whom God vouchsafed to take the flesh of man. If any Protestants," he continues, "have seemed to speak slightingly, it was not done in any the least contempt of her but with zeal they bear to the honour of their Saviour."[2] And translating from a Latin hymn he calls her the Mother of God.

[1] *A Mittimus to the Jubilee at Rome or the Rates of the Pope's Custom House.*
[2] *The Bespotted Jesuit.*

God to God and not to th' other [Nature]
Was Father but Mary to both was Mother.[1]

But oddly his language here departs from orthodoxy in the opposite direction so to speak. For he speaks here of Mary as Mother of Our Lord's Godhead.

Bishop Andrewes had supplemented the Prayer Book offices by a form for the dedication of churches. William Crashaw is with him in this. "Our religion," he writes, "doth solemnly and decently dedicate churches to God and useth them not for God's worship till they be set apart by solemn consecration."[2] It was just such a solemn consecration, probably according to Bishop Andrewes' rite, of St. Catherine Cree which brought down the wrath of Prynne on the head of Archbishop Laud, and this reverence for churches was remote from the fashion in which they were treated by the Puritans. But it was in harmony with his son's interest in church restoration as expressed in his Shelford verses.

When the church at Little Gidding was restored to serve as a chapel for Ferrar's community the pulpit and the reading-desk were made of equal height "to show that prayer was an ordinance of equal value with preaching". The High Anglican Shelford complained in his *Discourses* that "the beauty of preaching hath preached away the beauty of holiness; for if men may have a sermon, prayer and church service . . . may sit abroad in the cold". And Laud in his diary congratulated himself on obtaining from King Charles a promise not to come into his chapel, as his father had regularly done, just to hear the sermon, either at the end of prayers or to break them off. On this point the elder Crashaw was a Laudian. In fact he goes further than Ferrar's equalization of prayer and preaching. He gives precedence to prayer. In the *Milk for Babes* Catechism he says that public worship is "*first and chiefly* to call on God by prayer and thanksgiving. *Secondly*, to hear God's word read and preached." He praises two London churches for daily prayers[3] and hopes they will be practised in Virginia.[4] "They" (the Catholic regulars), he wrote, "all rise at midnight both men and women and go to their service in their churches, the devotion whereof should be honourable in our eyes, if it were not tainted with such gross

---

[1] *Manual for True Catholics.*
[2] *Sermon Preached at the Cross.*
[3] ibid.
[4] *Sermon preached before the Virginia Company.*

superstition and accompanied with so many miserable and monstrous inconveniences."[1] Since the night-watches at Little Gidding were not accompanied by these Catholic ceremonies and devotions, these words amount to an anticipated approval of them[2] and therefore of his son's share in them during his visits to Gidding, as also of his nightly prayer at Cambridge, where "in St. Mary's Church near St. Peter's college—like a primitive saint he offered more prayers in the night than others usually offer in the day".[3] Indeed in this fundamental point of religion from first to last father and son were in entire agreement, and the latter had no doubt learned from the former, namely, in the value they attached to prayer and their confidence in its power. God, the elder Crashaw preached, had blessed the Virginia plantation, "by moving all good men to pray for it. An enterprise so prayed for cannot fail, as holy old Anselm" (a curious slip, but proof that he could call a Catholic Archbishop holy) "said of young Augustine, a soul that cost his mother so many prayers cannot perish." He continues with that unexpected and inconsistent appeal to the efficacious prayers offered for the victory of Henry V's army. He concludes in an eloquent passage: "The power of the whole army of Angels" (he had been insisting on their protection of the enterprise) "be unto God but as a drop of water to the sea and the might of all men be inferior to the power of one Angel, yet the prayers of the good man are able to shake hell and make the devil tremble." In the *Milk for Babes* Catechism the question is asked "Why do you call prayer a chief work of piety? A. For two causes. First, prayer sanctifies all the rest. Again the rest are but sometimes to be done but prayer continually. Q. How can we always pray? A. We may always lift up our hearts to God and that is the chief thing in prayer." And in a beautiful Catholic prayer for the dying translated in the *Manual*, Our Lord is asked to "make the dying man partaker of all thy [? the] prayers and good deeds done in the whole Church". The translator not only bears witness here to the value of prayer, but without realizing it accepts the Catholic doctrine of the communion of all members of the Church in the prayer and good works of the saints. Here, as elsewhere, one is conscious of a

[1] *A Mittimus to the Jubilee at Rome.*

[2] Still living when the Ferrars settled at Gidding, he may have approved their rule of life, may even have assisted with advice. See below, pp. 178-9.

[3] Preface to *Steps to the Temple.*

conflict in William Crashaw between his virulent hatred of the
Catholic Church and a devotion, akin to his son's, which chafes
subconsciously against the theological barriers his Protestantism
imposed. From this point of view Richard Crashaw is not the
opposite of William but his emancipation and fulfilment. In the
impressionable and docile years of childhood his father taught
the poet to love and practise prayer. Had he given him the
complete Catholic creed with all its inexhaustible wealth of
religious truth, without the life of prayer, he would have given
him less. For it is for the sake of prayer that the Church exists.

On no point have I discovered any divergence of doctrine
between William Crashaw and the Ferrars or their friend George
Herbert. Neither the Ferrars nor Herbert belonged to the
advanced wing of Laudians. Whereas Dr. Owen, in the porch
he added to St. Mary's, Oxford, set up the statue of Our Lady
which remains to this day, Nicholas Ferrar refused to put into
his chapel even a stained-glass window representing the crucifixion, though he would, he said, have left it had it been there
already. Whereas at his trial Laud refused to state plainly that
the Pope is Antichrist and like the youthful Richard Crashaw
deprecated such invective, calculated, he said, to repel Papists
rather than win them over, Ferrar, as we have seen, held it as a
fundamental article of his creed. He cannot have liked Crashaw's
verses. Presumably the friends debated the point when the poet
visited Gidding. For in spite of his close friendship with the
family and his frequent visits Crashaw had already gone beyond
his friends in the Catholic direction. While still their Anglican
friend and fellow worshipper, he had paraphrased hymns and
offices distinctively Catholic, and had composed a poem to honour
the Assumption, a doctrine also affirmed by the Laudian Antony
Stafford in his little book of devotion to Mary, *The Female Glory*.
In so far as he had departed from Nicholas Ferrar, Richard had
departed from his dead father. But between Nicholas and his
father there was no significant difference of doctrine or practice.

Nor is this all. I have had occasion to quote from William
Crashaw's sermon before the Virginia Council in which he
displays the warmest interest in the colony and above all as a
missionary centre to evangelize the Indians. It was preached in
the first years of the Company and I have unfortunately failed to
discover evidence of a later connexion between Crashaw and the

Company. But it is, to say the least, most unlikely that he lost interest in an undertaking for which he was so enthusiastic and from which he expected so much. If, however, he remained in touch with the Council he must have been in touch with the Ferrars, the devout city merchant, the elder Nicholas Ferrar and his sons John and Nicholas. For the elder Ferrar was a shareholder in the Company, and John a member of the Council, later deputy treasurer. And the Council met every week in Ferrar's "great parlour". When Nicholas returned from abroad in 1618 he became at first an unofficial secretary to the Council, later in turn a member of the Council and deputy treasurer. Finally he took a leading part in the unsuccessful defence of the Council against King James, when that monarch, instead of continuing to play the rôle assigned him by the preacher, of a Constantine or Charles the Great, turned against the Council and finally revoked its patent. These events could hardly have left unconcerned so devoted a Virginian as William Crashaw. Moreover, the administrative policy pursued by the Council, which made ample provision for the Church in the new colony and founded a missionary college, was precisely that urged in his sermon. We are surely, therefore, justified in concluding—though we cannot to my knowledge strictly prove it—that William Crashaw was a friend of the Ferrars, visited their house and supported their Virginian policy. And if this, as we may presume, was the case, his son did not make the acquaintance of Nicholas and John Ferrar for the first time through his Anglican *milieu* at Cambridge, but long before, as a boy in his father's home, so that it was to his father that he owed his introduction to them. The family at Gidding is generally supposed to have helped him along the road which eventually led him to the allegiance of his father's bogey, the Pope. The belief is, I am convinced, mistaken. In fact the influence of Little Gidding did not draw him forward but held him back. As we have seen, he had already gone beyond Nicholas Ferrar in the Catholic direction. The attraction undoubtedly exercised by the devotion of the Gidding household which exceeded the practice of so many Catholic religious houses, weighed with him no doubt as possibly the most powerful, certainly the most striking, argument that, in spite of the aggressive Protestantism which already hurt him sorely, the Church of England must be a province of God's true Church and his spiritual mother. For she could appeal to the undeniable mark of her children's holiness.

It may be added that on a point where the elder Crashaw seems to us pre-eminently Puritan and agreed with Prynne against Laud—his fanatical hatred of the theatre—his view was shared by Nicholas Ferrar, who from his deathbed ordered a holocaust of the poetry and drama he had collected when still in the world, but had put away for years. When he thinks of the Quarto Shakespeares and other priceless Elizabethan and Jacobean plays and collections of verse which went up in flames that November day in 1637, the bibliophile finds it hard to forgive this disastrously misguided zeal.

For Puritanism of this kind was far from being bound up with the doctrinal variety. It was shared later by the Non-juror Collier and the Non-juring mystic Law. Nor is there any reason to suppose that the poet ever parted company with his father on this point. For this hostility to the players was entertained by perhaps the majority of devout Catholics. Bossuet would have heartily agreed with William Crashaw's denunciations of the stage.

In another way unintended, or rather contrary to his intention, the elder Crashaw may well have set his son's feet on the path to Rome. As his writings prove, he was well acquainted with Catholic literature both theological and devotional. In this matter indeed there is a striking contrast between the older English Protestantism of the seventeenth century, Anglican or Puritan, and the later English Protestantism whose heyday was the nineteenth century. The latter, hating and despising the Catholic Church, refused to look at her.[1] The former, with equal hostility, fixed its gaze upon her, and though primarily, by no means exclusively, to find fault. In a secondhand bookshop I dipped into a Protestant attempt at a *Summa Theologica* by the minister of a Somerset parish during the Commonwealth. I was amazed at his wide knowledge not only of the great Catholic doctors of earlier times such as St. Thomas, but of the later theologians, such as Suarez, Banez and Bellarmine. When Cromwell's favourite chaplain, the Independent Sterry, retired during the Plague to a friend's house, he took with him a few

---

[1] This of course is but a rough generalisation. Many nineteenth-century English Protestants were well acquainted with Catholic teaching and literature.

elected books whose names he listed. The list is headed "Thom. Aquin. Summes." Sterry was, I grant, an exceptional figure. A Platonist whose religion is aesthetic in colouring, he was obviously attracted on one side of his temperament to the Catholic religion —the stumbling-block in fact being authority and law. But I have found the same acquaintance with Catholic theology among those whose dislike of the Church was more wholehearted. And, as I have just said, it was not used solely for fault-finding. Culverwell, the Cambridge Platonist, discusses the respective merits of the Thomist view which places man's final beatitude primarily in the understanding and the Scotist which places it in the will. In matters indeed on which Protestant theology agreed with Catholic—in the judgment of Abbé Constant more than half the Thirty-nine Articles "are in conformity with Catholic doctrine"[1]—the Protestants were ready to make use of Catholic theologians. Rous, for example, a Presbyterian first, finally an independent, in his *Heavenly Academy*, appeals to a passage from the *Summa* on the higher light of grace superadded to the light of nature. The predestinarian Bradwardine was widely read.

Throughout the period, works of Catholic spirituality and devotion fed and influenced Protestant devotion. A bowdlerized and unacknowledged version of Parsons' *Directory*, though it was the work of a Jesuit particularly obnoxious to Protestants and widely disliked even by his fellow-Catholics, enjoyed a considerable success. In the last year of the Commonwealth a publisher in St. Paul's Churchyard published Serenus Cressy's edition of Hilton's *Scale of Perfection*. William Crashaw, it is true, denounced the reading of Catholic books if the Protestant answers were not read.[2] But his own bookshelves were well furnished with Catholic books. And, as we have seen, he translated Catholic devotions for the edification and use of Protestants. A boy with Richard Crashaw's alert intelligence and strong religious interest presumably made his first acquaintance with Catholic theology in his father's library.

In another way the elder Crashaw influenced his son, namely as a poet. In his *Manual for True Catholics* he translates a number of mediaeval Catholic hymns. True his verse is pedestrian and, normally, remote from his son's manner. But the fact remains that William set the example of translating Catholic hymns.

---

[1] *Reformation in England*, Vol. II, pp. 283–4.   [2] *The Parable of Poison*.

There is a hymn to the Father, the translation of which opens:

> First and last One God divine
> All men's God as well as mine.

"All men's God" is a felicitous addition by the translator.
From a hymn to the Son I quote:

> Temporal yet time defying,
> Ever living yet once dying,
> He rose and so to heaven ascended,
> Whence He shall come, when time doth call,
> Though judged Himself, to judge us all.

Another piece is entitled "A Devout and Holy Prayer":

> In this sea of dread and doubt
> My poor bark is tossed about
> With storms and pirates far and wide,
> Death and woes on every side.
> Come thou steersman ever blest,
> Calm these winds that me molest,
> Chase these ruthless pirates hence
> And shew me some safe residence.

Continuing this translation of a hymn by Hildebert he comes
to the well-known verses about heaven: "Me receptet Sion
illa":

> In Sion lodge me (Lord) for pity
> Sion, David's kingly city
> Built by Him that's only good,
> Whose gates are of the Crosse's wood,
> Whose dwellers fear none but the Lord,
> Whose keys are Christ's undoubted word,
> Whose walls are stone, strong, quick and bright,
> Whose keeper is the Lord of light.
> Here the light doth never cease
> Endless spring and endless peace.
> Here is music heaven filling,
> Sweetness evermore distilling.

We have noticed Richard's devotion to music, and the "sweetness", though not sentimentality, of his devotion.

Another piece is entitled "A Holy Meditation of Man's Misery
and God's Mercy".

> But oh humanity
> With how great vanity
> Art thou betost:
> To dote in care
> On things that are
> So quickly lost.
> If to thy fear
> The judge appear
> With angry face,
> Know He will lose
> Not one of those
> That beg His grace.

William also translated separately a product of the grimmer
aspect of mediaeval religion: *The Complaint or Dialogue betwixt
the Soul and Body of a Damned Man supposed to be written by St.
Bernard from a Nightly Vision of his.* It is not from St. Bernard's
pen. It achieves a measure of unpleasant force which the translation certainly has not lost. This is shown by comparison with the
original Latin, printed, as also in the case of the hymns, together
with the translation. In turn the soul and the body of the
departed blames his fate on the other.

> In silence of a winter's night
> A sleeping yet awaking sprite,
> A lifeless body to my sight
> Methought appeared thus addight.

.   .   .   .   .

> Wast but yesterday the world was thine
> And all the country stood at thy devotion,
> Thy train that followed thee?
> Oh, doleful alteration.

.   .   .   .   .

G

> Thou art not now
> Begirt with troops of friends.
> The flower of all thy beauty
> Lies in dust.
> The bands of every love
> Do here take end.
> Yea, thine own wife
> Now thinks all tears unjust.

The Latin jingles intolerably for so aweful a theme:

> O felix conditio
> Pecorum brutorum
> Cadunt cum corporibus
> Spiritus eorum.

It is the rhythm of the famous Goliardic verse,

> Mihi est propositum
> In taberna mori.

The translator with poetic feeling has substituted a more appropriate cadence:

> Happy are ye brute beasts, happy your state,
> You wholly die at once and only rot.

And at the beginning and the end he has altered to good purpose his own metre.

But the father's poetry approaches his son's more closely when he is translating to attack the original. One of his outbursts against the Jesuits, *The bespotted Jesuit whose Gospel is full of blasphemy against the blood of Christ*, consists largely of invective against a poem by a Flemish Jesuit, Bonarsch, addressed to Our Lady of Hal and the Child Jesus. It is a florid poem and we need not be anti-Catholic to find it distasteful. The desire spiritually to suck Our Lady's milk or, unless transmuted for the imagination into the wine of the chalice, the blood flowing from Christ's wounds, jars on my sensibility. But one should recognize that devotion is inevitably and rightly coloured by the taste of the period and environment to which it belongs and to which it must make its appeal. And the poem is in harmony with the devotional taste of Baroque Catholicism.

Precisely the same devotion is to be found in a contemporary emblem book: Fr. Hoyer's *Flammulae Amoris S. P. Augustini*—he was an Augustinian, not a "bespotted Jesuit". He depicts the saint on his knees receiving on his haloed head two streams, blood from Our Lord's side, milk from Our Lady's breast. And he expatiates on this emblem in two lengthy poems, the former stuffed with allusions to classical mythology, the latter in the same vein of devotional luxuriance as Bonarsch's poem.

To denounce the poem William Crashaw had to translate it. He did so in verse which, if, like most contemporary translation, it is not always an accurate rendering of the original, reproduces faithfully its substance and style—once more he has printed the Latin—so successfully, indeed, that one might have thought the translation the work not of an enemy but an admirer. It is difficult to avoid the impression that the poet did in fact admire subconsciously the poetry the theologian condemned. Indeed he may even consciously have relished the poetry, even the taste, and hated only the theology. And—this is most significant—it is the type of poetry which in his son's hands reached its highest achievement. That is to say, there is a poetic inheritance of the son from the father, conditioned perhaps by a temperamental affinity. I shall quote sufficient of the translation to enable students of the poet to judge whether my belief is justified.

> My thoughts are at a stand; of milk and blood
> Delights of breast and side which yields most good,
> And say, when on thy teats mine eyes I cast
> O Lady, of thy breast I beg a taste.
> But if mine eyes upon Thy wounds do glide
> Then, Jesu, I had rather suck thy side.
> Long have I mused, nor know I where to rest:
> For with my right hand I will grasp Thy breast
> (If so I may presume) as for the wounds
> With left I'll catch them; thus my zeal abounds:
> And of the milk and blood in mixture make
> The sovereignest cordial simple soul can take.
> These wounds corrupted ulcers mundifies [sic]
> Which none can cure unless he cauterize.

In a later edition the translator is at pains to correct this ugly
and ungrammatical couplet, the retouching of a poet careful for
the quality of his work, not of a controversialist hot after his
prey.

These breasts the fainting Ishmael well would cherish
Whom Sara scorned and Agar could not nourish.
Youngling that in Thy Mother's arms art playing
Sucking her breast sometimes and sometimes straying
Why dost Thou view me with a look of scorn?
Tis forceless envy that gainst thee is borne.

This is a mistranslation. The meaning is that envy in the
sense of grudging niggardliness is powerless to touch heaven,
cannot exist there.

Oh, hast Thou said, being angry at my sin
Dost thou desire the teats my food lies in?
I will not, oh I dare not, golden child:
My mind from fear is not so far exiled.
But one, even one poor drop I do implore
From thy right hand or side; I ask no more.
If neither, from Thy left hand let one fall,
Nay from Thy foot rather than none at all.
But ah I thirst: ah drought my breath does smother
Quench me with blood sweet Son, with milk good Mother
Say to Thy Mother: See my brother's thirst
Mother your milk will ease him at the first.
Say to Thy Son: Behold thy brother's bands
Sweet Son Thou hast his ransom in Thy hands.
Ah when shall I with these [the milk and blood] be satisfied,
When shall I swim in joys of breast and side.

William Crashaw's polemic, forcing poetry into the logic of
the theological textbook, concludes that this Jesuit "anointed by
the devil with the oil of mischief above all his fellows" teaches
that Mary's milk is more precious than her Son's blood—if I am
denied the former give me *at least* the latter. A less prejudiced
view would have seen that the certainly ill-judged language
meant no more than that the blood is necessary for our salvation

the milk a superabundant grace and consolation. But we can well believe that the imagination of Richard, eight years old when the second edition appeared, was struck by a poem held up to him as particularly naughty, and the luxuriance of its devotion to which his father's translation did justice, made, if only an unrecognized, appeal.

Did not the impression revive when in his paraphrase of the *Stabat Mater* he wrote:

> O let me suck the wine
> So long of this chaste vine,
> Till drunk of the dear wounds I be
> A lost thing to the world as it to me . . .?

"I swim in joys" is thoroughly in Richard's vein with his predilection for images drawn from water or other liquids, tears, wine, milk, blood. "Golden child", "Youngling that in thy Mother's arms art playing"—there surely we catch something of Richard's manner.

Indeed, his editor, Mr. Martin, points out that Richard's "My golden Lad" echoes his father's "Golden child" and "A drop, one drop craved" by his Dives, his father's "but one, even one, poor drop".[1]

Undoubtedly Crashaw was indebted to his father not only in his religion and prayer but as a poet.

---

[1] *Crashaw's Poetical Works*, Clarendon Press Edition, 1927, pp. 434, 435.

CHAPTER IX

DOM AUGUSTINE BAKER

Augustine Baker's life was, for the most part, such as he wished it to be, a life of retirement and seclusion. Not for him the martyr's crown or a prominent part in the apostolate of England. And though, over a period of many years, he was a prolific writer, he does not rank high as a writer of English. His style, though lucid and with a charm of its own, is of no outstanding merit. It is too diffuse, too rambling, too formless.

Even in his special field, contemplative prayer and mystical theology, Baker is not among the supreme masters. When he wrote, he had experienced of the mystical prayer which he terms passive contemplation only a single ecstasy. When towards the end of his life he entered permanently into this state of prayer he had long ceased to write. Of the summits of prayer he says little. His concern is with the "ordinary way" of contemplative prayer.

Nevertheless, no Catholic teacher of the spiritual life has a more valuable message for us than Baker. Others have been far greater, and to all appearance holier than he. But not one among them is a better guide to the life of prayer. By all but a tiny minority, the highest states of mystical prayer can be studied only for their witness to God's glory, to his achievement and manifestation in souls, as matter for adoration and a testimony to the truths of faith, not as having any practical bearing on our spiritual life. Moreover, to read the works of the great mystics, a Ruysbroeck or St. John of the Cross, for practical instruction, is not without its dangers. Guides to the supreme mystical union, they demand the utter renunciation indispensable to its attainment and describe the spiritual purgatory through which those alone can and must pass who are invited to enter the earthly paradise, which, like Dante's, is situated above purgatory.

As Baker shows, these sufferings are not given to souls of lower call who have not received the strength to endure them.

heir description, therefore, if regarded with personal application, nay frighten souls from the life of prayer.

Baker, while faithful to the principles worked out in their utmost rigour by a St. John of the Cross (whose works he had read), tempers their application to the weakness of the majority, even of contemplatives. Hence his writings can be put with safety and profit into the hands of any who are invited to contemplation.

The snow-clad peaks climbed by St. John of the Cross are likely to deter those who are not Alpine climbers of the spirit, so that they remain comfortably seated in their hotel garden. The more accessible uplands to which Baker summons us, the downs, or at most the high moors of his native country, encourage even those of moderate vigour to climb after him.

And if there be any called to even higher ascents, they will find his doctrine in conformity with the sublimer teaching they will need, a stage on their way to the Alpine peaks.

In this moderation, this consideration for human weakness, which nevertheless is never false to the immutable, because intrinsic, principles which determine man's union with God, Baker is true both to the spirit of his order—the discretion which renders St. Benedict's rule the masterpiece of wisdom that it is—and to the tradition of English mysticism.

His doctrine of contemplation follows closely the anonymous fourteenth-century *Cloud of Unknowing* on which he commented chapter by chapter. He also made considerable use of Walter Hilton's *Scale of Perfection*. He is thus in the direct line of pre-Reformation English mystics, as the Congregation to which he belonged is in the direct line of mediaeval English monasticism.

Baker's life is the record of his spiritual doctrine as lived by himself and taught to others. External events are of secondary importance. Its best source, as regards his life of prayer, is the disclosures he made under a thin veil of anonymity in his commentary on the *Cloud*, the *Secretum*. Making use of these, Serenus Cressy wrote his life, published for the first time a few years ago together with a shorter life by another Benedictine contemporary, Dom Peter Salvin. A third life by Dom Leander Pritchard has been published by the Catholic Record Society and with it an autobiographical fragment covering his earlier life.

Baker was born at Abergavenny in 1575, the thirteenth child of William Baker, Lord Abergavenny's steward. His mother Maud was the daughter of Lewis ap John, Vicar of Abergavenny, born however before the marriage of the clergy was first permitted in the reign of Edward VI. His baptismal name was David. His parents had conformed with no particular enthusiasm to the Established Church. He was educated at Christ's Hospital, London, and at Broadgates Hall, Oxford. He was then called to the bar, working with an elder brother.

Though his fastidious temperament kept him from gross vices, he lost hold of religion and even doubted the existence of God. On his brother's death, his father recalled him home and obtained for him the post of Recorder of Abergavenny. A project of marriage, however, fell through. In the year 1600, as he rode home absent-mindedly, he suddenly found that his horse had taken him onto the middle of a high and narrow footbridge over a mountain stream, the Monnow, where he could neither go forward nor turn. In this extremity "he framed such an internal resolution as this: 'If ever I escape this danger I will believe there is a God who hath more care of my life and safety than I have had of His love and worship.' Immediately he found his horse's head turned by no means that he could discover and the danger escaped." This brought him back to a serious practice of religion and to study the controversy between the Protestant and Catholic religions. The result was his conversion. At his first confession "there sprang up a desire of spiritual perfection to be purchased with the loss of all sensual pleasures and abandoning all secular designs." It was not long before he had converted his mother and sister.

Desirous of embracing the religious life, he met in London some English monks affiliated to the Italian Cassinese congregation. He went out to Italy and was clothed, taking the name Augustine, at the monastery of St. Justina in Padua on May 27th 1605.[1] Here he began the practice of mental prayer, his first "conversion". Knowing of no other method than meditation, little adapted to his temper, he soon found himself a prey to aridity and gave up mental prayer entirely. As his health was bad, his superiors sent him home, when still a novice, to his native air. Though he had intended to travel slowly and visit places of

---

[1] The feast of his patron, the Apostle of England.

interest, a powerful impulse made him travel post-haste, so that
he arrived in time to procure his father's deathbed reconciliation
with the Church. He made his profession in London. At this
time the English Congregation was restored, or rather continued,
by the affiliation to it and Westminster Abbey of two Cassinese
monks by the last surviving monk of Westminster, Dom Sigebert
Buckley. Though there is no doubt of this affiliation, its time
and circumstances are reported very differently by those in a
position to know the facts and with no motive for misrepresenting
them—an instructive warning against overconfidence in historical
details.

Dom Baker joined this revived Congregation, and when later
in 1619 it was fully organized, he became a monk of Dieulouard
Abbey in Lorraine, the parent of Ampleforth. Surprisingly,
however, he never lived there, though he spent later many years
at Douay, the parent of Downside. This great light of English
Benedictinism may therefore be claimed by both houses.

Two years later (1608) he returned to the practice of mental
prayer, his second "conversion", though in the *Secretum* he treats
it as his first, and after a few months was raised to "passive
contemplation", an ecstasy produced by "a speaking of God to
the soul". It lasted at most a quarter of an hour. He believed that
this rapid spiritual advance was assisted by the mortification of his
inability to satisfy his hunger without very serious effects to his
digestion. With a man's appetite he could digest no more than
a small child. Later in life his digestion became normal, though
his health was never robust. This ecstasy made his prayer "far
purer, far easier, less painful to nature and more abstract from
sense" than before, "yea, it wrought a stability or perfect settled-
ness of prayer". It also produced an interior illumination whereby
he understood the meaning of spiritual books. And it replaced
fear of death by an eagerness to die. Further, it gave him a personal assurance of the truth of Catholic doctrine. "I would tell
you of the wonderful proof and satisfaction that a soul hath of the
verities of Christian religion by one of the said passive contemplations . . . The soul most clearly seeth that all is most assuredly
true that in such work is manifested or told unto her, as are the
verities and mysteries of Christianity. O happy evidence of our
belief. No thanks to them that believe after such a sight. A man
may say that God is not beholden to them for believing that

which they have so clearly, evidently and manifestly, as it were, seen with their eyes and handled with their hands. Such sights of the soul are far more clear than are the sights or feelings of our outward senses."[1]

This apprehension of Catholic dogma, bound up, no doubt, with a penetration of its spiritual significance, is not a universal or even a normal feature of passive contemplation. It is, however, an occasional accompaniment. Malaval, the blind mystic of Marseilles, speaks of it in the same terms as Baker.

This contemplation was, however, followed by the desolation inevitable in the higher mystical way. Baker, having no experienced director, and not having yet studied the mystical theologians who treat of it, did not understand its nature or the attitude he should adopt. And at the same time he was the victim of a practical scruple. Perplexed and discouraged, he again abandoned interior prayer at the threshold of the Night of Spirit, as he had abandoned it before when faced with the Night of Sense. Years of life followed with no practice of mental prayer, the spiritual void being covered by legal practice, in itself useful and largely charitable, but not altogether in conformity with his vocation. "He did practise the office of a solicitor at law,[2] even in public courts, not only out of charity for his brethren, widows, orphans and distressed persons, but also for other more wealthy and greater personages." About the year 1613 he was ordained priest.

After twelve years, in the year 1620 he returned to mental prayer, never again to abandon it. This was his third, in the *Secretum* he calls it his "second", "conversion". Though he attained a high degree of what he terms active contemplation, he had not been raised again to "passive" when he composed his works.[3] A prayer of aspirations, acts of love elicited by God in his will, became his usual prayer, increasingly simplified and abstracted from all sensible images or even mental concepts. At the beginning of this renewed spiritual life he was in Devonshire, chaplain to Mr. Philip Fursdon. Here, by avoiding controversy and recommending a prayer of humble resignation, he converted

---

[1] *Confessions of Fr. Baker*, pp. 70–1. (Extracts, chiefly biographical, from the *Secretum* by Abbot Justin McCann.)

[2] Cressy, *Life*. " Solicitor " presumably means what we now term a barrister. This public exercise of the legal profession by a man who, as a Catholic priest, was by the law of the land guilty of high treason, is surprising.

[3] See, however, below, pp. 178.

Mr. Fursdon's mother-in-law, a staunch Protestant, whom the arguments of other priests had merely irritated. She asked him the reason of his silence, that whereas other priests "almost deafened her with their continual clamorous disputes", he never made the least attempt to persuade her to agree in belief with him. He answered her that he could promise but little good from disputes, but if she "would be assured on what side the truth lies", she "must join her prayers made with a pure submission of mind and indifferency", and at her request he gave her instructions for such prayer. Within three weeks he received her into the Church. "It fortuned that the good priest, her ancient adversary, met her as she was going out of the door and said to Father Baker that surely it was for no good that that perverse woman came to him. He answered that surely it was for no ill, unless the Sacrament of Penance were ill."[1]

From 1621 to 1624, he was in London engaged, by his superiors' command, in antiquarian research into the history of English Benedictinism. It is interesting and pleasant to notice that in these researches he had the assistance and sympathy of Protestant antiquaries, Selden and Sir Robert Cotton. To mobilize scientific research in the service of a state ideology has been reserved for the modern totalitarians, Nazi or Communist.

In 1624 he went to Douay but was at once sent to Cambray as a spiritual director to the English Benedictine nuns who had just founded a convent there, the present Stanbrook. Among the nuns was the great-great-granddaughter of St. Thomas More, Dame Gertrude More. In fact, the convent could not have been founded without the financial support of her father, Cresacre More. She had inherited a good measure of her ancestor's humour, love of learning, critical intelligence and mental curiosity. To these she added his strong will. All these qualities, reinforcing her position as the daughter of the practical founder, had made her a dominant influence in the convent. Moreover, they turned her away from the interior life to external interests, in Baker's terminology to extroversion rather than introversion. Even her religious vocation was not perfectly clear to her. It had been, in part at least, a distaste for marriage, the only practical alternative, and she had made her profession half-heartedly. However, she had also what Baker calls "a wonderfully strong propensity in her

[1] CRESSY, *Life*, Sec. 67.

rational will to seek after God and eternal felicity and a disesteem or contempt for all the transitory things of this life". This propensity, in which also she resembled her martyred ancestor, drew her inwards to seek God in the soul, towards introversion. Indeed, it was no doubt the true motive of her religious vocation, as it had drawn St. Thomas to make trial of the Carthusian life. Torn between these two conflicting tendencies and moreover harassed by the disease of scruples, Dame Gertrude was unhappy, restless, and in consequence rather bitter and very critical. At first, therefore, she would have nothing to do with this new director, to whom she was not bound to go, since he was not the nuns' official confessor. Indeed, we may suppose that it was to give the nuns the choice between two types of direction that he was not appointed confessor. At last, however, she came to him, for the first time, eleven months after her disconsolate profession. A few months later she returned to him and became his most enthusiastic disciple, as also was the nun elected Abbess while Baker was still at Cambray, Dame Catherine Gascoigne. He put her into a course of affective prayer, acts of love in which her propensity to God could find expression and exercise unhampered and unretarded by the multiplicity of images and concepts involved in meditation. It proved most beneficial, and its fruits are embodied in the outbursts of affective prayer known as *Confessiones Amantis*, a lover's confessions. Baker left her at liberty to follow the inner guidance of the Holy Spirit both in regard to her prayer and those external matters not regulated by her rule. Her weak health made her unable to undertake extraordinary mortifications; she could not indeed carry out the rule completely. And she found it necessary to continue a measure of secular reading and conversations and to engage in a large number of external activities. Since however these things were now regulated by the guidance of the Holy Ghost obtained by prayer and subordinated to a unifying, because simple, contemplation, she advanced rapidly. Her prayer was directed to the incomprehensible Godhead apprehended by faith. And although affective it was not sensible devotion, but an exercise of the spiritual will aspiring and adhering to God. Any sensible affections were secondary, the concomitant, and, so to speak, by-product of the exercise of will. Moreover, she was tried and purified by much sensible aridity, the Night of Sense.

Baker remained at Cambray nine years, 1624 to 1633. It was during this period that he began to compose the host of treatises, with translations and adaptations, in which his doctrine is contained. In the *Secretum* he tells us of some peculiar psycho-physical results of his prayer, motions of arms or legs and an apparent drawing of his prayer activity upwards to the head. Finally on Mid-Lent Sunday, 1627, "there happened upon his head and body such an alteration that he greatly wondered at it nor could he tell what to make of it". Of the phenomenon itself we hear no more. But whereas before he had suffered from a mental dullness due to the drawing of his spiritual activities into the centre of his soul, though it left him capable of all his duties, he now "had free use of his wits and senses in greater clearness and perfection than ever before". He "found himself enabled to write or discourse of spiritual matters". In the strength of this new light he produced all his writings. *Sancta Sophia* was com-piled by Cressy out of more than forty treatises. And the bibliography appended to Abbot Justin McCann's edition of the Salvin and Cressy lives enumerates no less than sixty-eight items. Of these, however, some are translations or adaptations, others fragments. Nevertheless, it was a most prolific output. Indeed, it would seem as though many mystics, knowing that they cannot adequately convey their sublime spiritual apprehensions, yet under a strong urge to impart their knowledge for God's glory and the benefit of others, cannot refrain from expatiating on the same topics, repeating themselves in the vain effort to express themselves to their satisfaction. Moreover, the instruction of the Cambray nuns was a powerful inducement to composition.

As always, a novelty or apparent novelty, however good, provoked opposition. The opposition at Cambray was headed by the nuns' regular chaplain, Dom Francis Hull. Though per-sonal jealousy may have played a subconscious part, the liberty left to the individual by Baker, the seeming illuminism of his insistence upon Divine calls and inspirations, the subordinate place assigned to meditation, then widely regarded as the ideal form of mental prayer, and above all his denial that Superiors had a right to prescribe their subjects' method of prayer, were grounds for genuine, though mistaken, alarm. Moreover, Dame Gertrude's enthusiasm and her naturally assertive temper, which, though subdued by prayer, could not have been wholly eradicated, may well have made her tactless and somewhat overbearing in defence of the doctrine which had liberated her soul. Father Hull, on his deathbed, declared to Dom Salvin that he had not opposed Baker's doctrine in itself but merely the abuse made of it by indiscreet disciples. In any case, the dispute produced two good results. It effected a final purification of Dame Gertrude's soul in view of her holy death from smallpox in August 1633, at the early age of twenty-seven. Not only did she bear with exemplary courage the pain and the loneliness of her disease, nauseating remedies and the deprivation of Communion until her final viaticum, but she proved how thoroughly she had assimilated Baker's teaching by refusing to see him, since it was unnecessary and she wished to be left alone with God.

The other good result was the formal examination of Baker's writings by order of the General Chapter of the Congregation. For it resulted in an unreserved and wholehearted approbation. In fact, *if* the English Benedictines can be said to possess any official body of spiritual doctrine, as the Jesuits the *Exercises of St. Ignatius*, surely it must be the doctrine of Father Baker. I hasten to add that although in his writings Baker had primarily in view the monks and nuns of his Order, he expressly points out that, *mutatis mutandis*, his doctrine is applicable to all, whatever their state of life, who are called to seek God by the practice of contemplative prayer. Of the sixty-five years he lived, he spent less than six in a monastery, and during his five years at Douay took no part in the choir. That is to say he was a monk rather in the spirit than in the letter. But it is for the spirit that the letter exists, not the spirit for the letter. For souls surrendered to God, Baker tells us, all employments undertaken by a Divine call are equally valuable, "even labouring for the conversion of souls is of no greater price with God than is the keeping of sheep".[1]

Though the General Chapter approved Baker's doctrine it was thought wiser to remove both protagonists in the controversy from Cambray. Baker therefore now spent five years at Douay. Except for his daily Mass and his meals he confined himself almost entirely to his room. This soon became a centre of spiritual

[1] This surely requires qualification. No doubt all employments performed in obedience to God are equally sanctifying. It does not follow that they are equally valuable in themselves, therefore in God's estimate, who must judge values as they objectively are.

guidance, not only for members of the house but for outsiders, the English Franciscans, for example, and the students and teachers at the seminary for secular priests. It may therefore be said that during these years Baker was training in the spiritual life confessors and martyrs of the English mission where the Civil War would shortly rekindle the persecution relaxed under King Charles.[1]

This unofficial influence, with the body of enthusiastic disciples it brought into being, alienated from Baker a powerful theologian who had hitherto supported him, but who was of too active and domineering a temper to practise his doctrine himself, Dom Rudisind Barlow.[2] Even so the trouble would not have come to a head had Baker not felt himself obliged to compose a treatise on the conventual life, aimed under the thinnest of disguises at Dom Rudisind. This error of judgment exasperated Dom Rudisind, to whom he had actually presented in person the attack upon himself, and, though infirm, he was sent to England in 1638.

We are not, however, entitled in Dom Rudisind's case, any more than in Father Hull's, to charge Baker's adversary with deliberate and conscious jealousy. As Baker himself points out, the good are often permitted by God to oppose the good for their spiritual profit without wilful fault, but from lack of light withheld by God. In this instance Dom Rudisind may well have regarded Baker as a centre of dissension in the house and as encouraging by his censure of himself an undesirable spirit of criticism and insubordination. Any personal jealousy or pique at work as a motive may well have been completely hidden from his conscious knowledge for want of the light to discover it, obtainable only by prayer. Though Baker was so infirm that he hardly expected to reach England alive, and could have appealed on grounds of health against the command of his immediate superiors, or even, it seems, could have gone to live at the Seminary for secular priests, he obeyed and sailed for England with his future biographer, Dom Peter Salvin. Dom Salvin "noticed his continued contemplations". Throughout the hardships and distractions of his journey—no holiday travel in the seventeenth

---

[1] But it was in earlier years that he converted to the Church the Benedictine martyr, Bl. Philip Powell.

[2] Brother of the martyr, Bl. Ambrose Barlow.

century—"he remained still in his interior conversation with God in his own soul".[1]

In England, Baker spent the last years of his life partly in Bedfordshire, partly in London. Towards the end he had often to change his lodgings to escape arrest. For the Long Parliament was bent on extirpating popery. But this banishment from Douay and its consequent sufferings were the purification enabling him to receive the "passive" contemplation he had lost so long. Since he had ceased writing we are ignorant of his final prayer. All we know is a revealing phrase in a letter that he was *totus in passionibus*, wholly in a passive state. When his correspondent misinterpreted these sufferings as privations and was arranging for a supply of money, he explained that the sufferings he meant "were the greatest tastes of heaven that this life is capable of, his prayer being now become wholly passive". The illuminations of passive prayer may account for his abstinence from writing, as an illumination of Divine Truth made St. Thomas unable to continue his unfinished *Summa*. Like St. Thomas he may have been impressed with the impotence of human language and thought to convey the Infinite Reality of Divine Truth.

We have, it is true, seen reason to believe that it was for the profit of souls, the vast majority of contemplatives, called only to a lower degree of mystical union, probably at most the Prayer of Quiet or Full Union which illuminations do not normally accompany, that Baker has said so little about the higher degrees of prayer and their concomitant illuminations and, therefore, also of the desolation, the Night of Spirit bound up with them. His motive, however, was more probably the sense of impotence to express them.

He died of a pestilential fever in the house of a Mrs. Watson, who described his peaceful and resigned death in a letter to her daughter. "His body was weak but his sickness violent and the pangs of death extreme strong; but perfect resignation and a total subjection to the will and good pleasure of Almighty God was plainly seen to be performed by him to his last breath. The day before he died he took a leaden pen and wrote thus: 'Abstinence and Resignation I see must be my condition to my very expiration.' His happy departure out of this world was on the

---

[1] Dom Peter SALVIN, *Life*, Sec. 38.

ninth of August, 1641, upon St. Laurence's Eve." He was buried
in St. Andrew's, Holborn. But his grave is as unknown to-day
as that of his disciple Dame Gertrude More, buried somewhere
in what was the Convent cemetery and is now a private
garden.[1]

Sixteen years later his enduring monument was to be erected by
Dom Serenus Cressy, *Sancta Sophia.*

Posterity owes Cressy a great debt for compiling *Sancta Sophia*
out "of more than forty treatises" left by Baker and digesting
them methodically with such success into a treatise so well
ordered and well proportioned that his arrangement admits
of little improvement. Nor would Baker's repetitive and diffuse
writings find many readers willing to plough through them in
their original state. His legal training and practice left their
mark upon his style, and not for good. Repetition and an
accumulation of synonyms to make sure that his meaning has
been accurately stated render it prolix and heavy. "Being in
such exercise . . . proceeding upon or from his said exercise of
aspirations", "secure and profitable and to be admitted", "upon
his seeking or procuring"—all those in a short paragraph: "when
that hereafter she shall be arrived at it, there will appear no such
distinction, all such distinction shall be gone", "the selfsame thing
without any distinction, division or separation", "that same
definition or description," "discover and show Himself", "the
which *union* in itself or in its effect is also called *transformation*",
"union sometimes called a *deification.* In these unions is sometimes
understood also *annihilation, the mystic death* of the soul". Such
writing smacks of a legal document. But it was unfortunate that
the laxer view then prevalent of obligation to an author's exact
words led Cressy to alter throughout the wording of the passages
excerpted and arranged. As Abbot McCann has shown,[2] he has
left hardly a sentence as Baker wrote it and on many occasions
has toned down and qualified language which seemed too bold
in the original. A new editor is needed to turn the extracts which
compose *Sancta Sophia* back into Baker's words while retaining,
substantially at any rate, Cressy's selection and arrangement.
Till he is found we must be content to read *Sancta Sophia* as
Cressy has left it.

[1] Or was in 1910. I know nothing of it later.
[2] In the *Downside Review*, October 1941.

· The substance however of what is perhaps Baker's most important work—the *Secretum* in which he comments on the *Cloud of Unknowing* and illustrates his commentary by a spiritual autobiography, an account of his life of prayer—has been published, in his own words; the commentary in Abbot Justin McCann's edition of the *Cloud of Unknowing*,[1] the autobiographical passages and some of the commentary in his *Confessions of Venerable Father Augustine Baker*.[2] But neither the commentary nor the autobiography has been published in its entirety. We have access also to a defence and practical example of his spiritual teaching, his *Inner Life of Dame Gertrude More*, his disciple at Cambray.[3] If these are read in conjunction with *Sancta Sophia* we may be sure of studying Baker's authentic doctrine.

Baker addresses himself to those with the gift and *attrait* for contemplative, unitive prayer; he calls it a propensity. It is "a thirst for God" which "leads the soul to seek God in an imageless manner in her own interior."[4] "It moves" the subject "to seek simplicity of soul, a denudation of all created images and one which renders her capable of immediate union with the Divine simplicity." And—it "urges the soul to seek after the simplicity of the pure Divinity, abstracted from all bodies or created images". For "the Divinity is the infinite, profound centre or resting-place of man's soul, to whom all other things . . . are narrow and unsuitable". "It is the proper vast element wherein the soul should find . . . an infinite life . . . Thus does the contemplative soul, in virtue of her propensity, ever aspire to her centre and proper element, the simple Divinity . . . She thirsts after the spaciousness and infinity of God."[5]

[1] Burns, Oates & Washbourne, 1st ed. 1924. Reprinted 1936, 1941, 1944, 2nd ed. 1952. I shall refer to the *Cloud of Unknowing* as *Cloud*, to the chapters in which Dom McCann has digested the substance of Baker's commentary on the *Cloud*, which he calls the Introduction, as "Introduction", to Baker's notes on the individual chapters of the *Cloud* which he calls the Commentary as " Commentary ". But all are published in the same volume.
[2] Burns, Oates & Washbourne, 1922. Unfortunately out of print.
[3] Ed. Dom. Benedict Weld Blundell, O.S.B. R. and T. Washbourne, 1910.
[4] In her *Life* of Dame Gertrude More, Chap. VI.
[5] ibid., Ch. XX. Unfortunately, since this propensity is not confined to Catholics and *a priori* prejudice denied supernatural prayer to those who are not visible members of the Church, Baker says that it is natural not supernatural. Here I most emphatically dissent from him. If this aspiration of the will to union with God is not supernatural I do not know what can be pronounced supernatural. For, as we shall see, even the supreme union of the great mystics is but the fulfilment and perfection of this propensity as Baker describes it.

The soul obviously cannot be united to the simple transcendent Godhead beyond image or concept by the imagination or understanding. The union therefore must be effected by the will, by following the *attrait* or propensity to it.

Baker's prayer was accordingly an exercise of the will. Acts of will, at first deliberately elicited, "forced acts", become gradually more affective and under the operation of grace ultimately become "aspirations", acts elicited by the Holy Spirit and produced, therefore, with greater facility, indeed, spontaneously, also fewer, since each continues longer. And there is a corresponding progress in their spirituality and simplicity. Moreover, these acts and aspirations are addressed to the incomprehensible Godhead apprehended by faith. The substance of this method can be found already in the *Cloud of Unknowing*, on which Baker commented. But it is worked out in greater detail and divided into stages. Although it was no novelty, it ran counter to the method of mental prayer then most popular, though not so universal as it became after the Quietist controversy had brought mysticism into discredit and supicion. This method was that of discursive meditation, of which St. Ignatius's Exercises were the most influential example. Baker himself agreed that for many souls of active and extroverted temper meditation is the best form of mental prayer, indeed probably the only form of which such souls are capable. And all souls, he thought, capable of meditation, should begin with meditation, even if they continued it no more than a few months, until they were called to replace it by acts of will.

There can be no doubt that meditation or an equivalent such as well digested reading, is indispensable.[1] For its object is to transform an exclusively or predominantly notional assent to the truths of faith into the real assent by which alone they are assimilated into our mental and spiritual life and move the will. Indeed, if our spirituality lacks the foundation of such realised doctrine, the exercise of the will elevated to the incomprehensible God which Baker recommends may operate in a vacuum of religious knowledge, may prove an unconfessional and undogmatic worship of a God not only above knowledge but wholly unknown,

[1] In my opinion for many people vocal and liturgical prayer is the best method of prayer from first to last and is capable of becoming a vehicle of contemplative or rather unitive prayer. See below, pp. 233–4.

in short, may be agnostic. When Baker wrote, however, ther
was a tendency to treat meditation not as what it is—prepar
ation for mental prayer and its food—but as being itself menta
prayer; though, as he shows, prayer is an act of will, not o
understanding. Indeed it was widely regarded as the sole menta
prayer.[1] This, I suspect, was largely due to the fact that th
Reformation had disclosed a widespread ignorance and at best
lack of effective realisation of Catholic truth. Because Catholi
doctrine had, too often, been unknown to Catholics or had no
been assimilated by them vast numbers had yielded to the assaul
of a heresy whose doctrine was the vital conviction of its adherents
The most urgent need, therefore, was to replace a formal and
customary Catholicism by an intelligent and living understanding
of the Catholic faith. For this purpose, in the contemporar\
intellectual and devotional environment, there could be no bette
instrument than the methodical meditation practised and preached
by the Jesuits, who set the tone of Counter-Reformatioi
spirituality.

But however valuable and indispensable meditation may be
if it is regarded as the sole or even the best method of prayer
indeed as being strictly prayer, it must prove a fatal hindrance to
the soul's Godward ascent. The mystics had never cease{
to protest against meditation when pursued beyond the poin
up to which it is necessary. Baker had many predecessors and
contemporary writers to support him, notably St. John of th
Cross. It was an uphill fight all the same, and destined to
prolonged, though not complete or final, defeat.

Aspirations are distinguished by Baker from forced or immedi
ate acts, as being chosen and produced by an operation of the Hol\
Spirit, "elevations of the mind towards God upon an enablemen
or impulse for them, from God working the said impulse in the
soul".[2] They are identified by him with the contemplation, the
"work" taught in the Cloud of Unknowing, and he terms thi
exercise "a mystic active contemplation".[3] In his Inner Life o

---

[1] Where meditation is and must be to the end a soul's method of prayer, the praye
is not the meditation itself but the resolutions and other acts of will which it produces
[2] Instruction given to Dom Peter Salvin. See SALVIN's Life, Sec. 11.
[3] Introduction, Sec. 5. In the instruction to Dom Salvin (see p. 12), however, Bake
reserves the term " active contemplation " for " an elevate quiet act of the soul, throug
an enablement for it from God, almost imperceptible whereby she is as it were immersin
and drowning herself in the profound and immense depth of the pure divinity ": in othe
words, what elsewhere he terms " active union".

Dame Gertrude More, he distinguishes another kind of prayer—
an alternative variety of immediate or forced acts which Dame
Gertrude practised and which he terms the prayer of sensible
affections. Unlike the immediate acts of the will alone, this prayer
begins by "sensible affections" to conclude with acts of the will.[1]
This variety however is not mentioned in the almost contemporary *Secretum* nor in the map of prayer given to Dom Salvin.

These aspirations lead to active union, a state in which the
spirit adheres so closely to God that for the time it loses consciousness of self and without image or concept, time or place,
is "lost" in God, aware of Him as the nothing which is also all,
emptiness which is also a "totality", indistinguishable from the
soul thus "lost" in God.

Thus the active way of ordinary contemplation, this exercise
of the will, leads the soul to the summit of union with God, is
the unitive way of mystical prayer. Well might Dom Salvin call
the life of the man who practised and taught it "nothing else but
inspiration from God and *aspiration* to God by continual contemplation at least virtual".[2] For this inspiration and aspiration
are the two inseparable poles, around which Baker's prayer and
spiritual doctrine revolve.

What then of the extraordinary way of passive contemplation
or union? How does Baker distinguish passive from active
contemplation? Passive union is not described in *Sancta Sophia*
as that union of the apex of the will or centre of the soul with
God known by faith which, for St. John of the Cross and other
mystics, is the essential mystical union. It consists of what are
but concomitants of that union, intellectual visions, touches
or locutions which are supernatural illuminations of Divine
Truth—for example the intellectual vision of the Trinity which
often accompanies the supreme degree of union, or at a lower
level the conviction of Catholic truth by which revealed
doctrines are known with a direct and indubitable certainty,
which was granted to Baker himself when first admitted to passive
prayer.[3]

[1] *Inner Life of Dame Gertrude More*, Chs. XI and XX. In Chap. XVI Baker calls
resigned persistence in prayer during the impotence of aridity, the Night of Sense, yet
another kind of prayer. It might well be called the prayer of resignation.
[2] *Life*, Sec. 40.
[3] *Secretum, Confessions of Fr. Baker*, pp. 70–1.

In an unpublished passage of the *Secretum* Baker speaks of passive contemplation as "the finding of the presence of God in the soul". He "doth in a supernatural and evident manner, though nothing so evident as is the sight in heaven, discover and show Himself to the soul". This experience of the Divine Presence is distinguished from the experience of God in active contemplation as the obscure Reality known to faith when "He is seen as nothing or as all in all". It must therefore be a manifestation of God by image or concept, as contrasted with the imageless and unconceptual awareness of His transcendent Reality in active contemplation.

And this is in fact the account of his passive union given by Baker in his *Secretum*. He there describes his passive contemplation as "A speaking of God to the soul".[1] That is to say it was a locution. And it was a "work" which "passed and was acted in the very substance of the soul".[2] That is to say it was presumably what St. John of the Cross calls a substantial locution, a locution which produces a vivid, deep and lasting effect upon the soul and "is of such moment and price that it works a greater blessing within the soul than all that the soul has itself done throughout its life",[3] an estimate of the efficacy of passive contemplation in which Baker entirely concurs. In default of the beatific vision all these illuminations are necessarily, Baker teaches, communicated by infused species imaginary or conceptual.

Nevertheless, most mystics and writers on mysticism regard as passive at least the higher stages of experienced union with God, and, as we shall see, Baker's language is not altogether consistent on this point. I propose, therefore, to examine more closely the evidence his writings afford and hope to show that his normal teaching, at any rate, is what I have stated it to be, namely that active contemplation, aspiration of the will and its perfection, active union, the imageless union of the will with God known by faith is the substance of mystical prayer and is the mystical way of progressive union with God which may even attain the most intimate union with God possible in this life.

When this active contemplation has reached the stage of "Elevations" "distractive thoughts of creatures either do not come at all, or if they do come, affect only the understanding and imagination

---

[1] *Confessions*, 59.   [2] ibid.   [3] *Ascent of Mount Carmel*, Bk. II, Ch. 31.

and not the will". [1] The latter, however, is St. Teresa's account
of the Prayer of Quiet, the former of its perfection, the Prayer of
Full Union. And both these states of prayer are mystical contemplation, commonly accounted passive.

The desolation discussed in chapter nine of the Introduction to
the Commentary on the *Cloud*[2] is regarded by Baker as a form or
degree of active contemplation. But "it may be an immediate
disposition" to the "State of *perfect* union" and in that case is
"the purgatory of love in this life". And elsewhere he speaks of
"the great privation or desolation which disposes a man for the
state of perfect union". This desolation, that is to say, includes
the Night of Spirit described by St. John of the Cross. But this
Night of Spirit is a state of prayer superior to the infused and
distinctively mystical prayers of Quiet, Full Union and Ecstasy
and following them in the mystical ascent. *A fortiori* therefore it
is the infused prayer commonly termed passive.

In a paper inserted in his *Remains*[3] Baker describes an "*Active
mystic union*" in the following terms. "By this," he writes,
"you may conceive what an active mystic union is . . . It is
caused by an application of the soul—being for the time void
of all images—to God apprehended according to faith, without
any image and above all images. And so, in this case of union,
there is nothing and nothing and they make nothing. For the
less there is apprehended by way of image in such an union, the
purer is the union, and, if it be perfect, there is neither time nor
place, but a certain eternity that is without time or place. So
the soul, in that case, discerneth neither time nor place nor image,
but a certain vacuity or emptiness, both as in regard of herself as
of all other things. And then it is as if there were nothing at all
in being saving herself and God; and God and she not as two
distinct things but as one only thing; and as if there were no
other thing in being. *This is the State of a Perfect Union*, which is
termed by some a state of nothing and by others with as much
reason termed a state of totality. Because there God is seen and
enjoyed in it and He therein as the Container of all things and the
soul as it were lost in Him". An unpublished passage of the

[1] Introduction, Ch. 9.
[2] The arrangement and divisions are Abbot McCann's.
[3] Published by Abbot McCann, *Downside Review*, October 1941, pp. 370-1, in part
as a note to his edition of the *Cloud* and its commentary—in full as an appendix to his
latest edition of the book.

Secretum gives a similar account of "the state of perfection and perfect union". "There will be so immediate and straight an union, that in the union" the soul "shall not discern herself from God; but it will seem unto her that God and she are but one and the selfsame thing without any distinction, division or separation between them. And it will seem unto her for the time, that she is turned to be God and to have lost her being of a creature."

The union thus described is so intimate and sublime that no closer union is conceivable on earth. It must be the supreme degree of mystical prayer. If it is the perfect active union, active union and the active contemplation which culminates in it are the way of mystic union usually termed passive. Dom Cressy in fact took from this paper the formula, a union of nothing with Nothing, which he introduced into the final chapter of *Sancta Sophia after* the account of what he terms passive union. Baker's active contemplation and union cannot then be identified with the acquired contemplation of other writers, but on the contrary comprise the entire course of their infused and passive contemplation and union, *in so far* as its essence—the experienced union of the soul with God—is concerned, and includes the perfect union called Transforming. Indeed in the *Secretum* he says the "active union" is also called "*transformation*" and like the passive, "a deification".[1]

Baker has in view this supreme union, when self-consciousness is replaced by God-consciousness, when he speaks of "the condition of saints in heaven and perfect souls in this life" whose prayer is an "abstraction wherein" a man "shall lose the feeling of his own being and shall have and feel a nothing kind of being which will be a being and living in God in whom he hath lost himself and his own being".[2] This abstraction in its highest degree "is from the soul and its powers into the top or height of the spirit and is above both soul and body". This is "the state of perfect union. In this degree a man has no feeling of his own being either as to soul or as to body, but all his feeling", as is explained later, only so long as he is in prayer, "seemeth to be only of the being of God".[3]

Moreover, Baker tells us also that this supreme union is attained only after "the great privation or desolation", which disposes the

---

[1] Unpublished passage.   [2] Introduction, Ch. 10.   [3] ibid., Ch. 10.

subject "for the state of union".[1] This "great desolation",
however, as we have just seen, is the Night of Spirit, the second
passive night of St. John of the Cross, and this perfect union the
Transforming Union which follows it and which its purification
makes possible.

In this passage[2] Baker says that, though, normally, the soul is
assisted to attain this supreme union by a passive contemplation,
God can and perhaps "doth bring" "some souls" to it "by means
of the active exercise", though in that case it will require a far
longer time. For passive contemplation takes a soul from the
hundredth mile of her journey eight hundred of the thousand
miles she must travel, leaving her to journey the last hundred on
foot.[3] That is to say that though passive contemplation, as
Baker understands it—namely, a supernatural illumination about
God and His revealed truth or a supernatural infusion of virtue[4]
—assists the soul to reach the Transforming Union, that union
is the goal and perfection of what he calls active contemplation.
The highest state of mystical union is thus a state of active
not passive contemplation, and Baker calls it in set terms an
active union. Indeed, he says that "the active contemplation
wherein God is seen as nothing or as all in all is nearer and
liker to the facial and true sight of God than is any contemplation had of Him by a particular species as is usually seen in a
passive contemplation."[5] Passive contemplation, though more
potent than active, is ancillary to the latter which is the regular,
indeed indispensable path to the summit of mystical union,
the summit of St. John's Mount Carmel. For Baker active
contemplation is the main route of mystical prayer. Though like
the *Cloud* he confines himself to active contemplation, the guide
book he offers is substantially the same as those composed by
SS. John of the Cross and Teresa, who have so much to say of
the contemplation he terms passive. But whereas the former
describe the goal of the mystic way, the Transforming Union,
from personal experience of it, Baker describes it from below,
from the midway of the Ascent, on the witness of others
and as the dimly seen terminus of the path he was engaged in
climbing.

[1] Introduction, Ch. 10. [4] See below, p. 218.
[2] ibid., Ch. 10.   [5] *Secretum*, unpublished passage.
[3] ibid., Ch. 10.

We may indeed conjecture that when, shortly before his death, he described his prayer as wholly passive, informing his correspondent that he was "in passionibus", he was receiving the illuminations which commonly accompany, though they do not constitute, the state of Spiritual Betrothal and that when on his deathbed he wrote that "Abstinence and resignation must be my condition to my very expiration" he was in the great desolation, the Night of Spirit, the purgatory which precedes the Transforming Union or, as is often the case (and presumably in his own), death—and, if at death its work has been completed, the beatific vision.

Failure to recognize that Baker's active contemplation is the substance of mystical prayer, its essential union and its progress to its highest earthly summit is probably due to the fact that it has been taken for granted that acquired and active contemplation are synonymous, as also infused and passive. But the union described by Baker as active, and the aspirative contemplation which leads up to it, are not acquired but infused, and described by him as infused. The soul, he writes, in this "active union" is hardly conscious of her operation, but receives what God gives as the senses receive their sensible objects.[1] And elsewhere "aspirations . . . do not lie in man's power to exercise at his pleasure, but depend upon the power of God, who moves and enables the soul to them".[2] This is infused, not acquired, contemplation, but active notwithstanding.

Baker expressly distinguishes between acquired and infused prayer, and moreover identifies the latter with perfect, as opposed to imperfect, mental prayer. But he does not identify infused with passive prayer. Though passive prayer is obviously infused, active prayer may also be infused. "Internal or mental prayer", he writes, "is either *imperfect and acquired or perfect and that which is called properly infused prayer*. The former is only a preparation and inferior disposition by which the soul is . . . made capable of the infusion of the other, to wit, the prayer of *pure contemplation which is the end of all* our spiritual and religious exercises."[3] We have already seen that for Baker the goal of religious exercises is the active union to which passive union is but an assistance. Therefore it cannot be the mere preparation and inferior disposition which he here calls acquired, as opposed to infused, prayer.

[1] Introduction, Ch. 9.   [2] ibid., Ch. 7.   [3] *Confessions*, p. 42.

In fact he proceeds to speak of the "Prayer of pure *active* contemplation or aspirations". And aspirations, as he has told us, are not in our power to exercise at pleasure, that is to say are not acquired, but depend upon the power of God who "moves and enables the soul to them".[1] And in another passage[2] he writes: "The exercise of aspirations has great variety in it, comprehending humiliations, exinanitions, annihilations, praisings, thanksgivings, elevations, adorations, as also *the state of* privation or *desolation*, *union* and other various conditions. And all of them are aspirings and tendencies towards God and *come by motion from God* [are infused] and are *active* and *not passive* exercises." Almost in set terms Baker here calls aspirations infused and active contemplation. And they include, be it noticed, the entire course of mystical contemplation, even the Night of Spirit, commonly called passive, and the Transforming Union which follows it. Therefore the prayer of active contemplation is the pure contemplation which is infused, not acquired. This conclusion is confirmed when we are told that aspirations, as contrasted with forced or immediate acts which are but the entrance into contemplation, "purely flow from an internal impulse of the Divine Spirit", that "the constant exercise" of them "is proper and perfect contemplation" and that "*mystic contemplation* or *union* comprises active and ordinary as well as passive and extraordinary contemplation".[3] There can surely be no doubt that Baker regards active contemplation, from the prayer of aspirations upwards, as infused. Indeed when he speaks of "a *mystic* active contemplation"[4] he equivalently speaks of "an infused active contemplation". The prayer of forced acts, on the other hand, is acquired prayer, though they depend for their fruitful exercise on a Divine call to their practice and are the entrance to the infused prayer of aspirations.

It may be asked, however, how could Baker regard active contemplation as infused? Is it not a contradiction in terms? Surely passive and infused mean the same. The answer is given in the *Secretum*: "In all passive contemplations God becometh the *sole* worker."[5] In active contemplation, on the other hand, in the exercise of "aspirations or elevations, the soul herself is the agent, though by interior motion or enablement from God . . ."

[1] Introduction, Ch. 7. [3] *Confessions*, pp. 42–6. [5] *Confessions*, p. 61.
[2] *Commentary*, Ch. 20.. [4] Introduction, Ch. 5.

who "both moveth the man's will immediately for to do it and teacheth him how to do it, in some sort even as a writing master doth move and guide the hand of his young scholar when he teacheth him to write. God inciteth, moveth and enableth the soul . . . for it to break forth immediately into such aspiration or elevation".[1] "This stirring", an aspiration, "proceedeth not from any discourse, premeditation or consideration, but merely from interior motion, impulse and information from God, moving and directing the will in it".[2] And elsewhere "Aspirations proceed suddenly and without any premeditation or cause, but *only* from interior motion and information from God who moves the will".[3] "They are produced without force, foresight or election, *purely flowing from an internal impulse of the Divine Spirit.*"[4]

And the author of the *Cloud of Unknowing* is, if possible, even more insistent upon the infused and in common parlance the passive character of the prayer of which he writes, a prayer however which Baker calls active and identifies with his prayer of aspirations. "Let that thing" (the work of God in the will) "be the worker and thou but the sufferer: do but look upon it and let it alone. Be thou but the tree and let it be the carpenter; be thou but the house and let it be the husband dwelling therein . . . It is only God that stirreth thy will and thy desire, plainly by Himself, without means either on His part or on thine."[5]

Nevertheless the soul freely obeys the Divine motion which invites and elicits the aspiration to which she is moved. In passive contemplation on the other hand the soul contributes nothing, so that it is wholly and entirely infused. And for that reason Baker holds that it is not meritorious. In one passage indeed he admits, as he ought to have admitted, an active factor even in passive contemplation. But he explains at the same time why it is nevertheless passive, not active. "It is called passive," he writes, "*not that the soul therein doth not actively contemplate God*; but she can neither when she pleases dispose herself thereto"—"*nor yet refuse it when that God thinks good to operate after such a manner in the soul* and to represent Himself unto her by a divine particular image not at all framed by the soul but supernaturally infused into her."[6] It is the inability to resist the Divine operation which renders this

[1] *Confessions*, pp. 63, 64.   [3] ibid., Ch. 36.   [5] *Cloud*, Ch. 34.
[2] *Commentary*, Ch. 4.   [4] *Confessions*, p. 44.   [6] *Confessions*, p. 46.

contemplation pre-eminently passive and devoid of merit. Since the soul is not free to do anything but accept the Divine communication her prayer is strictly passive. Nor can she merit by doing what she cannot help doing.

In active contemplation, on the other hand, the soul takes a more active part. For she produces the acts of will and is able to refrain from doing so, though invited and moved to produce them by God. Without the Divine motion she cannot, but with it she need not. Therefore notwithstanding this Divine motion, inasmuch as the soul freely accepts and follows it, producing the acts to which she is moved, when she could, if she chose, resist the invitation, her contemplation is rightly called active in spite of its dependence upon the invitation and action of God instructing and moving her. But, inasmuch as it is produced by the Divine motion and light, it is infused. True, to that extent it is also passive. And Baker, instead of distinguishing between active and passive contemplation, could have distinguished them as, respectively, partly passive and partly active, and wholly passive. But this is clumsy language. And the same meaning is conveyed by calling, as he in effect does, the former contemplation active and infused, the latter passive and infused.[1]

It is however impossible to draw too rigid a line of demarcation between acquired and infused contemplation. For the entire process of active contemplation and union, from imperfect to perfect, is the advance of a union in the course of which the action of the soul becomes progressively a reception of the Divine operation in her radical will, her centre, and is thus rendered increasingly the active-passive recipient of that operation.

Nevertheless the boundary, such as it is, between acquired and infused contemplation—if the former should not more correctly be termed a preparation for contemplation—is drawn by Baker between forced acts which are acquired, and aspirations which are infused prayer. For, as we have seen, "aspirations, though the soul herself is the agent, are produced by 'an interior motion from God'". "At first" in the prayer of immediate or forced acts—immediate, because not the result of previous meditation, forced, because elicited by the soul's deliberate effort—"the party should use some force (so far as he should need such forcement of

[1] Abbot Cuthbert Butler recognised that Baker's aspirations are infused not acquired. *Western Mysticism*, 2nd ed., Afterthoughts, XLI.

his will)" but "afterwards" in the exercise of aspirations he "should come to be able to exercise the same will"—a blind adherence to God as known by faith—"out of an interior impulse, motion and information". "The party should cease from acts, when he comes *to be moved* to aspirations."[1] Elevations, Baker explains, are but a higher form of aspirations, more spiritual, more subtle, and no doubt (though this is not stated explicitly) more infused, in common parlance, though *not* in Baker's terminology, more passive than aspirations strictly so called.

Immediate acts, moreover, as Baker points out, are not exercised without images. But from aspirations, images are absent. "The understanding is to carry with it no images or species."[2]

In his *Ascent of Mount Carmel*,[3] St. John of the Cross describes the loss of memory produced as the soul "progresses in contemplation" by the action of God bestowing contemplation and thus uniting "the memory with Himself". This contemplation is the mystical contemplation and union for which St. John would prepare and instruct souls called to receive it. For he speaks of God "working" this "Divine union" in the soul and of a "supernatural *infusion* and illumination of the faculties". The loss of memory is caused by the "transformation of the memory in God whereby it cannot receive impressions of forms or a natural knowledge of things. For its functions are all divine . . . and God Himself moves them divinely".

This evidently is mystical contemplation infused by God.

Baker, however, describing his own lapses of memory refers to "B. John de Cruce[4] . . . affirming how that usually a certain stupidity or dullness doth possess them who are in aspirations or other exercise of the will tending towards contemplation; yet not so, but that they are sufficient for the performance of what God or necessity layeth on them".[5] This is an unmistakable allusion to the passage in the *Ascent of Mount Carmel* from which I have just quoted, in which St. John discusses the contemplative's

---

[1] Introduction, Ch. 5. Forced acts are also, like all acts supernaturally good, produced by the operation of Divine Grace moving the will. But the soul is not aware of it.

[2] *Confessions*, pp. 91–2.

[3] *Ascent of Mount Carmel*, Bk. III, Ch. 2 (in Fray Gerardo's Edicion Critica).

[4] As he gives St. John's name a Latin form Baker presumably used the Latin edition of his works published at Cologne in 1622. But as he was not beatified until 1675 the " B." is hard to explain. The title may have been used loosely to denote a generally accepted sanctity. But modern editions of *Sancta Sophia* make Baker or Cressy speak of *St.* John of the Cross.

[5] *Confessions*, p. 117.

failure of memory and points out that it does not interfere with
the performance of duties. That is to say, Baker identifies the
active contemplation of which aspirations are the beginning with
the contemplation which, as St. John teaches, produces this loss
of memory; namely, the contemplation infused and effected by
the action of God, which is the substance of mystical prayer and
in its perfection the highest union possible in this life. True,
Baker does not seem to have experienced an oblivion so complete
or so intense as that described by St. John. Nor was it followed
by a similar divinisation of his faculties. For unlike St. John he
was not being raised to the Transforming Union. But it was
produced in a lesser degree by an inferior degree of the same active
but infused contemplation and union. Baker thus identifies
aspirations with St. John's onset of the contemplation produced
by God in the soul which causes the failure of memory, and therefore by implication the perfect active contemplation or union to
which they lead, with the state in which the soul's faculties are
deified and moved by God, namely the Transforming Union.

In the ascending sequence of infused contemplation mystical
writers place Ecstasy after Full Union, the perfection of the
Prayer of Quiet, before the Night of Spirit and the Transforming Union. Strictly speaking, however, it is the union which
enters into this sequence, not the accompanying anaesthesia
which is but the temporary weakness of a body unable as yet to
endure a state of union to which it is not naturally adapted. As
we have seen, Baker regards this sequence of progressive union
as the progressive development of active and infused contemplation. He should therefore regard ecstasy as a state of active
contemplation. And in fact the author of the *Cloud* tells us, it
would seem from personal experience, that it is often in a condition of ecstasy—"ravishment"—that a soul experiences "the
perfection of" the "work" which is the subject of his treatise.[1]
And that "work" is active, not passive, contemplation.

Baker, however, undoubtedly, considers ecstasy as a distinctive,
indeed, invariable characteristic of passive contemplation.[2] For he
says that the state of desolation is not a passive contemplation,
because the soul "remaineth still in the use of her senses".[3]

---

[1] *Cloud*, Ch. 71.
[2] His own passive contemplation had, he informs us, produced a state of ecstasy.
Confessions, pp. 70–4.
[3] Introduction, Ch. 9.

There is no reason why the progress of active contemplation from Full Union towards the Transforming Union should not, as the *Cloud* teaches, produce ecstatic anaesthesia. The active contemplation Baker describes as a "pure and total abstraction" in which the subject "seemeth to himself to be all spirit and as if he had no body"[1] may well involve anaesthesia. Indeed, what is said later in the chapter suggests that this state is the state of union which corresponds with ecstasy in the order of unitive ascent and is commonly so called. And the active union described in *Remains*[2] is, I suggest, this ecstatic union. Moreover a passive contemplation concomitant upon the Transforming Union does not produce accompanying ecstasy. Ecstasy, therefore, and passive contemplation are not invariable concomitants.

Perhaps the difficulty and the apparent disagreement between Baker and the *Cloud* may be explained by supposing that complete anaesthesia is produced only by the infused species of passive contemplation, involving as they do a Divine Operation in the soul of exceptional potency and which moreover commonly accompany the stage of active union which corresponds to ecstasy; whereas the active union alone produces only an incomplete and weaker alienation of the senses, a condition of dullness and involuntary inattention to external stimuli rather than total anaesthesia.[3]

A further confirmation, were further confirmation required, of my thesis that Baker's active contemplation is the mystical contemplation usually called passive, is his observation that "the perfect union of love" which, as we have seen, is the highest degree of *active* contemplation, "doth not end with this life but is continued in the future life. It was the same will and the self-same God that were united here and are united in the other world . . ." And the union is the same union here and there. "This happy state of active contemplation is *for substance* the most perfect that a soul is capable of in this life." And elsewhere *"the highest exercise of this life* is but an elevation of the will by which it willeth God to be that which He is", the active contemplation taught by the *Cloud of Unknowing*, without, as in passive contemplation, "any aspect of God or of any attribute

[1] Introduction, Ch. 9.
[2] See above, p. 205.
[3] Such, it seems, was the ecstasy of the youthful Elizabeth. See below, p. 260.
[4] Commentary, Ch. 1.

of His, otherwise than according to the confused and general knowledge of Him that our faith ministereth to us".[1] And this agrees with St. John of the Cross, who teaches that to the very end faith is the medium of union with God in this life, therefore even in the supreme degree of mystical union—a union effected by and through the will, or more strictly the radical will which is the centre of the soul, as it rises (in Baker's terminology) from active and acquired to active and infused prayer.

That the account given above of Baker's doctrine of active contemplation and its distinction from passive is true to his teaching, has, I think, been sufficiently proved by the evidence of his writings. There is however a difficulty, an apparent inconsistency which must be discussed here. There is a brief passage in *Sancta Sophia*[2] which speaks of an intellectual passive union without any perceptible images "in which God is not seen as He is, yet He is clearly seen that He is incomprehensible". It is a "union exercised more by the will than by the understanding", or rather it "passes above both the understanding and will, namely, in that supreme portion of the spirit . . . so pure, noble and divine, that it neither hath nor can have any name proper to it, though mystics endeavour to express it by divers, calling it the summit of the mind, the fund and centre of the spirit, the essence of the soul."

It seems quite impossible to distinguish the union here described from the active union described in the first chapter of section IV and in the *Secretum*. For the active union described in this first chapter is said to proceed "from the principle and fountain from whence the superior powers of the soul flow". It is "exercised wholly by the will" and its object is God known by faith. Moreover it is "above all particular images". "There is neither time nor place but all is vacuity and emptiness as if nothing were existent but God and the soul; yea, so far is the soul from reflecting on her own existence that it seems to her that God and she are not distinct but only one thing."

In all these respects the active union thus described agrees with the supreme passive union described in sections V and VI of chapter 4 quoted above and seems indistinguishable from it. We can hardly escape the conclusion that the two unions described as respectively active and passive are in fact one and

---

[1] Introduction, Ch. 2.   [2] *Sancta Sophia*, IV, 4, 5, 6.

H

the same, namely the essential mystical union with God known by faith, whose higher and more conscious stages are often termed by other mystical writers passive. Nor can we be certain that this duplication is Cressy's mistake. Not only is he unlikely to have misunderstood Baker so completely. There is positive evidence pointing to an inconsistency in Baker's language.[1]

In the twelfth chapter of his *Institutio Spiritualis*, translated in the *Secretum*,[2] Blosius describes the perfect union in terms indistinguishable from Baker's description of the supreme active union in the *Secretum* and in the paper in his *Remains* on the union of nothing with Nothing. "The loving soul," Blosius writes, "flows away and fails from herself, and, *as it were reduced to nothing*, she sinks into the abyss of the eternal Love where *dead to herself she lives in God knowing nothing and conscious of nothing save the love she tastes* . . . For she loses herself in the vast solitude and night of the Godhead. But thus to lose herself is to find herself." The state and union thus described are surely what Baker describes as "a certain vacuity or emptiness . . . as if there were nothing at all in being, saving herself [the soul] and God; and God and she as one only thing." For "God is seen and enjoyed . . . as the Container of all things and the soul, as it were, lost in Him". Moreover, Blosius insists on the transcendence of all images and distinct ideas thus excluding, *for the substance* of the prayer he describes, species of any kind. We should also notice that he supports his account of this union by excerpts from Dionysius' *Mystical Theology* which the author of the *Cloud* translated as the theoretical justification of the active contemplation he taught.

Nevertheless Baker apparently failed to recognize the obvious identity of these two states of prayer, that namely described by Blosius, and the state of perfect *active* union as described by himself. For he regards, indeed terms, the state of prayer described by Blosius as passive prayer as contrasted with active, a "divine passive operation. The which passive operation the

---

[1] The following are important passages in these books bearing on the distinction between active and passive contemplation. Introduction, Chs. 2, 7, 9, 10; *Commentary*, Chs. 1, 26, 28; *Confessions*, pp. 42–4, 46–9, 60–1, 63–5, 73. The sections in *Sancta Sophia* dealing with the passive union have drawn upon the *Secretum*. But the difficult passage, Ch. 4, § 5, 6 has been taken from another source. The description of the active union quoted above from Ch. 1 has been taken from the important paper in Baker's *Remains*, describing the perfect active union, published by Abbot McCann. I have also made a few quotations from unpublished passages of the *Secretum*.

[2] My quotations have been translated from the original Latin. Baker's translation has not been published.

aid Blosius doth describe".[1] And he did so no doubt on the authority of Blosius.

The misconception may have been assisted by Blosius's emphasis on the soul's experience of the Divine Presence and operation within her. For this is the passive aspect of Baker's active contemplation, namely the Divine motion and information which distinguish aspirations from forced acts and become most powerful and most sensible in the highest state of union. Blosius, however, stresses this passive aspect more than Baker. And unlike Baker he regards it as predominant over the active aspect. And this in turn may have disposed him to designate as passive a contemplation which Baker normally and rightly terms active.

But the confusion is due at bottom to Blosius's insufficient analysis of the contemplation he describes. For, as he describes it, it contains, over and above the passive aspect of its substantial active union-contemplation, another contemplation which is passive in Baker's normal understanding of the term. For Blosius speaks of "brilliant illuminations of the Sun of justice" received "in the soul's intellectual capacity". "Such an one God Himself teaches all things and opens to him spiritual and mystical meanings." These words describe a contemplation which *is* passive in Baker's sense, a contemplation through infused species which give knowledge of God's attributes and mysteries. Indeed, in another passage Blosius speaks of what must be an intellectual vision of the Trinity.

The highest active union is often, perhaps in most cases, accompanied by the illuminations of passive contemplation. This, for example, was the case with the Transforming Union as experienced and described by St. Teresa and St. John of the Cross. Blosius evidently takes the concomitance for granted, and describes the substantial active union and this concomitant passive contemplation as one and the same state of mystical union and contemplation, without making the necessary differentiation between them. And this in turn would seem to have misled Baker who, remarking the passive element in the contemplation described by Blosius, concluded too hastily that the entire contemplation was passive, and failed to take account of the identity between its active aspect and the active union he describes in the *Secretum* and *Remains*.

[1] Introduction, Ch. 5.

The mistake may have led him, in deference to the supposed authority of Blosius, to duplicate what is in fact one and the same union, namely active union as he describes it himself and Blosius's amalgam of that active union and a concomitant passive contemplation, as being respectively an active and a passive union. This duplication we have in fact found in *Sancta Sophia*. But Blosius' failure to discriminate between the active substance of the supreme active union and the passive contemplation which commonly accompanies it, and the confusion which it occasioned in Baker, cannot weigh against Baker' plain teaching as it is expounded in the *Secretum* and *Remains*.

For, as we have seen, except for one or two isolated passages the result probably of undue deference to Blosius, Baker's passive contemplation is an illumination of Divine truth, and preeminently the intellectual visions frequently concomitant on the higher degrees of mystical union, Divine attributes o mysteries of faith to the soul by "species or images infused by God, or by the images that already are therein which He maketh in some manner to represent Himself unto the soul". But she does not see Him "as He truly is in Himself".[2] In one passage, it is true, Baker speaks of a passive contemplation in which "God does not present Himself by some species or other but by His work".[3] It is a sudden and powerful operation of God in the soul "causing and creating in her all virtues, reforming her after this unspeakable manner and (as some term it) baptising her and renewing her in the Holy Ghost".[4] That is to say a passive contemplation of this type is an infusion of supernatural virtue. Baker, however, was not, in my opinion, justified in describing this Divine operation without species or intellectual illumination as passive contemplation. It should be regarded as a special case of his active contemplation in its higher stages, a peculiarly powerful and perceptible instance of the Divine motion which produces aspirations and the active union to which they lead. For, as Baker describes it here, it would seem to be a sudden acceleration of the active-infused contemplation-union, whereby the soul makes an instantaneous and far-reaching advance on the road she was travelling already as when a motorist drawing out the clutch of his car makes it

---

[1] Introduction, Ch. 4.
[2] *Commentary*, Ch. 26.
[3] Introduction, Ch. 7.
[4] ibid.

continue the ascent of a hill with a facility and speed otherwise impossible. If this view is correct, the infusion of virtue is not the essence of this contemplation but a result of the advance in her union with God made by the soul thus Divinely moved.

In this passage, be it observed, Baker evidently intends to classify all passive contemplations under these two types, illumination by species and the infusion of virtue, to the implied exclusion of any third type. He therefore leaves no room for the passive contemplation described in *Sancta Sophia* (IV, iv, 5, 6), which reduplicates as passive what is elsewhere described as the perfect active union.

Baker was criticised by Abbot Cuthbert Butler for teaching that mystical contemplation is not an immediate union with the Godhead but the supernatural infusion into the soul of species in some way representative of God, and thus making an unnecessary concession to a false psychology.[1]

As regards passive contemplation Baker was right in teaching this. Otherwise the vision of God would be possible in this life, which it is not. If however he taught that species sensible or conceptual are the medium of active contemplation and union, he was mistaken and the Abbot's criticism was justified. *Did* he? It must be admitted that he did, but only with reluctance, in the teeth of experience and as Abbot Butler observes, in deference to a false psychology. Even so he so qualifies his admission of species as practically to nullify it. In a passage in *Sancta Sophia*[2] it is admitted, though only as probable, "perhaps", that images play a part in the active union. But he tells us that this is a concession to the "Schools" which resolve that "operations" with "no use at all of the internal senses or sensible images cannot consist with the state of a soul joined to a mortal body". Experiments conducted by Professor Spearman and his pupils have proved that they can and do. Moreover he speaks of "obscure notions imprinted in our minds" in active contemplation "concerning God by which we do perceive that He is not anything that we can perceive or imagine but an inexhaustible ocean of universal being and good exceeding our comprehension".[3] A notion of this kind, it might be pointed out, is purely intellectual

---

[1] *Western Mysticism*, 2nd ed., Afterthoughts, LXVIII.
[2] *Sancta Sophia*, IV, 1, 12.
[3] *Confessions*, p. 48. A passage, however, excerpted from *Sancta Sophia*.

and therefore makes no use of "the internal senses or sensible images". And it is more negative than positive. In *Sancta Sophia*, however, this "general obscure confused *Notion of God*" is called "virtual" rather than "direct and express", and distinguished from "the main business", the essence or substance of the active union which is a union of the will.[1] That is to say the union itself, the substance of active contemplation, is not mediated by any species, not even an obscure and negative notion. It is an existential union[2] with the transcendent Godhead effected by the will. And Baker not only implies that the species in this active union of the will are imperceptible; when he calls them virtual, not express, he explicitly calls them so. "The images that the soul makes use of are so exquisitely pure and immaterial that she cannot perceive at all that she works by images."[3] "There is a mystic contemplation . . . by which the soul without discoursings, without any perceptible use of internal senses or sensible images, by a pure, simple and reposeful operation of the mind simply regards God as infinite and incomprehensible Verity and with the whole bent of her will rests in Him as her infinite universal and incomprehensible Good."[4] The experience, that is to say of other contemplatives and of Baker himself, is opposed to the hypothesis that images or even ideas are the medium of their active contemplation, which, as we have seen, is the substance of mystical prayer, "mystic contemplation which is truly and properly such".[5]

And the hypothesis is contradicted by Baker's other utterances on the subject, by his constant insistence on the absence of images from this active contemplation of the will. "The understanding is to carry with it no images or species."[6] And in the exercise of aspirations the soul "is to cast all images out of doors and to keep them out . . . and to admit only a general notion or remembrance of God, *wherein yet the soul doth not tarry, but speedily with her will passeth into or towards that same God. And thus, by and with such aspirations, she doth transcend all images* and created things whatsoever, aspiring to the union of

---

[1] *Sancta Sophia*, IV, I, 14.
[2] Union between existents, actual beings, not perception of the essence, the nature of form of any being.
[3] *Sancta Sophia*, IV, I, 12.
[4] *Confessions*, p. 45. A passage excerpted from *Sancta Sophia*.
[5] ibid.
[6] *Confessions*, p. 91–2.

the Creator Himself, who is without any image, and is the more perfectly had and found by how much all images both of Him and of all creatures are cashiered and done away out of the memory of the soul."[1]

Here even the general and negative notion of God is not the medium of the aspiration but a precedent condition which must be transcended and put away when the aspiration itself is produced by the will.

In another passage indeed Baker contrasts contemplation of God by infused species in the passive union with contemplation "with the light of faith only"[2] in the active union of the will, the prayer of the *Cloud*. And in another place he says that "The understanding in this life hath not" the "essence of God for her object, but some species or other in some sort representing Him *or else* sees Him *only* according to and *by* the light of faith".[3] That is to say he distinguishes a contemplation through the medium of species, passive contemplation and a contemplation "only by", that is through the medium of, "the light of faith", namely, active contemplation. Images and concepts are excluded from the latter, whose medium is faith, not species. If pressed by the scholastic doctrine of the indispensable image Baker would presumably have said that the species—"a general notion" of God—"is not totally eliminated but made imperceptible and merely 'virtual'," though a notion surely is not an image. But it is clear that, speaking from experience and the testimony of other mystics, he regards active contemplation from aspirations upward as imageless, devoid even of ideas, a union of the will alone. We are therefore true to the spirit and substance of Baker's doctrine in denying his occasional statements that a species, be it an image or a concept, and even if the latter is negative, "virtual" and imperceptible, is the medium by or in which the active union and the aspiration which is its imperfect beginning are produced.

Such "obscure notions" however "by which we perceive that God is not anything that we can perceive or imagine but an inexhaustible ocean of universal being and good infinitely exceeding our comprehension"[4] are the conceptual language into which the contemplative is compelled by his experience

[1] Introduction, Ch. 8.   [3] *Commentary*, Ch. 1.
[2] ibid, Ch. 4.   [4] *Confessions*, p. 48, excerpted from *Sancta Sophia*.

to translate the intuitive aspect of his existential union of will to his own intelligence, and when he communicates it to others. That is to say, Baker's error was no more than to mistake for its medium a preliminary and a consequence of active contemplation. And the fact that these general and negative notions precede the union of will and are also a subsequent conceptualisation, seemed to justify the supposition that they are its medium.

Active contemplation therefore may be described as a deliberate attention and adherence to God as He is known by faith without image or concept, a union which, when this contemplation is developed and infused, is evidently produced by the action of God. When however ill-health or excessive fatigue has weakened or impaired the nervous system, this attention becomes difficult or even impossible. A state of desolation results in which prayer is arid and distracted. Writing in an age which knew very little of the nervous mechanism of the human body, it is not surprising that Baker ignores the extent to which desolation is the product of overstrained nerves. Even so he recognises that good health is normally required to support the effort of contemplative prayer. But the desolation he seems to ascribe solely to the action of God. It is more surprising that the physiological factor has not been more clearly recognised by modern spiritual writers.

But although attention and, therefore, consciousness of union with God or aspiration to it is prevented by the effects of fatigue or infirmity, the will to attend to God and adhere to Him is not affected. Nor do they affect God's motion of the will to adhere to Him, though that motion is no longer perceived or *conscious* attention produced by it. And since the substance of prayer is the union of the will with God, not its conscious effects, nor even awareness of the union, the soul is advancing in her union with God in this state of desolation, though she is unaware of her progress. Indeed, since it requires a greater degree of charity and a more powerful motion of grace to persist in the will to attend to God, when that will appears impotent and fruitless, the desolation, though not directly caused by Divine action but by a psychophysical inhibition, is used and doubtless therefore, permitted by God, to purify the soul and advance her union with Him. By the pain felt at the loss of consolation from God, the desolation reveals the selfwill that is attached to this satisfaction and thus prevents the closer union of a will wholly surrendered. The persistent will to attend to God despite apparent inability to do so, and the humble acceptance of that impotence as permissively willed by Him, by overcoming that selfwill, progressively destroy it. And the desolation which so often supervenes as death approaches, though presumably produced by the failure of bodily strength and the effects of illness, serves nevertheless for a final purification, while the will is yet free, by its acceptance and right use, to merit, that is, to increase its union with God, and therefore the measure of the soul's eternal fruition of Him.

Baker's long immunity from desolation after his final conversion was probably due to his ability to order his mode of life to the benefit of his prayer and his prudence in avoiding excessive mortifications.[1] The final desolation which he experienced and disclosed on his deathbed was no doubt caused by the collapse of his bodily powers and his physical suffering. But it was the means of completing the purification which preceded and followed the return of passive contemplation and the high degree of active contemplation—probably the Spiritual Betrothal —which that passive contemplation accompanied and promoted.

God's permission and use of desolation however do not imply that it is in itself good or that the contemplative should desire it. On the contrary, though he should accept it, if it is inevitable, as God's permission for his spiritual profit, he should, as far as he can, avoid it, by avoiding to the best of his ability its causes, particularly excessive strain not required by his duty, and debilitating mortification. This was the wise precept and the example of Baker, a safer guide in this respect, I venture to think, than the greater continental mystics. It is therefore to be feared that the austere rule of life observed in contemplative orders, by producing excessive fatigue and weakness, produces avoidable desolation which, though it may and no doubt does serve the spiritual progress of heroic souls, for many, perhaps, most subjects is an obstacle to contemplative prayer, as serious as the persistence in meditation which contemplatives have always condemned.

These rules moreover were composed and approved when the effect upon prayer of nervous conditions was insufficiently understood. And in this connection I would suggest that if

---

[1] *Confessions*, pp. 114–15, 129–30.

"Balduke"[1] erred in regarding desolation as a proof of sin or at least imperfection and as God's penalty for it, his critic Abbot Chapman erred in the opposite direction by regarding it as in itself a desirable, indeed excellent state, God's gift and the effect of His operation, even as preferable to states of spiritual, as opposed to merely sensible, consolation.[2] For this he had no warrant in the teaching of Baker. And he ran counter to the doctrine of St. John of the Cross who devoted an entire book, his *Living Flame of Love*, to an enthusiastic account of the joys, primarily spiritual, but overflowing upon the bodily senses, which attach to the supreme degree of earthly union with God.

We may now sum up the conclusions reached from this survey of the available evidence.

(I) Baker's active contemplation, from acts upwards through aspirations to the active union which is their goal, covers the entire ascent of contemplative prayer to its summit, therefore those degrees of manifest union which are distinctively mystical prayer and are commonly termed passive and infused, but by Baker, implicitly at least, active and infused.

(II) Passive contemplation, as Baker understood it, consists of all forms of concomitant illumination, a revelation of God to the soul by image or concept, unveiling thus a Divine Presence, otherwise an obscure transcendent Reality, an intellectual vision of the Trinity present in the soul or other intellectual impressions of Divine Truth upon the understanding. These illuminations often accompany high degrees of active contemplation and powerfully assist the latter, are indeed the normal accompaniment of the Transforming Union. Mistakenly, however, Baker also regarded the sudden infusion, without images, of supernatural virtues, as passive contemplation.

(III) These intellectual illuminations are, and from their nature must be, given through the medium of infused species.

(IV) From undue deference to an erroneous psychology Baker assumed that the awareness of God as incomprehensible and "wholly other", unlike anything that can be imagined or conceived, which precedes the union of the will with Him which is

[1] Fr. John Evangelist, of Boisleduc, O.S.F.C., *The Kingdom of God in the Soul*, English trans., Capuchin Classics, Sheed & Ward, 1930.
[2] *The Spiritual Letters of Dom John Chapman*, esp. pp. 162–3.

the substance of active and infused contemplation, and which subsequently translates the experience of it to the understanding, is a medium of the union itself. But under the pressure of his own experience and the witness of mystical writers he admitted that during the aspiration or union this general and negative notion is no more than virtual, too subtle to be perceived, that is for practical purposes non-existent. Nor is he consistent.

(V) Since Blosius in his description of the supreme mystical union did not distinguish between its active substance—the existential union of the will with the transcendent Deity—and the passive contemplation which commonly accompanies and aids it, and which consists in illuminations of the understanding, Baker was on occasion misled into duplicating the same union as active and as passive. This confusion however does not retract his ordinary teaching which is clearly set out in the *Secretum*, as I have disengaged it. He can however hardly be acquitted of inconsistency when he denies that the contemplative is aware that he is in a state of grace. For "interior souls", he tells us, "*see* that they have corresponded with their light and impulses, *are prepared to follow the Divine will* in all that appears to be such, and see no impediment between their soul and God—that is, they do not consciously retain affection to creatures but *see* that they are immediately *united to God in will* and affection according to the manner of this life". Yet they have not "a clearer and more certain testimony" than other souls "that they are in a state of grace."[1] It is obvious that these dispositions are incompatible with the sole alternative to the state of grace, mortal sin, which is precisely a conscious and deliberate disobedience to God's will.[2] Therefore inasmuch as the contemplative sees that he possesses incompatible, indeed, contrary dispositions, he sees that he is in a state of grace.

We can hardly overestimate the value of Baker's teaching, in which he agrees with the *Cloud of Unknowing* and the meaning, if not always the language, of other mystical writers, that the substance of mystical prayer, its progressive union with God, is from first to last an exercise of the will adhering to God as it obeys and later is evidently moved by His grace. "The whole course and process . . . of the *Cloud* is but a prosecution of the

[1] In her *Life of Dame Gertrude More*, Ch. 19, p. 148.   [2] Moreover, in a grave matter.

exercise of the will, as a man would say: from top to toe".[1]
And the contemplation taught by the *Cloud* is the active contemplation which is the essence of mystical prayer. For it is
a progressive union with God and the awareness of it.

True, the effect of passive contemplation is so powerful that,
if the road to God be thought of as a journey of a thousand miles,
it takes the soul in an instant from the hundredth to the nine-
hundredth milestone. But its purpose is to enable the soul to
travel the final hundred miles of active contemplation.[2] That is
to say, passive contemplation is valuable only as an aid to the
active prayer which it accompanies and which follows it and
which is the process of sanctification and merit.

It is worth notice that Baker recognized that the illuminations
of Catholic truth apprehended in mystical prayer, are identical
in nature, though not in authority, with the illuminations, in
which God conveyed truth to the original organs of His public
revelation, to the prophets and apostles.[3]

Perhaps the most distinctive element in his spiritual teaching
is his doctrine of Divine calls and inspirations.[4] Here also he can
and does appeal to authority. Scripture, the liturgy, the Fathers
of the Desert, Cassian and his own Patriarch St. Benedict
have much to say of Divine guidance obtained by prayer.
Nevertheless, during the reaction against Protestant individualism,
to insist upon the necessity for spiritual progress of seeking and
obeying the inspirations of the Holy Spirit must have seemed
dangerous. Was it not the doctrine of the Spanish illuminists
and of the Quakers, who arose in England between Baker's
death and the completion of *Sancta Sophia*, and, moreover, had
not yet acquired their reputation for impeccable respectability,
and harboured eccentric enthusiasts who alleged Divine inspiration for such vagaries as walking nude through the streets?
Did not Baker's teaching refuse obedience to superiors and
directors in favour of selfwill masked as Divine inspiration?
Cressy thought it necessary to refute such objections in his preface
to *Sancta Sophia* and in particular the assimilation of Baker's
doctrine to heretical illuminism. It is in fact, as Baker pointed

[1] Introduction, Ch. 5.
[2] Introduction, Ch. 10.
[3] *Confessions*, pp. 71–2.
[4] The French Jesuit and mystic, however, Père Louis Lallemant, teaches the same doctrine as Baker and defends it against the same objections by the same arguments.

out, contained in the Collect which asks God to prevent, that is, precede our actions by His inspiration and does but expound St. Paul's text "as many as are led by the Spirit, they are the sons of God". It is a doctrine of spiritual liberty without the least taint of licence. Every heresy, it is said, is the revenge of a neglected truth. And the unguarded and exclusive emphasis laid by the Quakers on immediate inspiration was the revenge for the long neglect into which the genuine Catholic doctrine of inspirations, as Baker explains it, had been suffered to fall. Indeed, precisely by meeting and satisfying by anticipation what was true in the Quaker doctrine, it was the best antidote and remedy for what was false in it, though it must be admitted, that, as far as contemporary Quakers were concerned, the language Cressy used about them, by implication, was not calculated to make the remedy applicable in practice.

In our time the doctrine of Divine inspirations has become the distinctive and most prominent tenet of a contemporary religious movement, the Oxford Groups, now known as "Moral Rearmament". Every action of the day, it is taught, however trivial or secular, even the choice of a tailor or a train, must be decided by Divine guidance, to be sought by daily silent prayer and to be expected from it. And it is no doubt the truth and value of both practices, regular mental prayer,[1] and seeking Divine guidance, which has attracted so many to the movement and given it so much strength and vigour, in spite of the exaggeration and onesidedness with which the latter is presented. Baker's doctrine, which safeguards and incorporates in the entire body of Catholic truth the practice of seeking and following individual guidance, is thus the best answer to Group excesses, because it recognizes the truth they contain.

As against illuminism, Baker denies that we are to expect Divine illumination where public religious authority has already spoken. The illuminations of passive prayer are extraordinary, not to be sought, and, when doctrinal, confirmations or illustrations of truth declared by the public revelation in the Church's custody. Nor do the Divine inspirations concern actions already prescribed or forbidden by the duties of our vocation or the command of lawful superiors. They are confined to actions in

[1]Which, however, I venture to think may for many souls be clothed in vocal, particularly liturgical, prayer. See pp. 233–4.

themselves indifferent which can without sin be performed or
omitted. For, although such actions or omissions are in their
matter indifferent, they are not so in the concrete. A pure
intention makes them positively good, an impure intention
correspondingly evil. Moreover, a pure intention requires that
we should do or omit, as is, not necessarily in itself, but for us
here and now, the best choice. How are we to secure this pure
intention, and the choice of the right course for us to adopt such
as we are and in the circumstances in which we are placed?
The inspiration of the Holy Spirit alone will cleanse our motive
from the impurity of self-seeking and enlighten us to choose
rightly, where from the nature of the case no external rule is
applicable. Moreover it is necessary if we are to perform even
obligatory actions and omissions with a pure intention and in
the best way. Unlike the Groups, Baker does not extend inspirations to secular matters in so far as they have no spiritual relevance.
Perhaps, however, writing as he does, primarily for religious,
he does not sufficiently allow for cases in which success in a
secular undertaking is necessary for subsistence.

However that may be, the primary object of the Divine calls
and inspirations is our spiritual progress, our gradual emancipation from selfwill and attachment to creatures, by detachment
from self and creatures and abandonment to the will of God.
It is for this spiritual progress that every soul must observe her
individual calls, follow the inspirations obtained by mental
prayer for her guidance. "Observe," he tells the Cambrai nuns,
"your own way, spirit and call; and of books, take and practise
according as you shall find to be proper and answerable to such
way, spirit and call of yours and no more or further."[1] "These
matters of calls are various and almost infinite for their number
and varieties in matter and manner." They are "not in matters
that of themselves be of any moment but commonly are but of
very little moment as in regard of the matters themselves, but
in regard they are from God and are His will . . . they are all
of them of much moment and therefore never to be neglected."[2]
And Dom Salvin sums up his master's doctrine as obedience to
the Divine Teacher. "That we should seriously practise to
correspond interiorly and exteriorly with the Divine grace and
inspiration. And therefore this is the burden of all his lessons:

[1] Introduction, Ch. I.   [2] Confessions, Ch. 7.

Observe your call: which is all in all: everyone according to the measure of his grace."[1]

In contrast with the Groups Baker tells us we must not expect the inspiration and guidance to be given in our prayer itself. To expect it then would tend to distract our prayer from God to our needs and problems. Having laid our problem before God in prayer, we must banish it from our thoughts till our prayer is finished. Then the guidance will be given either by an enlightenment of our reason or, if, after careful consideration of the arguments in favour of both courses, the mind remains doubtful, by a blind impulse of the will. If neither form of guidance is received, we may choose at random, even by lots, tossing up, as we should say, and take the result as God's will. But, no doubt, Baker would have regarded this solution as applicable only where the pros and cons are balanced so evenly that there really is very little to choose between the alternatives. Indeed, as we have seen, he regarded all lawful actions as in themselves spiritually indifferent, receiving their value solely from our obedience to God's will in performing them.[2]

This indifference as to the matter of these acts and omissions is probably bound up with another significant difference between Baker's teaching and illuminism. Illuminism claims that if we follow Divine inspirations we shall always choose the course in itself the best and the wisest, that is to say, it promises infallible guidance. Baker admits that, even when we have sought Divine guidance in the way he prescribes, our choice may be mistaken. God may nevertheless allow us to choose what will prove the wrong or the less wise course. But the mistake thus permitted will be the best for our spiritual advancement. A choice itself an error or resulting in a failure will be more advantageous for our soul, more spiritually successful, than would have been the choice in itself better or more successful. We may, therefore, say that whereas illuminism promises infallible guidance, Baker promises only infallibly profitable guidance, profitable, that is to say, for our soul's progress to God. And objectively infallible guidance would not be infallibly profitable guidance.

---

[1] *Life*, Sec. 43.
[2] For Baker's doctrine of inspirations, calls and the inner light see *Sancta Sophia* Part I, Sec. 2, Chs. 4–9. Also for his exact words: *Confessions*, 110–13, 118–19, 124–6; Introduction, Chs. 1, 4, *Commentary* Ch. 23.

For constant objective profit would be inconsistent with the mortification and humiliation necessary for spiritual progress, and would foster the attachment, self-satisfaction and pride from which it is the object of prayer to deliver us. On the other hand such measure of objective wisdom, profit or success as is good for the individual under his particular circumstances, a variable unpredictable measure—is guaranteed by the infallibly profitable guidance taught by Baker. Even when, as sometimes happens, a sincere prayer for Divine guidance is followed by an act of material sin, that is of sin committed in invincible ignorance of its sinful nature, the Divine permission which has withheld the objective guidance sought will overrule the moral error to the spiritual profit of the innocent sinner. And mistaken choices of religious creed made after sincere prayer for guidance must be explained in the same way.

Baker's life affords, I believe, an instructive example of infallibly profitable, as opposed to infallible guidance. His well-intentioned but tactless criticism of Dom Rudisind, which led to his leaving Douay, was no doubt written after prayer for light and in accordance with what he believed to be the Divine Will. In itself his action was, so far as we can judge, mistaken. Nevertheless, it procured him that final purification of his journey to England which was, it would seem, indispensable for his advance to a higher degree of prayer. It was, therefore, by God's infallibly profitable guidance, that he was permitted to make what appears to have been the mistake of attacking Dom Rudisind. We may, however, wonder whether in the end the latter, however indignant at the time, did not profit by Baker's rebuke.

In Baker's opinion, the Divine inspiration inclines in case of doubt to omission rather than positive action. For a multiplicity of activities, not demanded by the duty of our state, hinders contemplation and the simplicity it induces. It turns us outward, makes us extroverted, instead of inward to the central spirit where God dwells and works. This inactivity contrasts strikingly with our modern worship of activity, the hustle and bustle of perpetual business and exciting amusement. But it is precisely what the modern world needs, if the spiritual life is to revive and the voice of God to be heard. Modern psychology tends to regard the introvert as a pathological case. He is in fact the

man who alone lives a worthy human life, possessing his own
soul and finding there his God. It must, however, be admitted
that introversion without prayer is indeed pathological. For
the irreligious introvert finds only his empty self with its day-
dreams and delusions. His state is even more unhealthy than
that of the extrovert. In extreme cases it may even lead to insanity.
The introversion Baker preached is Godward, not selfward.
Moreover, all works of obligation must be punctually performed, however many and however distracting and, if performed with the right intention, cannot hinder union with
God, though they may hinder, even entirely prevent, conscious
awareness of that union. And in the higher degrees of contemplation external activities no longer interfere with contemplation
in the apex of the spirit above their tumult of images and thoughts.
For there is no longer any attachment to them.

As regards the Sacraments, Baker keeps the happy mean
between the excess which believes that their use automatically
produces holiness and their depreciation, if not disuse, by many
Protestants. For, while duly valuing the Sacraments, he warns
us that without interior prayer they will not enable us to overcome our faults and advance far on the road towards God.
Only the assiduous practice of mental prayer enables the grace
they confer to operate effectively.

Baker's teaching on mortification is eminently prudent. The
mortifications he values are those he terms "mortifications
of necessity", that is to say, arising from the circumstances in
which we are placed, or imposed by the duties of our state.
Voluntary mortifications, mortifications assumed by the free
choice of the subject, he is reluctant to advise. "Had I a spiritual
disciple that had a body as strong as Samson's and whom I saw
willing and fit to pursue recollection and competent abstraction
of life, I should never be the . . . proposer unto him of voluntary
mortifications, unless it were . . . for remedy against some
temptation wherewith he were troubled. And such mortifications
were not to be termed voluntary but necessary".[1] In this attitude
Baker is in the tradition of English spirituality. Miss Allen
remarks that Margery Kempe did not practise the self-torture
so common among continental mystics. Nor, so far as we can
tell, did Dame Julian.

[1] *Confessions*, Ch. 8.

His doctrine of Divine guidance diminishes the role assigned by Baker to the human director. It is not for him to prescribe the details of prayer and conduct. For he cannot have sufficient knowledge of the soul's state and call. He can but supply general instructions whereby his penitent or disciple can enable himself to receive the guidance of the Divine Director. Consequently for contemplatives following the way of prayer through the will Baker opposes to the constant self-examinations and repeated confessions of the same faults then so popular in many quarters, though he does not deny that they may be useful in awakening and maintaining a tender conscience in those active souls whose consciences are not enlightened and cleansed by God in contemplative prayer.

The author of the *Cloud of Unknowing* is most emphatic that contemplative prayer, by which he means the aspirations preached by Baker, is impossible to those who live the active life. "That Martha should not think that she might both love God and praise Him above all other business . . . and also be busy about the necessaries of this life, Our Lord said that Mary had chosen the best part." The highest prayer possible habitually to those engaged in an active life is discursive meditation.[1] Baker seems to endorse this opinion when he says that even those with a natural disposition for an internal life but who cannot get "commodity of place" for it or are "in a state of marriage and worldly solicitude," are debarred from this contemplative prayer of aspiration.[2] This view is scarcely consistent with his view of contemplation. If contemplative prayer is an aspiration of the will towards union with God, is in fact unitive rather than strictly contemplative, and contemplation therefore but the intuition of the union effected by these aspirations, it should follow that this union of the will and the aspirations which are its exercise are entirely compatible with an active life, even if its activity may weaken or prevent the awareness of this progressive union, which is the contemplative aspect of unitive prayer. That is to say the doctrine of the *Cloud* and Baker as to the nature of "contemplative" prayer as an aspiration of the will should make us deny the limitations they would impose upon its exercise. In *Sancta Sophia* there is in fact a passage in which Baker himself seems to accept this wider view, which

[1] *Cloud*, Chs. 20, 21.   [2] *Commentary*, Ch. 27.

alone is in harmony with his view of the nature of active contemplation. "Though this solitude" indispensable for contemplative prayer "be found both more perfectly and more permanently in a well-ordered religious state . . . yet it is not so
confined to that state but that in the world also and in a secular
course of life God hath oft raised and guided many souls in these
perfect ways."[1] And Elizabeth of the Trinity endorsed this view
when she invited her married sister to live as she did in the
solitude of an interior communion with God.[2]

It has been widely debated in recent years whether all the
faithful are called to contemplative, that is to mystical, prayer.
The answer, I am convinced, is to be found in the nature of
contemplation. Since its substance is not strictly contemplation
but a progressive union with God through a will aspiring to
union with Him, the call to this unitive prayer must be universal.
For all are called to holiness and holiness and union with God
are identical. On the other hand, since the contemplative aspect
of this unitive prayer, the intuition of the union, is accidental
and dependent on factors other than the union itself, all are not
called to it but many, perhaps most, can and must possess the
union with little or no consciousness of it.

It must, I think, be admitted that Baker undervalued the
Divine Office as a means of sanctification. He was, indeed, well
aware that in primitive monasticism the vocal recitation of the
Psalter was the sole regular prayer of the monks. He also recognized that it is possible to say the Office as a prayer of aspirations,
if the Holy Spirit so enables and moves the soul. He had
in fact prayed it himself thus. He even says that such vocal-
mental prayer is the safest, being least liable to harm the head
and spirits, in modern language strain the nerves. He even says,
"Considered in itself, vocal prayer is undoubtedly the more
proper instrument to bring souls to contemplation. This, I think,
is one reason why the Church obliges religious and priests to
the recitation of the Breviary."[3] Nevertheless in his opinion
under contemporary conditions the recitation of the Office could
not normally be contemplative prayer, at any rate for souls not
far advanced in contemplation.

[1] *Sancta Sophia*, Part I, Sec. 3, Ch. 1.
[2] See below, p. 263.
[3] *Inner Life of Dame Gertrude More*, Ch. 16, p. 119.

If, however, the Office can be prayed aspiratively why can it
not, at a lower stage, be prayed as a prayer of forced acts? It
would seem eminently adapted for this. Some modern representatives of the Bakerite tradition maintain that the function of the
Office is not to be mental prayer, but solely to fulfil man's
obligation to worship God. What then is worship, if it is
more than external, but the raising up of the soul to God,
adoring surrender to His Majesty? Does not the *Gloria Patri*
involve in principle the complete abandonment to God which
the spiritual ascent with its degrees of prayer progressively
realises? And what is the 118th Psalm, recited on so many days
of the year, but a series of acts of submission to God's law and
aspiration to obey it, that is to say an aspiration of the will after
union with God, the substance therefore and purpose of the
immediate acts recommended by Baker? Certainly where the
Office is recited in choir at a pace allowing no return upon
distractions, or slowing down, and the regular life admits them,
there will and should be set times for mental prayer apart from
the Office, though, even so, a portion of the latter might well
provide the material of acts. Where, however, circumstances
do not allow more time for prayer, the Office recited in whole
or part is a sufficient, as it is the best form of prayer. For its acts are
made in unison with the Church and guided by her appointment,
in accordance with the scheme of redemption celebrated in her
liturgical year. Even Baker was not unaffected by the liturgical
decay which was already far advanced.

These disagreements do not affect my conviction that Baker's
spiritual doctrine is the most practically valuable that I am
acquainted with for all who desire a life inspired and guided by
prayer. Many writers hold up a lofty and difficult ascetical
ideal, without showing how it may be attained, others are too
emotional, if not sentimental, others are rather theoretical than
practical, others take our devotion no further than the Saints
and the Sacred Humanity,[1] and others describe summits of
prayer to which only a minute number are called. Baker,
especially if read together with the *Cloud of Unknowing* on which
he commented and his teaching illustrated by the inner life and
devotion of his great-hearted disciple, Gertrude More, leads us

[1] Like the author of the *Cloud*, Baker observes the Augustinian rule *per Christum
Hominem ad Christum Deum.*

with gentle yet firm guidance towards God. He asks us to correspond with grace, not to out-step it, to observe our individual call instead of burdening our souls with the practices and prayers of others, even if in themselves more perfect than ours. Though he does not hide from us that the ascent is rough and steep, he assures us that we shall be guided and supported by a Guide who will not ask for any exertion beyond the strength which He alone can gauge, since He gives it Himself. The principles of what was known in Baker's lifetime as Bakerism can be taught to all of ordinary intelligence, while inexhaustible by the wisest. They can and should be the foundation of the spiritual education of Catholic children. If this were the case there would not be such a lamentable tale of lapsed Catholics. Those trained in the school of the Spirit will have received the best security against the materialism of the modern world and its human idolatries. The conversion of Mr. Fursdon's mother-in-law would be repeated time and again by the employment of the same Bakerite method. No one to whom Catholicism had been presented, as Baker presents it, could suppose that priest, director or saint, not even Our Lady or the *Humanity* of Our Lord comes *between* the Catholic and God, or interferes with his direct access to the Triune Godhead, incomprehensible in His transcendence yet apprehended by faith and intimately present in the soul, as nothing created can be, however holy.

Baker's doctrine is so simple, so discreet, so replete with sanctified commonsense, that it is difficult to convey its distinctive quality, its traditional originality—if the oxymoron may be excused—and its homely sublimity. Bremond might have done justice to Baker and Bakerism, though he would perhaps have over-refined and subtilised them. His Holy Wisdom, safe, sober, solid, simple and sublime, is the ripe fruit of the English mystical tradition confirmed, clarified and enriched by the more scientific mystical theology of the Counter-Reformation. In the homelier language of Hilton and the *Cloud*, as restated by Baker, the doctrine of St. John of the Cross loses the terrifying quality of its Castilian ice and scorching sun. That Baker says so little of the illuminations of passive contemplation draws our attention away from these accidents of mystical prayer to its substance, the one thing necessary, the prayer of a will more closely united with God, as it is progressively emptied of self. His prudent yet emancipating instructions about the role of Divine Inspirations in the life of prayer and the paramount importance of obeying our call and *attrait* keep the golden mean between legalism and illuminism. I implore any readers who do not already know their Baker to make his acquaintance. If *Sancta Sophia* seems too large a mouthful to begin with, though selections could easily be made, there is his own abridgement of Bakerism in his *Inner Life of Dame Gertrude More*. Or if we would begin with his biography, there are the autobiographical portions of the *Secretum* excerpted and arranged by Abbot McCann under the title *The Confessions of Father Baker* and the two lives by Salvin and Cressy edited together by the Abbot. Dom Pritchard's life also with the unfinished autobiography. Finally, there is the book to which Baker owed so much and which we cannot separate from him, a book which has attracted, though not without serious misconception, Mr. Aldous Huxley. I mean the *Cloud of Unknowing*, now published with Baker's commentary. Those who desire to practise Baker's prayer of acts, assuming of course they have the requisite call, will find his own collection at the end of *Sancta Sophia*. And there are the acts from which he partly derived them, those compiled by Blosius. There are acts of affective prayer, forced acts, collected by Dame Gertrude More, published as *The Sainctly Ideot's Devotions* (1657), also devotional pieces in the form of prayers which she composed the *Confessiones Amantis* or *Ideot's Devotions*, published 1658. Her papers had been edited by Baker—and her writings exemplify and apply his teaching. In one way or another come to Baker. The result will not fail to be a considerable addition to the Bakerites. And I know no wiser or safer school of prayer. So with Abbot McCann, to whom all lovers of Baker are so deeply indebted, I conclude by repeating Baker's petition: "The blessed spirit of prayer rest upon us all."

BIBLIOGRAPHY

Holy Wisdom: Directions for the Prayer of Contemplation. Compiled by Dom Serenus Cressy. Latest edition Burns, Oates and Washbourne (1950)

The *Confessions* of Venerable Father Baker excerpted from the *Secretum*. Abbot McCann. Burns, Oates and Washbourne (1922).

The Cloud of Unknowing with Fr. Baker's Commentary. Abbot McCann. Burns, Oates and Washbourne (1924). Sixth and Revised Edition, 1952.

Life by Dom Leander Pritchard. The fullest Life. It includes Baker's fragmentary autobiography. Catholic Record Society, No. 33.

Lives, by Dom Peter Salvin and Dom Serenus Cressy. Ed. Abbot McCann. Burns, Oates and Washbourne (1933).

The Lives by Dom Pritchard and Dom Salvin with the autobiographical fragment were lost and came to light in 1927, discovered by Dom Orsmer Berlière in the Bibliothèque Mazarine.

The Inner Life of Dame Gertrude More. Ed. Dom Benedict Weld-Blundell. R. and T. Washbourne, Catholic Home Library. Imprimatur 1910.

Dame Gertrude More's collection of acts—*The Saintly Idiot's Devotions*, edited by Dom Hildebrand Lane Fox, before 1910.

The Writings of Dame Gertrude More: Confessiones Amantis, etc. Ed. Dom Benedict Weld-Blundell. Catholic Home Library, R. and T. Washbourne. Imprimatur 1910.

CHAPTER X

JOHN SMITH THE CAMBRIDGE PLATONIST

THE THREE constituents of an adequate religion distinguished by Von Hügel in his *Mystical Element of Religion* are now a commonplace of the philosophy of religion. They are, in his words, the experimental-mystical, the rational-critical and the historical-institutional. Of these three elements, John Smith had very little understanding or appreciation of the historical-institutional. It was a defect he shared with the other representatives—some his personal friends—of what is known as Cambridge Platonism and more generally with Puritans of the left wing. In consequence his insights of religious truth had little influence beyond an immediate circle of disciples. For they were not integrated into an organic and traditional body of religious doctrine and worship and thereby safeguarded and handed down intact. On the other hand he presents an admirable fusion of the other two elements, the experimental and the rational. For this and for the attractive and holy personality revealed by his works, and for the eloquent prose in which his deepest thought and loftiest aspiration found embodiment, he deserves to be far better known and far better appreciated than he is.

August 7th, 1952, was the tercentenary of his death. This study is offered as a tribute to his memory on an occasion which, one fears, may not have been celebrated as it deserves.

Smith's life was uneventful. Born in 1618 at Achurch near Oundle he went up to Cambridge in 1636 and spent the remainder of his life at the University. He was entered as a pensioner of Emmanuel College, a Puritan foundation and a stronghold of Puritanism. But already a wider and less dogmatic theology had found entrance into the college. For the father of Cambridge Platonism, Benjamin Whichcote, was Smith's tutor at Emmanuel. Smith took his B.A. degree in 1640, his M.A. four years later. The same year he was transferred to Queen's College by the Parliamentary commissioners engaged in purging the University of Royalists and convinced Anglicans. He was a lecturer at

Queen's for the remainder of his life. Though the commissioners' choice proves that Smith had no difficulty in accepting a Presbyterian service and discipline, his writings leave no doubt that he regarded such things with indifference and would have found no difficulty in conforming to any Protestant worship. He lectured on mathematics but was known for his wide erudition in philosophy, theology and oriental languages. He shews astonishing knowledge of Rabbinical and Cabbalistic Judaism. Another fellow of Queen's, Simon Patrick, later Bishop of Ely, in his funeral panegyric spoke of Smith as a "living library and a walking study". He left his college his library of over six hundred volumes, a considerable number in those times. But it is clear from Patrick's sermon that, as we should have expected from his writings, he impressed his associates even more by his holiness than by his learning. However, his career was cut short by an early death from consumption in his thirty-fifth year. All we have from his pen is a collection of ten pieces, "Discourses", largely from an unfinished series of sermons in the college chapel —conferences we might call them—in which he intended to expound and defend the fundamental truths of the Christian religion, of natural theology first, then of revealed. That he has left so little we need not regret. For he states sufficiently and in a noble English style views of truth which might otherwise have been buried, as they were by his fellow Platonists Cudworth and More, under a mass of obsolete erudition and longwinded discussions of contemporary philosophies, of Hobbes and the Cartesians, unrewarding, when there is so much to be read and life at the longest so short. The *Select Discourses*[1] were prepared for publication by John Worthington, to whom we are indebted for the arrangement, a translation of the Hebrew, Greek and Latin quotations of which Smith was lavish, and a detailed synopsis printed before each section of a discourse and in full at the beginning of the book. The first edition, which I was fortunate enough to pick up for a few shillings in the attic of a second-hand bookshop, was published in 1660.

The first discourse treats of the true way of attaining to Divine knowledge. It is not notional knowledge but real, vital, experimental. The second treats of superstition, the third of atheism.

---

[1] All, however, that Worthington could find. In his preface he promises to print more should they be sent to him. But nothing further has survived.

In those happier days it still seemed sufficient to refute the crude mechanical atomism of the Epicureans. The fourth discourse seeks to prove the immortality of the soul. The fifth is concerned with the existence and nature of God. The sixth discourse is a long discussion of the nature of prophecy, as we meet with it in Scripture. This is, not unnaturally, the most antiquated of the Discourses. But it illustrates admirably Smith's view of reason and its enlightenment by a higher Divine illumination. The seventh discourse treats "of the difference between Legal and Evangelical Righteousness". It must be read in connection with the two following, "A Discovery of the Shortness and Vanity of a Pharisaic Righteousness" and "The Excellency and Nobleness of True Religion".

Every year on March 25th a sermon must be preached at Huntingdon by a fellow of Queen's College against Witchcraft and Diabolical Contracts. The final discourse is the sermon preached by Smith "A Christian's Conflicts and Conquests over Satan". It is a fine performance. Though the possibility of witchcraft and a formal contract with the devil is not denied, very little is said of it. The bulk of the sermon is devoted to the spiritual struggle against evil spirits and the reminder that they can harm us only if they find an accomplice, diabolic evil, in our own souls. Smith insists on the impotence of devils, if the Christian resists them seeking God's help. And he remarks upon the diabolism of violence, even if cloaked by zeal for religion. For it results in divided aims, fosters confusion and irrationality. "The devil loves to be conversed with in a way of darkness and obscurity."[1] He seems here to be remarking on that ambiguity of the diabolic, brought out so well in a recent symposium on Satan, and on the diabolic irrationality such as contributors to the book have pointed out in certain manifestations of contemporary art.

Throughout his writings Smith reveals himself a candid soul, a luminous spirit, enamoured of light and therefore of the Divine Luminary, the Father of Lights from whom proceed alike the natural light of reason and the higher light of revealed truth. If man would be illuminated by this light, he must purify his spirit from all that may obscure it, impatience, violence, self-seeking and self-assertion, obstinate prejudice and the inveterate tendency even of

[1] *A Christian's Conflicts and Conquests*, Ch. V.

Christians to make God in their own image. "Divinity is a true efflux from the eternal light which, like the sunbeams, does not only enlighten but heat and enliven; and therefore our Saviour hath . . . connext purity of heart with the beatifical vision." "The knowledge of God which springs forth from true goodness brings such a Divine light into the soul, as is more clear and convincing than any demonstration . . . Those filthy mists that arise from impure and terrene minds, like an atmosphere perpetually encompass them, that they cannot see that Sun of Divine Truth that shines about them, but never shines into any unpurged souls."[1] "True religion teaches men to rise above that vaporous sphere of sensual and earthly pleasures which darken the mind and hinder it from enjoying the brightness of Divine Light. The proper motion of religion is still upwards to its first original."[2] "Religion, where it is in truth and in power, renews the very spirit of our minds and doth in a manner spiritualise this outward creation to us." It "teaches the soul to look at those perfections which it finds here below, not so much as perfections of this or that body, as they adorn this or that particular being, but as they are so many rays issuing forth from that first and essential Perfection in which they all meet and embrace one another in the most close friendship. Every particular good is a blossom of the First Goodness; every created excellency is a beam descending from the Father of Lights: and should we separate all these particularities from God, all affection spent upon them would be unchaste. We should love all things in God and God in all things, because He is All in all, the beginning and original of their being, the perfect idea of their goodness and the end of their motion. It is nothing but a thick mist of pride and self-love that hinders men's eyes from beholding that Sun which enlightens them and all things else. But when true religion begins once to dawn upon men's souls and with its shining light chases away their black night of ignorance; then they behold themselves and all things else enlightened, though in a different way, by one and the same Sun and all the powers of their souls fall down before God and ascribe all glory to Him. Now, it is that a good man is no more solicitous whether this or that good thing be mine or whether my perfections exceed the measure of this or that

---

[1] *The True Way or Method of Attaining to Divine Knowledge*, Sec. 1.
[2] *The Excellency and Nobleness of True Religion*, Ch. XI.

particular creature; for whatsoever good he beholds anywhere he enjoys and delights in it as much as if it were his own, and whatever he beholds in himself he looks not upon it as his property but as a common good; for all these beams come from one and the same fountain and ocean of light in whom he loves them all with an universal love: . . . in a particular being" he "loves the universal goodness. Thus may a good man walk up and down the world as in a garden of spices and suck a divine sweetness out of every flower". For "there is a twofold meaning in every creature, a literal and a mystical and the one is but the ground of the other".[1] "Because all those scattered rays of beauty and loveliness which we behold spread up and down all the world over are only the emanations of that inexhausted light which is above; therefore we should love them all in that, and climb up always by those sunbeams unto the Eternal Father of Lights."[2] "God made the universe and all the creatures contained therein as so many glasses wherein He might reflect His own glory. He hath copied forth Himself in the Creation . . . How to find God here and feelingly converse with Him, and being affected with the sense of the Divine Glory shining out upon the creation, how to pass out of the sensible world into the intellectual is effectually taught . . . by true religion: that which knits and unites God and the soul together can best teach it how to ascend and descend upon those golden links that unite, as it were, the world to God." "That Divine wisdom that contrived and beautified this glorious structure can best explain her own art and carry up the soul back again in these reflected beams to . . . the fountain of them." While "good men . . . are thus conversing with this lower world and are viewing the invisible things of God in the things that are made, in this visible and outward creation, they find God many times secretly flowing into their souls and leading them silently out of the court of the temple into the holy place".[3] One is sorry that this philosopher of true enlightenment was cut off by prejudice from the magnificent texts of the Catholic liturgy— for Christmas, the Purification, Holy Saturday—which speak of the Divine Light and its illumination of human spirits.

This philosophy or rather this theology of light, is remote

---

[1] *The Excellency and Nobleness of True Religion*, Ch. VIII.
[2] *The Existence and Nature of God*, Ch. VIII.
[3] *The Excellency and Nobleness of True Religion*, Ch. VIII.

from the dourness and sourness too often charged indiscriminately
on Puritan religion—in fact "sour" and "peevish" are Smith's
frequent epithets of censure. "Religion is no such austere, sour
and rigid thing as to affright men away from it. It is no sullen
Stoicism, no sour Pharisaism, it does not consist in a few melancholy passions, in some dejected looks or depressions of mind"—
the characteristic demeanour of the conventional Puritan—"but
it consists in freedom, love, peace, life and power, the more it
comes to be digested into our lives, the more sweet and lovely
we shall find it to be".[1] The "sweetness and light" of Matthew
Arnold's humanist culture are the attributes of genuine religion
as Smith knew it. This "enlightenment" involved the high
esteem of reason characteristic of this Platonist school. It is the
esteem of the Christian humanist. "God hath stamped a copy of
His own archetypal loveliness upon the soul, that man by reflecting into himself might behold there the glory of God. . . .
Reason in man being *lumen de lumine*, a light flowing from the
fountain and father of lights . . . was to enable man to work out
of himself all those notions of God which are the true ground-
work of love and obedience to God and conformity to Him."[2]
Reason however has been darkened by the fall and God has
therefore given man the revelation which has culminated in the
coming of Jesus Christ. It is not simply external. "There
is also an inward impression of it on men's minds and spirits.
We cannot see divine things but in a Divine light."[3] Here
as elsewhere Smith's language lacks an accuracy which was
the fruit of the progressive theological tradition of Catholic
schools and doctrinal definitions. But the illumination he has
in view is that infused faith without which the spirit cannot
apprehend God as the revealer of the truths to which it assents.
He fuses it is true, to the point of confusing, faith and charity. And
when he seems to identify faith with an assurance of God's love
he is once more inaccurate. When however he tells us that by
faith, "Moses-like conversing with God in the mount and there
beholding His glory shining out upon us in the face of Christ,
we should be deriving a copy of that eternal beauty upon
our own souls, and our thirsty and hungry spirits would be

---

[1] *The Excellency and Nobleness of True Religion*, Ch. XI.
[2] ibid., Ch. I.
[3] ibid., Ch. II.

perpetually sucking in a true participation and image of His glory,"[1] he intends what the Catholic mystics tell us of faith, a faith informed by love, as the means of union with God.

Smith was no rationalist. Reason as he understood it is not exclusively or primarily the manipulation of clear concepts which constitutes discursive ratiocination. Nor is it restricted to reasoning from data to data of sense perception.[2] He would have spoken of Humian empiricism and logical positivism in terms more scornful, if possible, than those in which he speaks of the Epicureans. For him the highest exercise of reason is the intuition of spiritual truth, metaphysical truth, moral truth, aesthetic truth and above all religious truth. Of the last he says: "When reason once is raised by the mighty force of the Divine Spirit into a converse with God, it is turned into sense . . . We shall then converse with God τῷ νῷ" by intellectual intuition, "whereas before we conversed with Him only τῇ διανοίᾳ with our discursive faculty. Before we laid hold on Him only with a struggling, agonistical and contentious reason . . . we shall then fasten our minds upon Him with such a serene understanding . . . as will present us with a blissful, steady and invariable sight of Him".[3] Locke, typically rationalist in temper, was well aware that Smith did not share his rationalism. For commenting on the *Discourses* he wrote that Smith's views savour too much of Enthusiasm.[4] A true, because a complete, empiricist, Smith accepts every category of human experience, and as an illumination of Divine Truth. And he accepts the unique experience of the divinely commissioned teachers and revealers, above all of Christ.

It must however, I think, be admitted that he is insufficiently aware of that dark and negative knowledge of God, the darkness of light too brilliant, which for the mystic is the highest form of Divine knowledge possible in this life. Certainly he is not ignorant of it. He speaks of the human spirit as flying "upwards . . . till it be swallowed up in the boundless abyss of Divinity . . . that divine darkness which the Areopagite speaks of, which the

---

[1] *Legal Righteousness and of the Righteousness of Faith*, Ch. VI.
[2] Not truly such, however, but mental perception of form through and in sense data.
[3] *The True Way or Method of Attaining to Divine Knowledge*, Sec. 2.
[4] Letter to Damaris Cudworth, quoted in J. A. PASSMORE'S *Ralph Cudworth*, p. 92. Smith's religion, however, was too individualist to do much to stem the current already beginning to flow in a rationalist direction.

higher our minds soar into the more incomprehensible they find it".[1] But this would seem to be rather a theoretical limit than a personal experience. For in his discussion of prophecy he appears to condemn all ecstasy indiscriminately. And he tells us "that God will only be conversed with in the way of light and understanding".[2] Nor in this life can our intuition of God ever be "steady and invariable".[3] Satisfied with present illumination he seems to have experienced the positive rather than the negative aspect of God as infinite and incomprehensible Truth, Goodness and Being.

With light the liturgy associates liberty and the same combination is to be found in Smith. He sees religion as the ascent to God of a spirit whose capacity cannot be satisfied otherwise. A depreciatory adjective common from his pen is "pinching", that which holds the spirit captive in the narrow confinement of some petty selfish aim or sensual pleasure. "Religion . . . does work the soul into a true and divine amplitude. There is a living soul of religion in good men which . . . enables them to *dilate* and *extend* themselves more fully upon God and all Divine things without being pinched or straightened within themselves. Whereas wicked men are of most narrow and confined spirits, they are so contracted by the *pinching particularities* of earthly and created things, so imprisoned in a dark dungeon of sensuality and selfishness, so straightened through their carnal designs and ends that they cannot stretch themselves nor look beyond the horizon of time and sense. The nearer any being comes to God who is that infinite fulness that fills all in all, the more vast and large and unbounded it is"[4]—the very opposite in fact of those narrowminded and petty folk too often regarded as distinctively religious.

Today the majority of mankind is content with material aims and an earthly destiny, many, perhaps, oppressed by the almost infinite extent of inorganic matter revealed by the telescope. In advance Smith condemns this slavery in one of his finest flights of spiritual aspiration. "There is nothing that so embases and enthralls the souls of men, as the dismal and dreadful thoughts

---

[1] *The Existence and Nature of God*, Ch. I.
[2] *A Christian's Conflicts and Conquests*, Ch. V.
[3] *The True Way or Method of Attaining to Divine Knowledge*, Sec. 2.
[4] *The Excellency and Nobleness of True Religion*, Ch. III. Cf. Fr. Baker, "the contemplative soul thirsts after the spaciousness and infinity of God".

of their own mortality which will not suffer them to look beyond this short span of time . . . or to look higher than these material heavens; which, *though they could be stretched forth to infinity*, yet would the space be too narrow for an enlightened mind, that will not be confined within the compass of corporeal dimensions. These black opinions of death and the nonentity of souls . . . shrink up the freeborn spirit which is within us, which would otherwise be dilating and spreading itself boundlessly beyond all finite being: and when these sorry *pinching mists*" (notice the joint dislike of darkness and confinement) "are once blown away, it finds this narrow sphere of being to give way before it; and having once seen beyond time and matter it finds then no more ends nor bounds to stop its swift and restless motion.[1] It may then fly upwards till it be beyond all orb of finite being, swallowed up in the boundless abyss of Divinity . . . Those dismal apprehensions which pinion the souls of men to mortality, churlishly check and starve that noble life thereof which would always be rising upwards and spread itself in a free heaven: and when once the soul hath shaken off these, when it is once able to look through a grave and see beyond death, it finds a vast immensity of being opening itself more and more before it, and the ineffable light and beauty thereof shining more and more into it."[2]

In the same vein is Smith's appeal to present experience of God as a final proof that the soul is immortal, with which he concludes his discourse on immortality, when he has retailed traditional proofs in which I, at least, can find nothing more cogent than plausibilities and persuasives counterbalanced by arguments equally strong for the opposite conclusion. This final argument which if it does not amount to strict proof—for individual survival might conceivably be an intrinsic impossibility—is nevertheless the ground on which, antecedent to any revelation, the spirit which is convinced of God and of present communion with Him may become assured of its immortality. "The soul" of a good man "being purged and enlightened by true sanctity is capable of those divine irradiations, whereby it feels itself in conjunction with God, and by . . . the light of divine Goodness mixing itself with the light of its own reason, sees clearly not

---

[1] Unceasing, not restless in its usual sense today.
[2] *Of the Existence and Nature of God*, Ch. I.

only that it may, if it please the supreme Deity, of its own nature exist eternally, but also that it shall do so: it knows that Almighty Love, which it lives by, to be stronger than death and more powerful than the grave . . . It knows that God will never forsake His own life which He hath quickened in it; He will never deny those ardent desires of a blissful fruition of Himself which the lively sense of His own goodness hath excited within it: those breathings and gaspings after an eternal participation of Him are but the energy of His own breath within us: if He had had any mind to destroy it, He would never have shewn it such things as He hath done; he would not raise it up to such mounts of vision, to shew it all the glory of that heavenly Canaan flowing with unbounded pleasures and then tumble it down again into that deep and darkest abyss of death and non-entity. Divine goodness cannot, it will not, be so cruel to holy souls that are such ambitious suitors for His love. The more they contemplate the blissful effluxes of His divine love upon themselves, the more they find themselves strengthened with an undaunted confidence in Him; and look not upon themselves in these poor bodily relations and dependencies but . . . as the sons of God who is the Father of souls, souls that are able to live anywhere in this spacious universe and better out of this dark and lonesome cell of bodily matter which is always checking and clogging them in their noble motions than in it: as knowing that when they leave this body they shall then be received into everlasting habitations, and converse freely and familiarly with that Source of life and spirit which they conversed with in this life in a poor, disturbed and straightened manner."[1] There are echoes here, though probably unconscious, of similar language on the lips of a contemporary Cambridge don of different beliefs and destiny, Crashaw:

> The selfremembring soul sweetly recovers
> Her kindred with the stars; not basely hovers
> Below: but meditates her immortal way
> Home to the originall source of *light* and intellectual day.[2]

Like other Platonists, Smith here and elsewhere speaks slightingly of matter and the body, not indeed as being positively

[1] *The Immortality of the Soul*, Ch. VII.   [2] *Description of a Religious House.*

I

evil but as least in value and as thwarting and imprisoning the spirit. He did not however deny the resurrection of the body, like the heathen Neoplatonists and even their Christian disciple Synesius, who when chosen Bishop of Cyrene told the patriarch, Theophilus of Alexandria, that though he was prepared to preach the doctrine for the benefit of his simple flock, he could not believe it himself. On the contrary Smith professes his belief in a final embodiment of the soul.[1] This body however will not be of the coarse-textured matter we know, but of a finer grain, such as will serve the life of an immortal spirit. In this, I submit, Smith and his fellow Platonists were right and in agreement with what St. Paul teaches of the risen body. In this life the spirit is the soul, that is to say the formative and informing principle, of the body, the principle of man's biological life. In so far as this is the case, the body is in truth an obstacle and a prison of which the spirit would be well free. That the major part of man's time and labour must be devoted to the satisfaction of the biological needs which he shares with the brutes, is a bondage and degradation for an intellectual and immortal spirit. This is not however the sole relation between the body and the spirit. Even now in this mortal life the body is also employed in distinctively spiritual activities, serves man's spiritual, not only his biological, life. Mouth, eye, ear, hand—they are instruments of spiritual as well as of biological functions and purposes. Morality, speculation, the acquisition of biologically useless knowledge, aesthetic appreciation and creation, prayer—all these use and require the body. That is to say, the spirit, which can survive death only because it exceeds its lower function as the informing principle of the body, not only ensouls but inspirits the body. Since biological life finally ceases at death, the risen body will be inspirited but not ensouled. It will therefore be adapted exclusively for this inspiration, will be what St. Paul termed a spiritual body, a body wholly and solely inspirited and therefore as unlike the present body as the oak its acorn. To have perceived this was not the defect but the merit of such Platonists as Smith.

Religion for Smith, as prayer for Baker (and prayer is essential religion) consists in aspirations to God and to union with God, the "breathings after Himself" to which "wheresoever God beholds them, He gives life as those which are His own breath

[1] *Of the Existence and Nature of God*, Ch. X.

in them".[1] "The spirit of religion is always ascending upwards."[2] "The spirit which is from Heaven is always . . . carried upwards again towards Heaven from whence it came."[3] "The proper motion of religion is still upwards to its first Original."[4] Religion, that is to say, is an order of spirits aspiring upwards to God like those human flames painted by El Greco to depict these spiritual aspirations. This aspiration to God is universal and inevitable. For all men seek happiness. And God alone can make men truly and permanently happy. "Thus when men most of all fly from God they still seek after Him."[5]

Smith insists on the peace of true religion, "a knowing of the truth in that sweet, mild, humble and loving spirit of Jesus",[6] "a serene understanding, intellectual calmness and serenity".[7] "Evil spirits are always turbulent and restless."[8] They must be resisted not by violence but by "a pacifying and quieting of all those riots and tumults raised by sin and Satan".[9] And in the same context he rebukes the bitter religious polemics of his time. "There is a pompous and popular kind of tumult in the world which sometimes goes for zeal to God and His kingdom; whenas men's own pride and passions disguise themselves under the notions of a religious fervency. Some men think themselves the greatest champions for God and His cause, when they can take the greatest liberty to quarrel with everything abroad and without themselves which is not shaped according to the mould of their own opinions, their own selfwill, humour and interest."[10]

Not the least part of the attraction exercised by Smith is his determination to keep aloof from controversy. Of set purpose he refrains from discussing the doctrine of justification by faith only and is content to contrast a purely external self-satisfied righteousness with an interior righteousness of loving faith in God and distrust of self. His fellow-Platonist and personal friend

---

[1] *A Christian's Conflicts and Conquests*, Ch. V.
[2] *The Excellency and Nobleness of True Religion*, Ch. I
[3] *A Christian's Conflicts and Conquests*, Ch. IV.
[4] *The Excellency and Nobleness of True Religion*, Ch. XI.
[5] *The Existence and Nature of God*, Ch. III. As Max Picard has pointed out in his *Flight from God*, a book which, were its tone less hysterical, would be most valuable in its illuminating and fundamental criticism of modern secularism.
[6] *The True Way or Method of Attaining to Divine Knowledge*, Sec. I.
[7] ibid., Sec. II.
[8] *A Christian's Conflicts and Conquests*, Ch. I.
[9] ibid., Ch. IV.
[10] ibid., Ch. IV.

Henry More mars his work by crude and violent outbursts of anti-Catholic bigotry. Smith discusses superstition without so much as alluding to Catholicism. On the contrary he shews us what superstition really is: to cherish unworthy notions of God. And he points out to his fellow-Puritans that zeal against idolatry is perfectly consistent with the interior idolatry which prefers the creature to the Creator. Only once in these ten discourses is there a note of anti-Catholic polemic, when, in face of the fact that while he was declaring that he had kept the law Jesus loved him, Smith attempts to show that Our Lord's invitation to the young man to sell his possessions was "not a *consilium perfectionis* in the Papal sense" but designed to expose his Pharisaic self-righteousness.[1] But this *obiter dictum*, pronounced without rancour, does but ruffle for a moment the surface of a peace too charitable, too deeply absorbed in communion with God, to desert prayer for polemics, contemplation for controversy.

This peace is the product of unity, a unity which progresses as the spirit is progressively united with the Divine Unity. "The good man in whom religion rules"—Smith would have had no sympathy with a secular morality—"is at peace and unity with himself . . . Grace doth more and more reduce all faculties of the soul into a perfect subjection and subordination to itself. The union and conjunction of the soul with God, that primitive unity is that which is the alone original and fountain of all peace and the centre of rest: . . . God only is such an Almighty Goodness as can attract all the powers in man's soul to itself . . . and so unite man perfectly to himself in the true enjoyment of one uniform and simple Good."[2] We may be reminded of the emphasis placed by Sister Elizabeth of the Trinity on the Divine work of progressive unification and the peace it brings. And again of her when Smith tells us that "the soul must . . . by a holy abstraction from all the things that pinion it to mortality withdraw itself and retire into a Divine Solitude".[3] For this is the solitude of interior detachment and separation to which Elizabeth invites us.

In this solitude the soul becomes Godlike by receiving the "efflux" of the Divine life. "This" is "the life" which "is nothing else but God's own breath within" the Christian "and an infant

---

[1] *The Shortness and Vanity of a Pharisaic Righteousness*, Ch. I.
[2] *The Excellency and Nobleness of True Religion*, Ch. VI.
[3] *The Shortness and Vanity of a Pharisaic Righteousness*, Ch. I.

Christ . . . formed in his soul, who is in a sense the shining forth
of the Father's glory".[1]

God's glory is nothing that can accrue to Him from any
creature; but the reflection of His Divine glory in the creatures
to whom He communicates it. "When [God] is said to seek His
own glory, it is nothing else but to ray and beam forth as it were
His own lustre . . . God does then most glorify and exalt Himself
in the most triumphant way that may be . . . outside Himself
when He most of all communicates Himself and . . . erects such
monuments of His own Majesty wherein His own Love and
Goodness may live and reign. And we then most of all glorify
Him when we partake most of Him, when our serious endeavours
of a true assimilation to Him and conformity to His image declare
that we think nothing better than He is and are therefore most
ambitious of being one with Him by an universal resignation of
our selves unto Him. This is His glory in its lowest humiliation
while it beams forth out of Himself; and our happiness in its
exaltation. . . . His honour is His love and goodness in paraphrase
spreading itself over all those that can or do receive it; and this
He loves and cherishes wheresoever He finds it as something of
Himself therein."[2] Salvation therefore, and this communicated
glory of God, are identical. "I doubt we are too nice logicians
sometimes in distinguishing between the glory of God and our
own salvation. We cannot in a true sense seek our own salvation
more than the glory of God which triumphs most and discovers
itself most effectually in the salvation of souls; for indeed this
salvation is nothing else but a true participation of the Divine
Nature. Heaven is not a thing without us nor is happiness anything distinct from a true conjunction of the mind with God in
a secret feeling of His goodness and reciprocation of affection to
Him wherein the Divine Glory most unfolds itself. And there is
nothing that a soul touched with any serious sense of God can
more earnestly thirst after or seek with more strength of affection
than this. Then shall we be happy when God comes to be all in
all in us. To love God above ourselves is not indeed so properly
to love Him above the salvation of our own souls as if these
were distinct things, but it is to love Him above all sinful
affections and above our particular beings and to conform

[1] *The True Way or Method of Attaining to Divine Knowledge*, Sec. 3
[2] *The Existence and Nature of God*, Ch. IV.

I*

ourselves to Him."[1] Smith's spiritual commonsense cuts the
ground in advance from the muddles and subtleties about pure
love which bemused Fénelon.

This progressive reception of God's life and assimilation to
Him is a progressive destruction of the self-principled life of
unregenerate nature. The life of evangelical faith, "true faith"[2]
"is begotten of the Divine bounty and fulness manifesting itself
to the spirits of men and it is conceived and brought forth by a
deep and humble sense of self-indigency and poverty. Faith arises
out of self-exinanition seating and placing itself in view of the
Divine Plenitude and all sufficiency and thus . . . 'we received
the sentence of death in ourselves that we should not trust in
ourselves but in Him'. The more this sensual, brutish and self-
central life thrives and prospers, the more Divine Faith lan-
guisheth; and the more that decays and all self feeling, self love
and self sufficiency pine away, the more is true faith fed and
nourished, it grows more vigorous; and as carnal life wastes and
consumes the more does faith suck in a true, divine and spiritual
life from the true 'life' who hath life in Himself and freely bestows
it to all those that heartily seek for it . . . We are told of Christ
being formed in us and the Spirit of Christ dwelling in us; of our
being made conformable to Him, of having fellowship with Him,
of being as He was in this world, of living in Him and His living
in us, of dying and rising again and ascending with Him into
heaven: because indeed the same Spirit that dwelt in Him derives
itself in its mighty virtue and energy through all believing souls,
shaping them more and more into a just resemblance and conformity to Him as the first copy and pattern".[3] "We can never distrust enough in ourselves nor ever trust too much in God."[4] Thus
self makes room for God, self life is replaced by the Divine Life.
"By self denial I mean the soul's quitting all interest in itself and
an entire resignation of itself to Him as to all points of service and
duty: and thus the soul loves itself in God and lives in the possession not so much of itself as of the Divinity; desiring only to be
great in God, to glory in His light and spread itself in His fulness";
"the Universal Fountain-fulness of One supreme Almighty
Goodness" "to be filled always by Him and to empty itself again

---

[1] *The Excellency and Nobleness of True Religion*, Ch. V.
[2] In Catholic terminology " of faith formed by charity ".
[3] *Legal Righteousness and the Righteousness of Faith*, Ch. VI.
[4] ibid., Ch. VI.

into Him, to receive all from Him and to expend all for Him; and so to live not as its own but as God's . . . It is the character only of a good man to be able to deny and disown himself and make a full surrender of himself unto God, forgetting himself and minding nothing but the will of his Creator; triumphing in nothing more than in his own nothingness and in the Allness of the Divinity", that naughting of self and alling of God of which the *Epistle of Privy Counsel* speaks "but indeed this his being nothing is the only way to be all things; this his having nothing the truest way of possessing all things".[1]

Smith's religion is thus distinctively mystical in type. The principles which for him determine the genuine religious life— a progressive influx of the Divine life, unity, interior solitude, complete reliance on God, profound distrust and progressive abnegation of self—are the principles which determine the way of Divine Union, as taught by Catholic mystics. Nevertheless not only has he not proceeded along that road so far as they; he does not even know by report its later stages, as they have traversed them. For he does not perceive what complete surrender to the Divine life, complete abandonment of self and entire conformity to the death and resurrection of Christ, must involve. That is to say, he does not clearly or consistently perceive what is implied by the nothingness of self and the allness of God which he teaches. In the passage just quoted he speaks of the soul's "resignation of itself to God" *"as to all points of service and duty"*. The qualification is significant. St. John of the Cross demands complete and unqualified surrender. It would seem as though Smith conceived after all of the natural self-principled life as made obedient to the inflowing Life of God, as being subdued, informed, purified and enlightened by the latter but not as totally destroyed by it. Its destruction, as he understands it, is in fact not strictly destruction but complete subordination. Though Sister Elizabeth and Smith say the same thing, she says it with a deeper and a fuller understanding of its meaning. In consequence we may picture Smith as plodding stoutly along the road to God whereas Elizabeth is cycling along it, so that he never reaches the point where the final stretch, the distinctively unitive way, comes into view. He is a mystic of the middle stage, the illuminative way.

[1] *The Excellency and Nobleness of True Religion*, Ch. II, also Ch. VI.

And as Evelyn Underhill has pointed out "illumination" is a
half way house which "cannot give final satisfaction".[1] Smith's
spirituality is predominantly radiant—the atmosphere of a
cloudless summer morning drenched with sunlight. But there
is a path leading upward into the cloud. He did not climb it.
For he lacked the guidance and instruction of the Catholic
mystical tradition. The only mystics he quotes are the Areopagite for his Platonism and the anonymous author of the
Theologia Germanica. When Evelyn Underhill speaks of "the
tepid speculations of the Cambridge Platonists",[2] as regards
many, even most of the school she may be right. So far
as my knowledge extends, to Culverwell, More and at second
hand to Cudworth, I have not found Smith's intense spirituality.[3]
I would hazard the opinion, though subject to correction by
wider knowledge, that alike for the profundity and fervour of
his religion as also for his literary quality, Smith far excels all
his fellow Platonists except for Sterry. In any case Evelyn Underhill does not do him justice. As the passages I have quoted must
have shown his religion was anything but tepid. And it was not
primarily speculative but practical. Speculation for its own sake
has no attraction for Smith. His religion is a life lived with God
and for God. Of the Cambridge Platonists he and Sterry
alone were mystics. If such a mystic as Elizabeth outstrips him
so far, it is not so much because she has given more, as that she
has been given more. Or rather, she gives more because she has
been given more. Smith receives all the light he is given, gives to
the utmost actually possible for him. This is not tepidity. Nor is
the illumination he reached of slight value because it is not the
final earthly union. Most of us have certainly not reached
it. And his illumination, let us not forget, is "a mount of
vision" where the soul is shewn "all the glory of that heavenly
Canaan flowing with eternal and unbounded pleasures". A lofty
eminence surely, though not the summit of St. John's Carmel.[4]

On one matter, to be sure, I must take issue with Smith. He
regards a purely sensible devotion as artificial, the mimicry of
genuine religion.[5] This is to confuse the superficial with the

---

[1] *Mysticism*, 13th ed., Ch. IV, p. 265.
[2] ibid., p. 72.
[3] Nor indeed his merit as a writer of prose.
[4] *The Immortality of the Soul*, Ch. VII.
[5] *The Shortness and Vanity of a Pharisaic Righteousness*, Ch. V.

artificial. We may be sure that Tom's love for Jane is no better than a passing excitement, that in a short time he will have transferred his affections elsewhere. His love, that is to say, for Jane is superficial. But it is not therefore artificial, a pose, a pretence. In his shallow fashion, for the time Tom does love Jane. He is not indifferent to her, still less does he dislike her. Those whose love for God is but a superficial emotion which will not survive the tests of time and temptation are in the same case. Their love is superficial. But such as it is it is genuine. While they feel it they cannot be indifferent to God, still less hate Him.

Much of Smith's reasoning is outmoded. His refutation of Epicurean atomism is no sufficient reply to the more subtle dynamic materialism of today, still less to the dialectical materialism which, as Berdyaev has pointed out, though irreligious is not strictly materialism at all. He shared the view of his friend and fellow-Platonist Cudworth that matter is inert. Inertia indeed is its very definition, all activity is spirit.[1] On the contrary, all being corporeal as well as spiritual is energy, a substance being a focus of energy. Matter differs from spirit, not because it is not also energy, but because it is energy of a lower order and inferior reality with corresponding differences of manifestation, quality and operation. Since the brutes possess sensation, memory, purpose, even a certain intelligence, Smith is proving too much when he argues from the immaterial character of analogous human operations to the existence of a human soul separable from the body and immortal.[2] For these psychical functions in animals are also immaterial, without spatial extent.

But his positive testimony remains to an intellectualism which is genuine, consistent and truly rational because it is not rationalist but spiritual, and to a vital knowledge of God which is His own illumination of the soul, a communication to her of His light and life.

Though critical exegesis of Scripture was still in the future—it was later in the century that Simon published his studies on the composition of the Pentateuch—many difficulties it would raise were answered in advance in Smith's study of prophecy. "Divine

[1] J. A. PASSMORE, *Ralph Cudworth*, pp. 21 et seq.
[2] *The Immortality of the Soul*, Ch. III.

truth hath its humiliation and exinanition as well as its exaltation." "It becomes many times in Scripture incarnate, debasing itself to assume our rude conceptions that it might converse more freely with us and infuse its own divinity into us . . . If 'God' should speak in the language of eternity who could understand Him or interpret His meaning? Or if He should have declared His truth to us only in a way of the purest abstraction that human souls are capable of, how should then the more rude and illiterate sort of men have been able to apprehend it? Truth is content when it comes into the world to wear our mantles, to learn our language, to conform itself, as it were, to our dress and fashions . . . it speaks with the most idiotical sort of men in the most idiotical way and becomes all things to all men, as every son of truth should do for their good. Which was well observed in that old cabbalistical axiom among the Jews *Lumen supernum nunquam descendit sine indumento* [The heavenly Light never descends naked]."[1] Here is neither fundamentalism nor shallow rationalism but the insight of reason spiritually illuminated. Smith however did not perceive that many Catholic legends and devotions which he rejected out of hand can be justified on the same principle.

BIBLIOGRAPHY

John Smith, *Select Discourses,* 1st ed. London, 1660; 2nd ed. (corrected) Cambridge, 1673 (ed. of both, J. Worthington); 3rd ed. Edinburgh, 1756; 3rd ed. (corrected) Glasgow, 1821; 4th ed. (corrected and revised) Cambridge, 1859.

[1] *Prophecy*, Ch. 1. "Idiotical" of course means here simple, unlettered, cf. Dame Gertrude More's *An Ideot's Devotions.*

CHAPTER XI

THE SPIRITUAL TEACHING OF SISTER ELIZABETH OF THE TRINITY

MYSTICS everywhere and always are concerned with what is substantially the same experience, experience of union with God. Moreover the Godhead with whom they experience this union is experienced as transcending every image or concept, blinding with its "light inaccessible" the weak vision of mortal man. It is not therefore surprising that there is comparatively little variety in their accounts, particularly when the mystics in question accept the same dogmatic theology and interpret their experience in terms of its doctrines. This inevitable uniformity, however, renders mystical literature more repetitive than any other. And the individual mystic describing his experiences has not many different things to say. Nevertheless the intensity of the mystic's experience, the infinite content of the absolute Reality he experiences, combined with the tormenting incapacity to communicate more than suggestive hints, impels him to repeat himself indefinitely, as though by mere insistence he could force into his readers' field of vision something of the glory he is seeking to convey.

Moreover the friends and disciples of one thus admitted to the secret of the King are convinced that everything he has written is worth our attention, even when he does but repeat devotional commonplaces.

Nevertheless it is far from true that to read one mystic or even one Catholic mystic is to read all. Not only does the degree of experienced union with God differ widely—and only a few have climbed the loftiest summits. Even when the experience is the same, the individual mystic may insist upon a particular aspect of it, may distinguish that aspect more clearly than others, and may possess a peculiar ability to give it expression.

The student of mysticism therefore must study a considerable number of mystics, though, except in the case of a few giants such as St. John of the Cross, if copious remains have been left, he would be well advised to select what is distinctive and leave much unread or skimmed with a rapid glance.

Only when this principle of selection has been applied to the remains, chiefly letters, of Sister Elizabeth of the Trinity, published with an account of her short life by the Prioress of her Carmelite convent at Dijon, is one fully aware of the outstanding value of her spiritual doctrine, its combination of profundity and simplicity, austerity and consolation, universal applicability and aim directed unerringly to the centre, personal experience and understanding of the spirit, or—shall we call it?—the substance, of Scripture. Fundamentally the spiritual way practised and taught by Sister Elizabeth is no doubt identical with the little way of her more celebrated sister of Lisieux. Since God and man are what they are, there cannot substantially be more than one way of union between them, the way of a surrendered and aspiring will. But Elizabeth presents it more contemplatively, as a way of prayer from which, when necessary, action and suffering will follow, as it were, automatically. And with a more penetrating speculative insight she bases it upon her apprehension of the two facts which condition it, the nature of God and the nature of the human soul. Moreover, although some of her earlier letters are tinged with the sentimentality of feeling or at least expression, which is such an unpleasant quality of modern French religion, she does not clothe the truths she sees, the sublimest and the ultimate, in tawdry devotional finery such as prevents one reader at least from appreciating the writing of St. Thérèse.

I may, I must, dislike a few excesses of untheological devotion which occasionally fell from Elizabeth's pen. She is willing to be damned to please God. She desires to make God happy: "Will you not comfort Me? I am left alone my daughter, do not forsake Me." "Can I rejoice when my Spouse is suffering? For my sake He is a prisoner in the Tabernacle." And to speak of the Three Persons of the Trinity holding their council in her soul is unfortunate language. But this amounts to very little in comparison with the profundity, solidity and sureness, intellectual and spiritual, of her doctrine—such indeed as to give her rank among the masters of contemplation.

But, before we consider it, a brief account must be given of the life of a friend of God, widely known, it is true, but far less known than she should be. Elizabeth Catez was born on July 18th 1880, while Mass was being offered for her mother's safe delivery. She came of that Catholic bourgeoisie whose religion, if too often narrow and stuffy, is strong and deep-rooted, and which has given many holy men and women in recent times to the French Church. Her father was a devout army officer. He died when she was still a child leaving behind him Elizabeth and another daughter two years younger, Margaret. Her mother, Marie Catez, *née* Rolland, was not only devout but an admirer and student of St. Teresa. It is in fact rather surprising that she opposed her daughter's Carmelite vocation, though finally yielding, when convinced it was the will of God.

To my knowledge no detailed picture of Elizabeth's family, home life or childhood has been published or even exists. There is little beyond a jejune and conventional account of a child, not by any means faultless, for she was self-willed and liable to display bad temper, but affectionate and exceptionally devout. Her father's death found his family at Dijon where, except for a few visits and journeys as far afield as Switzerland and Italy, Elizabeth passed the remainder of her short life. *Gloire de Dijon*, the name of the well-known rose, may therefore be applied most fittingly to a soul who named herself the praise of (God's) glory. For, as she will tell us, the praise of glory is the reception of God's glory by the creature, as the sunlight in a translucent crystal, so that the praise of glory is in fact no less than the Divine Glory itself manifest in a human spirit.

We hear of her skill in playing the piano, of its extent we cannot judge, used as an occasion to mortify a natural and, most of us would think, harmless, vanity. And from the age of seven there is a desire for the religious life. There is nothing that could not be said of a multitude of young Catholic girls brought up by pious mothers.

But from an early age Elizabeth was favoured with an extraordinary gift of prayer together with a powerful attraction to a contemplative life and to Carmel in particular. On the eve of her fourteenth birthday she made a private vow of virginity. "It was followed by profound graces of recollection. Nothing distracted her from God. Penetrated with His holy Presence and deeply moved by what she experienced she said to herself:

When I see my confessor I will ask him what is happening to me."[1]

The experience initiated her contemplation and was already the substance of its future development. Unfortunately, since, before she entered Carmel, she burned the greater part of her Diary, the dating of these early years is so inexact that we cannot tell whether she had already read St. Teresa's *Way of Perfection*. In any case her perplexity proves that her experience was not copied from her reading which at most helped her *later* to understand it. For she evidently did not recognise at the time that St. Teresa had described what she experienced. Otherwise she would not have felt the need to ask her confessor to inform her of its nature.

At eighteen in the middle of some festivity Elizabeth would suddenly become aware of her Master's Presence and be rapt into a prayer so deep that she lost consciousness of her surroundings. That is to say her prayer was ecstatic. Her recollection was so profound that an eyewitness has told us "that for an hour and a half she did not see her make a single movement".[2] She seemed to be surrounded by a distinctive atmosphere which cut her off from her surroundings. This surely was "the gaze of faith", of which she will speak, "simple and loving, that separates us from all things and interposes, as it were a cloud between ourselves and everything earthly".[3] Notes taken during a retreat made the following year 1900 contain a prayer whose fulfilment was her contemplative life. "Divine Master, may my life be a perpetual prayer, may nothing, nothing whatsoever, distract me from You, neither my occupations, nor pleasures nor suffering. May I be submerged in You. Take my entire being that Elizabeth may disappear, Jesus alone remain."[4]

When Elizabeth was nineteen Madame Catez told her that she would not prevent her entering Carmel at twenty-one. We have notes made during a mission at this time which tell us how she wrestled in prayer for the conversion of a free-thinker. But unlike Pranzini, the murderer converted at the moment of execution by the prayers of St. Thérèse, her sinner died as he had lived. Self-satisfied and respectable irreligion is

[1] *La Servante de Dieu Elizabeth de la Trinité, Souvenirs*, p. 50.
[2] ibid., p. 54.
[3] ibid., p. 216.
[4] ibid., pp. 61–2.

probably more obdurate than criminality to the solicitations of grace.

It was originally intended that Elizabeth should be sent to a Carmel at Paray-le-Monial which the Prioress of Dijon was about to open. At the last moment, however, to make the separation easier for her mother, she was chosen for the Dijon Carmel which she entered as postulant on August 2nd 1901.

Life in Carmel did not disappoint her expectation. It was what she had desired, "silence and adoration". Nothing suggests the abuses of the Lisieux Carmel, a temperamental, indeed unbalanced Prioress, hostile factions among the nuns. Her Prioress, who was also her Mistress of Novices, Mother Germaine of Jesus, understood her vocation and prayer. This is evident from the *Souvenirs* she compiled after Elizabeth's death in which she included spiritual notes written at her command. But like St. Thérèse, Elizabeth became very shortly the victim of a painful and fatal disease. It was a serious disease of the stomach.[1] During her last years she was unable to take an active part in community life or, save for a rare exception, join her sisters in choir. But she had always been a hermit of the spirit and her life of seclusion, inactivity and suffering was a life of perpetual prayer and a central joy beyond the pain.

She had never wished for a long life and she was only twenty-six when she died in the early morning of November 9th 1906. It was the feast of the Dedication of the mother church of Christendom, St. John Lateran. As she often reminded herself, her name means "the house of God" and this first and last she had desired to be and had been. And the liturgy of the day dwells on God's heavenly house, the communion of the blessed who are filled with the glory which is Himself. There was every indication that her last moments were a foretaste of eternal joy. "Reclining on her right side, her head thrown back, her eyes wide open and fixed upon a point above our heads, Sister Elizabeth seemed not to be in her agony but rapt in ecstasy."[2] Nevertheless a multitude of religious has lived and died in holiness. What distinguishes Elizabeth is her spiritual teaching, a permanent legacy to the Church and all souls drawn to a life of prayer.

---

[1] So Fr. Philipon informs us in his study of Elizabeth's spiritual doctrine. But he does not tell us its exact nature. The *Souvenirs* are completely silent.

[2] *Souvenirs*, p. 264.

Shortly before her death, when asked if, like Thérèse, she would come back from heaven to do good on earth, she replied that this was not her mission. She would plunge deeper and deeper into the glory of the Trinity. Nevertheless she too would have a special mission to her fellows on earth—"to lead souls into interior recollection". The pledge is repeated in a letter: "In heaven, I believe, my mission will be to attract souls, to help them to go out of themselves and cleave to God by a perfectly simple movement of pure love and to keep them in this great interior silence which enables God to impress Himself upon them and transform them into Himself."[1] No mission could be better suited to our needs today, no spiritual teaching more opportune. Drawn by the myriad influences of a secular and utilitarian civilisation to the flashy and noisy unrealities of our environment, enslaved to economic necessity, dazzled by scientific discovery and achievement, isolated and diminished as a unit of subhuman masses, man today is hard put to it to maintain his human dignity, fulfil his Divine vocation. Elizabeth invites the soul to enter into herself and in that "fortress", secure from the outer world, to make contact with Reality. On the eve of her entrance into Carmel she became acquainted with a Dominican, Père Vallée. Like the other Dominican, Bañez, who assured St. Teresa that God was present in her soul substantially, not merely by His grace, Père Vallée assured Elizabeth of this Divine inhabitation and of her vocation to attach herself to it. God however is not only One. He is also a Trinity and it was to the indwelling Trinity that Elizabeth directed her devotion, an *attrait* recognised by her Prioress when she was commanded or permitted to take as her name in religion Elizabeth of the Trinity. Towards the close of her life, after an interior locution, she was granted an intellectual vision of the Blessed Trinity within her soul. Otherwise, it would seem, in the light of her Catholic faith she gave a Trinitarian interpretation to the obscure Presence she experienced in prayer. But on this point our information is less precise than one might wish.

Elizabeth is aware of God as an overflowing fulness of Being who may even be said in a loose and human manner of speech "to need to communicate all He is and all He has to the soul that will receive Him", a soul which is "like a crystal through

[1] *Souvenirs*, pp. 234–5.

which He can shine" and in which "He can contemplate His
own splendour".[1] It is for the soul to respond to this pressing
invitation of infinite Love and Full Being. Whether the soul
feels consolation or the aridity of desolation, no matter; let her
abide fixed in the central direction of her will upon the Divine
Presence which never changes, in a loving abandonment to His
good pleasure. "The good God has no need of the Sacrament to
come to me, I have Him, it seems, as fully without It. How
satisfying is this presence of God. In this depth, this heaven of
my soul I delight to find Him . . . For He never leaves me.
God in me, I in Him. That is my life. How good it is to consider that, except for the vision, we possess God already as the
Blessed possess Him above."[2] No wonder she loved this interior
silence, this solitude where she found God. "I am God's little
anchoress . . . How I love solitude alone with Him where I
lead the truly delightful life of a hermit."[3] Nor is this hermitage
the exclusive privilege of the contemplative nun. She invites
her sister Margaret, married and the mother of children, to enter
it. "Our Father's house, this heaven is in the centre of our soul.
Whatever your occupation, in the midst of a mother's cares you
may withdraw into this solitude and surrender yourself to the Holy
Spirit that He may transform you in God, and imprint upon you
the image of the Divine Beauty."[4] This indeed is the peculiar
value of Elizabeth's teaching for us today, that it brings the
Thebaid into the midst of our cities, erects the hermitage in the
office or factory, enthrones contemplation in the heart of action.

   This solitude is like that of God Himself who though
intimately present in His creatures as the source of all their
activities is solitary in His transcendence of them all. *Rerum
Deus tenax vigor, Immotus in te permanens*.   "God," St. Denys
tells us, "is the great solitary. My Master asks me to imitate this
perfection and pay homage to Him by being a great solitary. The
Divine Being lives in an eternal and immeasurable solitude from
which He never emerges, though providing for His creatures'
needs. For He never goes out of Himself and this solitude is
His Deity. That nothing may withdraw me from this lovely
inner silence my condition must always be the same, the same
isolation, the same separation, the same poverty. Unless my
desires, my fears, my joys, my sorrows are wholly directed to

---

[1] *Souvenirs*, p. 116.   [2] ibid., p. 67.   [3] ibid., p. 194.   [4] ibid., p. 158.

God, I shall not be solitary, there will be noise in my soul."[1]
No trials from within or without can expel the soul from this
fortress where she is held a willing captive. She must therefore
on no account quit this central recollection, even if God
withholds any sign of His presence. "If only I could make all
souls understand what a source of strength, peace and happiness
they would find, if they would but consent to live in this
intimacy [with God]. But they will not wait. If God does
not give Himself in a sensible fashion," does not make His
presence perceptible, "they leave Him; and when He comes laden
with all His gifts, He finds no one at home. The soul is abroad in
outward things, not living in her own centre."[2] We are reminded
of Crashaw's Poem "On a Prayer Book sent to Mrs. M. R."

> If the noble Bridegroom when he come
> Shall find the loytering heart from home.
> Leaving her chast aboad,
> To gadde abroad:
> Doubtlesse some other heart
> Will get the start,
> Meanwhile, and stepping in before
> Will take possession of that sacred store
> Of hidden sweets and holy joyes,
> Words which are not heard with ears
> (Those tumultuous shops of noise)
> Effectual wispers whose still voice
> The soul itselfe more feeles than heares.
>
> An hundred thousand goods, glories and graces
> And many a mystick thing,
> Which the divine embraces
> Of the deare spouse of spirits with them will bring
> For which it is no shame
> That dull mortality must not know a name.
> Of all this store
> Of blessings and ten thousand more;
> If when He come
> He find the heart from home,
> Doubtless He will unload
> Himself some other where.

[1] *Souvenirs*, p. 362.   [2] ibid., pp. 213-14.

Down the centuries contemplatives speak the same language. For they speak from the same experience, the same knowledge, for which the human spirit has been created.

Elizabeth's experience of this central solitude and her meeting there with God was the experience of a double abyss, a phrase which, it would seem, she derived from St. Catherine of Siena but made her own.[1] One abyss is the soul—"a bottomless abyss, as it were, into which [God] can flow and spread Himself".[2] The other abyss is God. "We must descend day by day down into the abyss which is God. The one abyss calls to the other. There on this sea floor the Divine encounter will take place, when the abyss of our nothingness, our wretchedness, is confronted with the abyss of mercy, the immense all of God. There we shall find the strength to die to ourselves and losing count of ourselves be changed into love."[3] "We must be recollected within ourselves, remaining silent in God's presence, while the soul sinks into the abyss, expands, takes fire and melts into Him in an unbounded plenitude."[4] For the abyss of our comparative unreality is capable of being filled with the Divine fulness. "As I see it, to be plunged in humility is to be plunged in God. For God is the bottom of the abyss."[5] "Interior souls, beings God has chosen, to live within, in the depth of the bottomless abyss."[6] "The simple soul, raising herself by the power of the gaze she directs inwards, enters into herself and beholds her own abyss, as the sanctuary where she makes contact with the Holy Trinity. She has thus penetrated her death to its floor which is the gate of eternal life."[7] This abyss is plumbed progressively at levels successively deeper, as the soul penetrates deeper into God present in her deepest self. "When the soul knows God perfectly, that is to the utmost of her capacity, and loves and enjoys Him without reserve, she has reached the deepest centre she can attain in Him. Before she reached this point she was, it is true, already in God who is her centre, but not in her deepest centre. For she could go further."[8] "As you may read in St.

[1] *Souvenirs*, p. 99.
[2] ibid., p. 116.
[3] ibid., pp. 312-13.
[4] ibid., p. 327. Cf. Rous: "My very faintings shall be inflamed towards Thee and melt into Thee." See above, p. 155.
[5] ibid., p. 335.
[6] ibid., p. 336.
[7] ibid., p. 324.
[8] ibid., pp. 313-14.

John of the Cross, when we are in the deepest centre we are in God."[1] A mystic of St. John's order and school whose writings Elizabeth could not have known (for none were printed till after her death) Mother Cecilia of the Nativity, speaks much in her language of "the intimate will and essence of the soul created by God in His image and likeness and therefore of a depth so unfathomable that it is like a sea or bottomless well in which the deeper a man may plunge the further he is from touching the bottom. For the human spirit is grounded in the being of the Creator and derives its life from His". "The soul has been raised . . . to her centre, called truly the empyrean heaven where God dwells in her and where she enjoys Him as in heaven . . . God is tasted and enjoyed in this heaven of heavens . . . the most secret depths of the soul, set apart for God's abode, in which divine centre we resemble Him and which He alone fills and satisfies. Though no man in this mortal life can grasp its nature, God has disclosed to some after a divine fashion this divine centre wherein He dwells."[2] Once more over the centuries an identical experience has evoked the same testimony from souls wholly unacquainted. This centre, Elizabeth tells us, is "the depth where God dwells and will give us the repose of the abyss".[3] "The soul rises" (in the order of spirit, as Baker points out, height and depth are identical and mystics therefore are not averse to mixed metaphor[4]) "rises above the senses, above nature; she transcends herself, passes beyond every joy and every sorrow, and piercing the clouds does not rest till she has penetrated into the interior of Him she loves and He Himself has given her the repose of the abyss."[5] "The repose of the abyss." It cannot be claimed for Elizabeth that she is a gifted stylist, though the sublimity of the things she says so simply, without sentimental fripperies or cheap rhetoric, elevates her style by her theme. But, "the repose of the abyss". Here truly is a masterstroke of expression not unworthy to indicate the ultimate inexpressible reality she is trying to express. "The repose of the abyss"—it is the last word of human experience and human

---

[1] *Souvenirs*, p. 158.

[2] Mother Cecilia of the Nativity, *Transformation of the Soul in God*, Cantos 1 and 4. Printed in the Edicion Critica of St. John of the Cross, edited by Padre Gerardo de San Juan de la Cruz (1914), Vol. 3, pp. 359, 382–3.

[3] *Souvenirs*, p. 324.

[4] As we may also observe in the passage just quoted from Mother Cecilia.

[5] *Souvenirs*, pp. 376–7.

destiny. It describes the peace which is almost a satisfaction, solemn and sublime, which we experience at the close of a great tragedy, *Oedipus Rex* for example, or *King Lear*, when, as we contemplate the spectacle of human greatness brought down to the depths, we are obscurely aware of a Reality which has somehow been touched in the fall; in fact could we but know it, are aware of that encounter of the two abysses, human emptiness and Divine fulness, of which Elizabeth speaks.[1] But art is not prayer. This is but confrontation not conjunction. In the contemplative, or more accurately the unitive, prayer Elizabeth practised and preached, the abyss of human receptivity is progressively emptied of its self-principled life to be filled and satisfied with the inflowing Godhead. Nevertheless there is a mysterious relation between human emptiness, revealed as capacity unfulfilled and will frustrated, and the Divine plenitude and satisfaction. The vista therefore of art, the distance it glimpses afar, is the revelation of prayer—the repose of the abyss, the repose of the abyss of human capacity and need, the repose of the Divine Abyss which fills it and alone can fill it.

For God "invades" the created abyss, as it is emptied of the old self-principled life, "flows into it, spreads through it"[2] until it is pure, wholly a receptacle of the Uncreated. The "crystal" shines with the Uncreated light shining throughout its translucent purity. The soul now is "an additional humanity" of Christ "in which He can reveal His mystery[3] and in which He can still suffer for His Father's glory and to assist His Church in her needs".[4] "The soul has endured the mystical death in which she annihilates herself and forgets herself so completely that she dies in God to be transformed into Him . . . For everything which belongs to self must be destroyed and replaced by God Himself."[5] This, to be sure, is the traditional doctrine of Christianity on which Elizabeth's favourite doctor, St. Paul, insists. "You are dead and your life is hidden with Christ in God." Yes, but too often this is heard, as though it were but a manner of speech, rhetorical hyperbole. Elizabeth lived it so wholeheartedly, that it comes alive in her statement of it and possesses once more the freshness and the force it must have had

---

[1] See above, pp. 51–2.
[2] *Souvenirs*, p. 133.
[3] ibid., p. 135.

[4] ibid., p. 201.
[5] ibid., p. 195.

for those who first heard it from the Apostle's lips or read it in
his letters. Where the eternal verities are concerned the sole
novelty possible is realisation. And in virtue of her personal
realisation of it, the old doctrine lived and expounded by
Elizabeth is truly new, truly original. " 'I die daily', St. Paul
exclaimed. This doctrine of dying to self, a law binding every
Christian soul, though it seems so stern, becomes deliciously
sweet when we consider the result of this death, the substitution
of God's life for our own life of sin and wretchedness."[1] The
soul "dies and flows into God".[2] When this substitution has
been effected "the Father sees in the soul" only His Christ and
can truly say of her "Behold my dearly beloved daughter in
whom I am well pleased."[3] "Abide in Me" is the command of
God to the soul, "pray in Me, adore in Me, love in Me, suffer
in Me, work, act in Me." To such a soul "God gives Himself;
all her movements then become Divine, and though they are
God's, they are just as much the soul's. For Our Lord performs
them in her and with her".[4] "When love has been made perfect,
the soul will be transformed so thoroughly, that she will be
very like God. To such a soul whose life is interior may be
addressed the words addressed by Père Lacordaire to Magdalen
'Ask no man for your Master, no one on earth, no one in
heaven. For He is your soul and your soul is He'."[5]

These words are almost a verbal repetition of the famous
conclusion of Indian Vedanta: "The soul—Atman—is The
Absolute—Brahman. Thou art It." But although the same
experience of an identification with God is expressed in words
almost the same their meaning differs widely. The Vedantic
meaning misinterprets the experience it seeks to understand.
Elizabeth's interprets it truly. For the Vedantist is asserting a
natural identity between the soul and God disguised by an illusion
of distinctness which contemplation removes. Elizabeth is
telling us that precisely because the soul is of her nature so
remote from God in her comparative unreality, she can by His
free grace in Christ be filled with His Godhead until she is wholly
a receptacle of God, living with His life in her, knowing with His
knowledge, loving with His love.

---

[1] *Souvenirs*, p. 227.   [4] ibid., p. 313.
[2] ibid., p. 376.   [5] ibid., p. 314.
[3] ibid., p. 158.

Because it is in unbroken contact with the Divine eternity such a soul "lives in the likeness of the immutable Trinity in an eternal present always adoring the Trinity for Its own sake and, by a look ever more simple, and producing a closer union, becomes the resplendence of Its glory . . . a perpetual praise of the glory of Its adorable perfections".[1] Thus Elizabeth understood her device, the praise of glory which she had taken from St. Paul's Epistle to the Ephesians. All things, all events are now sacraments of God's Divine communication, transparencies through which He manifests His glory. Everything therefore which befalls may and will be accepted as God's gift of Himself. "We must rather accept our difficulties than seek deliverance from them. Our acceptance will be our deliverance. We must even will the consequences of our faults and infidelities as a satisfaction paid to the justice of God who from the situation thus produced will draw glory for Himself, profit for us."[2]

The soul's descent to the central God is also a progressive liberation, expansion, an ever widening horizon. In Carmel Elizabeth writes "My horizon widens every day".[3] "In God I recover all those far horizons" of mountain ranges.[4] "On the other side of the convent grill, what a magnificent horizon! It is infinite, and therefore expands daily."[5] This is the liberty of the spirit in God, with its unbounded vision of which Smith spoke so eloquently, his "true and divine amplitude, the dilation and expansion of the spirit aspiring Godward, beyond all finite being", as it looks "beyond the horizon of time and sense".[6] Elizabeth's experience fulfils Smith's aspiration. "God," Baker wrote, "doth not heed the greatness or worth of the works wherein the soul is employed, I mean as to what these works are in their own nature; all are alike to Him; even the labouring for conversion of souls is of no greater price with Him than is the keeping of sheep or other cattle. All one with Him for you to be pricking on a clout or to be curiously working a veil or pall for the altar."[7] Elizabeth repeats in effect what Baker taught the nuns he directed, relating it to her teaching about the inner life with God. "We must realise," she writes, "God's intimate presence

[1] *Souvenirs*, p. 377.
[2] ibid., p. 224.
[3] ibid., p. 84.
[4] ibid., p. 58.
[5] ibid., p. 148.
[6] See above.
[7] *Confessions*, Ch. 7.

in our soul and perform all our actions in His company. Then our life is never commonplace, even when we are engaged in the most humdrum occupations. For the soul does not live in her occupations but passes through them. *A supernatural soul does not deal with second causes but with God alone.* Her life is correspondingly simplified."[1] A "simple intention" to do God's will here and now "gathers into unity all the scattered powers of the soul and unites the spirit itself to God. The spirit penetrating itself and passing through itself, passing through all creatures and penetrating them finds God in its depth . . . I call the intention simple which looks to God alone and relates all things to Him. It places man in His presence. This simplicity is the incline that leads the soul inwards and the foundation of the entire spiritual life. It bestows peace and silences the inane noises which make themselves heard in our souls".[2] Simplicity is unity and the soul is made one with God. "On these divine summits Unity—the Divine Unity—is perfected between God and the soul."[3] "The soul must be in peace, her powers put to sleep, her being must be unified." Then "the King will be enamoured of her beauty. For beauty is unity, the Divine Beauty at any rate".[4] Awareness of an ultimate Unity and the need to attain it, which is the final truth alike of Platonic philosophy and of mysticism, is Elizabeth's experience expressed by her doctrine. Platonic also is her apprehension of the eternal ideas, the exemplars of creatures. "In the abyss of His fruitfulness the Father contemplates Himself and by this very act of comprehending Himself engenders another Person, the Son, His eternal Word. The exemplar of all creatures which had not yet emerged from nothingness has from eternity resided in Him and God saw and contemplated them in their exemplar, in Himself. This eternal life which our exemplars possess apart from ourselves in God is the cause of our creation. Our created essence craves to be reunited with its principle. The Word, the resplendence of the Father, is the eternal blueprint and in conformity with it creatures are fashioned at their creation. Accordingly it is God's will that, delivered from ourselves we should

---

[1] *Souvenirs*, p. 108. Cf. Dame Julian: "There is no Doer but He" (God). See above, p. 84.
[2] ibid., pp. 323–4.
[3] ibid., p. 137.
[4] ibid., p. 363.

aspire to our exemplar and rising above all things to our model
should possess it."[1]

Suffering, to be sure, will continue to the end. For the work
of immolation is never complete on earth or, if it should be,
there remains the member's vocation to share the redemptive
suffering of the Head. But the peace, the joy is at a deeper level
than the pain. In a memorable phrase in which Mother Germaine
achieves the accent of great literature,[2] Elizabeth's soul, she
tells us, "turned towards *the summits which overtop suffering*".[3]
Art, tragedy in particular, descries those summits, though it
cannot tell us the path that climbs them—"In spite of her sufferings
Elizabeth seemed already a denizen of celestial glory." "Beside
her King," she wrote, "the Queen in royal majesty climbs
the slope of Calvary: 'The Queen stands at Thy right hand'."
"This is the station of my soul. She climbs Calvary on the right
of her crucified King, annihilated and humbled, but always
strong, calm, regal."[4] Here the suffering whose grim visage
lost Darwin his faith in God and made Jefferies deny his own
vision is vanquished by a peace and a glory which transcend
and transfigure it. *Solvitur orando*. A problem which resists the
solution of thought is solved by prayer, the prayer which finds
in suffering itself repose and joy, the peace and the joy of God.

Sister Elizabeth had no concern with the problems and the
panaceas, the causes and the aims which occupy the world and rule
it so tyrannously. She knew nothing of politics or economics, cared
nothing for social justice, had nothing to say of national rights or
aspirations. Of this world she prized only the natural beauty
which reflects God. In her convent garden "Nature seemed full
of God".[5] Of art we hear only of her musical accomplishment.
She does not even appear to have concerned herself much with
the external work of the Church, her active apostolate, her
victories and defeats. Like Mary of Bethany she is absorbed in
the one thing necessary, contemplative love of God. Like her
she chose the best part and her choice rebukes the noise and bustle
of our Marthas. For she knows that all they seek so busily is
found by prayer, is given by prayer. For prayer, her unitive
prayer of love, gives God to herself and to others and He is all.

[1] *Souvenirs*, p. 325.
[2] Much as Dean Burgon's memorable line of poetry.
[3] *Souvenirs*, p. 245.
[4] ibid., p. 351.
[5] ibid., p. 165.

CHAPTER XII

HENRY VAUGHAN

WHEN FIRST as a boy I made the acquaintance of *Silex Scintillans* in the Temple Classics I was charmed with its frontispiece, a picture of the church in which Vaughan used to worship at Llansantfraed. It was what one would expect the church of a remote mountain valley to be; white walls with a simple window, a roof of stone slabs rising in quaint slopes, and a low round tower. Unfortunately I failed to notice or at any rate to take in the words written below the picture "The Old Church". When therefore on a summer's day in 1947 I approached in pilgrim temper the church of Llansantfraed, I expected to see at last the building so long known. I was bitterly disillusioned. It exists no longer and its place is taken by a particularly pretentious and hideous specimen of Victorian-Gothic built in 1884. But the poet's grave is still to be seen beneath a yew, "No shade but yew", its inscription recut as the result of the endeavours of one of the poet's most faithful admirers, Miss Imogen Guiney, the American Catholic, so devoted to the English poets of the sixteenth and seventeenth centuries. It is a simple, humble, deeply Christian inscription, the poet's choice: "Servus inutilis, peccator maximus, hic jaceo. Gloria. Miserere." *Gloria,* for the glory of God had been the theme of all his best verse; *Miserere,* a prayer surely for the repose of his soul. A little further along the road is the farm-house, though much altered, of Newton, where he lived the greater part of his life.

Two women—a local Anglican, Miss Gwenlian Morgan, and Miss Guiney—spent years of labour collecting materials for a life of Vaughan, working in collaboration. Unfortunately neither was able to write the life planned. But their work was not lost. For after Miss Morgan's death the materials she and Miss Guiney had collected were sent to the late Dr. F. E. Hutchinson who made use of them to produce what is no doubt the definitive life of the poet, enriched moreover by the biographer's appreciations and interpretations of his work.[1] The year following its publication Dr. Hutchinson joined in "the world of light" Vaughan and the women whose devoted labours had made his work possible. For them all *Gloria, Miserere.*

Vaughan came of an old Welsh family, the Vaughans of Tretower. Their mansion, only a few miles from Llansantfraed, survives and is in charge of the Office of Works. His paternal grandmother Frances was the illegitimate daughter of Thomas Somerset, a son of the second Earl of Worcester. Thomas was a staunch Catholic who for his loyalty to his faith spent some twenty-four years in the Tower. It cannot be said that the example of his great-grandfather aroused in the poet the least inclination towards the Catholic Church. That he read and translated devotional works by Jesuits has no significance. Books of Catholic spirituality were frequently translated by Protestants and were widely read by them. They were indeed the channel through which Catholic devotion watered the spiritual life of Anglican and Puritan. The poet was not merely an Anglican, but an Anglican devoted to the Church of England. In the days of the Commonwealth so dark for Anglicans, when Anglicanism had been officially abolished and Anglican worship forbidden, his loyalty became fervent, as passionate as anything in him could be. He was upheld and exalted by the conviction that he was a faithful member of the true British Church, exiled and driven underground by the Puritans. Nor had he the consolation of Catholics under a more relentless and a bloody persecution, that the Church here dispossessed flourished elsewhere and ruled. His ordeal, however, was brief, though all his religious poetry was written while it lasted. And the distinctive charm of Anglicanism as a religion of the devout and cultured gentleman invests his life and work.

Vaughan grew to manhood and except for some four or five years spent all his life among the beautiful scenery of the valley of the Usk. He was deeply attached to his native river and the first considerable volume of poetry he published was entitled *Olor Iscanus*, the Swan of Usk. He never departed from his first loyalties imbibed as a child, ecclesiastical and political, local patriotism and love of the landscape into which he was born.

[1] *Henry Vaughan: A Life and Interpretation.*

Henry Vaughan was born with a twin brother Thomas in 1621 and another brother William was born a few years later.

The twins were fortunate in escaping the brutalities of the contemporary public school. For they were educated within a few miles of home by Mathew Herbert, Rector of Llangatock. Herbert, whose Anglicanism and Royalism would later cost him his benefice, imparted a thorough knowledge of Latin and a fair modicum of Greek. Dr. Hutchinson may very well be right in his conjecture, that it was to him that the brothers were indebted for their first interest in the occult or Hermetic philosophy, with its alchemy and astrology, which we must consider later. For *Silex Scintillans* was considerably influenced by it and its doctrines are often presupposed and allusion made to them.

In 1638 Henry and Thomas went up to Oxford to the Welsh College, Jesus. But whereas Thomas stayed at Oxford for many years, Henry went down at the end of two years without taking a degree and proceeded to London where he studied at one of the Inns of Court. As he was never called to the bar, he did not presumably intend to adopt the legal profession but, like many others of his social position, to acquire sufficient legal knowledge for the needs of a country gentleman, likely to be made a justice of the peace. In fact on his return to Wales he acted as clerk to Judge Lloyd, another devoted Royalist and Anglican.

The poem "Abel's Blood" seems on the face of it to show that Vaughan was a pacifist:

> If single thou,
> Though single voices are but low,
> Couldst such a shrill and long cry rear
> As speaks still in thy Maker's ear,
> What thunders shall those men arraign
> Who cannot count those they have slain,
> Who bathe not in a shallow flood
> But in a deep wide sea of blood? . . .
>
>   O accept
> Of his vow'd heart, whom Thou hast kept
> From bloody men.

Or again, "The Men of War":

> The sword wherewith Thou dost command
> Is in Thy mouth, not in Thy hand,
> And all Thy Saints do overcome
> By Thy blood and their martyrdom.
> But seeing soldiers long ago
> Did spit on Thee and smote Thee too . . .
> I'll marvel not at aught they do
> Because they used my Saviour so.

And he prays that

> I may be found preserved by Thee
> Amongst that chosen company,
> Who by no blood here overcame
> But the blood of the blessed Lamb.

And in Latin verses prefixed to *Olor Iscanus* he appears to disclaim having taken any part in the Civil War.

Poems however in this collection prove that, like his brother Thomas, he joined the Royalist forces, that he took part in the battle of Rowton Heath, when a comrade was killed, and was later in the garrison of Beeston Castle when it surrendered with military honours. In the light of these facts his condemnation of soldiers cannot have been intended universally, but must refer to Cromwell's army which seized power after the King's overthrow. On the other hand these and similar passages strongly suggest that when he composed the poems of *Silex Scintillans* in the fervour of his conversion, he had become convinced that not war but suffering was the weapon Christians should employ against the Saints militant whose sincerity, even, he could not admit. In any case his language about a deep wide sea of blood shed by those who cannot count those they have slain is applicable with a truth he could not have foreseen to those who even in a good cause massacre and maim with their bombs multitudes of innocent civilians. Loud indeed must be the cry of the blood shed in saturation bombing or at Hiroshima.

In 1646 a slender volume of verse appeared by Henry Vaughan

and, although *Olor Iscanus* was not published until 1651, it was ready, though, Dr. Hutchinson argues, in a considerably different form, by the end of 1647. As it was eventually published it consists mainly of free translations of Ausonius' *Cupido Cruci Affixus*, the poems contained in Boethius' *Consolation of Philosophy*, three poems by Claudian, a poem in praise of country life by the Polish Jesuit Casimir and four prose treatises, "Of the Benefit we may get by our enemies", from a Latin version of Plutarch, two treatises of the Diseases of the Mind and the Body respectively by Plutarch and Maximus of Tyre and the Praise and the Happiness of Country Life from the Spanish of Don Antonio de Guevara, Bishop of Carthagena. Incidentally the final translation illustrates the point, made so insistently by Christopher Dawson, that even the religious cleavage of the Reformation did not dissolve the common culture of Western Europe.

In the preface to the second part of *Silex Scintillans* Vaughan, with the zeal of the recent convert, will condemn his own secular verse. But it could not have been more innocent. There is no touch even of sensuousness, still less of sensuality, in the *Poems to Amoret* in the volume of 1646 and, even so, Amoret, as Dr. Hutchinson shews, was certainly his fiancée, probably his wife. In these charming trifles which deserve to be better known, he already speaks of the sympathies binding together all natural creatures. Though no record of his marriage has been found it was certainly about this time, the middle forties, that he married his first wife Catherine Wise, daughter of Richard Wise of Coleshill, Warwickshire. He probably met her when she was visiting a neighbour.

About this time his brother Thomas became Rector of Llansantfraed.[1] But he did not hold the living for long. For the Puritans, not likely to forgive his service in the royal army, soon expelled him and with charges against his morals. He retired to Oxford, making no attempt even at the Restoration to resume his clerical life, and devoted himself to alchemy and chemical experiments in which he was assisted by his wife, and poured out a series of books under the *nom de plume* Eugenius Philalethes.[2] Lucid passages scattered here and there prove that

---

[1] St. Bridget's church.
[2] Reprinted in one volume with an introduction by A. E. Waite.

Thomas Vaughan might have taken an honourable place among writers of English prose. And his verse is by no means devoid of merit. But he deliberately adopted a cryptic jargon which makes his writings unreadable, indeed unintelligible. Their successive publication however proves that they all found readers at the time, that there were circles who could interpret this strange lingo.[1] We must say more of them later for the better understanding of his brother's poetry. Their publication led incidentally to a public contest of vulgar mudslinging between their author and the Cambridge Platonist Henry More, a lamentable performance by two men who were gentlemen and scholars and professed most sincerely a spiritual philosophy and Christian faith. At the Restoration Thomas assisted Sir Robert Morray, who presided at the first meetings of the Royal Society, in his chemical researches. That is to say, a professed occultist assisted in the growth of modern science. It cost him his life. For in 1666 he died suddenly near Oxford as the result of an experiment with "strong mercury".

The death of his younger brother William in 1648 would seem to have been the prelude and, at least in part, the cause of the decisive event in the life of Henry Vaughan, without which he would never have been the poet he was, but at best a versifier, on occasion ingenious or charming. It was his conversion. It was not a conversion from a life of sin. Nor was it a conversion from scepticism to religious faith or from one form of faith to another. He had always lived a moral life, had always been a convinced Anglican. It was conversion from mediocrity, from a respectable worldliness, to a profound and fervent religious life. In addition to his brother's and shortly afterwards his wife's death, the overthrow of the monarch and the Church of his allegiance, and consequent damage to his private fortunes and future prospects, had their share in detaching him from the world and impelling him to seek in communion with God a peace and consolation of which no external disaster could deprive him. Positive influences were a renewed study of the Bible, which had become for Protestants the most effective channel of Divine Grace and, as he tells us himself, the sacred poetry of George Herbert, who exerted the joint appeal of poet and pastor.

---

[1] A present revival of popularity in circles interested in the occult is even harder to understand.

Under the impetus of this powerful experience Vaughan produced in succession the first and the second part of *Silex Scintillans*. The first part appeared in 1650, the second was added in a second edition published in 1655. After this the poetic afflatus deserted him. Most of the pieces of religious verse contained in *Thalia Rediviva*, published in 1678, are considered by Dr. Hutchinson from internal evidence to have been more or less contemporary with the later poems of *Silex Scintillans*. Yet he lived until 1695, forty years after the publication of the complete *Silex*. Like Wordsworth, with whom he has considerable affinities, he was a poet only for a few years out of a long life. But, unlike Wordsworth, he did not continue to pour out verse.

In 1652 Vaughan published a prose volume, *The Mount of Olives or Solitary Devotions*, a meditation on death and judgment, *Man in Darkness* and a translation of a treatise on the blessed in Heaven mistakenly attributed to St. Anselm, which he entitled *Man in Glory*.[1] In 1654 he published under the title *Flores Solitudinis* translations of two treatises by the Jesuit Nieremberg, respectively on Temperance and Patience and on Life and Death, a tract by Bishop Eucherius of Lyons *The World Contemned*, and a life of St. Paulinus of Nola compiled from the original sources and entitled *Primitive Holiness*.

In 1655 he published *Hermetical Physick or The Right Way to preserve and to restore Health*, a translation from the Latin original of Henry Nollius (Nolle). A translation of another treatise by Nolle, known to have existed from a letter from Vaughan to Aubrey, has been lost. This Hermetical Physic, an application to medicine of the Hermetical Philosophy or Theosophy was, like homoeopathy today, a medical heresy. Though drugs were used, faith healing played a considerable part in the treatment. "Let [the patient] certainly believe that there is communicated and infused (by the gift of God) into the medicine such an innate virtue as is effectual and proper to expel his Disease. If he doth this, the event will be answerable to his faith and the medicine will in all circumstances work successfully. A firm credulity, cheerful hope and true love and confidence towards the Physician and the medicine conduce as much to the health of the patient, yea sometimes more, than

---

[1] Miss Guiney published an edition of *The Mount of Olives* (1902).

either the remedy or the physician. Natural faith . . . imaginative faith . . . is so powerful that it can both expel and introduce
diseases . . . To the faithful all things are possible . . . who-
soever believes in God he operates by the power of God and to
God all things are possible . . . Cogitations or thoughts surpass
the operations of all elements and stars, for while we imagine
and believe such a thing shall come to pass, that faith brings
the work about and without it is nothing done. Our faith
that it will be so, makes us imagine so. Imagination excites a
star, that star, by conjunction with imagination gives the effect
or perfect operation. To believe that there is a medicine which
can cure us gives the spirit of medicine and that spirit gives the
knowledge of it and the medicine being known gives health."[1]
Apart from the astrological fantasy about the star this is a substantially true, though exaggerated, statement of the power
of suggestion, "imagination" as it has been studied in recent
times. By three centuries Nolle anticipates Coué.

About this time Vaughan turned from poetry to medicine
and practised as a doctor for the remainder of his life. It has
proved impossible to discover the source of the degree of doctor
of medicine which he claims on his tombstone and which is
given him in official documents. But he was not the man to
claim it falsely.

His first wife died about 1655 and very shortly he married
again. Here we are confronted with the most perplexing
problem in his life, with a fact which, if fact it be (and it is
not easy to deny it) must teach us to distrust *a priori* arguments,
however strong, for or against the truth of an event, and not to
expect consistency in human behaviour. For he married Elizabeth
Wise, who, it appears, was his deceased wife's sister. Though no
record has been found of the marriage, his father-in-law's will,
in conjunction with entries in the baptismal register of Coleshill,
would seem to prove that his new wife was indeed the sister
of his former wife. Dr. Hutchinson at any rate has no doubts.
Yet this fact, well established though it would appear to be,
involves accumulated improbabilities. Vaughan, so devoted to
the Anglican Church, contracts nevertheless a marriage forbidden
by her law, as set out in the table of kindred and affinity incor-
porated in the Prayer Book. He does so in the first fervour of

---

[1] *Hermetical Physic. Works of Henry Vaughan*, ed. L. C. Martin, p. 591.

his conversion when he condemns even innocent secular verse as unworthy of a Christian. And, as Dr. Hutchinson points out, he is able to do so only by taking advantage of the fact that his enemies the Puritans had abolished the authority of the Anglican Church and with it of her canons, that is to say of the defeat which he laments so bitterly. When the Restoration re-established the Church and once more gave her matrimonial legislation the force of law no action whatsoever was taken to render the marriage void. Vaughan, a regular communicant, was not refused communion by the Anglican clergy, though, when marriage with a deceased wife's sister had been legalised in 1907, Mr. Bannister was refused communion for contracting it. Moreover when, after the restoration of Anglican worship, he attended his parish church, every prayer book would pronounce his marriage unlawful, incestuous, and no marriage in the sight of God, a declaration repeated by a wooden table of the same prohibited degrees. When in later years Thomas, his son by the first marriage, quarrelled with his father and took legal proceedings against him, because he considered that his rights were being infringed for the advantage of a half-brother and half-sisters, though he complained of indecent haste in contracting the second marriage, he made no suggestion that it was or could be declared invalid because his stepmother was also his aunt. Neither Thomas nor his sister Catharine, though they did not shrink from public action against their father, made use of what must have been their most powerful weapon to secure the financial settlements they sought—the threat to take proceedings to make his second marriage void and their half-brother and sisters declared illegitimate. In face of these cumulative improbabilities, as powerful in their combination to produce dissent, as cumulative probabilities to produce the assent studied by Newman, I cannot but wonder whether, after all, the two wives were not sisters, but cousins. In the extract from Richard Wise's will printed by Dr. Hutchinson[1]—it is unfortunate that the entire document is not available— although the language used seems to imply that the children of the first marriage as well as those of the second were the testator's grandchildren, the testator does not explicitly use the term of the children of the first marriage as is the case with Lucy, a

[1] *Henry Vaughan*, pp. 204–5.

daughter of the second wife. And there could be more than one Richard Wise in the same family. If, however, the evidence compels us to credit what seems for so many reasons incredible, the sole explanation of the enigma that has suggested itself to me is that the prohibition in Leviticus is restricted to the lifetime of the first wife and in the last resort even such a churchman as Vaughan might have regarded the Bible rather than any ecclesiastical ruling as authoritative. But this explanation is far from meeting all the difficulties.

Vaughan's later life was as uneventful as poetically unproductive. His last years were darkened by sordid family quarrels. Evidence is insufficient to enable us to pronounce upon the merits of the case. We can only regret that the poet to whose poetry and piety we are so greatly indebted did not in his old age receive, whether through his fault or theirs, the regard and affection of all his children.

But it would not be long before he would leave a scene dear for its long-loved beauty but marred by the noise of dissension and "obscured by the 'Mists which blot and fill'" the "perspective as they pass" to go forward towards the "country afar beyond the stars" where "above noise and danger sweet peace sits crowned with smiles", the city "whose shining spires" are departed saints, with a fortunate but unusual humility leaving his body to be buried not, as was customary for a gentleman, in the church (doomed to destruction) but in the churchyard.

Vaughan's admiration for George Herbert was expressed by imitation. In *Silex Scintillans*, Dr. Hutchinson points out, "He borrows or imitates not only subjects and titles but phrases and whole lines. He uses Herbert's words freely . . . There is no example in English literature of one poet borrowing so extensively from another."[1] But the resemblances are on the surface. In spirit, in the insights to which it gives poetic expression, in the temperament it reveals, in its vision of the world, in the religious experience which gave it birth, *Silex Scintillans* is unlike the *Temple*, even remote from it. Herbert's poetry expresses the reaction of a sensitive, delicate and devout soul to the Christian scheme of salvation, as it was understood by contemporary Anglican theology. Such a reaction is certainly an element of *Silex Scintillans*, but it is not what gives it its character,

[1] *Henry Vaughan*, pp. 102–3.

not what is deep, wide and enduring in it; it is not the source of its poetry.

The Herbertian Vaughan would have passed into oblivion, read only by specialists in minor seventeenth-century verse. The Vaughan who has his abiding place in English poetry is of another stamp, moves in another world. To him belong the lightning flashes, the sparks struck from the flint, which illuminate landscapes invisible to Herbert, spaces beyond his span, depths to which he never penetrated. Herbert was no mystic. Vaughan is commonly so called. Was he? If by a mystic we mean, as strictly we should, one who in contemplative prayer experiences a union with God effected by the will, as it receives His communication of Himself, a union with God present in his central depths and exceeding image or concept, Vaughan was not, in my opinion, a mystic. For in the celebrated stanza which concludes "The Night" he says:

> There is in God, *some say*,
> A deep but dazzling darkness.

Some say—it is but the report of another—doubtless the pseudo-Denys—not personal experience. The poet had not himself entered that darkness, had not beaten with longing love upon this Cloud of Unknowing. Certainly he knew the joys of devotion, delights of prayer. He can write from personal experience:

> O Joyes, Infinite sweetnes! with what flowres
> And shoots of glory my soul breakes and buds!
> All the long houres
> Of night and rest
>
>   .   .   .
>
> This dew fell on my breast;
> O how it blouds
> And spirits all my earth.[1]

This, however, is but sensible devotion, accompanying, as the poem proceeds to tell us, an awareness of nature, of all natural objects, adoring the Creator. It is excellent praise, genuine

[1] "The Morning Watch".

insight, an illumination of the Divine Glory. But it is not the unitive prayer which alone is mystical in the strict sense.

In a wider and laxer sense however Vaughan may be accounted a mystical poet. For his poetry, if not the product of the mystic's unitive prayer, expresses a personal illumination, an illuminated vision of the world in its relation to God together with a personal apprehension of Christian truths, notably of that world of light just beyond our mortal horizon where the departed dwell with God. If the prayer traditionally described as contemplative were called by its true name unitive, Vaughan should be called a contemplative. For he contemplates truths concerning God and the things of God, whereas the unitive experiences God Himself above any conceivable truth.

But I am speaking of course of the only Vaughan of whom can speak, the writer of *Silex Scintillans*. Of the later, the dumb Vaughan we know nothing. We cannot know what his prayer became, whether or no he rose from contemplation to union and thus became in the strict sense a mystic. So far as we are concerned the only Vaughan is the poet.

The view of things expressed by *Silex Scintillans* is very largely conditioned by the Hermetic Philosophy such as it was stated in the writings of Henry's brother Thomas to which I have already referred.[1] In a series of treatises, *Anthroposophia Theomagica, Anima Magica Abscondita, Magia Adamica, Coelum Terrae, Lumen de Lumine, Aula Lucis, The Fraternity of the Rosy Cross* and *Euphrates,* Thomas attempts the contradictory task of publishing a secret wisdom without communicating it to the profane. To understand him in detail is therefore impossible. But a general notion of this Hermetic Philosophy is attainable and fortunately is sufficient for our understanding of the poet.

Though it styled itself magic, Hermetism is not the magic of conjuring tricks masquerading as produced by spirits or occult powers, still less the black magic which seeks to compel or cajole evil spirits. It is an esoteric doctrine which claims to impart to its initiates, together with spiritual and philosophic wisdom, a knowledge of the secret forces of nature. Its name derives ultimately from a series of tracts which baited their philosophy of a Neoplatonic type to the taste of a mystery-

---

[1] Miss Elizabeth Holmes has given us a monograph on " Henry Vaughan and the Hermetic Philosophy " which should be read by all students of the poet.

loving public by presenting it as the secret revelation of the
Egyptian God Thoth, identified with the Greek Hermes.
But its proximate source was presumably a treatise on alchemy
also presented as a revelation of thrice great Hermes.[1] For the
Hermetic mystery or art was concerned with alchemy, with the
search for the tincture or stone which could transmute base
metal into gold. This alchemy however was regarded as the
symbol, because the material copy, of a spiritual alchemy, the
process whereby a Divine tincture transmutes the soul into a
godlike being, and thus deifies it. Sometimes, as with Boehme,
alchemy is simply a symbol of mystical doctrine. Normally,
as in the case of Thomas Vaughan, it is both literal and symbolic.

This Hermetic wisdom was not an esoteric Christianity as it is
understood by modern theosophists. For it was not a religion
or a philosophy incompatible with Christianity, presented as
being the true, interior Christianity. It was regarded as truth
additional to Christianity as taught by Christian churches, not as a
substitute for it. It claimed to be a contemplative Christianity,
an interior and vital understanding of Christianity, and as such,
a deeper understanding of it than the ordinary Christian's.
Thomas Vaughan professed himself "a true resolute Protestant
in the best sense of the Church of England". And the master
he chiefly followed, Cornelius Agrippa, despite his bitter conflicts with the clergy, never renounced his Catholic faith. The
errors of this Hermetic theosophy were in fact of detailed
application and not of principle, historical and scientific rather
than theological or philosophic. For the broadly mystical religion
of the Hermetists, the spiritual alchemists, and of Thomas
Vaughan in particular, not alchemy alone but in general the
processes of nature reflect and therefore symbolise the communion between the soul and God, her regeneration, purification
and illumination, her restoration to the likeness of God, her transfiguration by and in His image and glory.[2] This religion, this
wisdom, was for the substance of it true, solid, even profound
though, one may suspect, it was more contemplative than
unitive. That is to say, like Henry Vaughan's poetry which
expresses it, it belonged to the illuminative, not to the unitive

[1] Evelyn UNDERHILL, Mysticism, 13th ed., p. 143.
[2] See in particular Evelyn UNDERHILL, Mysticism, Part I, Ch. VI, " Mysticism and
Symbolism "; also Ch. VII, " Mysticism and Magic". Also R. D. GRAY, Goethe the
Alchemist, in particular Ch. I.

way. For the Hermetist saw creation truly as a hierarchy in which the inferior orders of being, down to seemingly lifeless matter, are communications, reflections of the superior. The lower and the higher orders of being are mutually analogous. Thomas Vaughan could therefore conclude, "In the summer translate thyself to the fields where all are green with the breath of God and fresh with the powers of heaven. Learn to refer all naturals to their spirituals *per viam secretioris analogiae* [by the way of a more hidden analogy], for this is the way the magicians went and found out miracles."[1] No less true was the Hermetist's view of the world, as in a true sense an organism, not a mere aggregate of material units, but informed and moved by a vital, indeed a spiritual, principle. It is however not easy to decide whether the Hermetists regarded this principle as a created world-soul, a universal life, as a quintessence or tincture of spiritualised matter or as the Holy Spirit functioning as a world soul. They probably wavered between these views of it or attempted to combine them. Of a quintessence natural research affords no evidence. A created world-soul is difficult to conceive. But, though the Holy Spirit cannot be the soul of a creature, that He performs the function of a world soul is an orthodox and credible belief. It had been stated long since in the twelfth century in a fine composition of St. Hildegarde's, a sequence in honour of the Holy Ghost. "Most mighty passage that hath penetrated all things in the heights, on earth and in all depths. Thou dost compose and bind together all. By Thee the clouds glide, the upper air flies, stones are moist, the waters pour forth streams and earth exudes greenery."[2] *Spiritus Domini replevit orbem terrarum.* And the Hermetists' awareness of a spirit immanent throughout nature is Wordsworth's awareness, though he conceived it too pantheistically, when he

> felt the sentiment of Being spread,
> O'er all that moves and all that seemeth still.[3]

his

> . . . a sense sublime
> Of something far more deeply interfused . . .
> A motion and a spirit that impels,

---

[1] *Anima magica Abscondita.* Quoted by L. C. Martin in a note to his edition of Vaughan's works, Vol. II, p. 697.
[2] *The Hundred Best Latin Hymns*, ed. Prof. J. S. Phillimore.   [3] *Prelude*, Book II.

> All thinking things, all objects of all thought,
> And rolls through all things.[1]

Because the created universe is thus conceived as an organism, not only is there a correspondence between objects of a lower and objects of a higher order, as indeed was concluded from the fact that the lower is the reflection, the analogy of the higher. Throughout, all things in every order and department whatsoever are linked by a bond of subtle and potent reactions and sympathies:

> Sure there's a tye of bodies.
> Absents within the line conspire.[2]

This cardinal principle of Hermetic doctrine and its expression in *Silex Scintillans* has been memorably stated by a modern Catholic poet.

> To the new eyes of thee
> All things by immortal power,
> Near or far
> To each other linked are
> That thou canst not stir a flower
> Without troubling of a star.[3]

These indeed are almost the words of Thomas Vaughan in his *Magica Adamica*.[4] "There is not an herb here below but he hath a star in heaven above and the star strikes him with her beam and says to him Grow." Stellar influence for the Hermetist played a part even in the operation of faith healing. "Our faith that it shall be so" a cure effected "makes us imagine so". "Imagination excites a star, that star by conjunction with imagination gives the effect or perfect operation."[5] This hierarchical order of reflections and correspondences is a universal harmony, a universal hymn to its Creator and Ordainer

> all is hurl'd
> In sacred hymns and order. The great chime
> And symphony of nature. Prayer is
> The world in tune.[6]

[1] " Lines written above Tintern Abbey."
[2] Untitled poem in *Silex Scintillans*.
[3] Francis THOMPSON, " The Mistress of Vision ".
[4] Quoted by Miss Holmes, " Henry Vaughan and the Hermetic Philosophy," p. 39.
[5] See above, p. 279.
[6] " The Morning Watch."

In common once more with Wordsworth, who thought that the flower enjoys the air it breathes and that the stones by the wayside are alive, the Hermetist was inclined to animism, the belief that all material objects live and feel. Henry Vaughan in particular rebelled against the accepted view that there are inanimate objects and appealed against it to St. Paul's text which he quotes in Beza's Latin version, which I translate "For things created watching with head uplifted await the revelation of the sons of God".

> And do they so? have they a sense
> Of aught but influence? . . .
> . . . My volumes sed
> They were all dull and dead;
> They judged them senselesse and their state
> Wholly inanimate.
> Go, go; seal up thy looks
> And burn thy books.[1]

At worst a harmless and a pleasant fancy, far less irrational and more amiable than the opposite Cartesian error that even animals are automata without sense or life. But in fact this animism is not altogether untrue. Inorganic objects are not inert, not wholly dead. They are energies, reacting to their environment by attraction and repulsion, and therefore well termed by Professor Lossky psychoid, that is to say subanimate, as the plant is subsentient, the animal subintelligent.

The serious errors of this theosophy were, as I have said, of detailed application, were historical and scientific. The alleged tradition reaching back to the origins of humanity had no existence. No exact reference of a particular "natural" to a particular "spiritual" is possible. The fact that the lower reflects the higher and therefore signifies and symbolises the higher does not permit precise or detailed correspondences to be established between the two orders or between individual objects in one order and the other. Alchemy, though founded on the truth that material elements are in principle transmutable, was completely unscientific, and the astrology which seemed to corroborate the

---

[1] Untitled poem in *Silex Scintillans*.

Hermetist belief in the bond uniting even the most remote objects was not even true in principle. Knowledge of physical nature from above, qualitative, vital, spiritual, is a concrete and a more real knowledge, in fact truer than the abstract quantitative knowledge from below which for the rich reality of experience substitutes measurements and formulae, Eddington's "pointer readings". But these theosophists were mistaken when, like M. Guénon recently, they concluded that this vital and qualitative knowledge could be developed as a scientific knowledge of nature and as such be the foundation of its practical manipulation, the white magic they professed. For though— or rather, because—it is concrete, not abstract, it is not clear, is not exact and therefore is not scientific. When therefore the alchemist undertook chemical experiments, he had perforce to employ the quantitative and wholly material procedure of modern science. Though there is a philosophic understanding of corporeal nature from above, there is not a scientific. The conviction of theosophy that there is, was mistaken. And though the "natural" is a reflection and analogy of the "spiritual", since we are unable to grasp an exact and particular correspondence between objects of the two orders, we cannot with Thomas Vaughan's white magicians employ it to work natural miracles. The marvels effected by modern technology derive from below not from above, from material measurements and mechanism, not from knowledge of spiritual analogies. The latter however can alone satisfy the human spirit and its profounder intelligence. This at any rate has been true up to the present. There is however more than sufficient evidence of vital, even of spiritual energies operative in the world, of which we are as ignorant as our forefathers until recently were ignorant of the material energies— electricity for example—which compose the corporeal universe. We may perhaps hope that these in turn will be discovered and their operation exactly determined. They would thus at last become amenable to a scientific understanding and treatment, the subject matter of a type of science hitherto impossible and the white magic of the Hermetist thus be transformed into a novel science.[1]

These Hermetic errors, though in part perhaps anticipations

---

[1] In which case Guénon, mistaken as to the science of the past and present, may have forecast the science of the future.

of a remote future, were however no detriment to a poetical view of the world, a view seen by the spirit and shown to it, anima's profound obscure knowledge, not the knowledge of animus with its superficial clarity. The same theosophy which for his brother was so largely unintelligibility and frustration stimulated and enriched Henry's poetic vision and statement, as he employed it in the restricted measure compatible with his scope and purpose as a poet. Most Hermetic is the poem "Cock-crowing" where the cock is said to greet the approach of dawn, because it contains a particle akin to the sun, a "sunny seed", a "busy ray", "a little grain expelling night" which "shines and sings as if it knew the path unto the house of light", "a candle tinned and lighted at the sun". And the Hermetic term "tincture" is applied to it. Hermetic too is the poet's conception of "a preserving spirit in nature" which "doth still pass untainted through this mass, which doth resolve, produce and ripen all that to it fall" and will finally raise man's body from the grave. But whether this spirit is a world soul, a quintessence or the Holy Spirit is not clear.[1] To its operation must be ascribed the hidden survival of natural life in winter, its resurrection in spring "the dear secret greenness" of the "seed growing secretly" "nursed below", the living root of the flower laid bare in winter by the poet's spade, "the warm recluse" "that lived fresh and green of us unseen".[2] Here the preserving and quickening spirit seems to be identified with the Spirit of God that formed the poet's body and gave it life. "Greenness" and "green" however are difficult to understand. The underground part of a plant, be it seed, root or stem, is not and cannot be green. For the production of chlorophyll light is indispensable. One must conclude that for all his love of nature Vaughan was by no means an accurate observer. The association in his mind between greenness and life was so powerful, that not only did he think of the buried root as green; he even imagined that he had seen a green root under the earth. Could he however have known of the part played by light in plant chemistry, the knowledge would have fitted well into his view of nature as seeking light.

The Hermetic doctrine of individual correspondence finds expression in "The Starre" attracted by some terrestrial beauty

[1] " Death and Resurrection ". For all this I am much indebted to Miss Holmes's study.
[2] " I Walked the Other Day ".

"whose pure desire and longing for thy bright and vitall fire",
"are the magnets which so strongly move and work all night
upon thy light and love". All things indeed aspire upwards:

>   Waters that fall
>   Chide and fly up . . .
>   . . . trees, herbs, flowres, all
>   Strive upwards still.
>
>   Plants in the *root* with earth do most comply,
>   Their *leafs* with water, and humiditie,
>   The *Flowres* to air draw neer, and subtiltie,
>   And *seeds* a kindred fire have with the sky.

"All have their keyes and set ascents." And by this ascent they
are purified.

>   How do they cast off grossness? . . .
>   Waters refined to Motion, Aire to light,
>   Fire to all three.

Only earth like man is content to stay below.[1] This is the
Hermetic doctrine of a natural purification and refinement akin
to the spiritual regeneration and purification of the Christian.

It is to a Hermetic search for truth through a vital knowledge of nature, just such a search as that which occupied his
brother all his life, that Vaughan alludes when he tells us:

>   I summon'd nature; pierc'd through all her store,
>   Broke up some seales which none had touch'd before,

(Surely original experiments)

>   Her wombe, her bosome and her head
>   Where all her secrets lay abed,
>   I rifled quite.[2]

But unlike Thomas, Henry did not stop at this point but left
theosophy to devote himself to poetry first, then medicine.

[1] " The Tempest".   [2] " Vanity of Spirit".

The Hermetic awareness of a universal life culminates in Vaughan's experience of the spiritual life of a regenerate soul—the true life which contrasts with the false life of the world.

> Life is a fix'd discerning light
> . . . ever bright
> And calm and full.

> 'Tis such a blissful thing, that still
> Doth vivifie,
> And shine and smile . . .

> . . . life is, what none can express.
> *A quickness, which my God hath kist.*

To the universal life of nature, as the Hermetist saw it, is superadded a supernatural life from the same Divine Source. Hermetism is crowned by mysticism, of principle at least.[1]

Vaughan's Hermetic theosophy was bound up with a profound love of nature, of the landscape in which he spent almost his entire life. In this he has the advantage of Crashaw who, a townsman from birth to death, was content like St. Augustine to know God and the human soul. The rays lingering on a hillside after sunset in the valley below, the mist rising lazily from the "drowsy lake" to fall later back to earth in a weeping shower,[2] walks "primrosed and hung with shade", the stars in their silent and orderly motion across the sky or looking down upon a "Gloomy grove"—all these are as dear to Vaughan as his native scenery to Wordsworth. Like Wordsworth Vaughan watched and loved falling water:

> With what deep murmurs through time's silent stealth
> Doth thy transparent, cool and watery wealth
> Here flowing fall
> And chide and call
> As if his liquid, loose retinue staid
> Lingring, and were of this steep place afraid.

[1] " Quickness". The italics are in the original.
[2] " The Showre". But once more Vaughan's observation is inaccurate. The mist over the lake which turned to rain could not have risen from the lake, could not have been its birth.

> The common pass
> Where, clear as glass,
> All must descend
> Not to an end:
> But quickned by this deep and rocky grave,
> Rise to a longer course more bright and brave.[1]

> Dear stream! dear bank, where often I
> Have sate and pleas'd my pensive eye[2]

This "dear stream" is no doubt the river in whose honour Vaughan wrote the poem printed first in *Olor Iscanus*, "by the river Isca". The swan of Usk scarcely quitted the river he loved so well. The motion of its flowing water is the undercurrent of his verse.

When contrasting it with Crashaw's palette of warm colours I had occasion to speak of Vaughan's love for white and the explanation of it given by Dr. Hutchinson that in Welsh, spoken by Vaughan from infancy, white (gwyn) bears also the connotation of "blessed". Next to white in his preference is green and the gold of a clear sky at sundown. Purity and peace, not, as with Crashaw, ardour and passion, find expression in his colour scheme. His temper is subdued, serious, melancholic, and, like Milton's *Il Penseroso*, or Burton, he hugs his melancholy. Such a temperament was akin to the soft lights, the half-tones, the cloud and mist of our British climate and pre-eminently in the west where the light is softer, the atmosphere mistier and contours less definite than in the eastern counties. How often, not only in his allegorical pilgrimage, must his eye have "Measured the melancholy skye".[3]   High noon on a sunny day is not Vaughan's hour. When after sunrise,

> The unthrift sunne shot vitall gold
> And heaven its azure did unfold
> Checqurr'd with snowie fleeces[4]

we are conscious of an exception. Normally his brightest light is the golden light of dawn or sunset, rich and clear but not

[1] " The Waterfall".   [3] ibid.
[2] " Regeneration".   [4] ibid.

dazzling or even brilliant, without warmth and so far from exhilarating that it can foster his sad and pensive mood. "Fair and young light", the early light of daybreak,

> My guide to holy
> Grief and soul-curing melancholy.

Though the light is here, it would seem, a symbol of his deceased wife, its natural effect is presupposed.

Above all Vaughan loves a "calm golden evening", such as he imagined for the pastoral Patriarchs, and early morning daybreak. The dawn is dear with its renewal of nature's life, its pure and calm light, if the weather is fine, and its expectancy of sunrise; also the sun rising in its tempered light.

> "I see a rose
> Bud in the bright east and disclose
> The Pilgrim Sunne."[1]

> Mornings are mysteries; the first worlds youth
> Mans resurrection and the futures bud
> Shrowd in their births: The Crown of life, light, truth
> Is styled their starre.[2]

The stillness conveys a sense of God's hidden Presence:

> Walk with thy fellow creatures; note the hush
> And whispers amongst them . . .
>   Each bush
> And oak doth know I AM.[3]

There is expectation here, the expectation of a hidden glory, a hidden Deity to be revealed. It is explicit in "The Dawning", a poem which suggests daybreak as the most suitable and likely time for Our Lord's second Advent.

> Ah, what time wilt Thou come . . .

[1] Untitled poem in *Silex Scintillans*.
[2] "The Search".
[3] "Rules and Lessons".

. . . Shal these early, fragrant hours
Unlock thy bowres,
And with their blush of light descry
Thy locks crown'd with eternitie?
Indeed it is the only time
That with thy glory doth best chime,

. . . The whole creation shakes off night
And for thy shadow looks the light;
Stars now vanish without number
Sleepie planets set and slumber
The pursy clouds disband, and scatter,
All expect some sudden matter:
Not one beam triumphs but from far
That morning star.

Vaughan's religious perspective was dominated by three intuitions which together determine the emotional tone of his religious poetry, its distinctive pathos: awareness of a hidden splendour, indeed of God Himself, concealed behind the veil of creation; regret that it is now concealed, its primitive manifestation lost by man's sin whose fall dragged the world in his train: expectation of its final restoration when Christ returns to revive the dead and renew heaven and earth, their matter once again pure, refined, become the fit vehicle of spirit. The regret and the expectation are double, individual and racial. The lost paradise of the individual is childhood,[1] the morning of his life; of the human race, the paradise where God conversed openly with Adam and Eve.

Like Traherne and Wordsworth, Vaughan idealised childhood as a lost paradise of innocence, of a pure and spiritual vision and enjoyment of the world. That the father of a family could entertain such a view is hard to understand. Experience of children proves that, as far back as they can express themselves to us, they display in germ the evil passions and selfish desires of the adult which the abuse of freewill will transform into actual sin. For the vast majority at any rate the alleged vision does not exist. If Vaughan, Traherne and Wordsworth, as they tell us, saw the world invested with a glory invisible to the adult, they were

---

[1] Comparative however not in the strict sense. See below.

the rarest of exceptions. They must surely, one thinks, have
idealised a remote past, have mistaken imagination for memory.

Vaughan at any rate has no doubt of the radiance, the bliss,
the high privilege of childhood. He would have agreed with
Wordsworth that "heaven lies about us in our infancy":

> I cannot reach it; and my striving eye
> Dazles at it, as at eternity.
> Were now that chronicle alive,
> Those white designs which children drive.
> And the thoughts of each harmless hour,
> With their content too in my pow'r,
> Quickly would I make my path even
> And by meer playing go to heaven.
>
> . . . Dear harmless age! the short, swift span
> Where weeping virtue parts with man;
> Where love without lust dwells, and bends
> What way we please, without self-ends.
> An age of mysteries! which he
> Must live twice, that would God's face see.[1]

And if possible the well-known "Retreate" is even more emphatic:

> Happy those early dayes when I
> Shin'd in my Angell-infancy
> Before I . . .
>   . . . taught my soul to fancy aught
> But a white celestiall thought.
>
> . . . When on some gilded cloud or flowre
> My gazing soul would dwell an hour
> And in those weaker glories spy
> Some shadows of eternity;
> Before I taught my tongue to wound
> My conscience with a sinfull sound
>
> . . . But felt throughout this fleshly dress
> Bright shootes of everlastingnesse.

[1] " Childhoode".

The lost Paradise is however not strictly childhood but a prenatal state. For this earthly life is called our "second race" and even the infant has already walked a "mile or two from" his "first love". Such language implies that the individual soul, before birth, had enjoyed the open converse with God enjoyed by Adam in Eden. That is to say, childhood is already exile from Paradise, though the soul is so close to her prenatal bliss that its glory still lingers and its innocence. Thus there is a complete parallel between the history of the individual and the race. For although the Fall expelled man from Eden its light lingered and the Patriarchs were favoured with an open communion with God and His Angels. The world's infancy, a lingering reflection of Eden's light and purity, is thus parallel to the infancy of the individual invested with glory lingering from prenatal vision.

This demiparadise of the race is attested by Scripture, as the childish demiparadise by memory:

> Sure, It was so. Man in those early days
> Was not all stone, and earth.
> He shin'd a little and by those weak rays
> Had some glimpse of his birth.
> He saw Heaven o'r his head, and knew from whence
> He came (condemned) hither.

So the child looks back a mile or two and catches a glimpse of his first Divine love:

> Things here were strange unto him . . .
>
> They seemed to quarrel with him; for that act
> That fel him foyl'd them all;
> He drew the curse upon the world, and crackt
> The whole frame with his fall.

A belief not then disproved by the fossil record:

> He sigh'd for Eden and would often say
> Ah! what bright days were those?
> Nor was heaven cold unto him; for each day

The vally or the mountain
Afforded visits and still Paradise lay
In some green shade, or fountain.
Angels lay leiger here; each bush and cel
Each oke, and highway knew them;
Walk but the fields, or sit down at some wel
And he was sure to view them.[1]

Those angelic visitations are no more.

. . . Thy curtains are close drawn; thy bow
Looks dim too in the cloud,
Sin triumphs still and man is sunk below
The center and his shrowd.[2]

"Religion" is concerned with the same theme.

My God, when I walk in those groves
And leaves thy Spirit doth still fan[3]
I see in each shade that there growes
An angell talking with a man
In Abraham's tent the winged guests,
O how familiar then was heaven,
Eat, drink, discourse, sit downe and rest
Untill the coole and shady even.

If this blessed communion has ceased, it is because religion, though deriving from a "Secret golden mine", as history proceeds, deteriorates: "In passing through the earths darke veines, Grows still from better unto worse" and mingles her water with "Veines of sulphur underground". Today therefore we have but "a tainted sink".

In "The Jews" Vaughan suggests that the apostasy of the Gentile Christians may result in a restoration of the Church to the Jews, as Herbert, to the scandal of the Archiepiscopal censorship, concluded that "Religion stands on tiptoe in our land, Ready to pass to the American strand". But Vaughan's normal hope was the second Advent. At the close of "Corruption" he hears the angel sounding the trump of doom. And the same

---

[1] " Corruption".   [2] " Corruption".   [3] The pages of Scripture.

expectation concludes the "Rainbow". "The Dawning" looks
forward with the same hope. Vaughan saw the Puritan victory
as the final apostasy which will be the prelude of the end. Thus
regret for Paradise lost passes into expectation of Paradise re-
gained, the expectation in which, inspired by the text of Romans,
he sees even creatures supposedly inanimate taking their part.
Then at last regeneration will be complete, the work of Hermetic
alchemy accomplished, heaven and earth purified and renewed,
the secret no longer hidden behind curtains "close drawn" and
the veil that permits "only gleams and fragments", fragmentary
apprehensions of it, removed.

This is Vaughan's hope, his expectation for humanity, for the
Church. But what of the individual? Though there was reason
to think the end near, there was no certainty. The poet might
well die before daybreak. He cherishes his hope for the individual, for himself, parallel once more to its racial counterpart. If the body must lie in the grave, the soul need not wait
for her partner. Vaughan shares his century's obsession with
death and the grave. But his eyes are fixed on the "mysteries"
that "lie beyond" its "dust". Glorious mysteries, of that at least
he is sure—for he sees the departed "walking in an air of glory"—
"the world of light", golden and clear beyond the dark cloudhung horizon of mortality.

> I saw eternity the other night
> Like a great ring of pure and endless light
> All calm, as it was bright.[1]

It is no dazzling scorching blaze but the Patriarchs' "Calm golden
evening", immobilised as an everlasting present.

Vaughan seems unconcerned with poetic craftsmanship as
such. He is content, when from time to time the spark is struck
from his flint and fuses intuition and expression in poetry,
confined it may be to a line or two, sometimes enduring for a
stanza or even more but very rarely throughout an entire poem.
"The Timber", which begins with a compelling evocation of
the vanished life of a tree, now a lifeless trunk, peters out into
banalities.

But even when he is a versifier not a poet, something of

[1] " The World ".

Vaughan's peculiar charm lingers. And when he writes poetry it is a spell to bind us to him. It is the charm of his personality but even more the charm of his landscape, the physical landscape of his Welsh valley and, blending with it harmoniously in its mixture of shade and soft light, the shade of regret and the light of faithful expectation, his spiritual landscape, the prospect in which he contemplates God and His revelation to man, man's fall and recovery.

Vaughan was not a Baroque poet. He was not sensuous to spiritualise sense, not passionate to be aflame with the fire of Divine love, not playful to sport with the ingenious far-fetched resemblances of the conceit.[1] Nor, like Crashaw, does he lose himself in adoring contemplation of the mysteries of Christian faith. A distance is always maintained between himself and the object of his contemplation, a distance in which he is aware of himself and can return upon himself or the cause with which he has identified himself. It is always Henry Vaughan and Christ, or the Church seemingly doomed and Christ. Crashaw loses himself and even the earthly prospects of religion in the mystery he contemplates and adores. Vaughan's spirit is a lamp which casts mild and shifting beams onto the scene it illuminates, Crashaw's a conflagration flaming upwards. This is not said in criticism of Vaughan. Poetry, like other forms of wisdom, is justified of all her children. But the distinctive endowment of both poets is elucidated by the contrast between them. And although in Crashaw Britain produced the greatest of Baroque poets, Vaughan is in the normal tradition of British poetry. Crashaw's muse has no local habitation. Vaughan's was born in the Usk Valley and haunts it still. He truly named himself the Silurist.[2]

So I end where I began, in the churchyard where under his native hills the Silurist rests beneath the yew.[3]

---

[1] Herbert's example, however, and the literary environment, are responsible for an occasional conceit, notably in " Sundayes ", a copy of Herbert's " Prayer ".

[2] From the Silures, a British tribe inhabiting South Wales.

[3] It is strange that there is nothing to mark the resting place of his wives.

BIBLIOGRAPHY

The Works of Henry Vaughan. Ed. Leonard Cyril Martin (the editor also of Crashaw's *Poems*), 2 vols., pagination continuous. The Clarendon Press, 1914.

Silex Scintillans. The Temple Classics (Dent).

Henry Vaughan, A Life and Interpretation. Dr. F. E. Hutchinson. The Clarendon Press, 1947.

The Mount of Olives. Ed. Louise Imogen Guiney, 1902.

The Works of Thomas Vaughan, Eugenius Philalethes. Edited, Annotated and Introduced by Arthur Edward Waite. The Theosophical Publishing House, 1919.

Henry Vaughan and the Hermetic Philosophy, Elizabeth Holmes, Basil Blackwell, 1932.

CHAPTER XIII

URANIA: THE POETRY OF MISS RUTH PITTER

A REVIEW in *The Observer* by Lord David Cecil introduced me to *Urania*, the volume in which Miss Ruth Pitter has selected from earlier collections of her verse the poems in her judgment the best. The expectations raised by the reviewer were more than fulfilled. Here is a poetess who, when the indispensable condition of poetry is so widely believed to be originality at all costs, even of intelligibility, writes in the traditional idiom and in common with the poets of the past is content with the originality of an individual vision and an individual employment of the accepted vocabulary.

Consequently there are no obscurities of language wilfully misused. What obscurities there are are but the veil drawn by a modesty of spirit about the poet's most intimate beliefs. Language and rhythm are limpid, lucid like the pure water Miss Pitter loves so well. Her poetry is simple but with the simplicity not of artlessness but of art. For she is a fastidious artist who has weighed carefully every word chosen.

As an artist should be, she is enamoured of perfection: "Dear Perfection" she calls it in the poem so named. Here's where (she) "perfection" is wholly mine:

> Up from the line
> Of lovely verse she leaps, and takes
> In her strong hand my soul that shakes,
> That faints and dies,
> Yet lives by looking in her eyes.

> Call not to me when summer shines,
> Death, for in summer I will not go;
> When the tall grass falls in whispering lines,
> Call not loud from the shades below;

> While under the willow the waters flow,
> While willow waxes and waters wane,
> When wind is slumbrous and water slow,
> And woodbine waves in the wandering lane.[1]

Here is the tone, the rhythm of high summer and the effect is largely due to alliteration.

Alliteration assists Miss Pitter to picture a swan swimming alone:

> But solitary he sails, moving unmated.

Or again in the same poem:

> She shall not pine, nor shall time's tedious passion . . .

> The fiery doom is falling, fear and horror . . .

> Bloom in brief pride then sink away in squalor . . .

> Losing the separate self the seed of anguish.[2]

Or yet again:

> Poetry, like all passion, seeks for peace[3]

> Leads the fond feet to the familiar places[4]

> There stole two silent children to my side
> And sat down with a still attentive air;
> The younger smiling five years old and fair.[5]

Miss Pitter even experiments with unrhymed Sapphics, a metre little used since Isaac Watts employed it so effectively in his tremendous poem on the day of judgment.

> Fairest is water, when the heart at evening
> Leads the fond feet to the familiar places:
> Fairest is water when it falls in silent
> Dew where thou liest.[6]

---

[1] " Call not to me ".
[2] " The Cygnet ".
[3] " Passion and Peace ".
[4] " Fair is the Water ".
[5] " The Fishers ".
[6] " Fair is the Water".

Here where the cold pure air is filled with darkness
Graced but by Hesper and a comet streaming,
Censed by the clean smoke from a herdsman's hearthstone
    I stand with silence.

Void of desire but full of contemplation
Both of these herds and of the gods above them
Mindful of these, and offering submission
    To those immortal.[1]

To speak of Miss Pitter as a contemplative may seem to say
nothing distinctive of her work. For the poet as such is a contemplative, as the mystic as such is a unitive. But there is a distinctive
quality in her contemplation, though only a careful reading of
her poems can bring it home. It is blended of simplicity, lucidity
and intensity. It is contemplation focused on its object, an object
or landscape of natural beauty for the most part, or a simple
person of no outstanding quality, but seen in some revealing and
significant speech or action. The object, natural or human, is
picked out from its context, immobilised and under the lens
of contemplation its significance, the beauty, content and
meaning of its form are magnified in the poet's and the
readers' vision. It is thus that perfection is seen in "the least
flowering weed".

Did you see nothing that could seem
Perfect, as life should be?
Yes; for the birds were like my dream,
And the leaves on the tree.
And the dear, stainless buds of spring
When upward they did move;[2]

Water in particular is dear to the poet. It is the subject of the
charming poem in Sapphics from which I have quoted. And
elsewhere:

Water shall bless them, water out of heaven
Washing from earth the stains of wicked creatures.

[1] " Of Silence and the Air ".
[2] " Lament for One's Self".

Water in rain, water in dew at evening
Falling through clear air, stealing through clean grasses,
Dwelling in darkness in our mother's body,
In secret springs welling and murmuring through her,
Gathering in brooks and lapsing into rivers,
Rolling magnificent down glorious tideways . . .

Pouring predestined to unfathomed ocean.[1]

Fruit trees are dear; in particular the apple tree from its flowering
in spring to the fall of the first green apples in summer; three
poplars are celebrated, a yew, the yew to the north of the
cottage falling into ruin, the strawberry plant. Two poems are
dedicated to swans. The poor old woman speaking of the beauty
of the moonlight, as it shone into her bedroom, the halfwitted
girl gathering a bunch of violets and ivy berries: the small
plant, "love's pilgrim and poor suppliant" which

> With a flower like a blue eye
> Propounds love's dreadful mystery;
> With a weak triumphant spire
> Soars to a peak of pure desire:[2]

all these are fixed and penetrated by this contemplation, the
contemplation which has lifted from the flow of change and time
the memorable scene when sitting by a moat the poet met the
two little fishers.

> The embattled towers, the level lillied moat,
> Between the lily leaves the inverted sky,
> The impending alders and the quivering float
> Charmed the vexed spirit.[3]

The "impending alders"—impending is the *mot juste*, for sound
and sense alike, slowing down movement to a stop, as "o'er-
hanging", for example, could not.
This loving vision of the simplicities, unfolding their wealth,
is akin to Wordsworth's vision of nature and man. Such rich

---

[1] " The Cygnet ".
[2] " The Small Plant ".
[3] " The Fishers ".

simplicities are the flowers of which Miss Pitter writes, the funeral wreaths visiting with a gleam of beauty the sordid surroundings and lives of the factory girls. The aged and noble poor who are one with the nature to which they belong are as dear to her as they were to Wordsworth. The old woman speaking of the moon is a Wordsworthian figure as is another old woman, childless and husbandless, who lavishes her loving care on another old woman whom she has nursed till her death and when she has performed the last offices lies down to sleep beside her friend's body. Wordsworthian too is another old woman who forgets her poverty and lonely toil as she watches a sparrow sitting on her eggs. But most perfectly Wordsworthian not only in herself but in the poem which celebrates her is "The Old Woman":

> She reigns in the tarred cottage in the corn
> Clothed on with power, where her docile mate
> Haunts rather than inhabits . . .

> These does she counsel, smiling without scorn:
> And for these wretched, from her look severe
> And winter-bright shines forth Philosophy
> A mind still satisfied with what must be,
> Nobility of faith and quiet breath.

She is own sister to the Leechgatherer or the guide of the *Excursion*. And Aged Cupid, the old yokel of seventy-four full of laughter and jest, would have delighted Wordsworth.

> Yet, star within a tomb—the painter here
> Bursts the strong sepulchre.[1]

> In a foul sepulchre a star.[2]

Here surely are reminiscences of Vaughan.

> If a star were confined into a tomb,
> Her captive flames must needs burn there.[3]

[1] " My God Beholds Me": " The Spanish Painting ".
[2] " Caged Lion ".
[3] " They are all gone into the World of Light".

Miss Pitter must find in the Silurist a kindred spirit sharing her hatred of noise, violence and war, her love for the beauties of landscape, water and flower and, as we shall see, awareness of the spiritual reality they reflect and signify, a pre-occupation also with death and what lies beyond it. But we are also reminded of Blake, not the Blake of the enigmatic prophetic books but the author of the "Songs of Innocence and Experience":

> To love the lion I will dare
> He waves in heaven his flames of hair:[1]

Or the lines just quoted, about the flower which

> . . . like a blue eye
> Propounds love's dreadful mystery;
> With a weak triumphant spire
> Soars to a peak of pure desire.

Or "The End of Fear":

> When a man has cast out fear
> All is indifferent, and dear.
> When desire has fled away
> Then the little mice can play.
>
> He can lay his head upon
> Another's bosom or a stone,
> And the stone is well beloved,
> And the breast by love unmoved.

And in the same strain "Weeping Water, Leaping Fire":

> I am damned and drowned in rue—
> With love then what have I to do?
>
> . . . With chaste stillness, blessed peace . . .
>
> Lulled in morning's lap I lie
> And mend my sorrows in the sky.
> I am redeemed and flown above
> Then what have I to do with love?

[1] " My God Beholds Me ": " The Lion-Seraph ".

An echo surely of Blake's words

> The death of Jesus set me free
> Then what have I to do with thee?[1]

Or again "But For Lust":

> But for lust we could be friends,
> On each other's necks could weep:
> In each other's arms could sleep
> In the calm the cradle lends . . .
>
> From the gold to the grey hair
> But for passion we could rest,
> But for passion we could feast
> On compassion everywhere.

What Blake intended by his paradoxical antinomian utterances is expressed in "The Task":

> With love of love now make an end;
> Let male and female strive no more;
> Let good and bad their quarrel mend
> And with an equal voice adore;
> The lion with the lamb adore.
>
> . . . Bow lofty saint, rise humble sin,
> Fall from your throne, creep from your den:
> The King, the Kingdom is within.

In one aspect Blake's belief, it is true, is diametrically opposed to this rejection of passionate desire. But it accords with another aspect never reconciled by Blake with the former, that the lust for exclusive possession whether of things, persons or of love itself must be rejected, if the pure vision of the artist and the truly religious man (who are confused by Blake) is to be achieved and preserved. For the time of artistic creation or aesthetic contemplation a temporary suspension of desire is sufficient. But neither Blake nor Miss Pitter is satisfied with a passing vision. Mystics, at least in the wide sense, as well as artists, they wish to dwell permanently

---

[1] *Songs of Experience:* " To Tirzah ".

in the heavenly places, where the ideas descried by the artist's intuition in their significant images, abide in living reality.

What Miss Pitter's professed philosophy may be, if indeed she owns allegiance to any philosophic system, I do not know. In one poem she employs the Kantian terminology of phenomenon and noumenon. But she is in fact a Platonist. Under her intent gaze, focused by a desire, not less but more intense, because it is not the possessive desire of earthly good, its object is seen for what it is, a projection onto the corporeal plane of a spiritual reality, discerned within and beyond it, the substance of which it is a shadow. The poet

> sees the changeless creature shine
> Apparelled in eternity:
> . . . She knows the constancy divine;
> The whole of life sees harvested,
> And frozen into crystalline
> And final form.[1]

A moment of intuition reveals this immortal order of forms.

> All was as it had ever been—
> . . . the oak beyond the hawthorn seen,
>
> . . . When suddenly heaven blazed on me,
> And suddenly I saw:
> Saw all as it would ever be,
> In bliss too great to tell,
> For ever safe, for ever free,
>
> . . . Saw as in heaven the thorn arrayed,
> The tree beside the door.[2]

For not only the ideas signified by sensible forms but those forms themselves are eternal in the Divine Mind. And to this ideal world the poet has access:

> Hate me or love, I care not, as I pass
> To those hid citadels,
> Where in the depth of my enchanted glass
> The changeless image dwells.[3]

[1] " The Eternal Image".   [2] " Sudden Heaven".   [3] " The Unicorn ".

The stone, the weed, the destroying insect "stream with light in heaven, where for ever their God beholds them".[1]

This exemplarism Miss Pitter professes in common with the Catholic mystic whom we have studied earlier—Sister Elizabeth of the Trinity. For she also contemplates the exemplars through and in which God made the creatures of earth and time.[2]

I have just quoted from the poems entitled "My God Beholds Me or Hymns to the Noumenon". For Miss Pitter knows that ideas cannot subsist of themselves, but only in the spiritual reality which she terms the Noumenon, the ideal world as it exists in God and, it would seem, as His first production, an order of spirits. The earthly lion is but the phenomenal appearance of a celestial counterpart. Stone, weed and insect are glorious in their ideal existence in God. In El Greco's "Burial of the Conde Orgaz" (for this is the Spanish painting of which she writes) the soul of the deceased rises to the heaven where the "pentecostal dove"

> strikes dead in the heart
> the fell phenomenon, burns it away
> Leaving *Noumenon* pulsing above time:
> which triumph my eternal God beholds.[3]

This world of spirits, an outcrop, as it were, of the ideal world in God, an innocent unfallen world; the celestial counterpart and fulfilment, as it is the original, of this fallen sinful world, is revealed in passing vision.

> . . . each one shows
> Worthy of love;
> How each toward the end his spirit knows,
> Doth calmly move!
>
> The cloud closes, the candid eye
> Is dimmed, is gone,
> But by the gleam left in the sky
> I'll wander on

[1] " My God Beholds Me ".
[2] See above, p. 270.
[3] " My God Beholds Me ": " The Spanish Painting ".

Till . . .
> . . . wrapped in gold
> I the world's innocence upon the breast
> Of God behold.[1]

And it will be "an ultimate innocence born of pain".[2]

It is not however easy to decide whether this order of pure spirits is understood as an order of spirits actually existing in God or, as is suggested by "My God Beholds Me", it is purely ideal, the exemplars of human souls existing eternally in God, each idea to be realised by a soul when the work of restoration is complete.

I have had occasion already to remark a resemblance with Vaughan. Here it is close; the innocence of Eden, lost, but to be finally restored. The golden world of innocence beyond the cloudy sky, the gleam left to guide us home to it, these belong to the spiritual landscape of *Silex Scintillans*.

> A swordlike gleam
> Kept man from sin
> First out; this beam
> Will guide him in.[3]

Silence is the truth.

> Shall not I also stand and worship silence
> till . . . the heart, the housewife
> spin no more, but sit down silent in the presence
> of the eternal?[4]

This appreciation of silence is another link with Sister Elizabeth.

But Miss Pitter is of our time and with her contemporaries has questioned the sufferings and frustration of humanity more insistently than our forbears. "The frail" jars with "peacock glaze" which are our mortal bodies are soon and lightly broken.[5]

"The universal curse" is "abroad":[6]

> . . . when I mourn
> . . . seated amid corruption,

---

[1] " My God Beholds Me ".
[2] " Seaborn ".
[3] *Silex Scintillans*, " Joy of My Life ".
[4] " Of Silence and the Air ".
[5] " The Bridge ".
[6] " To J. S. Collis".

In the expanding universe hope too recedes,
Or in the diminishing sinks to a dying ember.

. . . I behold the filthy orts, and the carcases
The gobbets, the offal of slaughter about me:
Then I behold myself, both savage and feeble,
Covered with creeping despairs.[1]

The thought lies heavy of

> all these millions
> Mind-infected, mother-betrayed.[2]

And the prospect of "1938" is grim to despairing:

> The greatest harvests of time

> . . . Are burned or thrown in the sea:
> The mind, with its burden of love
> Corrupting now heavily weighs
> The means of a myriad deaths.

Truer this than ever in 1953:

> The gentle are ground into earth
> And the tender despised

> Let us go down together
> Having despaired of wisdom
> . . . we
> Have failed to love and must perish.[3]

The sordidness in which multitudes are doomed to live, by the polluted Thames, no longer the crystal stream sung by Spenser, or in a factory, intrudes, insistently, on the poet's vision of beauty:

> In those dark places beauty is imprisoned;
> Beauties . . .
> Bloom in brief pride, then sink away in squalor,
> Die battling against the fall of filth unceasing.[4]

[1] " Elegy to Mary".   [3] " 1938".
[2] " The Tigress".   [4] " The Cygnet".

The force of the last line is strengthened by the alliteration, "fall of filth", and the assonance "battling . . . unceasing". And to crown the evil come the horrors of an air raid. .

> The fiery rain is falling, and the vision
> of love is lost in the funereal blackness: . . .

> . . . The fiery doom is falling; fear and horror
> engulf me as the wave of steel roars over.[1]

> In the life the people led,
> With sorrow day and night
> Vast wars, babes slaughtered, wicked bread—
> O there was nothing right.[2]

"O Come out of the Lily" is a cry to God to shew Himself appearing from the lovely things He has made and thrusting aside the veil of the world's evil "hate and anger and woeful pain" to walk once more with man as at the first in Eden, Vaughan's Eden. The poet touches here the enigma, insoluble to human knowledge, why the subhuman world reveals God's beauty but not His love.

At times there is the temptation to yield to despair and surrender an indefensible faith.

> I am spent, I have no more strength to swim

> . . . Cease then your striving, sink and go down.[3]

Or the poet will wish she had no soul to trouble her, envying the soulless fairies or the cattle without the burden of thought, the flowers and trees perfect in themselves and seeking no heaven beyond.[4]

For it is no longer possible for us to take the future life for granted as an obvious certainty, unassailed by doubt. The weighty arguments against it, the disbelief so widespread have produced a mental atmosphere in which many of us often, all of us at times, must hold to the belief by sheer faith. It has been truly said that, whereas the devout in the past were tempted to

---

[1] " The Cygnet".
[2] " Lament for One's Self".
[3] " Sinking".
[4] " To the Soul".

believe themselves doomed to damnation, today they are tempted with St. Thérèse to believe themselves doomed to extinction.

Confronted with the spectacle of sordid sin and suffering without apparent meaning Miss Pitter wrestles with these doubts. In "1938" she seems to be yielding:

> The good man's goal is the grave,
> His secret longing extinction.[1]

Elsewhere we witness the struggle. The tempest is followed by a calm when

> beauty new and naked opens and shines . . .
> and all surviving things wax great and blow,

But

> the sudden storm in the mind
> Conceived of anguish brooding wastefully
> Heaping the sullen forces baulked by life[2]

has not been followed by a similar calm renewing the life of the spirit. There is but the hope, a faint hope, of the soul

> making her landfall in the unknown place
> Where the miraculous freshness falls like dew, . . .

> . . . And on her face the sun incredible
> Longfabled, legendary and unhoped for shines.[3]

> O truth is it death there over the river
> Or is it life, new life in a land of summer?[4]

On the surface of things the evidence or the lack of it seems to disprove survival. But the deeper knowledge of the spirit affirms it indomitably. This is the theme of "The Paradox":

> Our death implicit in our birth
> We cease or cannot be;
> And know when we are laid in earth
> We perish utterly

---

[1] " 1938".
[2] " Storm".
[3] ibid.
[4] " The Bridge".

And equally the spirit knows
The indomitable sense
Of immortality which goes
Against all evidence.
See faith alone whose hand unlocks
All mystery at a touch
Embrace the awful Paradox.[1]

So it was with Richard Jefferies. His superficial reason doubted, perhaps denied, survival; his experience by the prehistoric tumulus affirmed immortality as a present fact, not admitting of question. "Recognising my own inner consciousness, the psyche, so clearly, death did not seem to me to affect the personality . . . It is eternity now. I am in the midst of it. Now is eternity; now is the immortal life. Here this moment by the tumulus, on earth now; I exist in it, I am in eternity now, and must there remain. Haste not, be at rest, this now is eternity."[2] This experience of immortality as an experience of present eternity passes over into the kindred proof of survival, stated so eloquently by John Smith, from a present experience of the eternal God and communion with Him.[3]

With aching heart and eyes wide open to suffering, frustration and death the poet penetrates to the obscure Godhead, to the experience which assures us that we are not wholly mortal. In 1940, when the fall of France threatened England with conquest, she plunged into the divine darkness:

Even so dread God!

. . . I must gather up my soul . . . and flee
Into the heart of terror, to find myself in thee.[4]

In her latest book *Receive the Joyfulness of your Glory* Miss Maisie Spens tells the story of a captain in the China Seas who saved his ship by driving her head on into a typhoon, till she reached the "oasis of silence and calm" in the centre of the typhoon. Similarly, she continues, God drives fallen and sinful man right through the typhoon of "violence, war, death . . .

[1] " The Paradox".
[2] *Story of My Heart,* Pocket Edition, 1907, pp. 38, 43, 45.
[3] See above, pp. 246–7.
[4] " The Sparrow's Skull".

and every ill begotten of sin" to find His peace and the Divine
glory begun here in the midst of evil, to be perfected, when
death has been faced and conquered, in the immortal joy of
the Heavenly Jerusalem.[1] Such an experience of God and His
peace in the heart of the typhoon of sin unleashed and the suffering
it produces, is expressed in Miss Pitter's words just quoted "flee
into *the heart of terror* to find myself in Thee".

"A Solemn Meditation", however, is her fullest expression of
this experience, is indeed for her religious experience the central poem in this collection.

Amid the storms of autumn with their prophecy of nature's
death in winter Miss Pitter, like Vaughan contemplating the root
still alive beneath the earth, is aware that life cannot perish, but
will return with the spring:

> This hydra life will not take no,
> More withering now, more blossoming by and by.

Meanwhile it sinks down to the depths and with it the spirit of
the poet must descend into the depths of death and darkness:

> Into the black of life unfathomable;
> Down to the nethermost dive.

But already this depth of apparent death is experienced as "life
unfathomable". In death life is discovered:

> Naked upon the bosom of my God,
> Bereft of all save the Unmanifest . . .

> In the great bitter dark I touch his breast:

In this utter abandonment, this Dark Night of the Soul, the poet
attains "the secret of the strong", "the knowledge of the wise",
has "thrust" her "way to where the immortal lies enwombed
in dust". She can therefore cry out the Alleluia of resurrection,
"in her Lord's likeness terrible and fair" and the Alleluia is echoed

---

[1] *Receive the Joyfulness of Your Glory*, pp. 106–8.
  I cannot let this opportunity pass without a word to advise my readers, if they have
not already done so, to become acquainted with this book of profound spiritual
insight, a " prophetic " message to us to receive the transfiguring glory offered us in the
transfigured and transfiguring Christ.

by the world that has risen or will rise. It is the Pauline death and resurrection with Christ, the mystic's dark night experienced, as befits such a lover of nature, in conjunction with nature's annual death and resurrection, celebrated the world over by those pagan rites of the dying and rising god which prefigure their spiritual and supernatural fulfilment.

In similar vein, in the midst of the air raid described in "The Cygnet" the poet is aware "even in extremity", "in this utter night", of "the secret", of a "seed of latent bliss" the "seed" of a "new beauty" to come, "the germ of hope undying", a "seed" which is "the key of the undiscovered kingdom", a symbol suggested by the "small winged seeds shaped like keys". This is the grain which must fall into the ground and to all appearance die, if it is to bear fruit. The poet however cannot hold fast the experienced union, which is and must be imperfect:

> Under the dual I divine
> The one, but cannot make it mine.[1]

Here and in the words already quoted "losing the separate self, the seed of anguish" influences of Indian Vedanta may perhaps be detected. But it is but a matter of expression or at most conceptual interpretation. The experience could be stated otherwise without falsifying it. For God is wholly simple, and though the distinct self cannot be destroyed (otherwise its existence would be inexplicable), when union with God has been perfected it will no longer be self-affirming and self-asserting—and thus a principle of separation—but will be pure receptivity of the one Divine Being and Its self-knowledge.

As *The Cloud of Unknowing* states it, though the contemplative better named the unitive "liketh right well to be", he "desires . . . to lack the knowing and feeling of his being", "the which knowing and feeling" (self-consciousness) must be destroyed.[2]

Sister Elizabeth's quotation from Lacordaire[3] "Ask for Him no more from any one on earth or in heaven. For He is your own soul and your soul is He" also has a superficially Vedantic flavour, yet can and must be interpreted in a Christian sense.

[1] " Buried Treasure".
[2] Chs. 43, 44. Cf. *Epistle of Privy Counsel*, Ch. 8. Also Baker's Commentary on the *Cloud of Unknowing* arranged by Abbot Justin McCann, Part I, Ch. 10.
[3] See above. p. 268.

Miss Pitter's experience and aspiration are sufficiently explained by this orthodox though, I admit, unusual teaching.

But the spirit "Clothed in the weeds of her [earthly] nonage", a vesture woven of "space and time", cannot, thus clad, surrender and unite herself to the ascending "glory" proclaimed by a true spiritual philosophy, better perhaps called a mystical wisdom; cannot descend from the tower of her distant contemplation to enter "the sacred desert of silence" which she contemplates.[1] Nevertheless the mystics and saints have descended and surrendered by a self-sacrifice ever renewed, not only by a passing experience of self-oblivion which, after all, is a surrender of the intelligence more than of the will. The very fact that contemplation yields such pregnant and satisfying intuitions of spiritual truth may even make it harder for the contemplative, the poet, the artist, to go forward to the life of the unitive, the mystical life which consists primarily and substantially, not in knowledge, however spiritual, profound, sublime, but in adherence of the will, in a love often savourless.

No less valuable on that account are the moments of illumination recorded in Miss Pitter's verse with such beauty of expression, such delicate discretion of statement, and with the aid of symbols seldom puzzling, and lovely for their own sake. But often symbolism gives place to simple statement, the statement of a triumphant conviction of God and the final victory of the immortal spirit.

There are days when mourning is done with, Mary
Strange is my sorrow to thee: how far stranger my joy! . . .

. . . Who then are those, in glittering spiral ascending? . . .

. . . Even the eagles of God, the translated spirits, . . .

. . . All paradox seized and resolved, all evil consumed,
All fear soared above, the depth and the height reconciled,
The ultimate claimed, the great cry of unity uttered.[2]

Where is the spring of my delight
Now every spring is dry? . . .

[1] " On a Certain Philosophy".   [2] " Elegy to Mary".

> And yet the spring of my delight
> Leaps up beyond belief . . .
>
> —The secret stream of grace
> Flows on and swells the same
> As if from out another place
> Where sorrow has no name.[1]

I have quoted the verse in "Lament for One's Self" bitterly exclaiming that in human life as led today there is nothing right. But the poet continues:

>   Another seeing
> Makes me not all forlorn
>
> No matter what the body felt,
> No matter what it saw,
> My inmost spirit ever knelt
> In a blind love and awe:
> And dead or living knows full well,
> Sick or whole it knows
> The secret it may never tell
> Of joy and of repose.

Therefore she can look forward to the "Ultimate innocence . . . born of pain", the purpose for which earth was created, of which poetry is the promise, prayer the pledge.

These illuminations however, valuable as they are, are not her last word. We have read lines from *Urania* which record not a contemplative but a unitive experience, the mystic's adherence in the "great bitter dark" to the "Unmanifest".

In the tradition of English mystical verse and so worthy a representative of it, Miss Pitter takes poetry to the point where the poet's contemplation must yield to the mystic's union, which fulfils it by a realisation, practical, concrete and, if not revoked, permanent, in a word, existential.

[1] " The Spring".

DATE DUE

JAN 4 '78			
JAN 15 78			
GAYLORD			PRINTED IN U.S.A.